THE LAST POLITICIAN

THE LAST
POLITICIAN

INSIDE JOE BIDEN'S
WHITE HOUSE *and the* STRUGGLE
FOR AMERICA'S FUTURE

FRANKLIN FOER

Penguin Press
New York
2023

PENGUIN PRESS
An imprint of Penguin Random House LLC
penguinrandomhouse.com

ISBN 9781101981146 (hardcover)
ISBN 9781101981160 (ebook)

Printed in the United States of America
1st Printing

Designed by Amanda Dewey

To Jonathan and Josh

CONTENTS

PART THREE

LEAVING

June–August 2021

PART FOUR

THE BOG

September–December 2021

THE LAST POLITICIAN

Prologue

Joe Biden's inauguration was an image in his mind. It took hold there decades earlier, and it looked something like a brisk winter's day, when the nation's establishment huddled around him, wrapping its arms around the kid from Scranton. It was a triumphalist scene, but also a revenge fantasy, since Washington's liberal elite had long rolled its eyes at him—for his loquaciousness, for his stories that were too folksy by half, for his blaring insecurities—and he knew it.

The consistent underestimation of Joe Biden was his diesel. It propelled him to keep chasing the image, over the course of three presidential runs. He pursued it into his late seventies, even though diminishingly few of his peers considered it plausible—and even though his inability to surrender his ambitions occasionally verged on the undignified.

He believed that fate—a word strewn across his monologues—sometimes required him to travel the ugly path to success. At every station in his adult life, joy marched in lockstep with trauma. And when the image in his head transposed itself into reality on January 20, 2022, it seemed entirely fitting that the inauguration, which he had so long desired, deviated so wildly from his expectations, and was stalked by death.

In the dream version of the day, he solemnly strides onto the stage erected on the west front of the Capitol, through doors held open by marines.

But when that day arrived, the glass in those doors was shattered. Two weeks earlier, right-wing paramilitaries battered them with flagpoles and purloined police shields in a violent quest to prevent him from ever taking office. The inaugural dais looked down onto steps, where police officers trying to fight off the surging mob had slipped in pools of blood.

Instead of a democratic extravaganza, his inauguration was surrounded by wire fences and Jersey barriers, guarded by armored vehicles and twenty-six thousand members of the National Guard who descended on Washington for the event, determined to prevent a reprise of the violence of the sixth of January.

Even if the public had been permitted to pass through the checkpoints surrounding the city center, it wouldn't have come. Through the winter, it sheltered at home, worried that it might die by inhaling particles of disease wafting in the air. A global pandemic was at its lethal peak. On January 19, the eve of his inaugural, COVID's death toll surpassed four hundred thousand. Despite the development of effective vaccines, the government had scant doses—and no effective plan for distributing them. To fill the expanse of the unoccupied Mall, inaugural planners planted two hundred thousand flags across the lawn, representing the absentees. Biden couldn't address an adoring crowd, just sheets fluttering in the wind.

This was not the image in his head. It was a postapocalyptic tableau—and the nation that he inherited.

THE ELECTORATE turned to Joe Biden as a balm. Postmortems of his victory ascribed his success to the fact that voters hoped the kindly grandfather might impose calm and decency, a bit of boredom, and a dose of competence, after four erratic, enervating years of Trump.

But voters' expectations for Biden didn't line up with his own.

Born in the middle of World War II, raised in the tense early days of the Cold War, he viewed himself as thrust by events into a successor struggle to preserve democracy. To stave off the authoritarian enemy, he would need to contain the rising force of China and ward off the revanchist ambitions of Russia. It required him to tangibly demonstrate that the American system wasn't the antiquated relic its rivals portrayed. He said that he would prove that democracy could still deliver for its citizens, that it hadn't lost its capacity to accomplish big things.

This was a much steeper, much riskier task than helping the country muddle through its tangle of immediate crises, which was job enough. But it suited Biden's heroic self-conception, his belief that he would prove the establishment naysayers wrong by proving himself great. He believed that he could save American democracy by transforming the country—passing monumental legislation, breaking with economic orthodoxy, redirecting its foreign policy to the challenges of the future.

For Biden the process and the substance were intertwined. Although he liked to brag about being a constitutional scholar—on the basis of seventeen years Biden had spent as an adjunct professor at Widener University Delaware Law School—he really had one primary profession in his career: he was a politician. His expertise was nose counting, horse trading, and spreading a thick layer of flattery over his audiences.

Over the decades, his profession, never truly respected, had fallen deeply out of favor. The nation elected consecutive presidents (Barack Obama, Donald Trump) who posed as antipoliticians, figures who emerged from outside the system, without much experience in Washington and with an abiding disdain for it. Both Obama and Trump came to office with the belief that they led mass movements, independent of political parties. In very different ways, both men profited from and intensified the old moan that politicians were the problem, corrupt, unresponsive, lacking in necessary boldness.

But the public wasn't just rejecting a profession; it simultaneously discarded a set of practices. Politics is the means by which a society mediates its difference of opinion, allowing for peaceful coexistence. It's an ethos that requires tolerance of competing truths—and permits the possibility of social change. It's a set of rules whereby the side that fails to prevail in democratic decision-making accepts its defeat.

The insurrection—stoked by Trump's refusal to accept the outcome of the 2020 vote—was the most worrying evidence of the demise of politics. Witnessing such horrific behavior, it felt reasonable to ask, Was it possible to cooperate with the political party that coddled Trump, let alone coexist in the same society as the people who voted for him?

Biden set out to prove the eternal relevance of politics. In fact, it was the way out of this mess. He wanted to show that dealmaking, coalition building, and persuading the other side were still effective ways to get things done. But on certain days of his presidency, it seemed like nobody else in the country sincerely believed in his faith. It felt as if he naively assumed the good faith of malevolent adversaries, that he believed in salvaging institutions beyond repair. His faith in his profession looked like it might doom him to become a historic failure, at the moment when America could least afford for him to falter.

But in the story of Joe Biden, a pattern keeps reasserting itself. Just after he is dismissed as past his time, written off because of his doddering detachment from the zeitgeist, he pulls off his greatest successes. He shocks those who only think they know him.

I FIRST pondered this book in the summer of 2020, when it seemed likely that Joe Biden might become president. I wanted to chronicle his administration's first hundred days as it sought to tame the pandemic and undo the legacy of Donald Trump. But that milestone came—and went. I struggled to grab hold of an assessment of the Biden presidency that I trusted. Each time I pondered stopping my project, it felt like a premature terminus. I worried the book's judgments would be stale by its publication date.

But after two years, I knew that I had my story and faith in my conclusions. In the modern presidency, the first two years of administration are the narrow window in which presidents can realize their highest ambitions. It's nearly an iron rule of politics that incumbents are punished by the electorate in their first midterm election, losing their congressional majorities, thus ending the possibilities for grand legislative achievements.

At the beginning of 2022, it seemed as if Joe Biden's window might close without much to show for his efforts. Despite the success of the vaccine rollout and the passage of a massive stimulus bill, his messy presidency looked like it would be best remembered for its failures—a disastrous withdrawal from Afghanistan, the humiliating collapse of his Build Back Better legislation, and the rise of inflation. Comparisons to Jimmy Carter, the benchmark for a presidency stuck in a ditch, felt reasonable, if not yet fully deserved.

But then redemption—and a profound legacy—came unexpectedly, splayed across the second half of his second year, as he orchestrated the most fertile season of legislation in memory and rallied the world to Ukraine's defense.

During Biden's long period of flailing, I had feared that he had missed his chance to avert the worst consequence of climate change—and that another opportunity to protect the planet wouldn't come around for years, after it was far too late. But then in the summer of 2022, Congress passed the Inflation Reduction Act, a banally named bill that will transform American life. Its investments in alternative energy will ignite the growth of industries that will wean the economy from its dependence on fossil fuels.

That achievement was of a piece with the new economics that his presidency had begun to enshrine. Where the past generation of Democratic presidents was deferential to markets, reluctant to challenge monopoly, indifferent to unions, and generally encouraging of globalization, Biden went in a different direction. Through a series of bills—not just his investments in alternative energy, but also the CHIPS Act and his infrastructure bill—he erected a state that will function as an investment bank, spending money to catalyze favored industries to realize his vision, where the United States controls the commanding heights of the economy of the future.

The critique of gerontocracy is that once politicians become senior citizens, they will only focus on the short term, because they will only in-habit the short term. But Biden, the oldest president in history, pushed for spending money on projects that might not come to fruition in his lifetime. His theory of the case—that democracy will succeed only if it delivers for its citizens—compelled him to push for expenditures on unglamorous but essential items such as electric vehicle charging systems, crumbling ports, and semiconductor plants, which will decarbonize the economy, employ the next generation of workers, and prevent national decline.

With Ukraine, his creative diplomacy mobilized an alliance—and an American public—that not so long ago exuded indifference to autocracy. He persuaded them to engage in selfless acts of solidarity, paying higher prices to sanction Russian aggression. By quietly arming the Ukrainians, he helped them fend off invasion, while avoiding the worst dangers of fight-ing a proxy war against a nuclear power. It was a bravura display of states-manship.

IT SEEMS only right to admit that I began this project sharing the Washing-ton establishment's skepticism of the man. I viewed him as a bloviator who dangerously fetishized bipartisanship.

But as I reported on him at close distance—through several hundred interviews with his White House inner circle, his cabinet, his oldest friends, and members of Congress—my respect for him grew. I came to appreciate his ability to shelve his ego and empathically understand the psychology of the foreign leaders he sparred with and the senators he wooed. In negotia-tions with these figures, he could be shrewdly self-effacing, accepting the fact that sometimes it was better if he wasn't the center of attention. He forced himself to sit back and let proxies do his bidding.

I found myself especially surprised by his capacity for absorbing criticism in the short term to achieve the objectives he considered most important. There was a patience, born of experience, that I never knew he possessed. It helped guide him to his greatest successes, and it carried him through his lowest moments. Despite the fiasco of the Afghan withdrawal, he never apologized or deflected blame onto his aides. He stubbornly owned the decision that scarred his legacy.

None of this healed the nation's divide, although after two years of the Biden presidency, the political scientists predicting civil war began to sound more alarmist than prophetic. With a slight cooling of the political climate, bipartisan-minded senators passed a raft of legislation, confirming Biden's instincts that creaky institutions could be rendered functional, that consensus was still possible in America. And in the midterm election, despite Biden's inability to tame inflation, Trumpist election deniers largely failed in their attempt to seize control of state governments. Biden hadn't defeated authoritarianism once and for all, but he pushed back the threat for the time being. It was hard to imagine any president doing much better under the circumstances.

Above all, watching Joe Biden at work renewed my respect for a profession, and its craft, unloved and in some ways unlovable, "the strong and slow boring of hard boards," as Max Weber famously described it. That, in the end, might be his profound achievement, providing an instructive example of the tedious nobility of the political vocation. Unheroic but honorably human, he will be remembered as the old hack who could.

PART ONE

DARK WINTER

January–March 2021

1

Day One

INAUGURATION DAY BEGAN at 8:30 a.m., with an occasion that unofficially, grudgingly marked the transfer of power. Donald Trump's loyalists gathered at Joint Base Andrews, in suburban Maryland, to hear their leader rant one last time in front of the seal of the president and watch him clamber aboard his valedictory flight on Air Force One, carrying him to his beach club in Florida. This was the lone inauguration in recent American history, with the exception of Gerald Ford's swearing in, where the outgoing president avowedly declined to participate in the official ceremony itself.

But for all the rhetorical force with which Trump battered the legitimacy of the election—all the rancor he stirred, all the violence he inspired—he left without making any more of a scene than usual. "Hopefully, it's not a long-term goodbye," he said wanly. The fact that he was leaving Washington of his own volition was the closest he ever came to explicitly conceding the fact of his defeat.

Minutes after Trump ascended to the airplane, Joe and Jill Biden arrived at St. Matthew's Cathedral for mass. They strolled past their friends and family, past the vice president elect, Kamala Harris, and her husband, taking their place in the front pew, just in back of an engraving in the floor commemorating the spot where John F. Kennedy's corpse rested during his funeral service in the building.

Even before the horror of January 6, Biden intended to invite the congressional leadership of the country to the event. But the invitations weren't extended until after the insurrection, and the presence of the Republican leaders, Mitch McConnell and Kevin McCarthy, suddenly felt loaded with outsize meaning. He granted his adversaries admission to the most intimate moment of the day.

As the service ended, the priest told the congregation, "Would the president elect and vice president elect and congressional leadership please remain in their places." All the friends and relatives piled into buses to the Capitol, but the leadership of the nation waited together for a separate motorcade. For fifteen minutes, Mitch McConnell, Nancy Pelosi, Steny Hoyer, Kevin McCarthy, Chuck Schumer, Kamala Harris, and Joe Biden mingled in an empty church. It was a moment of polite coexistence, of vacuous chitchat, a hopeful suggestion that perhaps Washington might actually revert to the folkways that prevailed before Trump, to something that could be described as normal.

AT 10:00 A.M., two hours before he officially started his new job, Ron Klain arrived in the West Wing for his third administration, to assume a post that his friends knew he had long coveted: White House chief of staff.

When Klain was twenty-eight, in 1989, Joe Biden hired him to serve as chief counsel of the Senate Judiciary Committee. He had worked, on and off, for Biden ever since. While Biden proudly touted the fact that he went to a state school, he took pride in the Ivy Leaguers, like Klain, on his rosters. They were his meritocratic trophies—and Klain his eternal wunderkind, even as he neared sixty. Words streamed from Klain's mouth in paragraph form. In a frustrated mood, Biden sometimes posed questions for the purpose of testing his staff, to gauge its grasp of minutiae. Klain, who projected the confidence of a high school quiz bowl champion, almost always knew the answer.

Biden not only admired Klain, he might have even seen familiar traits in him. Back in the last Democratic administration, the inner circle around Barack Obama undervalued Klain, as they did his boss, for lacking the qualities that the in-crowd prized. They thought he tried too hard, that he needed to better contain his verbal virtuosity in meetings, that he always had his eyes on a bigger job.

Obama and his acolytes professed to hate Washington, and they considered Klain a creature of the place. He certainly felt like an omnipresent fixture in the White House. Those who worked with Klain knew him by the sound of his gait as he walked through the halls in the early morning. He would wear his dress shoes as if they were clogs, with his feet smashing down the backs. His instantaneous responses to incoming email came with date stamps that suggested insomnia.

On the morning of January 20, Klain might have preferred to attend in person the inaugural ceremony of the man whose political career he worked so hard to advance. But he was missing it, stuck in the building at the behest of Trump's chief of staff, Mark Meadows.

Ever since the November election, much of the Trump administration acted as if the Biden people were engaged in a hostile takeover of the government. They refused to share the most basic details that would allow the incoming administration to prepare for the monumental tasks in front of it. A pandemic was raging—and the Trump people withheld access to civil servants and government data that would have provided the Biden White House with a basic sense of the government's vaccination program. When Biden officials asked Trump's trade negotiator for details about the state of conversations with China, he refused. Trump appointees at the Office of Management and Budget broke with generations of practice and prevented civil servants from helping Biden aides prepare the budget that they were legally required to submit to Congress in February.

After all of that petty obstruction, Meadows's invitation to meet felt like an act of comity that shouldn't be shirked.

When Klain arrived at the White House, he found it emptier than he had ever seen. Only a handful of workers were moving furniture around. He knocked on Meadows's door, then jostled the knob. It was locked.

Eventually, an aide emerged and asked Klain to come to the Situation Room. He handed him a phone.

"Mark, where are you?" Klain asked.

"You know . . . President Trump left late. I'm late. Just sit and wait."

Half an hour later, Meadows emerged in the corridor and walked toward Klain and warmly greeted him. He ushered Klain into his office. "I don't have time to sit with you," he apologized. "Trump signed one last pardon, and I have to deliver it to the Justice Department before noon to make sure that it's valid."

With that, Meadows told Klain to call if he needed anything and left to perform a task better suited to an intern. The whole encounter felt like a fitting coda to the most shambolic transition of power in American history.

For the next hour and a half, Klain lingered in the West Wing. His administration was on the brink of launching one of the most complex government programs of all time, distributing hundreds of millions of doses of vaccine; it needed to prevent the free fall of the economy and restore a government, which had fallen into disrepair; it promised to end the longest war in American history. But that was ninety minutes away. All of his governmental devices were scheduled to be activated at 12:01 p.m. So the man who would soon run the building had to run down the clock, waiting for his turn.

WHEN BIDEN walked out onto the West Front of the Capitol just after eleven thirty, his eyes fixed on Bill Clinton, George W. Bush, and Barack Obama, the men who had held the job before him. These were presidents he had known, observed up close. They weren't demigods or fundamentally superior to him. Their presence reassured him. As he later related the moment to aides, he told himself, *If they could do this job, so can I.*

At an earlier stage in his career, faced with a big moment like this, Biden would have felt the anxiety of influence. As a young senator, he gave rousing addresses that aspired to the lush lyricism of the Kennedys, rife with verbal pyrotechnics, moments of soaring eloquence. They seemed a source of pride for him, evidence of how he mastered public speaking, the very thing that had once debilitated him. This desire to prove his eloquence landed him in trouble back in 1987. As he sought to transcend himself through oratory, he came to inhabit another man's story. He inadvertently plagiarized sentences from the British politician Neil Kinnock, as if he were subconsciously confirming that there was something inauthentic about his grandiloquent style.

But as he walked down the steps of the Capitol, he stared into the teleprompter at much simpler language.

The prototype for the presidential speechwriter is a young person who dreams of having words immortalized in anthologies. That wasn't Mike Donilon. For starters, Donilon, rumpled, with untamed eyebrows, wasn't young. Like Ron Klain, he had worked for Biden since the eighties. For most of his career, Mike Donilon toiled as a political consultant—a *hack*, as he self-effacingly described himself, and Donilon was neurotically self-effacing—who did the workaday stuff of his profession. He scripted ads, commissioned polls, and wrote messaging memos. But his great skill was channeling his boss. Devoid of ego, an observant introvert, he could place himself in Biden's mind and anticipate his thinking. As Biden once described Donilon, "He understood me without saying it."

When Donilon sat down to write the inaugural, he began sketching before consulting Biden. The big theme was screamingly obvious to him, because Biden had hit it relentlessly through the campaign: unity. Biden's calls for unity were often mocked on Twitter as nostalgia for the bipartisanship that prevailed when he first arrived in Washington in the seventies but had long since dissipated. As Donilon wrote the inaugural, he aimed to sharpen the big theme. It was not a longing to escape differences of opinion, nor was it a call for treating racism with civility. Biden would rally the nation to form a popular front against the common enemies of disease and hate.

Biden and Donilon had just about finished the speech before January 6, a catastrophe that confirmed the choice of themes. He had set aside time to practice the speech with his friend the historian Jon Meacham and his younger sister, Valerie, who persistently pressed him to be plain-spoken. ("Don't say 'hyperbole,' when you mean 'exaggeration,'" she liked to chide.) But Biden wanted to tweak the draft to account for the trauma. He wanted to both acknowledge the tenuousness of American democracy and also note that it had just survived its greatest modern test, as evidenced by the very fact of the inauguration ceremony itself: "So now, on this hallowed ground where just days ago violence sought to shake this Capitol's very foundation, we come together as one nation, under God, indivisible, to carry out the peaceful transfer of power as we have for more than two centuries."

As Biden explained his conception of unity, there was an unintended element of autobiography to the argument. The lifelong politician implicitly made the case for politics as the best available mechanism for avoiding deadly fracture. In politics, success stems from the capacity to persuade, not conquer or punish, those who disagree. He wasn't longing for the country to be made whole again, so much as pleading for it to avoid the temptations of violence. "Disagreement must not lead to disunion," he said.

The fact that he suggested the plausibility of disunion—the same word Lincoln used to warn against civil war—illustrated the magnitude of the task.

EVERYTHING ABOUT arriving on Inauguration Day—in the middle of the pandemic, in the aftermath of Trump—had required an unusual orchestration. That work fell to Jen O'Malley Dillon, the manager of the campaign, now slated to become deputy White House chief of staff. Where Trump and his administration had infested the West Wing with disease, Biden instructed O'Malley Dillon to come up with the protocols that would model how to responsibly manage a workplace.

O'Malley Dillon had never worked in the building before. But she pored over architectural schematics to figure out how staff could move through it in a socially distant fashion. There was another reason, aside from the stubborn refusal to mask, that COVID spread through the White House under Trump. It's a densely-populated building, especially the poorly ventilated warren of the West Wing. To mitigate the possibility of viral spread, she limited the number of personnel in the building. A chunk of the incoming staff would continue working from home.

Those who arrived at work received a list of firm instructions. They were told to eat lunch at their desks behind closed doors. West Wing conference rooms should hardly be used. Most meetings would be conducted via Zoom, even if a colleague sat next door. Meetings in the Oval Office were capped at fifteen participants—the couches were limited to four people. Before each meeting in the Oval, staff had to devise and distribute a fresh seating plan.

The transfer of power is a high ideal of the Constitution, and a logistical pain in the neck. White House staff had six hours to move the Bidens' belongings into the building—to "flip the house"—not enough time to fully unpack, given the chaos.

In the weeks leading up to the inauguration, the Biden transition received calls from Trump staffers urging them to fire the chief White House usher, who had previously served as the rooms manager at Trump's Washington hotel. At 11:30 a.m. on Inauguration Day, Trump's own White House counsel did the deed. The absence of a chief usher further harried the day. When Joe and Jill Biden finally arrived at the White House at 3:45 p.m., his first time entering the building as president, they stood at the door. Protocol dictated that the entrance swing open, but for a painfully awkward beat, the couple stared blankly ahead, waiting for access to their new home.

BIDEN ENTERED the Oval Office for the first time in four years. On his desk, he found a letter left by Donald Trump. After reading it, he placed it in his pocket, without describing its contents, except to note its surprising graciousness.

At 5:00 p.m., aides piled seventeen folios in front of him, each containing an executive action awaiting his signature. Biden had always claimed that he felt squeamish about the imperial presidency, which so diminished his beloved Senate. During the campaign, he liked to muse to his aides about how he wanted to recalibrate the balance of power in Washington, to restore Congress to its proper place. He toyed with the idea of traveling to Capitol Hill each week to hold office hours, an act of presidential deference.

But now he embarked on what advisers referred to as the Days of Action, a ten-day torrent of unilateral orders. As his pen slid its way across the folios, the new president systematically undid the old president's legacy, ending the ban on travel from certain Muslim countries and pausing construction of the border wall. He restored the United States to the Paris climate agreement and the World Health Organization.

To combat COVID, Biden mandated the use of masks in interstate travel and on federal property; he ordered his administration to issue guidance for the reopening of shuttered schools. To combat climate change, he signed an order requiring the bureaucracy to consider the implications of the crisis in every policy decision; he canceled the Keystone XL pipeline. To blunt the economic crisis, he extended moratoriums on evictions and the collection of student debt.

Presidential historians speculated about how he might surpass Franklin Roosevelt's tally for executive actions. Such comparisons to FDR were a reach, but they also felt strangely within reach, especially to Biden. Despite the commentariat's modest expectations for him, Biden emphatically believed that he could pass massive pieces of legislation that would win him a place in the pantheon of great Democratic presidents. Biden hadn't waited his whole professional life for the job just to be a placeholder.

AT 6:58 P.M., Jen Psaki entered White House communications director Kate Bedingfield's office. Having consumed coffee all day, Psaki exploded with energy. Bedingfield and Psaki first worked together in 2006 as regional press secretaries for the Democratic Congressional Campaign Committee. They were bridesmaids in each other's weddings. Now, Bedingfield was psyching up her already-amped friend for her debut briefing as press secretary, in prime time no less. As Bedingfield barked encouragement, Psaki shuffled her feet to expunge the yips, then entered the briefing room.

In truth, Psaki didn't especially care for the traditional press conference, which she considered stilted and in desperate need of updating. If these were normal times, she might have tweaked the format. But when Biden first spoke to her about the job, he told her that he craved a return to the time when the White House stood as an authoritative voice, when the public regarded it as a purveyor of reliable facts. To revive an ethos that prevailed before the age of social media, she gravitated to the antiquated format.

As she stood at the podium, Psaki kept turning the pages of her self-curated briefing book, with a plume of Post-it notes protruding from it. Yet she self-consciously admitted moments that she didn't have the answer at her fingertips. She promised that she would research the question and return with an answer. "Let me circle back," she kept repeating.

When Psaki contemplated her first day on the job, she realized that her predecessor had seemingly broken with tradition. Ever since the Ford administration, each White House press secretary had passed their successor a bulletproof brocaded vest, the flak jacket—eventually replaced by a blazer—with a note of advice and encouragement tucked into its pocket. Psaki couldn't find the jacket and, in fact, never did. If the Trump administration had plundered the rest of the government, it might very well have absconded with that ceremonial relic, too.

To CONFORM with the instructions of public health officials, there were no inaugural balls, no gowns or tuxedos, just a bland prime-time televised celebration, hosted by Tom Hanks on the steps of the Lincoln Memorial. Joe

Biden made a brief appearance and then left to watch the festivities unfold from the warmth of the White House residence while Kamala Harris remained on the frigid set of the production.

At every moment of the day, Harris had self-consciously sought to commune with history. That morning she dressed in purple as an homage to Shirley Chisholm, the Black congresswoman from Brooklyn who had run for president in 1972. (Chisholm used the color in her campaign logo.) When Sonia Sotomayor administered the vice presidential oath, Harris put her hand on a Bible that had belonged to Thurgood Marshall. As she watched the fireworks display at the day's end, she carefully positioned herself at the spot on the steps where Martin Luther King Jr. had delivered his "I Have a Dream" speech.

Where Biden felt like a high school senior returning from summer break, Harris was bursting with enthusiasm. Her exuberance carried her through the day's surreal moments. After the inauguration ceremony, Mike Pence, one of the few Trump officials to attend the event, cornered her in the Capitol and began peppering her with mundane questions—"When do you move in? . . . How will you spend the evening?"—as if he hadn't just been part of an administration that had deployed every unprecedented tactic to prevent this day from ever arriving. Harris smiled through the exchange.

In a normal transition of power, Harris would have spent the night in the vice presidential mansion on Massachusetts Avenue. But repairs to the building prevented her from moving in. Instead, she returned to her condo in the West End, where she had woken up that morning. It was a strange liminal state of existence, and the whole day—its promise of normalcy and calm, of democracy functioning as designed—felt like a reverie.

2

Taking the Call

THE CALL WAS UNEXPECTED. On the second full day in the White House, emissaries of an old enemy left word that he wanted to talk. The enemy didn't hint at what he wanted to discuss, but Biden's aides just as soon would have ignored his unwelcome presence. It was perfectly in character for Vladimir Putin to ruin a honeymoon.

In the opinion of Jake Sullivan, Biden's forty-three-year-old national security adviser, the conversation could wait. As part of the preparation for the presidency, Sullivan had edited a list of the phone calls to foreign leaders that Biden was obliged to make, for the sake of repairing the damage of the Trump years, rebuilding old alliances, devoting a little loving attention to bruised friendships in Europe. The list of calls required careful curation, because each one had the potential to consume unexpectedly large chunks of Biden's schedule. Schmoozing foreign leaders was Biden's happy place.

When Sullivan informed Biden about Putin's request, he recommended that there was no harm in letting Putin wait for his turn in line. But Biden's response surprised him. The president told him, "You know, where I come from, when a significant world leader, a friend or adversary calls you up, unless you have a damn good reason not to, you take the call."

Sure, it would be satisfying to leave Putin hanging, especially after everything he had done to mess with American democracy in recent elections.

But the call, Biden argued, was an opportunity. There was every chance that Putin would attempt to wreak fresh havoc, mischief that would derail Biden's expansive plans to refocus American foreign policy on the strategic threat posed by China. If Biden had any prayer of minimizing the danger that Putin posed, he needed to personally tend to Putin's ego.

In Biden's retrospective opinion, the Obama administration had erred by gratuitously thumbing its nose at Russia. His old boss referred to the old Cold War rival as a "regional power" acting "out of weakness." Biden wouldn't make that mistake. He felt that Putin responded to both displays of strength and tokens of respect. Though it was difficult to combine both in the same breath, Biden told Sullivan that he intended to indulge Putin's sense of self-importance by returning the call, while using it to deliver a stern warning.

FOUR DAYS LATER, Biden had the Russian leader on the line. He began with an existential piece of business. In less than two weeks, an arms control deal, the New START Treaty, would expire. Biden told Putin that he didn't want that to happen. Whatever their differences, they needed to safeguard the planet from the old menace of nuclear Armageddon.

Having dispensed with the easy part of the conversation, Biden pivoted to the sources of tension.

"I want to be direct with you," he told him.

In the last months of the Trump administration, Russia had allegedly engaged in a series of nefarious misdeeds. With the SolarWinds hack, the Russians had slipped a bit of malicious code into a ubiquitous software update, allowing its intelligence services access to the servers of thousands of American corporations and government agencies. There was the poisoning of the dissident Alexey Navalny in August and the lingering matter of election interference, as well as reports that the Russians had placed bounties on the heads of US soldiers in Afghanistan.

Biden told Putin that he wasn't pointing a finger, at least not yet. The intelligence community would review the accusations against Russia. In a month's time, Biden would receive a report. If the evidence against Russia was compelling, punishment would be forthcoming.

To Sullivan's ears, Putin seemed taken aback by the blunt tone. Rather than pushing back on any of the allegations, the Russian president strangely seemed to accept them as fact. Putin ended the call with a polite "thank you." But it was hard to know how he absorbed the conversation, since it was unclear what he hoped to accomplish by scheduling it in the first place. There was always the sense that Putin was poking and prodding, searching for a weakness that he could exploit, in service of some sinister plan kept out of view, a gambit that would change everything. No token of respect would be able to avert that.

3

Visions of Rescue

O N FEBRUARY 5, Nancy Pelosi watched as the new president stood and brought his guests glasses of water. Of course, the guests were the chairs of the congressional committees whom Biden needed to steward his first massive piece of legislation. Then again, he was the commander in chief, and they were sitting in the Oval Office. *Just relax*, Pelosi thought. But the son of a car salesman had settled into a mode he clearly relished. There was no such thing as too thick. He told his guests, "This is your house."

Back when he was vice president, members of Congress liked to quietly beat up on Barack Obama as a distant introvert who didn't golf with them or invite them over to watch the Super Bowl. Joe Manchin once confided this complaint to Biden. Obama had just called the West Virginia senator to commend him for putting together a gun control bill. Manchin confided that it was his first interaction with the president. Biden reassured him, "It's a long line."

Finally, Joe Biden, an Irish raconteur, had the chance to do it his way, to exploit the majesty of the Oval Office to create a home court advantage for himself. He asked his friend, the historian and occasional speechwriter Jon Meacham, to curate the Oval Office so that he could use it as a stage for storytelling.

In the corner of the room, Meacham placed portraits of Alexander Hamilton and Thomas Jefferson so that Biden could point to them and say, *If you think we've got deep differences of opinion now, you should have seen what politics was like in their time.* He put Bobby Kennedy's bust near Martin Luther King Jr. so that Biden could argue, *See, Kennedy ordered the wiretapping of King, but he eventually became a champion of the civil rights movement. It's possible for a human being to grow.*

The portrait that Biden gave pride of place was a massive oil-on-canvas painting of Franklin Roosevelt, which hung above the mantel and which he liked to proudly show to visitors. When he did, he was really telling a story about himself, what he dreamed of becoming.

THE ECONOMIC conditions in late January 2021 were objectively terrible, but hardly akin to the depression Roosevelt inherited. When FDR became president, the government hadn't taken sufficient action to avert economic catastrophe. By the time Joe Biden took office, Congress had already passed multiple COVID relief bills, some of the most expensive pieces of legislation in history. It had spent nearly $4 trillion propping up an economy that shuttered itself in March 2020.

Just over a week into the collective shutdown that began in the second week in March, *The New York Times* published a chart on its front page, to capture the economic toll. It showed a line rocketing straight up the entire length of the newspaper, illustrating the growth of unemployment claims. Some twenty million Americans suddenly lost their jobs.

Once all the government money began circulating through the economy, and after the nation began to regain its bearings after the initial horror of the pandemic's descent, businesses started to hire back employees. The COVID recession hardly counted as one, since it *technically* lasted only two months.

That upswing of job growth continued until approximately the moment that Joe Biden became president. The problem is that physical health and economic health of the nation were intertwined. An understandable human impulse to preserve ritual, to commune with parents and siblings at Thanksgiving, permitted the virus to ricochet across generations and through families. But as the pandemic entered its deadliest phase, Donald Trump retreated into his television set and cut himself off from the parts of the world that didn't share his dark theories or his smoldering rage. The occupant of the White House had nothing to say about the nation he ostensibly governed, as it hurtled to catastrophe.

By December, COVID deaths began shooting upward. Nineteen thousand Americans died Christmas week. The surge in COVID cases stalled the economic recovery. Of the twenty million jobs lost at the outset of the pandemic, only ten million had returned, and it wasn't clear when the rest would come back.

The magnitude of human suffering was captured in the police blotters. In early December, *The Washington Post* reported, shoplifting was spiking across the country. Diapers, baby formula, and dried pasta were all being swiped from the shelves. Food banks were running short of funding, since they were perpetually emptied by the constant demand.

When Biden's top economic adviser, Brian Deese, briefed Biden on a disconcerting jobs report in early December, on his first day on the job, he told him that it was possible that businesses would begin to shed workers in massive numbers, yet again. He told the then president elect that there was a chance of economic collapse: "The bottom just might fall out."

BIDEN'S PRIMARY POINT of comparison wasn't really Roosevelt; it was Obama. By the end of their presidency, Biden was so in sync with his boss that the pair had what the journalist Jonathan Alter described as "secret code." When Obama tipped back his chair in meetings, Biden took that as a cue to ask provocative questions that Obama wanted answered but didn't want to raise himself for fear of shifting the tenor of a meeting.

But Biden also chafed at the constraints of his job—and if Obama sometimes rolled his eyes at him, he would roll his own right back. There was the tinge of class rivalry to their gibes. The lunch-pail cornball and the effete professor culturally chafing each other. Biden told a friend that Obama didn't know how to say *fuck you* properly, with the right elongation of vowels and the necessary hardness of his consonants; it was how they must curse in the ivory tower.

Now Biden was reliving the Obama presidency, but as the boss. Like Obama, he needed to pass a massive piece of economic stimulus upon entering office. During the transition, the Biden team had assigned a wonk named David Kamin to conduct an oral history of Obama's massive stimulus bills, the Recovery Act, to internalize all the learnable lessons.

Over time, Biden had come to regret the inadequacy of the Recovery Act, although he said so only obliquely. He wished that Obama had heeded the economic advisers who told him that the crisis required closer to $1.7 trillion in stimulus, if the administration hoped to regenerate all the jobs that had evaporated in the recession. But rather than making the case for a solution adequate to the problem, Obama negotiated with himself. Worried that Congress would never pass such massive legislation, he agreed with aides urging him to aim lower. In the end, the Recovery Act spent $787 billion.

The deficiencies of the bill haunted Biden. He frequently talked about the scarring effects of unemployment, which he had experienced himself when his own father lost his job and the family's socioeconomic status slipped. This was very near a central philosophical tenet for him: that work provides meaning, that it is at the core of the sense of self and a wellspring of dignity.

This time, Biden told Deese that he was going to go big. If Obama erred on the side of underreaction, Biden was going to err on the side of overreaction. He wanted to recover as many jobs as fast as possible, to push in the direction of full employment.

THE LEGISLATIVE strategy for Biden's presidency was set in mid-December, when the incoming administration didn't know the most elemental fact about its future. It wasn't sure whether Democrats would control the Senate. A majority felt improbable, since control of the body hinged on two runoff elections in Georgia, held simultaneously on January 5. Given the immediacy of the crisis, Biden aides couldn't afford to wait around for the results. It was far safer to assume that Republicans would remain in charge, that the filibuster would remain a primary obstacle—and that Biden would need eleven of their votes to pass his relief package.

From her home in suburban Maryland, Anita Dunn virtually presented him with the outlines of a plan. In the lore of the 2020 campaign, it was Dunn who salvaged the operation from disaster. After the humiliations of Biden's fourth-place finish in Iowa and his tumble to fifth in New Hampshire, Biden asked her to retool his operation, to give him an organization and strategy that might resuscitate him, however unlikely. The campaign's abrupt reversal of fortune earned her a special place in Biden's small universe, and she became the nexus of nearly everything.

What Dunn presented to Biden was the consensus of his inner circle. She laid out how Biden could audaciously cram his biggest plans into one mega-bill. They proposed spending roughly $1.3 trillion addressing the pandemic and its economic fallout, money for unemployment insurance and vaccine distribution, aid for depleted state and local governments, and $1,400 checks that would be sent to much of the country. On top of all that, they wanted Biden to simultaneously include another $1.1 trillion in spending on rebuilding infrastructure, incentivizing green energy, and subsidizing childcare. In one swoop, one single piece of legislation, the administration would seek both massive stimulus and to realize a large swath of Biden's domestic agenda.

Back when he served as chief of staff for Barack Obama, Rahm Emanuel quipped, "The presidency is like a new car. It starts depreciating the moment you drive it off the lot." That summed up the consensus of the inner circle. While sending direct checks to struggling families was necessary, it wasn't a permanent achievement. And it wasn't the basis for winning elections. People would spend their stimulus check, perhaps feel a moment of gratitude, then get on with their lives. If there was one shot at passing a monumental spending bill, it needed to include the lasting investments Biden had proposed on the campaign trail.

Aides braced for the possibility that Biden might react negatively at the $2.4 trillion figure they attached to the legislation. But by the time Dunn made it to the third slide in her deck, Biden had seen enough.

"I don't want to be dead on arrival," he sniffed.

The size of this package, he predicted, would cause Republicans, even the ones whom he considered friends, to throw up their hands and flat-out reject his entreaties. "This is too much for people to absorb."

Everyone on the Zoom knew there would be no budging Biden from his convictions about legislative strategy, since he considers himself to be his own best tactician. He was the only one in the room who had been a protégé of Mike Mansfield and Hubert Humphrey.

"I won because I promised to beat the virus," he said. That, and that alone, was his first priority.

When he talked about the institution of Congress, it sounded as if he were describing a human being with feelings and a temperament, a thing to be respected and romanced. It could be brought along to the bigger stuff, step-by-step, all in the right time and order. After passing a COVID package, he would quickly follow with bills to make massive investments that fulfilled his promise to "build back better." The first months of his presidency, he declared, would unfold in two acts: what he deemed "relief" and "recovery." He would nurse the nation back to health, then set about transforming it. Because Biden favored simple declarative names, Dunn called the first piece of legislation the American Rescue Plan.

Some big decisions, like selecting a vice president, paralyzed Biden with indecision and dragged past self-imposed deadlines. Others he made in a flash. On the Zoom, he bucked the detailed plans of his staff and quickly rendered the most consequential strategic decision of his not-yet presidency.

————

THEN, on January 5, the contours of the presidency shifted. Both of the Democrats candidates in Georgia—Jon Ossoff and Rev. Raphael Warnock—prevailed, handing the party its forty-ninth and fiftieth senators. A bare majority is still a majority, and that changed everything. Suddenly, the fate of Biden's first legislative proposal was no longer tethered to the whims of a small coterie of Republicans, who may or may not have been willing to cut a deal.

Two days later Chuck Schumer idled in his town car on a side street in Queens. He was supposed to be sitting in the Colombian restaurant just across the block, having a coffee and a schmooze. Instead, he was stuck in the back seat waiting.

Schumer had just experienced some of the wildest vicissitudes in American political history. He woke up on January 6 as the unlikely majority leader. Then that afternoon he narrowly escaped a brush with an insurrectionist mob, averted by a member of his security detail grabbing him by the collar and spinning him around to run in the other direction. Schumer recounted the moment to nearly everyone he encountered in its aftermath. And though they might have listened skeptically to his retelling, given his reputation for relishing melodrama, video evidence graphically confirmed his version of events.

Whatever lingering trauma, he quickly returned to the comforts of politicking. Even though the election in Georgia had endowed him with the title of majority leader, he continued to take provincial meetings in outer boroughs. Inside the restaurant, a newly elected state assemblywoman was sitting at a table expecting his imminent arrival. But he needed to stay in a quiet place for his first conversation with the president elect since the Capitol riot.

When the phone finally rang, Biden told him, "My heart goes out to you." Since it was already late in the day, neither man wanted to dwell on the horrors of the very recent past, even if the events of that day made their work considerably more complicated. A chunk of Joe Biden's honeymoon—and Chuck Schumer's debut as leader—would now be consumed with articles of impeachment filed against Donald Trump, for his role in instigating the riot.

As Joe Biden spoke to Schumer from his home in Delaware, he told him that he had Ron Klain in the room. He wanted Klain to pass along the latest thinking about the COVID relief package taking shape.

Schumer had been eager to see how far the ambitions of the new president would stretch now that he controlled the Senate. And, more to the point, he wanted to learn the size of the COVID relief package in the works. But when Klain unveiled the number, it took Schumer aback. It wasn't nearly high enough, in his estimation. Klain had proposed spending $1.3 trillion, lower than Schumer anticipated. The senator took a moment to regain his bearings. He paused to figure out how he would express his misgivings.

Over the course of the past nine months, the Senate had already passed multiple COVID relief bills. Schumer had negotiated them all. The first majority leader to preside over his caucus in the spirit of a *bubbe* pushing matzo ball soup, he liked to brag about how he tended to his senators. Since he doesn't trust the nuance of written communication, he shunned sending his senators text messages or emails. He spoke to them on his flip phone, an antiquated device he's unlikely to ever upgrade, it's so entrenched in his shtick. Few things made him prouder than announcing that he has memorized the phone numbers of his fifty senators.

As he cut deals with the Trump administration, Schumer kept a mental tally of the pent-up demands of Democratic senators, all the measures that never made it into previous iterations of COVID relief packages. Now that the Democrats held the Senate, they would want to realize their thwarted ideas. But as soon as he heard Biden's number, he knew it wasn't big enough to cover them all. Schumer told the president that he thought the package would probably balloon to $2 trillion.

"All right," Biden told him, "I hear you loud and clear." He said that he would give a speech on the following Thursday unveiling his plan. "I'm going to tell a story more than talk about the specifics about what we need to do."

"That's what you need to be doing as our new president," Schumer replied. "Just make sure this is a much bigger number."

THE BIGGEST item on the congressional wish list was something called the Child Tax Credit, and it was passionately desired by Connecticut congresswoman Rosa DeLauro—an implacable, powerful member of Nancy Pelosi's inner circle, nearly Joe Biden's age but with streaks of purple in her hair, a look that *The New Republic* described as "cool art mom."

What DeLauro wanted was nothing less than a revolution in social policy under the guise of the IRS. Ever since Bill Clinton reformed welfare, the government had demanded that poor families work in exchange for cash assistance from the state. But in recent years, Republicans had tentatively embraced the idea of giving families with children a subsidy in the form of a tax credit. Democrats, not just DeLauro, had seen the potential in this idea, and aimed to push it aggressively forward. Instead of giving that money at tax time, they proposed that the government send parents a monthly check. What they were proposing was an allowance, a guaranteed income for families, a variation of what European welfare states provide.

Thanks to DeLauro's tenacity, the Child Tax Credit made its way into the bill. Low- and middle-income families with kids would be eligible to receive monthly payments, up to $300. And the bill began to swell with other provisions, including $5 billion in loans and grants for Black farmers, intended to correct for the historic racism of the Department of Agriculture, a bureau that activists called the "Last Plantation."

This wasn't legislators cramming a bill with pork. Democrats were pushing American social policy into places it had never ventured. And it wasn't just the direct cash transfers. Money for Black farmers was, in essence, a form of reparations. Most of the provisions were funded for a year or two, but intended as demonstration projects, with an eye toward cementing them for the long term. And in the end, the administration proposed a bill that fell just short of fulfilling Schumer's prophecy. It would cost $1.9 trillion.

As they went about honing the package, Jared Bernstein, Biden's long-time economic adviser, kept shipping the outlines of the proposal to his old dissertation adviser, Irwin Garfinkel, who ran the Center on Poverty and Social Policy at Columbia University. Garfinkel had spent years honing a model to forecast the social reverberations of policy—and Bernstein was curious how their plans might register in the actual world.

As aides convened for a Zoom to coordinate the rollout of the bill, Bharat Ramamurti, tapped to be deputy head of the National Economic Council, instructed the group to stop and check their inboxes. The numbers had come back from Columbia. In the rush to polish the legislation, the details kept them blindered. But the email pulled them out of their spreadsheets and allowed them to view the legislation from a panoramic vantage. According to the Columbia tabulation, the American Rescue Plan would cut child poverty in half. Ramamurti found himself without the vocabulary to capture his astonishment at the magnitude of their handiwork and could only exclaim, "Holy shit."

Having constructed a bill that was worthy of his self-conception, Biden needed to shepherd it through the Senate as quickly as possible. In addition to the economic relief and idealistic provisions, it contained the funding for his plans to end the pandemic. It was the pathway from death.

4

Waiting for the Jab

THE VACCINE was salvation—a miracle that could lift the plague. It was there, approved for use, tantalizing in its proximity. With the vaccine, life could resume. The elderly could wrap themselves around grandchildren, rather than peering at them through nursing home windows or waving to them from a digital distance. Children could escape the intellectual numbness and social retardant of Zoom school. Restaurants could welcome back customers. An economy could fully awaken from its induced hibernation.

But the fact that the vaccine existed didn't mean that it could be obtained. In Florida, retirees slept overnight in beach chairs, waiting their turn for the needle. Children of aging parents shared the common experiences of government websites crashing just as they were about to secure vaccination appointments.

The promise of the Biden administration was competence. After the shambolic Trump years—where presidential whim guided bureaucracy—the new team would apply calm expertise. It would be akin to a wartime mobilization, Biden promised. And in the first hundred days, the administration would provide one hundred million shots. It wasn't the most ambitious goal he could set. But in its relative modesty, in the desire to avoid overpromising, there was the logic of keeping expectations from racing beyond the capacity to fulfill them.

Biden assigned the task of unleashing the vaccine to Jeff Zients. He wasn't a public health expert—or experienced in managing complicated supply chains that produced specialized products like needles or the lipids used in vaccines. And in some sense, he picked himself for the job, or at least volunteered his services. He had overseen the transition organization, including the operation that hired staff and vetted cabinet members. But this was the job he wanted most, the type of assignment he always craved.

Zients was the archetype of a new breed of Washington fixer. He grew up in DC in the seventies, the son of a psychiatrist, attending St. Albans, the finishing school for the establishment's male progeny. (For a time, his father worked at the school.) Despite having a Brahmin's impeccable manners, Zients never quite carried himself with perfect suavity. When he wore neckties, they were often loose around the collar, even at televised events. His hair was usually sprawled in a desultory fashion that advertised his indifference to such trivia.

The Washington of Zients's youth maintained an aristocratic disdain for money, or at least it professed to shun such base motives. But Zients burbled with entrepreneurial zeal. As a kid, he traded baseball cards so shrewdly that his collection grew to be worth $30,000. As a young management consultant, he ran a series of research firms, which he helped take public. In 2002, *Fortune* placed Zients on its list of the forty richest Americans under forty, estimating his net worth at approximately $200 million.

But he was still a businessman in Washington, DC. Having succeeded in the private sector, he hungrily sought out the public one. He wrangled a gig in the Obama administration, a new position called chief performance officer. The job description essentially invited a management consultant to descend on the federal government to improve hiring processes and modernize IT, to supply officials with better data. But his responsibilities morphed over time. Zients became the help desk for the administration. He acquired a reputation as the troubleshooter who could rescue a flailing program. When there was a backlog in GI Bill payments, he fixed it. He rallied a team to repair the humiliatingly ill-functioning healthcare.gov website, thus saving Obamacare itself.

Zients was an evangelist for the religion of process. Any problem could be solved with good management, or what might be described as hyper–anal retentiveness—relentless list making, the constant monitoring of dashboards filled with data, the setting of daily goals, the ruthless prioritization of decisions, treating the little details with outsize care. "It's all about the execution," he liked to exclaim. He would prepare for every call, no matter how junior the person on the other end. He would ask for briefings about his interlocutor and outline his goals for the conversation. When he listened, he took notes on index cards, using sharpened pencils that he kept in a bowl in front of him.

There were plenty of reasons why the job of COVID czar qualified as an impossible challenge. An entire political party was stoking hostility toward masks and expertise—and sowing doubts about the harm that might come from vaccination. The decentralized American system didn't lend itself to quick action or harmonious implementation of national policy.

But what made the job especially tricky is that Zients couldn't simply plan from scratch. The Biden administration hadn't inherited just the pandemic from Trump, but also a set of plans for combating the pandemic. It wouldn't be so easy to extricate itself from pre-existing systems for collecting data, contracts with suppliers, and strategies for deploying the vaccine. Zients was like a contractor getting called to complete a botched construction project in the middle of a hurricane.

ZIENTS LIKED to surround himself with protégés, whom he nurtured early in their careers, who shared his temperament. For his deputy, he picked one of them, Natalie Quillian. During the campaign, she served as the organization's second-in-command. Now Zients was plucking her from her exhausted postelection haze and heaving her into managing the response to the once-in-a-century pandemic.

Before Zients and Quillian could begin to devise a plan, they needed to understand what they were inheriting. They knew the contours of Operation Warp Speed, the Trump administration plan to subsidize the invention of vaccines, in exchange for first dibs on the product. But how did the Trump administration plan to take the stockpiles of vaccines, which had just been approved for use, and jab them into arms?

There are well-established protocols for an incoming administration to learn about the outgoing administration's plans. By law, the new administration gets to create what are called agency review teams. These are groups of volunteers who spread out across government, meeting with career bureaucrats to glean the state of play.

Among the most pressing tasks for the agency review teams was obtaining a copy of the vaccination distribution plan that Quillian so badly wanted. Logic suggested that plan resided at the Department of Health and Human Services.

When the Biden agency review team arrived at HHS, they were hopeful that the venerable traditions of cooperation during presidential transitions would prevail. Their point of contact was the deputy surgeon general, Rear Admiral Erica Schwartz. Her naval title derived from her long career in the public health service. Her résumé led the Biden volunteers to think that they had caught a lucky break. That sense of optimism, however, didn't survive their first meeting. From the start, the Biden teams were told that they could talk with career civil servants only in the presence of a Trump-appointed minder, a requirement that seemed designed to intimidate the bureaucrats and prevent them from speaking freely. The Biden volunteers weren't even allowed casual conversations with officials they had known for years without prior clearance from the department. Schwartz told them, "There is only one government at a time, and the current administration has a right to know what the next one is learning."

The whole point of the agency review teams was to receive a behind-the-curtain sense of the government that the new administration would inherit. But Schwartz told the Biden volunteers that they could receive only publicly available information, since the Trump administration didn't want to violate executive privilege. Never mind that the Trump administration had required that Biden teams sign nondisclosure agreements. When the leaders of the Biden team complained to Schwartz about the lack of cooperation, she told them that they could come down to the agency's headquarters to meet in person to discuss their issues—which seemed aggressively imprudent to them, given the pandemic and the aversion to mask wearing that they witnessed in their Zoom conversations with HHS officials.

As the Biden volunteers tried to charm their way into Rear Admiral Schwartz's good graces, Natalie Quillian kept prodding them to track down the Trump plan for vaccination distribution. At first, she worried that the wrong questions were being asked of the wrong officials. Perhaps the plans weren't at Health and Human Services, after all. So she made inquiries at the Defense Department. Then she began to speculate that the administration wasn't sharing its plans because they weren't finished. By mid-December, she had lost patience with the fruitless searching and arrived at an inescapable conclusion. She hadn't been able to find the plan because there wasn't one.

ON NEW YEAR'S EVE, Zients's team made contact with CVS and Walgreens. It was astonishing that the Trump people hadn't thought to reach out to them. The companies were eager to join the vaccination effort—and they solved essential problems that experts agreed would hobble the administration's work. They had storage facilities, distribution networks, and personnel with experience injecting flu shots. And with that, the pharmacies became central to the Biden plan.

The reality of the pandemic was race. Blacks, Native Americans, and Latinos were disproportionately dying. Zients and Quillian sketched a plan to erode that inequity, disseminating shots through Community Health Centers in poorer neighborhoods—and enlisting churches to spread the gospel of vaccination, vouching for its safety and necessity.

All through early January, Zients's team ran simulations attempting to anticipate the first week on the job, refining the techniques they would use to implore bureaucrats to quickly reverse course and implement a new plan for beating back the pandemic. Most of the plans consisted of common sense; the struggle consisted of realizing them quickly enough to avert death.

WHITE HOUSE COVID protocols limited Zients to two deputies who could work in person with him. In addition to Quillian, he brought along Andy Slavitt, a stubble-faced former health care executive from the suburbs of Chicago. Zients first worked with him in the Obama administration on the small team that rescued healthcare.gov.

Like Zients, Slavitt had trained as a management consultant. But he also dreamed of becoming a foreign correspondent. During the earliest days of COVID, he channeled that reportorial energy into his Twitter feed. In long threads, Slavitt would write up everything he learned in the course of his days spent phoning government officials and epidemiologists, a narrative he punctuated with paroxysms of raw-but-relatable emotion. Zients assigned him to deploy his explanatory skills, but in a more official capacity. Among other tasks, he would serve as the primary spokesman for the COVID team.

Slavitt didn't especially want the job. He turned it down twice before finally agreeing to move to Washington. He felt as if the public was stuck in a cycle of perpetual disappointment. Trump kept assuring the nation that it was on the cusp of turning the corner, but it never did. It was exhausting to wake up and learn things were worse than ever.

In Zients's plan, Slavitt would brief the public about the state of the pandemic during that first week. But before Slavitt could deliver information, he needed to extract it from the bureaucracy. On his first day in the White House, Slavitt set up a meeting with General Gus Perna, who had headed the Trump administration's vaccine distribution program.

Now that Slavitt had Perna and a handful of top wonks from the Centers for Disease Control and Prevention on the phone, he deluged them with a list of basic questions: "How many doses have been produced? How many have been sent?"

As they walked through the data, Perna mentioned that only 46 percent of the doses delivered to states had been injected into arms.

"That can't be right," Slavitt told him. He knew that problems like that existed, but not quite on such a scale. And if Perna was right, it represented a terrifying breakdown in the system.

Slavitt sat dumbfounded. The vaccine was the best hope for stalling the virus, which was killing 3,500 people each day, yet the vast majority of the doses were sitting in freezers unused.

"How could this be?" he asked.

The wonks on the call told him there was no good answer. The federal government shipped the vaccine to states, but there was no mechanism for tracking a shot. A well-devised system would have put a barcode on each vaccine, but this wasn't a well-devised system. *Walmart knows more about its stockpile of blue jeans*, Slavitt thought.

Perna's best guess was that hospitals and states were hoarding the vaccine. Because each patient required two shots, separated by approximately three weeks, none of the health care providers wanted to get caught short. And they didn't trust the federal government to replenish their supply if they ran low. It was hard to restore trust in the system if the system didn't trust itself.

As Slavitt absorbed the problem, he began to ponder solutions. The administration could guarantee states the number of shots they would receive each week, which would dampen the sense of panic. That was a patchwork fix, however. Zients had preached that the only way to solve a shortage, and the anxiety it provokes, is abundance. And that would require the government to be bullheaded in expanding its vaccine stockpile.

Despite his own hesitations, Zients agreed to assign the task of expanding vaccine supply to a well-known operator, a renowned pugilist with a long list of enemies.

———

BACK IN MARCH 2020, as COVID struck Seattle, then tinged the inner suburbs of New York City and began to steam across the country, it became apparent that the campaign would need to bolster its roster of experts. Ron Klain suggested enlisting a doctor named David Kessler.

Kessler hadn't officially worked in Washington in decades, but the memory of him still lingered. When Kessler, then aged thirty-nine, was running a hospital in the Bronx, George H. W. Bush had tapped him to be the nation's most powerful regulator of medicine, the director of the Food and Drug Administration. Kessler believed the job was even more powerful than his boss realized, and he set out to test its limits. He once seized twelve thousand gallons of Citrus Hill orange juice, which the company deceptively labeled as "fresh" or "pure squeezed." For the first time in the FDA's history, Kessler ordered the agency to regulate the sale of tobacco. To challenge an industry like tobacco, represented by a well-financed, exquisitely connected lobby, is an act of monumental chutzpah, a quality that Kessler's critics said he exuded from his every pore. Kessler didn't mind brawling with cabinet officials. In fact, he moved so quickly that he occasionally neglected to consult the White House. His work ethic was the stuff of lore. Because he couldn't ever find time to jog during the day, he would run the streets of Washington in the middle of the night.

At the onset of the pandemic, Biden asked Kessler, along with Kessler's old student, the former surgeon general Vivek Murthy, to begin virtually briefing him. Biden referred to the pair as "my docs." While Biden chafes at experts who speak in obscurantist jargon—and whom he feels use their academic lingo to belittle him—he hoists scientists onto pedestals. And he seemed to absorb Kessler and Murthy's counsel as if he were receiving advice from his own internist. Indeed, he was also charged with protecting his health. They designed the rules that governed who could enter Biden's bubble; they advised him on how to structure his public appearances; they organized a testing regime for the campaign.

Kessler made it his business to understand what he could about the vaccines in development. He worked with campaign lawyers to shape confidential disclosure agreements that he signed with pharmaceutical companies so that he could monitor the clinical testing of vaccines in real time and pass along reports to Biden. On the night that Pfizer reported it had successfully tested its vaccine, Kessler was on the phone with the company's executives, pumping them for information—a fact that infuriated Trump when he learned of it.

In the new administration, Kessler was placed at the Department of Health and Human Services, but he effectively reported to Zients. He wasn't the sort of figure that Zients normally recruited for his teams. Since Zients extolled the virtue of "low-ego teams," he wasn't inclined to pick a controversialist like Kessler, who somehow managed to question authority even when he was the authority. But with his relationships with the vaccine manufacturers—and Biden—he became an unavoidable member of Zients's inner circle.

IF THERE'S one Trump decision that receives universal praise, it is the creation of Operation Warp Speed. In the spring of 2020, the Trump administration invested billions in the development of vaccines, subsidizing private firms and giving them the security of knowing that the US government would purchase the fruits of their science in profitable bulk.

But Kessler and Zients began to learn that for all the nobility of the objective of the project, it was tainted by the fact that it emerged from the Trump regime. The name itself, borrowed from *Star Trek*, was a problem. Polling showed that the public distrusted the idea of a vaccine developed in haste, which would be thrust into their arms without the scrutiny normally applied to pharmaceuticals. By emphasizing speed, the name unnecessarily stoked that anxiety. One of the Biden administration's first official acts was to stop using the name Operation Warp Speed.

Then there was also an inherent problem with the government enmeshing itself so deeply in industry. When the state is placing big bets on certain companies, it is playing favorites. The model easily gives way to cronyism—especially when the head of that state is Donald Trump. As the Trump administration protected favored companies, the government also punished their competitors.

While Moderna, Sanofi, Johnson & Johnson, and three other companies took government subsidies for their research, Pfizer eschewed it. It didn't want the state interfering with its plans or micromanaging its process as it rushed to develop a vaccine. But the Trump administration—especially the secretary of Health and Human Services, Alex Azar—didn't ever forgive Pfizer's refusal.

In July 2020, Pfizer offered to sell the government hundreds of millions more doses of the vaccine that it was testing. (The Trump administration had already purchased one hundred million.) But instead of leaping at the chance, the Trump administration passed. Moncef Slaoui, the head of Operation Warp Speed, told Pfizer's CEO, Albert Bourla, that the government didn't need them. After the government declined, Pfizer warned that its offer was fleeting. If the US didn't want the doses, Pfizer would sell to Japan, which hoped to amass vaccines in preparation for the postponed Olympics it would host in 2021.

Even more ominously, the company believed that Azar was depriving Pfizer of the supplies it needed to produce vaccines. Pfizer had ordered disposable filters, essential to completing each dose, but Azar used the Defense Production Act to redirect those filters to Moderna. Azar's intervention so badly set back the company that Bourla worried that Pfizer would be unable to even deliver the one hundred million doses that the US government had ordered from it.

On November 9, less than a week after the election, Trump's least favorite vaccine maker published the results of its clinical studies, which were an unimpeachable triumph—its efficacy was beyond what a flu shot managed.

Pfizer filed papers with the FDA for an emergency use authorization, the beginning of the end of the full-blown pandemic. Despite that triumph, Trump remained as spiteful as ever. Trump felt cheated by the fact that Pfizer hadn't reported its result until after his defeat, thus depriving him of a success story that could have salvaged his presidency.

Even though Pfizer was ready for mass production, it continued to suffer from the black sheep status that Trump accorded it. The Operation Warp Speed companies that had accepted government money were granted certain privileges. That is, Trump had used the Defense Production Act to give them "priority status." If they needed to order a part for their factories, the government jumped them to the front of the queue, ahead of customers who may have placed their order long before them. Pfizer, meanwhile, needed to wait in line for machinery that would allow it to rapidly expand production. The Trump administration showed scant interest in giving the company the same helping hand that it had supplied its competitors, even as the virus's body count kept on rising.

THE NEW ADMINISTRATION needed to quickly ramp up Pfizer's production. Zients assigned that job to Tim Manning, whom he gave the title supply chain coordinator.

The son of a firefighter from the south suburbs of Chicago, Manning never strayed far from the family business. Even as he worked as a field geologist in New Mexico, cleaning up contaminated groundwater sites, he volunteered as a fireman and learned the art of mountain rescue. He once disappeared for days, combing the Sandia Mountains for survivors of a plane crash. Hazards, large and small, became his thing, which eventually landed him a job at FEMA.

From all his years responding to once-in-a-century storms and toxic spills, he had learned how to make things happen in cramped conditions, how to move fleets of utility repair trucks across the nation overnight, and how to find housing for refugees fleeing from all manner of apocalypses. He was trained to transcend the everyday practices of government.

Pfizer had the potential to be a workhorse vaccine, but its factories weren't robust enough to churn out the doses of vaccine that the government needed. Manning worked with the company to quickly buy mobile clean rooms, which were like mini-factories that it could append to its facility in Kalamazoo, Michigan, an instant expansion of capacity. But the mobile clean rooms weren't all that mobile. They were quite massive, in fact, and built in Texas. Manning coordinated the shipment of the units up the spine of the country. His team procured permits that normally took months; it suspended rules that would have required allocating time for drivers to sleep.

Producing billions of doses of vaccines taxed the entire supply chain. Vials are made of glass, made from sand. Needles are hewn from steel, covered by safety caps molded from resin. A failure at any link of the production process—any slowdown in production—would reverberate along the entire chain. From his perch at the White House, Manning acquired a god's-eye view of the entire industry. He could see bottlenecks as they emerged. From his days at FEMA, Manning was fluent in the esoteric canon of law that governed the use of the Defense Production Act. He knew how to invoke the state of emergency to quickly obtain exotic products and to prioritize the production across the sprawling supply chain.

The challenges came in worrying succession. In his first week on the job, he received a report that the supply chain couldn't produce both the COVID vaccine and sufficient flu vaccine. Then, a cold snap in Texas closed petrochemical plants, potentially hobbling the manufacturing of syringes for months. It was his job to troubleshoot, keeping the system oriented to achieving production goals, and to sometimes serve as a ruthless taskmaster. The administration pushed Johnson & Johnson to order one of its subcontractors, Grand River Aseptic Manufacturing, to begin operating nonstop, every hour of the day, no break for the weekend.

But Manning's works couldn't solve a core problem: the Trump administration hadn't purchased enough vaccines from Pfizer and Moderna—and the companies claimed that they had commitments to other countries, which precluded them from selling more.

ON JANUARY 26, a day when 4,013 American died of the virus, Biden officially ordered Kessler and Zients to go on a shopping spree, to buy the shots that the Trump administration had declined to purchase. He wanted them to obtain one hundred million doses from Pfizer—and another one hundred million from Moderna, a Massachusetts-based biotech company, which had received an emergency use authorization for its vaccine from the Food and Drug Administration in December.

At nine o'clock that night, the pair set up a Zoom with Moderna's CEO, the intense and intensely confident French-born Stéphane Bancel. Kessler played the heavy: "The president has said these doses will be available by the middle of May. They will be available by the middle of May."

"We're not doing that," Bancel told him. "We're going to sell them on the commercial market." The United States had missed its opportunity to buy them in the previous administration, he said. Now the Biden administration would have to wait in line, along with the rest of the world.

After everything the government had done to nurture Moderna, a company that had never brought a product to market before, this was a galling rebuff. And Bancel's unwillingness to sell would make it nearly impossible for the administration to realize its plans.

Kessler tried to muster his iciest voice. "That's not going to happen."

He waited for a response in awkward silence.

The Defense Production Act granted the government capacious powers that hadn't been fully tested in the crisis. Kessler didn't want to wave any explicit threats. But he hoped that subtext and implication would cause Bancel to consider the possibility that the government might force his hand. And by the end of the conversation, Bancel agreed to sell the doses.

Progress showed itself in Biden's speeches. At first the president promised the nation would have enough vaccine supply for every citizen by July; then he moved that date forward to early May. With the guiding hand of an activist state, factories churned out vaccines at a higher volume than any analyst predicted.

Within months, the state, in whose capacities the public held so little trust, made it possible for any adult to walk into a pharmacy and obtain a lifesaving shot. And even in its aftermath, the program operated so seamlessly that the public took it for granted. Technocracy—roundly maligned—had produced one of the best designed, most important government programs of all time.

5

The Nod of the Head

ALL THE PLANNING in the world is not enough to correct for the human tendency toward overeagerness. Nine days into the Biden presidency, Kamala Harris recorded a television interview with local news stations in West Virginia and Arizona. Her prestige was supposed to lend shine to the American Rescue Plan, helping bolster support for the bill in the home states of two moderate Democratic senators, Joe Manchin and Kyrsten Sinema.

But the plan to deploy Harris was slapdash. Nobody bothered to run it past the White House Office of Legislative Affairs, let alone the senators who Harris intended to help. And it backfired spectacularly. Manchin told the world that he had been blindsided, and he didn't particularly like it.

Less than two weeks into the Biden presidency, Ron Klain found himself groveling on the phone with Manchin.

"Our mistake," Klain said.

"Look, you guys lost my state by forty points. If you really think that coming and doing TV in my state's gonna change my mind . . ." The thought hung in the air. Rather than betraying his hurt, Manchin tried to project an air of bemusement, marveling at the ham-handedness of the White House.

But as he accepted Klain's apology with ostentatious generosity—and as Klain apologized again—Manchin couldn't help but append a dig. "I want to help President Biden to be successful. I want to beat the pandemic in my state. I want to get the economy in my state moving. But don't try to muscle me, because you can't."

BIDEN WAS FURIOUS that the White House had needlessly alienated Manchin, a terrible opening entreaty to a man who could very well prove decisive to the fate of the administration, not just with this piece of legislation, but with every other significant bill that the Democrats hoped to pass.

The Manchin blunder came in the midst of an internal debate. Now that Biden had his majority in the Senate, should the White House even bother courting Republicans? Biden had just delivered an inaugural address where he argued "history, faith and reason show the way, the way of unity." Some of his small inner circle, including Ron Klain, thought he shouldn't waste his time. They kept hearing stories from Democrats on Capitol Hill, especially in the House, about the vivid trauma of January 6. Congressional Democrats' anger billowed with such intensity that they couldn't even abide a hallway conversation with their colleagues on the other side. Working collaboratively on a monumental piece of legislation, therefore, seemed like a wild implausibility.

Even if the insurrection hadn't occurred, Klain would have regarded outreach to Republicans with extreme skepticism. Like every other veteran of the Obama White House, Klain could recall the torment of wooing Maine's Susan Collins and moderate Republicans in pursuit of health care reform. The moderates endlessly dangled the possibility of voting for the bill. But as Obamacare hung in the balance for months, the administration's adversaries used the extended negotiations to hone critiques that stuck in the public's mind. That, Klain vowed, wouldn't happen again.

With no real hope of winning the sixty votes for the American Rescue Plan required to overcome a Republican filibuster in the Senate, Klain wanted to dispense with pretense and embrace a parliamentary procedure known as reconciliation. An outgrowth of an obscure 1974 budget bill, reconciliation allowed the Senate to pass spending bills and tax cuts without having to garner sixty votes. Reconciliation allowed for a bill to clear the Senate with a simple majority, so long as the bill rigidly confined itself to items with "fiscal implications."

The use of the term *reconciliation* for a procedure that allowed the majority to ram legislation through on party line votes captures a certain irony. Then again, the Senate was no longer the deliberative body that Joe Biden knew from his youth. It was badly broken, a playground for vindictive partisans, a graveyard for legislation. Reconciliation was never intended as a routine vehicle for passing legislation, but it had become one.

The question of whether to pursue reconciliation divided the quintet of aides that sat at the pinnacle of the White House org chart. The top of the org chart was, in fact, a crowded place. In addition to Klain, it included two others who had served as Joe Biden's chief of staff during his vice presidency, Bruce Reed and Steve Ricchetti. Along with Mike Donilon and Anita Dunn, they constituted the group that knew Biden's mind best and had the best shot at swaying it.

In other circumstances, a group like this might vie for the affection of the president, leaking damning accounts about one another to the press. But in the clannish spirit of Joe Biden, they were intertwined with relationships that went back forty years. Ron Klain was the godfather of Reed's child. Donilon and Klain went to Georgetown together, where Klain covered Donilon's bid to become student body president in the student newspaper. Whatever jealousies they harbored were deeply submerged for the sake of their shared father figure.

Still, there were differences among them. During the Trump years, Klain had grown a bit more progressive than the rest—a stalwart on MSNBC, a biting presence on Twitter, and broadly more confrontational in his politics. Tactically and ideologically he began to diverge from the approach favored by the Obama administration. Obama seemed to treat his party's resurgent left as a bunch of professional bellyachers who didn't appreciate his hard-won victories.

Klain wanted to chart a more conciliatory relationship with the Left.

Over the campaign, he had formed an easy relationship with Bernie Sanders, who appreciated how quickly he responded to his calls and how he seemed open to suggestions. With appointments to administration jobs, he helped Elizabeth Warren place her protégés in top posts. He said explicitly that he wanted to avoid fights with the Left, on the cusp of a moment when the administration would need its support.

Ricchetti and Reed leaned slightly more to the center. (Reed had been president of the Democratic Leadership Council, the ideological organ of the party's moderate wing, although he also had evolved in a leftward direction.) And Donilon considered himself a guardian of the Biden brand, with its emphasis on healing the nation.

So when it came to the subject of reconciliation, Donilon and Reed were against deploying it too quickly. They felt Biden needed to at least gesture in the direction of bipartisanship, an argument that reflected Biden's own thinking. "Democrats aren't going to win every election for the next forty years," the president said. "We need to model how to coexist with the other side, even if it's not possible."

While he wouldn't wait around forever, he sensed a deal could be had. But he vowed that he would pursue it with his eyes wide open, aware of the pressure imposed by the clock.

IN JOE BIDEN'S telling of his life, the Senate represented salvation. After his wife and daughter perished in a car crash in 1972, his colleagues lifted him up. The members of American politics' most exclusive club wouldn't let their brother wallow in the dumps. Good old Fritz Hollings from South Carolina kept pestering him until he accepted a dinner invitation. Hubert Humphrey would listen to Biden pour out his soul, and then the happy warrior would collapse into an empathetic bawl. When he became vice president and left his beloved colleagues on Capitol Hill, Biden proclaimed, "I will always be a Senate man."

Sometimes, he seemed stuck in a daydream about the glory days of the deliberative body. When he saw Virginia senator Mark Warner on a Zoom, he called out, "John!" It was an understandable slip. John Warner had been Biden's longtime colleague in the Senate, but had retired twelve years earlier.

There weren't many senators left from Biden's time in the Senate. Susan Collins was one of the few. Over the years, they had traveled the world together as part of Senate delegations and shared committee assignments. When Collins won an award from an Irish heritage group, Biden recorded a swooning tribute video. "I'm crazy about her," he declared. As she ran for reelection in 2020, she took note of her Democratic colleagues who said nasty things about her. It stuck in her mind that Biden had refrained from criticizing her, even when he endorsed her opponent.

During his first days as president, Biden kept calling her. In public, he boasted that he had secured her vote for Obama's stimulus—a claim that Collins regarded as not wholly accurate, but she let it slide. It was flattering that the president of the United States kept talking about her as such a prize.

On January 31, it seemed as if she might reward his implacable pursuit of her cooperation. Collins organized a letter, cosigned by nine other Republicans, offering Biden a deal on COVID relief. Getting nine other signatories hadn't been easy, but she wanted to send an unmistakable message. Deal with her, and there were enough votes to break a filibuster.

Where the president proposed $1.9 trillion, the Collins group countered with $618 billion. Biden invited her group to the Oval the very next afternoon.

For four years, Collins had been on the outs. As a Republican from a bluish state, she couldn't afford to embrace Trump, but she didn't ever really denounce him, either. With Trump's defeat, she felt as if she were back in the game. In the last lame-duck days of the Trump presidency, in the stark absence of any leadership from the White House, Collins banded together with a bipartisan group of moderates to pass a $900 billion COVID relief package. She felt as if she were restoring the Senate back to its sensible traditions.

Upon her arrival in the White House, everything about the president's mood suggested she was right. He seemed thrilled to see her in the flesh. Playing the solicitous host, Biden encouraged his guests to discourse at senatorial length, disregarding the time allocated on the schedule. For two hours, he let Collins and her colleagues riff at will. Ron Klain watched it all from the corner of the room.

When senators talked among themselves in the cloakroom or in text exchanges, they doubted Joe Biden was running his own show. Because of his advanced age, they whispered that he was a marionette, waggling his arms as Klain manipulated him from above. Aides to Mitch McConnell were blunt in their analysis. They dubbed Klain "prime minister." Because Klain was an avid user of Twitter, Republicans studied his feed with the close-reading techniques of Kremlinology, scouring his Likes and retweets for hidden subtext.

In truth, it didn't take extraordinary skills to glean Klain's thinking. Even when a mask covered his mouth, as it did in the Oval Office that day, he didn't disguise his reactions. As he listened to the extended disquisitions of the Republicans, he couldn't quite believe that they were lining up to lecture the new president. More than three thousand Americans were dying each day; one million workers had just filed new unemployment claims. And the thrust of each of their monologues was that the piece of legislation Collins had helped broker in December had set the country on a perfectly fine course.

As Collins spoke, Klain couldn't help but use his head to fact-check her in real time. When Collins claimed that her new proposal contained just as much funding for combating COVID as the American Rescue Plan, Klain's face began swinging from side to side. He thought, *There's nothing in your plan to sequence the DNA of the new COVID strains coming from Britain, Africa, and Brazil; your party's president stopped sequencing the new cases of COVID last*

June. Her proposal would leave the nation in the dark about the next waves of the virus.

He began shaking his head furiously again when Mitt Romney, following Collins's lead, launched into a lengthy monologue about how to divide funds to state and local governments. *That's strange*, Klain thought. The plan Romney cosigned didn't contain a single dollar of state and local aid. Why was he so passionately explaining how to better spend dollars that he didn't want spent in the first place?

But when Susan Collins left the meeting, she was exuberant. For a brief moment, she felt a deal was imminent. Then she asked her colleagues about the masked aide shaking his head in disagreement. She didn't recognize him, but she complained about his rudeness. Her staff told her that she had just described the president's chief of staff.

In truth, Klain reflected a sentiment that the president would later admit he shared. Although Biden resisted the impulse to chide the Republicans, he was surprised that they didn't meaningfully test his impulse to compromise. There was a deal waiting for them. The president would have shaved hundreds of billions from the proposal if they had suggested a plausible place to meet in the middle. But the pandemic didn't lend itself to prolonged haggling. His exploratory mission had shown him that reconciliation was the only viable path. Hours after the Republican visit, congressional Democrats introduced a resolution that would allow them to pursue the American Rescue Plan through the reconciliation process.

Despite the limp offer of the moderate Republicans, Biden still wanted to cultivate one member of the visiting delegation, with an eye to the future. For decades, Biden had served with the Alaska Republican Frank Murkowski. In 2002, his daughter Lisa took his place. Biden liked her and how she remained steeped in the old folkways of the Senate, how she maintained an old-fashioned Alaskan streak of independence. Biden quietly asked his aides to include money for the cruise ship industry and Alaska Native Corporations. He told them, "Listen, she can't vote with us this time. Mitch isn't going to let anybody vote with us. And I get that. But I'm going to put stuff in anyway because down the road she'll remember that."

The task had clarified itself. Biden would be pursuing a strategy that hinged on his ability to corral his own party, which meant that his fate really rested with one senator, the one who warned he couldn't be muscled.

6

Take Me Home

JOE MANCHIN'S VISIT wasn't on the public schedule. But after Kamala Harris's poorly received interview on West Virginia television, Biden needed to shower attention on the senator. When Manchin entered the Oval Office, the vice president and president were locked in conversation. Manchin asked if Harris would be staying. "No, no, it's just the two of us," the president replied. Harris stood and exited the room. Manchin felt as if she hadn't acknowledged him on her way out—not a handshake, not a salutation—which surprised and wounded him, because they had served together in the Senate.

Manchin, a chummy pol with the frame of an old quarterback and a helmet of graying hair, didn't enjoy conflict. In fact, he considered defusing it to be his raison d'être. He lived on a houseboat moored at the Capital Yacht Club named *Almost Heaven*, a nod to the John Denver lyric about his home state. In the age of polarization, his boat was the last bipartisan clubhouse in politics. It was a place you could find Chuck Schumer kicking back with Lamar Alexander. Ted Cruz might show up. After January 6, Joe Manchin told friends that he would try to preserve the political center with even greater zeal. In the old saying attributed to George Washington, the Senate was the saucer that cooled the House's hot tea. Manchin saw himself as the saucer's saucer.

In February, Manchin announced he was going to vote against Neera Tanden's nomination to become director of the Office of Management and Budget, because he didn't like her tweets. And he especially didn't care for the fact that they targeted Susan Collins, his good friend on the other side of the aisle. His opposition sank Tanden's nomination. Progressives found it a bit rich to hear him preach civility with such rectitude when the television ad that helped catapult him into office in 2010 showed him loading a cartridge into a rifle and firing clean through a copy of a climate bill supported by Barack Obama.

But Manchin's continued existence in the Senate defied every trend in American politics. West Virginia, once a blue bastion, was now fervently Trumpist. His party, once a coalition of conservatives and liberals, was now marching leftward. Yet he stubbornly held on to his anachronistic place.

Still, when he professed his anxieties about the American Rescue Plan to Biden, he wasn't speaking just for himself. Other moderate Democrats might not have had the guts to say so out loud, but some of them didn't like the provision boosting the hourly minimum wage to fifteen dollars, either. And some of them even shared Manchin's concerns that pumping so much cash into the economy at once might awaken the long-dormant beast of inflation.

As Biden attempted to work Manchin over, he assured him that he shared the West Virginian's deep desire for bipartisanship. But it just wasn't possible on this piece of legislation, he told him. "I worked with them for seven or eight months trying to get a compromise on the Affordable Care Act, and at the end of the day I didn't get any Republicans. Now we have a COVID pandemic and it's time sensitive. I can't negotiate for six or eight months."

While Manchin didn't agree, he wasn't going to raise too big a stink. Biden was talking to him with an intimacy that conveyed respect. Manchin liked that Biden was trying to bring him along, not coerce him. After he left that evening, he told a friend, "I can do business with that guy."

———

BUT THERE were anxieties that Manchin couldn't shake, however much he personally liked Biden, and they weren't irrational. Along with every other Democrat, Manchin had read an op-ed in *The Washington Post* by Larry Summers, the former Treasury secretary, the former president of Harvard, the longtime economic oracle of Democratic administrations. Biden's post-inaugural glow insulated him from criticism from his fellow Democrats. But Summers, who prided himself on his contrarianism, wrote the verboten thing: the Rescue Plan had dangerously swelled.

Intellectually, this was a tricky critique for Summers to level, a fact he admitted in his piece. Back in the Obama administration, Summers was a lead architect of the inadequate Recovery Act of 2009, and he agreed that his stimulus package should have been larger. But his worry was that the Biden administration had overlearned the lessons of that mistake.

According to Summers's calculations, Biden was about to spend six times more than what the economy needed to recover, what he described as "macroeconomic stimulus on a scale closer to World War II levels." By placing so much money in workers' pockets, workers would become pickier about the job offers they accepted—or might decide not to work at all. To attract employees, firms would have to jack up wages—and then pass along the costs to consumers in the form of higher prices. The American Rescue Plan, he argued, "will set off inflationary pressures of a kind we have not seen in a generation, with consequences for the value of the dollar and financial stability."

There was another argument submerged in the op-ed, which attracted less attention. By pressing forward with such a large piece of legislation, Biden would make it harder to win his next congressional victory. He was blowing his capital on a bill filled with temporary measures, while making it harder for the likes of Joe Manchin to tolerate future spending on long-term investments required to address climate change and ease the burdens of working-class life.

Larry Summers mattered to Joe Biden. He was an elite whose respect Biden craved. In the Obama administration, Biden lobbied to make him chair of the Federal Reserve, a job that ultimately went to Janet Yellen. But Biden also couldn't help but imagine that Summers would always consider him an intellectual inferior. Even when he courted Summers, Biden told aides that he suspected him.

Instead of brushing aside the criticism, or wrestling with it, Biden called Summers and unloaded on him. His younger aides, many of whom had worked for Summers in the Obama administration, pumped their fists when they learned about the president's feisty rebuttal. Biden had put their old mentor in his place. But whatever sense of catharsis Biden's call provided, Summers's argument would remain fixed in Manchin's mind—and it was a plausible analysis—whether the younger aides chose to admit the fact or not.

RACKED BY the fear that he couldn't afford to lose a single vote in the Senate, that the Biden presidency might fail before it truly began, Ron Klain couldn't manage to sustain more than three hours of sleep.

But by the first week in March, nearing the expiration of a temporary boost in unemployment benefits passed at the beginning of the pandemic, Chuck Schumer devised a bargain to bridge the remaining difference between the factions—and seal the bill's victory. The moderates wanted unemployment benefits reduced from $400 to $300. Schumer could give them that. In exchange, he persuaded them to agree that those benefits would be exempted from federal income tax, thus increasing their value and pleasing progressives. Early on Friday, March 5, Schumer brought the bill to the Senate floor for a vote, convinced that it would quickly pass.

That morning, however, Manchin read the bill and didn't much like where it landed. He told Schumer that he might vote for a Republican amendment with far stingier unemployment benefits than contained in the bill—an amendment that would have shattered Schumer's finally poised compromise and threatened the very survival of the bill.

Worse, Manchin had expressed his misgivings after the Senate had begun to vote on the bill. In Schumer's Capitol office, with its oil canvases and rococo chairs, expletives began flying across the room. The fiftieth and decisive vote for the bill was demanding changes that would explode the Biden agenda. Without any quick fix in sight, Schumer's policy director, Gerry Petrella, shouted, "Fuck it. Let's throw the damn thing into a quorum call." In effect, Schumer would have to leave the vote in a state of suspended animation as he attempted to placate Manchin.

By Friday afternoon, the Senate remained stuck in a quorum call. A parade of Democrats attempted to gently peer pressure him into retreat. Republicans waxed gleeful about his predicament. John Thune, the senator from South Dakota, joked, "I hope the Geneva Convention applies to him."

Biden had refrained from applying personal pressure. But there was a limit to his patience. He picked up the phone and delivered a stern message to Manchin. He stated the obvious: "Joe, if you don't come along, you're really fucking me. I need you on this. Find your way to yes on this."

To give Manchin a face-saving victory, Schumer agreed that the bill would end unemployment benefits several weeks earlier than the last draft of the bill allowed, just enough for Manchin to ease back from the brink.

When the bill passed the next morning—after the longest session of voting in the recent history of the Senate—Biden allowed that the finale "wasn't always pretty." While Manchin resisted the impulse to ask for home-state goodies, Biden tried to reward him with some. Two weeks after the Rescue Plan passed, Biden appointed Manchin's wife to be cochair of the Appalachian Regional Commission, a paid post. More than a month later, Jill Biden visited Manchin in West Virginia, accompanied by the actress Jennifer Garner—the presidential version of the Schumer visits to *Almost Heaven.*

But the messiness wasn't what caught the eye. It was Biden's aggression.

He had proposed one of the most expensive, most self-consciously progressive pieces of legislation in American history and passed it quickly without any significant concessions. Biden pressed the limits of what his fifty votes in the Senate could accomplish. The headline of an essay in *Slate* declared the bill the "first step toward an FDR-style presidency."

7

Normal People

S ITTING IN THE OVAL Office with COVID advisers, Biden wanted to know, "What's he's saying?"

Everyone knew whom he meant. Biden had committed himself to expunging the words *Donald Trump* from his vocabulary and (wishfully) from public discourse, as if he would unintentionally increase his predecessor's power by innocuously incanting his name. Biden joked he would speak only of the "Former Guy." But he wondered aloud if he might need Trump after all.

"How am I going to persuade all these people who didn't vote for me to take the vaccine?"

The numbers were pretty dismal. In December, the Kaiser Family Foundation conducted a poll showing that only 34 percent of the country personally wanted the vaccine, with a massive gap between Democratic enthusiasm for the shot and Republican hesitance.

The scale of the problem meant that Biden was, at least, willing to chew over the idea of asking the Former Guy for help. If Trump's voters attended his rallies as if they were religious services, then they might be willing to listen to their spiritual leader, who had bankrolled the vaccine's development and taken the shots himself.

ANDY SLAVITT knew that a bunch of like-minded Democrats, spitballing in the White House, were unlikely to understand vaccine-hesitant Trump voters. He was desperate for an interpreter to supply a more native understanding of their thinking. On January 21, he called the Republican pollster Frank Luntz, whom he had never met. Slavitt knew that Luntz had been conducting focus groups with the vaccine hesitant to figure out how they might be persuaded to roll up their sleeves. To Slavitt, it felt like a small victory, a symbolic crossing of the partisan divide, when Luntz responded straightaway and offered to fly to Washington to meet in person.

Back in the nineties, Luntz had engineered Newt Gingrich's right-wing revolution. Luntz helped devise the Contract with America, one of the most potent gambits in the history of political consulting. But when Luntz connected with Slavitt, he told him that he wasn't his old self. In January 2020, while leading a focus group for *The Los Angeles Times*, he had suffered a stroke. Three weeks before his collapse, his doctor had warned that a catastrophe was only a matter of time. He was overweight, and ate as if he were a teenager. The stroke had scarred him. Luntz occasionally slurred a word. He tended to keep one of his hands, which sometimes felt numb, stashed in his pocket.

That experience spurred him to delve into the question of vaccine resistance. He considered himself a kind of Paul Revere, warning the world to treat COVID with the seriousness that he had neglected to apply to his own health. Luntz would tell his students that they had seventy-two hours to get vaccinated or he wouldn't talk to them again.

Luntz tried to deploy his dark arts for good. He began to develop a sense of what assured the vaccine hesitant—and what unnerved them. In the closing months of the Trump administration, he kept trying to find someone in the White House to listen to his findings, but to no avail.

When Slavitt met with Luntz, the pollster supplied a definitive answer to Biden's proposal to enlist Trump. The Former Guy's own supporters were guided by a sense that the elite had politicized the virus—which they viewed as a phony crisis, hyped by the media and Democrats to discredit Trump. But even with that paranoid view of the world, they weren't blindly following their leader. According to Luntz, to assume that they would obediently execute Trump's instructions was condescending, it disrespected the complexity of their thinking, and it would fail.

That tracked with Slavitt's thinking. Every time he turned on the television, he felt like he stumbled across pundits and cable news hosts disparaging the unvaccinated. But that sort of talk only served to make the unvaccinated shrink into their own filter bubbles, to become even more resistant to appeals to take the shot. Using Luntz's research, the White House arranged a briefing with cable news executives, urging them to soften their language.

Not every Biden adviser shared this view. Some wanted the president to speak to the unvaccinated with a sterner voice, to chastise their intransigence. But every time they urged tougher language, Biden rejected it. And in his self-conception of the job, he couldn't write them off. He needed to stick with the long slog of persuasion.

WHEN THE PRESIDENT assembled his COVID team, he would jokingly direct Anthony Fauci to sit in the vice president's chair.

In the earliest days of the administration, the doctor struggled to contain his exuberance, both out of affection for Biden, whom he had worked with in the past, and his sense of catharsis. When Fauci made his way to the podium in the White House briefing room for the first time after the inauguration, he felt a surge of traumatic memories wash over him. Jen Psaki asked him, "How long do you need? What do you want me to say?" For the first time in years, he was no longer in the awkward position of having to correct the administration he served.

During the first month, Biden kept calling on Fauci to get his help answering a challenging question: "When would the nation return to normal?" In anticipation of the question, Kate Bedingfield worked with the administration's public health officials to draft an answer. But then Biden would disregard them and ask to speak with Fauci so that he could go over the data in detail and understand it for himself.

Biden had a theory that guided his approach to the answer. The nation was suffering from a crisis of authority. There were pockets of trust to be found, and they mostly existed outside Washington, in communal relationships, with doctors and faith leaders and neighbors. While there was little Biden could do to reverse a problem that had been percolating for decades, he could unintentionally inflict harm. He needed to avoid the sin of over-promising.

During the first months of his presidency, he sounded caught between soaring optimism and unwarranted pessimism. In one breath he touted the progress of his vaccination program, in the next he warned the public not to let its hopes run wild. In February, he warned the nation that it might not be able to return to mask-free socialization with loved ones until the following winter. That might sound miserable, or unscientifically pessimistic, but Biden said that he was delivering on his vow to "shoot straight from the shoulder."

How to return the nation to a semblance of normal? The greatest imperative was addressing the disruption of childhood. For more than a year, kids had been barred from their classrooms, discouraged from playdates, and largely confined to their homes. In their isolation, they were struck with a terrifying fear. They had a rational basis for worrying about the death of their loved ones. When parents lost jobs—and millions of them did—households plunged into instability and even hunger. Through the pandemic, social scientists at Harvard tracked 224 kids, ages seven to fifteen, and found that two thirds of them exhibited symptoms of anxiety and depression, the same percentage as could be described as hyperactive or inattentive.

The academic dislocation imposed by COVID touched the Biden household, too.

Over the decades, Jill Biden's schedulers knew to regard Tuesdays and Thursdays, her days teaching English composition at Northern Virginia Community College, as inviolable. Her class was populated by immigrants, and she became enmeshed in their lives. They would text her questions like, "I'm not going to be in class today, because my car was stolen. What should I do?" She helped a student who had been kicked out of home and was living in a motel.

But in 2019, for the first time in her career, Jill Biden announced that she would skip a semester. She did so for the sake of the coming campaign. This was a gesture that surprised her longtime advisers. As a self-described introvert, she would quip, "It's my nature to walk into a diner and read by myself." The idea of walking up to strangers and taking a selfie filled her with anxiety, even if she could appreciate its value.

When she wanted to cheer up her husband, she would tape passages of poetry or inspirational quotes to the bathroom mirror. As she prepared to campaign, it was as if she needed to tape motivational messages to herself in her interior monologues.

In past campaigns, she could carve out time for teaching. But this time the Biden operation was poorly financed. In past campaigns, she flew private jets to Iowa. Now, she waited in line like everybody else for flights and strolled the corridors of O'Hare on layovers. But this was likely her husband's last campaign, and she was willing to pause her own career for it.

Still, she would declare to her staff, "If we win, I'm going to teach." The notion of a First Lady teaching twice a week posed inherent complications— and like everything else in America in 2020, the pandemic exacerbated those complications. Her college required her to take a course certifying her ability to conduct class via Zoom. Every Sunday night, she blocked off time to complete her own assignments, lessons in how to effectively teach via screen.

Jill Biden calls her staff the "Girls Team," even though one of her most trusted advisers is Anthony Bernal. The day before inauguration, the Girls Team whisked her away from her house in Wilmington, which was filled with relatives, dogs, staff, and the din of movers packing for the White House. They took her to a flophouse that had been rented for senior staff, which had been emptied so that she could have the necessary quiet to host her first day of class.

Her role as First Lady was always going to be different. Joe Biden was the oldest president in American history. Jill Biden, who is eight years younger, committed to serving as a vigorous proxy. Unlike Michelle Obama or Hillary Clinton, she wasn't really the subject of Republican attacks. It gave her space to actively take part in the substantive work of the White House.

Education wasn't just her vocation; it was her policy passion. She proudly self-identified as a rank-and-file stalwart of the National Education Association, one of the nation's most powerful unions. Even as she moved into the White House, she carried (and used) the Mastercard issued by her union, emblazoned with the seal of the NEA.

As Joe Biden mulled picking his secretary of education, Jill would listen to recordings of the interviews the transition conducted of candidates, and would relay her reactions. She let it be known that she didn't want the president to nominate an enthusiast for charter schools. In her view, the president had promised to nominate a champion of public education—and she didn't believe that advocates of charter schools fit that bill. None of the initial candidates that the transition unearthed excited her—or the rest of the president-elect's advisers, for that matter—so it went in search of a new list, which included one name that she greeted with enthusiasm, Miguel Cardona, the superintendent of schools in Connecticut, Biden's ultimate pick for the job.

Arriving at the White House, she knew her first significant assignment was to help her husband fulfill a campaign promise. He had vowed that he would get kids back in classrooms by the hundredth day of his presidency. In a way, this was the most challenging of all his pandemic promises. School had become a heated skirmish in the culture wars, an issue that didn't split just along ideological lines, but sundered his own coalition, pitting liberal parents against liberal unions. Even if it was never explicitly declared, a central pillar of Joe Biden's plan was Jill Biden.

ON JANUARY 21, Jill Biden invited the heads of the two largest teachers' unions—Randi Weingarten of the American Federation of Teachers and Becky Pringle of the National Education Association—to the White House. As she sat with them in the East Wing, in a room filled with bouquets of freshly cut flowers, she told the union chiefs, "I said I was going to bring you with me into the White House. And on day one, you're here."

A chunk of the country would have liked to see Dr. Biden dress them down. In upper-middle-class neighborhoods—and among newspaper columnists and television hosts—there was a sense that the unions were acting in a spirit of selfishness. According to their critique, teachers were, in fact, essential workers. But unlike warehouse workers and nurses, the teachers allowed their anxieties to get in the way of doing their jobs. Instead of allaying the worries of their members, the unions were indulging them for the sake of cultivating a spirit of militancy.

In Chicago, Mayor Lori Lightfoot demanded her district's teachers return to school. Her order was born of despair. The children of the city's vast immigrant population weren't getting the English language instruction they needed—and in fact seemed to be regressing. Large numbers of students, especially in the most economically disadvantaged families, weren't even logging on. But the unions resisted her pleas and wielded the threat of a strike.

As she sat with the heads of the union, Jill Biden didn't even nod in the direction of the tensions. Instead of pressing the union chiefs, she paid tribute to them, reserving her highest praise for Weingarten. Although the Right regarded Weingarten as a villain, Jill Biden praised her as the "type of general who is never far from the front lines."

Randi Weingarten had a history with Jill Biden's husband. In 2010, she confronted him in a meeting of the AFL-CIO Executive Committee in Florida. That year, the school board in Central Falls, Rhode Island, voted to fire every faculty member of a school with appalling test results, and Barack Obama publicly applauded it. Weingarten was furious that the administration had cheered the sacking of ninety-three teachers.

In the Florida meeting, Weingarten poured her anger onto Biden. As Biden absorbed her barbs, he grew animated in his boss's defense. Angrily rebutting her attack, he moved across the room in Weingarten's direction. *There's going to be a scuffle*, she thought. But when Biden stood next to her, he leaned in and whispered, "I hear you. Give me time, and I'll work this out." His anger was dutiful and performative. Despite Biden's loyalty to his boss, Weingarten felt as if she had discovered a genuine ally.

Seven days after Weingarten appeared at the White House with his wife, Joe Biden called her at her home in New York. He told her that he knew she was taking a lot of heat around the reopening of schools. Biden assured Weingarten that he was an abiding friend. "I am not abandoning you on schools. I want you to know that."

Biden wanted to ease the unions into accepting his goals, avoiding that sort of confrontation that might explode in a strike. He was never going to force teachers to return to school. His plan was to give them time and space to get comfortable with the idea, to smother them in the love of Jill Biden.

It was a policy that tracked with his approach to all the other culture war skirmishes of the pandemic. He, largely, sidestepped these fights. Hectoring red America into wearing masks was never going to work, so at a certain point, he stopped pressing. He spent months resisting the mandating of vaccines and never considered a vaccine passport, which could be used to verify inoculation as a prerequisite for travel or admission to sporting events.

After Trump had unleashed the furies, Biden's task was to restore as much calm as possible. Despite his expansive agenda, Biden managed to get slapped with the label "boring" by friends and critics alike—which is not far from what he aimed to achieve. Politics, which had consumed so much of the nation's collective consciousness for four years, suddenly didn't. Data showed a precipitous collapse in media readership and cable news viewership. When Ron Klain tweeted a link to this data, he quipped, "Sorry not sorry."

For the sake of avoiding conflict, especially conflict with an ally, the Biden administration trimmed its goal of returning kids to school to a fraction of what had been promised on the campaign trail. The announcement came as an aside in a press conference. Jen Psaki explained that Biden had really meant that he wanted more than half of the pre-K-to-8 schools to attend at least one in-person session a week by the end of his first hundred days. He was, in effect, conceding that for thousands of students, the rest of the school year would be lost to the pandemic. It was the price of peace.

8

The Captain Cook Incident

THE TWO most powerful leaders of the world finally connected on February 10. Xi Jinping, the Chinese president, began to chat with Biden as if he were dipping back into the middle of a running conversation among chums.

Indeed, the pair had history. In 2011, Barack Obama had dispatched Biden to China for the sake of getting to know Xi. At the time, Biden and Xi were the second-highest-ranking men in their nations. While the United States knew that Xi would eventually become head of state, it didn't have a deep sense of his mind. Biden's mission was, in part, a journalistic one. He would observe and listen, for the sake of a psychological and ideological understanding of his subject.

Trade meetings dotted the schedule of Biden's visit, but so did time for bonding. In addition to hours of scripted meetings, the pair traveled together to Dujiangyan City to visit a school rebuilt in the aftermath of an earthquake; they had dinner together at a restaurant in Chengdu.

To serve as Joe Biden's traveling companion is to be his caged audience. When his aides hit the road with him, they knew that they were buckling up for story time, for tales about Grandpa Finnegan and Senate majority leader Mike Mansfield, a back catalog of vignettes robust enough to cover the circumference of the globe several times over.

In the course of Xi's preparation for the call with Biden—their first chief-to-chief dialogue—his aides had clearly studied notes from Biden's vice presidential visits, or at least that's how it seemed to the White House officials listening in. Trying to project fondness, the Chinese president quoted Biden's maxims back to him. "I remember during one of our conversations years ago, you told me that your father once said, 'The only thing worse than a conflict that one intends is a conflict that one does not intend.'"

The time the pair spent together in 2011 had itself become the subject of one of Biden's well-worn tales. A good Biden story often gets better with time. He liked to say that he traveled seventeen thousand miles with Xi, although the trip they took together logged only a fraction of that. His public portrait of Xi seemingly had a similar sense of looseness. When he spoke about Xi, it felt as if he were talking a little too freely. He liked to tell crowds, "He doesn't have a democratic—with a small 'd'—bone in his body, but he's a smart, smart guy." Other times, he referred to Xi as a "thug."

But, in private, Biden assured aides that he thought hard about his public descriptions of foreign leaders. Biden believes that narrative is the foundation of good politics. If he relied on think-tank bromides to explain grand strategy, he would never persuade the public to support his positions. He needed to bring the public along by supplying it with vivid characters and compelling anecdotes. Such storytelling would help him conduct diplomacy, too. By speaking so bluntly, he sent clear signals to his adversaries. They wouldn't have to speculate about what he really thought of them.

So after Xi tried to soften him up with stories about the good old days, Biden shifted the subject. He didn't want to leave Xi guessing about his true intentions, especially as it related to the repression of the Uighurs, a Muslim minority, in the province of Xinjiang. Biden told Xi, "It's important that you understand my reasons for criticizing you." Any American president, he said, would take this position. Defending equality is in the nation's DNA, even if the country often fell short in living up to its high ideals. The important thing was to persist in the pursuit of those ideals.

Perhaps he couched his criticism in too much explanation. Chinese diplomats later surprised Jake Sullivan when they relayed that they considered the Biden-Xi call to be warm. It was a characterization that perplexed Sullivan, who couldn't understand how they could plausibly consider the time that Biden spent decrying the plight of the Uighurs to be anything but sharply critical.

To be fair, the point of the conversation wasn't blistering excoriation. It was to signal that the moment for that was imminent. Aides had begun preparing for what they knew would be one of the tenser meetings between China and the United States in recent memory. Like superpower summits of the past, it was scheduled for a slightly exotic and chilly locale: Anchorage, Alaska.

WHEN THE WHITE HOUSE'S top China hand, Laura Rosenberger, began planning for the meeting, the realization slowly dawned. The Chinese didn't get it. They seemed convinced that the Biden administration would want to leave behind all the acrimony of the Trump years and pick up where Barack Obama left off. As she sat in China's embassy in Washington, her counterparts kept brandishing copies of agendas from meetings that the two countries had held in 2015 and 2016. Those events were carefully scripted and culminated in communiqués filled with promises to hold further carefully scripted dialogues.

The Chinese didn't use the word reset, but that's how they viewed the change of administrations. "Let's rinse off the toxic residue of the past," they pleaded. By "toxic residue," they meant the layer of sludge coating Sino-American relations that accumulated during the Trump years.

As the Biden administration prepared for Anchorage, it hoped to clearly suggest that a reset wasn't plausible. By sending both Jake Sullivan and Tony Blinken to the meeting, the administration self-consciously intended to project a unified front. In the past, the Chinese liked to exploit the tendency toward rivalry between the White House and Foggy Bottom; Beijing sought out the friendliest voice in an administration and assiduously cultivated it.

They preyed on the vanity of officials who sought to personally monopolize the China portfolio. During the Trump administration, the friendliest voice was Jared Kushner. This time, the Biden administration wanted to physically demonstrate that there wasn't an ally for China to pry away.

WHEN KURT CAMPBELL, the swaggering diplomat and strategist Biden had personally recruited to the National Security Council to run his Asia policy, closed his eyes and thought about the Alaska meeting, he conjured wilderness cabins and tundra. But there's nothing cozy about the Hotel Captain Cook, where the administration booked meeting rooms. Arriving in Alaska, Campbell encountered a modern slab of glass and steel hulking above the water in downtown Anchorage.

As Campbell moved about the hotel, he saw members of the Chinese delegation from a distance. These were officials he had known over the decades. They had worked on countless contentious issues together. But the atmosphere felt different, almost gladiatorial, and it made him wistful.

When the meeting began, Campbell sat at a table, a few seats away from Sullivan and Blinken. Across from them, separated by several feet of hotel carpet, were China's two highest-ranking diplomats, Yang Jiechi and Wang Yi. Set against a black scrim rigged for the occasion, Sullivan and Blinken were about to launch into an exchange that deviated from everything they had learned on their ascents to their jobs.

Both Jake Sullivan and Tony Blinken came of political age in a different epoch in the history of the Democratic Party. They grew up in a world shaped by Bill Clinton and the faith that China should be a welcome guest at the feast of global capitalism. By stitching China into the fabric of international markets, China would evolve from its old doctrinaire ways. It would begin to respect property rights and develop a bourgeoisie of its own, which would inevitably crave political freedoms.

During the Obama years, that faith was tested. China was succeeding like crazy in markets, but it scoffed at capitalism's supposed rules. It acted as if intellectual property wasn't a thing; it manipulated its currency; the state kept subsidizing domestic industry. But instead of confronting China, Obama preferred to keep his criticism on the mild side. "I settled on a strategy to thread the needle between too tough and not tough enough," Obama wrote in his memoir. Although he accepted the critique of Chinese behavior, the financial crisis prevented him from doing much about it. He wanted to avoid a trade war that would "spook the jittery financial markets." Instead, he sought Chinese cooperation on battling climate change and in brokering an arms deal with Iran.

By Obama's second term, Joe Biden began to doubt the wisdom of the administration's position. Organized labor considered Biden its most sympathetic car in the Obama White House, and he began to echo what he heard from unions that complained about unfair Chinese trade practices. In 2014, he had pulled Jake Sullivan and Ben Rhodes, Obama's deputy national security adviser, into his West Wing office, not something he did regularly. And he began to rail. "The Chinese think they've got this figured out," he exclaimed. "They're betting on their model being better." He poked his finger in Rhodes's chest and said, "Don't bet against America."

Donald Trump had campaigned for president as the defender of the American working class against an elite that did nothing to protect the nation from the predator that is China. During his presidency, Chinese behavior seemed to prove his case, or at least disprove the old theories about globalization. Trade was supposed to have yielded a more benign China. Instead, China seemed to be trampling human rights with greater impunity. When China took over Hong Kong from the British in 1997, it promised to preserve the island's political freedoms for the next fifty years. But now, it brazenly stripped them away—shattering its promise of "one nation, two systems."

An official government slogan decreed, "Mao made the Chinese nation stand up, Deng made the people of China grow rich, Xi Jinping will make the people of China grow powerful." The government made the slogan tangible by creating fortress islands across the South China Sea—and by occasionally humiliating the United States. On Obama's final trip to China, the Chinese declined to pull stairs to Air Force One, forcing him to depart through foldout stairs in the belly of the aircraft.

As Sullivan watched China's behavior, he began to wonder if Trump, despite his xenophobia and hateful rhetoric, wasn't at least a little right. Wasn't it actually the case that China was "eating our lunch," as Trump put it? And if globalization wasn't yielding peace and democracy, then what was the point? If free trade wasn't advancing American interests, then why not pursue a more mercantilist trade policy?

In the haze of introspection that followed Sullivan as he recuperated from the 2016 defeat, he began to rethink the fundamentals of American foreign policy. He participated in a research team at the Carnegie Endowment for International Peace, a Washington think tank, that journeyed into the heartland and conducted focus groups in Ohio, Colorado, and Nebraska. How did Americans out there understand foreign policy as practiced by elites back here? What those groups told the researchers was a quietly devastating critique of elites like, well, Jake Sullivan.

Foreign policy had existed in an exalted sphere of grand strategy, with residual traces of the era when diplomats wore tails and sipped from coupes, a realm filled with abstruse taxonomies about idealists and realists. The discipline had tried to insulate itself from domestic politics, from concerns about how its policies implicated the average citizen. The Carnegie report argued for shattering the intellectual barriers that separated foreign and domestic policy. It proposed a new slogan, which Sullivan made his own: A Foreign Policy for the Middle Class.

Obvious implications flowed from the slogan. Rather than pursuing free trade for its own sake, the government should practice a once-fashionable doctrine known as industrial policy. That is, the government should explicitly boost its native firms and domestic industries. Globalization had dispersed supply chains across nations, a widget here, a battery there. Instead, the state should seek to concentrate those supply chains at home, or spread them among allies. That was a lesson of the pandemic, when the United

States didn't have domestic capacity to produce its own surgical gloves or ventilators. And it was the harsh reality of a semiconductor shortage that struck America in the first months of the Biden administration, as auto manufacturers had to temporarily close plants because they didn't have the chips to install into the vehicles sitting on the assembly lines.

Since September 11, the United States had fixed its gaze on the Middle East, directing its military and diplomatic attention there. But how did the American middle class benefit from wars in Yemen or Afghanistan, especially with the threat of terrorism receding? Barack Obama had intuited this twelve years earlier. He promised a pivot to Asia, a term and strategy minted by Kurt Campbell. But instead of extricating the nation from the Middle East, it remained hopelessly mired there.

Biden advisers entered office intending to complete the Asian pivot, but with an awareness of the irony that his policy wasn't all that different from the one Trump pursued, wrapped in the same protectionist rhetoric and the same dim view of Chinese intentions. Instead of reversing the tariffs Trump imposed on China, Biden left them in place. The Biden administration was making good on a strategy that Jake Sullivan and Kurt Campbell described in an essay that they cowrote for *Foreign Affairs* in the fall of 2019: "The era of engagement with China has come to an unceremonious close." Anchorage was planned as a moment to tell that to China's face.

ANTONY BLINKEN, the descendant of diplomats, has a gentle voice and impeccably polite manner. Even in flashes of anger, he maintains total control, still speaking with a slight hesitation, as if silently reading back his words to himself before they emerge from his mouth. Welcoming his Chinese counterparts to Alaska, he wanted to make clear that he wasn't welcoming them too warmly. Rather than sublimating American criticism of China, he said, "Our intent is to be direct about our concerns, direct about our priorities, with the goal of a more clear-eyed relationship between our countries moving forward." It was hard to tell from his voice, which contained not a trace of audible rancor, but he then proceeded to accuse the pair across the table of threatening global stability with cyberattacks and the coercion of US allies.

As he spoke, he looked across the room at Yang Jiechi. A former translator for the longtime leader Deng Xiaoping, Yang had served as an ambassador to Washington. Yang could be suave, but he also had earned the nickname "Tiger Yang." In the past, at similar such meetings, he had uncorked diatribes against the US. And though the Americans hadn't expected it, he tore up the prepared remarks he planned to deliver after Blinken's welcome.

To understand Yang, Sullivan waited for a translation. But he had a good sense of what was coming. Yang had far exceeded the two minutes allotted for his opening statement, clearly extemporizing, his face reddening, his eyes fixed on his American counterparts.

Sullivan passed a note to Blinken. "We have to respond," he wrote. That meant they would have to break with the carefully negotiated agenda for the meeting. Blinken agreed and began to scribble on a piece of cardstock.

When the translator finally had the chance to begin, it confirmed Sullivan's instincts. "Because, Mr. Secretary and NSA Sullivan, you have delivered some quite different opening remarks, mine will be slightly different as well." He chastised the pair for reverting to a "Cold War mentality," which he said reeked of hypocrisy. "The challenges facing the United States in human rights are deep-seated. They did not just emerge over the past four years, such as Black Lives Matter. It did not come up only recently. So we do hope that for our two countries, it's important that we manage our respective affairs well instead of deflecting blame on somebody else in this world."

When he finished, aides began to escort the press from the room, because the meeting was scheduled to enter into a closed session. But Blinken and Sullivan simultaneously held up their hands, asking the cameras to wait. It took a moment for the room to absorb the spontaneous change of plan. Blinken paused, then turned to the Chinese. "Given your extended remarks, permit me, please, to add just a few of my own."

Extemporaneous moments in international diplomacy are rare, by design. There was no time to comb Blinken's remarks to make sure that they were free of unintended implications. After launching into an extended defense of American foreign policy, Blinken answered Yang's criticism of the American society: "There's one more hallmark of our leadership here at home, and that's a constant quest to, as we say, form a more perfect union. And that quest, by definition, acknowledges our imperfections, acknowledges that we're not perfect, we make mistakes, we have reversals, we take steps back. But what we've done throughout our history is to confront those challenges openly, publicly, transparently, not trying to ignore them, not trying to pretend they don't exist, not trying to sweep them under a rug." As he wrapped up his retort, he quoted Biden, "It's never a good bet to bet against America."

WITH THE IMPROVISED REMARKS, Blinken and Sullivan were flying. The adrenaline coursing through them didn't quickly dissipate. And they envied how, once the press left the room, Wang and Yang quickly settled themselves, as if the whole confrontation had been a well-rehearsed sketch that permitted them to go in and out of character.

That evening, as the pair recapped the opening session, they began to worry that they had perhaps gone too far. Their confrontation in Anchorage coincided with another episode. Earlier in the week, in an interview, George Stephanopoulos had asked Biden, "So you know Vladimir Putin. You think he's a killer?" Biden replied, "I do." That morning, Putin issued a rebuttal to Biden: "The name you call is what you are yourself."

Blinken and Sullivan worried that the administration was edging into dangerous territory. They hadn't intended to rattle sabers, but perhaps it sounded that way. In all the strategic documents about the evolving relationship with China, the phrase managed competition kept recurring. But if the rhetoric grew too hot, would their anger sound as if it were truly being managed?

To prevent the next day from spinning beyond their control, they suggested convening with Wang and Yang in a more intimate setting, kicking out the retinues of aides. Each side would have a translator and notetaker. Stripping away the wider audience, there would be less incentive for theatrics.

When the Biden team first pondered the idea of the Anchorage meeting, they decided to wait until mid-March, anticipating that the American Rescue Plan would be signed into law by then and that COVID would be in abeyance. Joe Biden liked to talk about how the Chinese were under the impression that the United States was a sickly former hegemon. Challenging that assumption required concrete evidence of renewal. Behind closed doors, Sullivan and Blinken wanted to explicitly explain to Wang and Yang all the ways in which the American economy was not just on the mend, but being structurally remade to compete against China.

But it was exceedingly difficult to know if the Chinese were actually absorbing the message—or any of the messages the Americans hoped to deliver. At the end of the meeting, Yang approached Blinken.

"We appreciate your hosting. Protocol dictates that the next meeting is in China. We invite you and National Security Adviser Sullivan to China."

"Thank you," Blinken replied.

All through the meeting, the Chinese kept suggesting that the two countries cooperate. They proposed "dialogues" on health care, removing plastics from the Pacific, forest management, caring for the elderly—everything but the big issues that separated the two nations. Kurt Campbell felt as if the Chinese were trying to ensnare the United States in busywork, that the Chinese really did view America as a tired former superpower that they could preoccupy with vapid communiqués and the illusion of progress while China went about achieving dominance.

So instead of accepting Yang's invitation, Blinken tried to politely punt.

But as each side retreated to prepare a summary of the meetings for public consumption, Yang approached him again. "When I invited you to come to Beijing, you said, 'Thank you.' I would like to understand the meaning of the word 'thank you.'" Yang then sidelined his translator and broke into perfect English. "Does 'thank you' mean that you're agreeing to come?"

"'Thank you' means that I'm expressing appreciation for the invitation."

Yang kept going. "That means you're committed to come?"

After the room cleared, the Americans marveled at Yang's persistence. But it was evidence of a deeper problem. No matter how hard Blinken tried to suggest the emergence of a new reality, the Chinese kept insisting on the version of reality they preferred. There was no moving them.

9

Border Crush

"COME ON JOE," the president muttered to himself. He couldn't quite get his answer out cleanly. Ever since boyhood, when he struggled to overcome his stutter, Joe Biden strove for self-improvement. As a kid, he would stare into the mirror and recite lines from Emerson and Yeats, until the words flowed from his lips without pauses, hitches, or repetitions. Now he stood in the East Room of the White House, flagellating himself as he prepared for his debut press conference, scheduled for March 25, more than two months after his inauguration.

Everyone in the White House understood that the new administration benefited from relatively soft coverage during those opening months. A press corps suffering from post-traumatic stress disorder welcomed the relative professionalism of the Biden communications operation. With such favorable treatment, there was little rush for the White House to subject Biden to a ceremonial grilling, which would present endless opportunities for unintentional headlines.

Another concern weighed on Biden advisers as they hesitated to schedule the press conference. Biden's style of preparation chewed up enormous chunks of his schedule. Despite a history of improvising statements—or perhaps because of it—he didn't like to step in front of the cameras without extensive deliberation about what he might say.

Five days before his press conference, he met with White House communications director Kate Bedingfield to begin drafting his responses to likely questions from reporters. Biden likes to grope his way to his answers through conversation, preferably with top advisers in the room. As he talks through a potential answer, he routinely realizes that there are finer points of policy that he would like to better understand, so more experts are summoned. Suddenly, he isn't just preparing to answer a question, he's digging into regional variations in poverty statistics, and his morning schedule is in turmoil.

After Biden arrives at a formulation he likes, his advisers type up his words, which he edits at home that evening. When he returns the document, it is covered in his scrawl. Having been stung by accusations of plagiarism early in his career, Biden became obsessive about homework. All those train rides back and forth to Wilmington, during his Senate years, he pored over briefing books. Never again did he want to be accused of superficiality or borrowing someone else's words.

Where Obama would abhor prep sessions—advisers jokingly remember having to chase him down the hall—Biden insists on them. Yet, his relationship to those sessions is somewhat ambivalent. He deeply craves advice, but is often stubbornly resistant to it. At a press conference, or in response to a reporter's question, he'll begin an answer with "I'm not supposed to say this . . ." It's as if his subconscious can't help but advertise, *Hey, if I say something that gets me in trouble, don't blame my aides who didn't want me saying it in the first place.* Because Biden's staff has stuck with him for decades, they know precisely when he will go rogue.

On the morning of a press conference, Biden schedules one last prep session. "I want to get my motor running," he says. "Fire questions at me." For all his confidence and stubbornness, he's open to critique. In fact, he invites it. "Am I talking too fast?" "Am I stumbling?" "Does it feel comfortable?" At age seventy-eight, he was still staring in the mirror as he practiced.

POLLING SHOWED BIDEN had every reason to feel great about his standing with one exception. He was getting terrible marks for his handling of immigration, which meant that the press would inevitably gravitate to the subject.

The issue happened to be the place where he was most out of step with his evolving party's leftward trajectory. Activist groups chanted slogans like "Abolish ICE." But Biden had always styled himself a friend of cops. He worried aloud about the political consequences of progressive policy and how it might cost Democrats the Rust Belt.

But winning the Democratic nomination required Biden to commit himself to a wholesale reversal of Trump immigration policy. During the campaign, he said that he would loosen a provision known as Title 42. The Trump-appointed head of the Centers for Disease Control and Prevention invoked the public health emergency, which allowed Border Patrol agents to expel any foreigner entering the country, in order to prevent the spread of COVID. Whatever the justifications for the policy, it was exceptionally cruel. Kids who crossed the Mexican desert alone were turned away at the border, flung back into a netherworld of smugglers, gangs, and befouled refugee camps.

The plight of these children offended Biden's sense of decency. What gave him comfort were the plans he saw that his transition had sketched for dealing with the inevitable surge of unaccompanied kids. While Trump had shattered the government's infrastructure for caring for young migrants, the plans showed where money could be quickly found to rebuild that infrastructure. Slide presentations outlined how the new administration could address the influx as if it were a natural disaster, deploying FEMA, an agency expert in caring for the displaced.

But the president hated to see how his campaign proposals were being translated into policy. Just as he promised, Homeland Security imposed a hundred-day moratorium on deportations executed by Immigration and Customs Enforcement (ICE)—an organization that the Left vilified as an overzealous paramilitary force. But Biden hadn't realized that reforms would go so far. When he learned that ICE might stop targeting fentanyl dealers, sex offenders, and other felons, he exploded in anger. Plans were quickly changed.

Meanwhile, his administration was struggling to house the surge of unaccompanied minors. The plans to cope with the influx were lost in transition. Advisers who scripted the policy didn't enter the administration—or took jobs unrelated to immigration. It was as if all the planning never happened. Border Patrol agents weren't trained to care for children and were overwhelmed by the numbers in their custody. In theory, kids would stay in Border Patrol facilities for only seventy-two hours, and then the Department of Health and Human Services (HHS) would take care of them. HHS had a workforce trained to deal with the psychological complexities of scared children and the tools to reunite them with family members living in the United States. But as officials disregarded the transition planning, HHS couldn't keep pace. Children remained stuck in Border Patrol facilities for weeks, sleeping on gym mats covered by foil sheets, deprived of showers.

CLEANING UP this mess was a terrible first assignment. And HHS secretary Xavier Becerra tried to avoid it. As the former attorney general of California, he had ample experience with immigration, enough to know that it's the most thankless policy portfolio of them all. Because the Senate didn't quickly confirm Becerra, he came to the crisis late. His staff told him that HHS was being unfairly blamed for the problem—and he vowed to push back.

On a phone call with more than two dozen White House officials, Susan Rice, the head of the Domestic Policy Council, insisted that Becerra's department expand the number of children in its custody. But Becerra objected. In order to properly care for children, his department needed a ratio of one caregiver for every eight children. But if he adhered to Rice's request, that ratio would be skewed. HHS, he argued, wouldn't be able to properly tend to the children.

Rice tried to persuade Becerra. Transferring more children to HHS might not be ideal, but it was better than keeping them in overcrowded Border Patrol facilities, where they were living off Doritos; in the moments of anxiety and sadness, kids were consoled by officers carrying guns.

"I'll do it if I get a request from the president in writing," he finally volunteered.

His passive aggression irritated Rice. "You won't get a request in writing. That's not how the president of the United States operates. He's given you an order."

"I wasn't there for it," Becerra responded.

"The rest of us were," Rice told him. "You need to deliver."

Later that week, in the course of preparing for a meeting with Becerra and other advisers working on the issue, Biden heard about the call, and it put him in a foul mood. "Who am I going to fire in this meeting?" he said.

Biden felt as if he needed to make it unambiguously clear to Becerra that he needed to take more children into the department's custody.

Still, Becerra seemed to only grudgingly accept his responsibilities. "I will do what's requested of me," he told the president.

Kamala Harris told him, "It's good of you to do your job."

WITH THE SURGE of children, Biden was no longer sure that he wanted to follow through on other immigration promises. During the campaign, Biden had vowed to increase the number of refugees that the United States would resettle. Trump had capped the number at 15,000, a historic abrogation of the mission of welcoming the "huddled masses." On February 12, the administration told Congress that Biden would raise that number straightaway. In the next six months, the administration would resettle 62,500 refugees, victims of political oppression, targets of genocidal tyrants, and bystanders displaced by war.

It was an important symbolic reversal. And all that it required was Biden signing paperwork approving the funding for it. But in his cantankerous mood, he doubted whether he should. In an early March meeting that included Tony Blinken, he nodded in the direction of his longtime adviser, a passionate proponent of raising the cap. "They want me to increase the number of people in the country, but that's kind of crazy."

Biden swatted at every objection to his argument. He said that voters would never appreciate the difference between refugees fleeing tyranny and economic migrants from Central America. Since he was already getting pulverized on immigration, boosting the cap would just make things worse. His obstinacy deterred aides who might have otherwise challenged him, for fear of wasting precious capital on a hopeless fight. On April 16, the White House briefed reporters that the caps would remain fixed at Trump's level for the remainder of the fiscal year.

The cries of betrayal were instantaneous. "Say it ain't so, President Joe," the mild-mannered senator Dick Durbin tweeted. "This cruel policy is no more acceptable now than it was during the Trump Admin," Senator Richard Blumenthal complained. Biden wasn't getting hammered by Alexandria Ocasio-Cortez, but by old friends and true allies.

Ron Klain said that he wanted Joe Biden to change his mind; so did Susan Rice. But they weren't going to actively guide him there, at least not for the time being. They knew he needed space, so they didn't schedule any meetings to address the refugee cap. But it was perfectly clear that Biden would keep raising the subject himself, usually in meetings about the border crisis, usually with an edge of aggression. He moaned, "Can you believe that they want me to go back to those high numbers?" At a moment like that, Susan Rice would shoot a glance across the room, which told aides, *Don't take the bait.*

While Biden's angry moods made for uncomfortable meetings, they also prodded his administration to move quickly, to implement a version of the sensible plan drawn up in transition to more humanely manage a border surge. Kids were no longer stuck in Border Patrol facilities for weeks. As the crisis eased, conversations about immigration no longer ended in outbursts of anger.

In late April, Jake Sullivan sensed the moment had come to push on refugees. He wasn't scheduled to attend the weekly meeting on the border. But his assistant went in search of Amy Pope, a longtime Biden staffer who worked on immigration. Sullivan's assistant handed Pope the paperwork authorizing a rise in the refugee cap. "If you get the chance . . ."

Pope knew that she would have the chance. The same bureau charged with caring for migrant children also managed refugee resettlement. Indeed, Biden started asking questions about whether it had sufficient resources to carry out its mission.

"I've done a review," she told him. "There's enough money for children and enough to cover the resettlement of refugees."

"How can you tell me that the same guys that can't manage children coming are going to manage 125,000 refugees?" Biden asked.

Pope explained that the office had the ability to slow down the number of refugees it admitted into the country, if it ever started to get overwhelmed.

"Besides, there's symbolic value in keeping this number high," she pleaded. "This is important for your legacy."

"I don't care about my legacy," he shot back.

In the moment, Biden's logic shifted. All he cared about, he said, was treating the refugees humanely.

"Can you promise me that we're doing right by these people?"

"I promise," Pope told him and handed him the paperwork.

Without any further discussion, he took the document that had caused him so much consternation and signed it.

PART TWO

GREEN SHOOTS

April–June 2021

10

Biden's War

WHEN IT came to foreign policy, Joe Biden believed he was the business. For decades, in casual conversations, he would knock the strategists, diplomats, and pundits who pontificated on panels at places like the Council on Foreign Relations and the Munich Security Conference. He called them risk averse, beholden to institutions, lazy in their thinking. Listening to these complaints, a friend once posed the obvious question to him: If you have such negative things to say about these confabs, then why attend so many of them? Biden replied, "If I don't go, they're going to get stale as hell."

From twelve years as the top Democrat on the Senate Foreign Relations Committee—and then an additional eight years as the vice president charged with assignments like ending the Iraq War—he had acquired a swaggering sense of his own wisdom about the world beyond America's borders. Biden believed he could scythe through conventional wisdom, unlike the hidebound creatures of the foreign policy establishment who he encountered at think tanks or in the State Department. He took pride in this skill. If the moment demanded it, Biden had the courage to be contrarian.

He distrusted the mandarins, even when he had hired them to serve on his staff. They were trying to muddy things up with their abstractions and theories. He had once told a member of his Senate staff, "You foreign policy guys, you think this is all pretty complicated. But it's just like family dynamics." Diplomacy was just like persuading a pain-in-the-ass uncle to stop drinking so much. His point was that foreign affairs was sometimes painful, oftentimes futile, but really it was emotional intelligence applied to people with names that were sometimes difficult to pronounce.

Above all others, there was one subject that provoked him, triggering his contrarianism: the long war in Afghanistan. His strong opinions were grounded in experience. Soon after the United States invaded in late 2001, Biden began visiting the country. He had spent nights in sleeping bags on the floors of conference rooms; he had stood in line alongside marines and junior foreign service officers, wrapped in a towel, waiting his turn to shower.

On his first trip, in 2002, Biden met with interior minister Yunus Qanuni in his Kabul office, a hollow shell of a building. Qanuni, an old mujahideen fighter, told him, "We really appreciate that you have come here, but you should know that Americans have a long history of making promises and then breaking them. And if that happens again, the Afghan people are going to be disappointed."

Biden was jet lagged and irritable. Qanuni's comments set him off: "Let me tell you, if you even think of threatening us . . ." Biden was worked up, and his aides struggled to calm him down. The meeting went so badly that the American envoy Zalmay Khalilzad had to persuade Biden to return to the Interior Ministry later that evening to apologize.

According to Joe Biden's moral code, ingratitude is a grievous sin. The United States had evicted the Taliban from power, it had dispatched young men to die in the nation's mountains, it had given the new government billions in aid. But Afghan officials kept hectoring him about how the US hadn't done enough.

On two separate visits, in 2008 and 2009, he had dinners with President Hamid Karzai that went disastrously off the rails. Karzai had legitimate complaints with the US operation in his country. But he lodged his protests with spite and hostility, triggering Biden. In the middle of the first dinner, Biden dropped his napkin and stormed out of the room. "This dinner is over," he fumed.

Despite his flashes of temper, Biden is not a grudge holder, which is why he returned for dinner with Karzai one year later. But the frustration had stayed with him, and it helped to clarify his thinking. He began to draw unsentimental conclusions about the Afghan war—conclusions that the rest of the foreign policy elites resisted. He could see the Afghan government was a corrupt, failed enterprise. He could see that a nation-building campaign on the scale of Afghanistan was beyond American capacity.

After his second stormy dinner in Kabul, Biden experienced what one aide described as his "fuck-this-shit moment." He could no longer envision a successful end to the war and began to clamor for withdrawal.

As vice president, he would corner General David Petraeus, one of the true believers in the war, in the Situation Room. After meetings ended, Biden would grab Petraeus by the shoulders and refuse to let go, pleading with the general to heed his arguments for drawing down America's troop presence. Petraeus would just stand there, unable to extricate himself from the vice president's grasp and his impassioned monologue, as his schedule for the afternoon fell into disarray.

For eight years as vice president, Biden kept hearing the same set of pleas from the generals and State Department planners: *Just one more year, that's all it will take to create a stable political system; just one more year and the military will be self-sustaining; just one more year and corruption will fade.* Biden became convinced that the United States could stay for decades and nothing would ever change.

Biden also watched as Barack Obama was talked into sending thousands of additional troops to salvage a doomed cause. His old boss felt the pressure of the military. While Obama agonized over his Afghan policy, Biden pulled him aside and told him, "Listen to me, boss. Maybe I've been around this town too long, but one thing I know is when these generals are trying to box in a new president." He pulled close to Obama and whispered, "Don't let them jam you."

Over the decades, Biden had developed a theory of how he would succeed where Obama failed. He wasn't going to let anyone jam him. With his lifetime of experience, he had a plan to resist the pressures to stay. America didn't know how to win the war in Afghanistan, but Biden knew how to win the bureaucratic argument.

MAY 1, 2021, was the date enshrined in the Doha Agreement, which had been negotiated with the Taliban by the Trump administration. If the Taliban adhered to a set of conditions—to refrain from attacking US troops and to engage in political negotiations with the Afghan government—then the United States would remove its troops from the country on that date.

The agreement had all the hallmarks of the Trump administration. It was slapdash and the negotiators hadn't bothered to include the Afghan government—nominally, the rulers of the country in question—in the process.

What the agreement did successfully was create the illusion of peace, at least from the vantage of Washington. The Taliban stayed true to their promise that they wouldn't attack American soldiers. Their army advanced through the countryside, but refrained from capturing provincial capitals. The treaty gave the Americans a taste for peace—and it carried the threat of an escalation in the war. If the United States stayed beyond May 1, the Taliban might resume hostilities against American troops.

And it imposed a choice on Biden: he could honor the Trump agreement to leave Afghanistan or break it, just as Trump had undone the Obama administration's deal with Iran. It was a serendipitous deadline. The first major foreign policy decision confronting Biden was the one he seemed to feel most strongly about.

ON FEBRUARY 3, Biden invited his secretary of defense, Lloyd Austin, and the chairman of the Joint Chiefs of Staff, Mark Milley, into the Oval. At the beginning, Biden wanted to acknowledge an obvious emotional truth. He told them, "I know you have friends you have lost in this war. I know you feel strongly. I know what you've put into this."

Biden didn't know Milley or Austin well, although his son Beau had served under Austin in Iraq, where they sat next to each other at Catholic mass. Over the years, Biden had traveled to military bases, where he would occasionally run into them, sometimes accompanied by his fellow senator Chuck Hagel. On those trips, with their long plane flights, Hagel and Biden dipped in and out of a long-running conversation about war. They traded theories about why the United States would remain mired in conflicts in the Middle East. One problem was the psychology of defeat, the hardest thing for a commander to admit. Generals lived in terror of being blamed for a loss, living in history as the one who waved the white flag.

It was this dynamic, in part, that kept the United States entangled in Afghanistan. Politicians who hadn't served in the military could never summon the will to overrule their generals, and the generals could never admit that they were losing. So the war continued indefinitely as a zombie campaign. Biden seemed to believe that he could break this cycle, that he could master the psychology of defeat.

That's why he told Austin and Milley that he understood their emotional attachment to Afghanistan. Biden's great strength is his empathy—his ability to understand the baggage of the person sitting across from him.

Biden wanted to avoid having his generals feel cornered—even as he was guiding them to the outcome he desired. He wanted them to feel heard, to appreciate that he was acting in good faith. They would never agree with his decision, but he hoped they would feel a sense of co-ownership of it. He told them, "Before I make a decision, you'll have a chance to look me in the eyes."

The May 1 deadline was, in a way, a gift. Nearly twelve years earlier, in the Obama administration, the debate over Afghanistan had dragged on for months. Details from the deliberation leaked. Obama had begun to feel pressured to ignore his own instincts and to defer to his generals. The Pentagon set the terms of debate.

Biden wouldn't let that happen. This time, the decision was going to be a dash. It would be made as Biden still basked in the glow of his inauguration. Rather than asking his generals for a plan, he wanted them to participate in an intellectual exercise. He wanted them to answer four questions—Jake Sullivan called them the "inputs" that would inform a final decision. He wanted to know: What was the terrorism threat globally—and in Afghanistan? Could the government in Kabul survive if the US withdrew? Were the Taliban abiding by the deal they brokered with Trump? And finally, what were Russia, China, India, Iran, and Pakistan thinking about Afghanistan?

Back in the Obama administration, Biden was a strident participant in discussions. This time, he tried to play the role of facilitator. He presented himself as someone keenly aware of the dangers of groupthink. "Whoever disagrees, speak up now," he would say. Or, when he mustered an opinion in meetings, he would add, "Someone challenge me here."

And he was challenged. Just as he anticipated, his generals presented a grim portrait of the aftermath of the war. Milley warned him that Kabul might fall to the Taliban, which would erode all the good work that Americans had done in the country. The United States would, in effect, hand the country over to a political movement that had once happily provided a sanctuary for terrorism. He believed a contingent of about 2,500 troops, 4,000 at the outermost, would be sufficient to hold off the Taliban and support the Afghan government, until the United States brokered a political agreement with the Taliban.

After meetings, Biden kept Jake Sullivan in the room and only then revealed his inner thoughts. "The way I'm hearing, the argument for staying is . . ." And then Biden would recapitulate what he heard, before asking, "Is that good enough?" The answer was always "no." As Biden summarized the debate, everyone kept telling him that staying in Afghanistan was an insurance policy against the threat that the country might become a terrorist harbor again. But in his conversations with Sullivan, he was adamant that the premium was too high.

ON MARCH 4, Sullivan ended the day with his deputy Jon Finer and Yohannes Abraham, the chief of staff of the National Security Council. Normally, he liked to sit with them and breezily review every crisis that had crossed their desks. But Sullivan wasn't in a schmoozy mode. He was red in the face and raining expletives.

One of Sullivan's priorities during the Afghanistan decision-making process was to prevent leaks. In a White House that hardly ever spoke without permission, Sullivan wanted to place this decision in an impenetrable lockbox. Yet, word had gotten out. Someone—and he wasn't pointing fingers—had told a reporter at *Vox* about the Oval Office debates. The piece contained details about how Milley was making a passionate case for staying. And it was obvious that the leak hadn't come from Milley, since it described his arguments as lacking substance.

Leaks were evidence of a debate conducted in bad faith. A damning quote delivered on condition of anonymity was the opposite of the *I'll give you a chance to look me in the eye* process that Biden promised.

Sullivan summoned the NSC's chief flack, Emily Horne. If the leaker wasn't brave enough to put their name to a quote, he would expose their cowardice by talking on the record to refute the anonymous account.

It was unnerving to see Sullivan break character like this, but it was also obviously theatrical. Sullivan had presented an object lesson, showing how he would rip the head off anyone who conducted freelance conversations with journalists.

The last administration had destroyed the inter-agency process, through which the White House traditionally consulted with departments and agencies for feedback and expertise. With Afghanistan, Sullivan aspired to model how the new administration would immaculately involve all the right parties and hold all the right meetings, to avoid all the wrong sorts of rivalries.

It was perfectly consistent with his character that Sullivan—the institution-alist, the young aide trusted by older leaders—was the model Process Guy.

But the obsession with process risked rendering the debate about Af-ghanistan soulless. It was the warrior Milley who interjected with his fears about the fate of women and girls if the Taliban returned to power. But that concern was only tangential to the four questions that Biden had asked his aides to consider. Biden hadn't just grown disillusioned with the war; he had turned against the whole project of nation building, with its emphasis on implanting the foundations for liberal democracy in Afghanistan. In George Packer's biography of the late Richard Holbrooke, there's a moment in 2010 when Biden vents, "[I am] not sending my boy back there to risk his life on behalf of women's rights, it just won't work, that's not what they are there for."

In the course of the 2020 campaign, CBS's Margaret Brennan asked Biden if he felt any responsibility for what might follow the American with-drawal from Afghanistan. He brought his forefinger to his thumb. In an ir-ritated voice, he told her, "Zero responsibility."

ON MARCH 22, Blinken traveled to Brussels to meet with NATO foreign ministers. Biden wanted him to share a sense of his thinking with the allies and to gauge their reactions.

Afghanistan had a special place in the history of the transatlantic alli-ance. The attack of September 11 was the only time in NATO's history when it invoked Article 5 of its charter, which declared that an attack on one member state was an attack on them all. Its long involvement in Afghani-stan was a deviation from the alliance's founding mission.

Historically, the United States had played the role of exuberant idealist, enthralled with the prospects of democracy promotion and nation building, while the Europeans were hardened realists, tempered by a tragic sense of history and commercial instincts. As Robert Kagan had famously put it, "Americans are from Mars, Europeans are from Venus."

But Blinken found himself startled by a reversal of roles. He came to Brussels to inform America's European friends that Biden wanted to abandon the old blueprint for remaking traditional societies in a Western image, a message of humility, restraint, and prudence. Instead of a rapturous reception, however, Blinken was greeted by scathing objections.

For more than three hours, he sat in NATO headquarters madly scribbling, recording everything he heard. The Europeans, especially the Germans, were furious at the prospect of abandoning the women and girls of Afghanistan. They worried about a revived Afghan civil war, which would inevitably culminate in refugees overwhelming European borders.

The Europeans were adamant that the United States should stay longer. They proposed an idea that Joe Biden disliked. Instead of leaving in September, they wanted the United States to condition its departure on a negotiated political settlement between the Afghan government and the Taliban. In other words, the Europeans wanted the United States to leverage its remaining troop presence to extract a promise from the Taliban to participate peacefully in a pluralistic Afghanistan.

When the session ended, Blinken went to the US embassy so that he could call the president on a secure line. Biden was eager to hear what the Europeans thought. But Blinken's description of European skepticism wasn't what he expected. At the end of the call, Biden said, "Well, we'll need to factor that into the decision."

The European reaction shook Blinken. When he returned to Washington, he set out his own thinking in a memo. The vehemence of the European reaction had changed his mind. While he had initially agreed with Biden about the necessity of ripping off the bandage and unconditionally withdrawing, he was no longer so sure. In part, he found himself persuaded by the substantive European objections. But more than that, he worried about the health of the transatlantic alliance. Wasn't restoring that alliance a primary objective of the Biden administration? If they were sincere about that, how could they ignore such passionate objections?

Blinken proposed that the State Department take another stab at talking with the Taliban. The US would assert that its troop presence remain until the Taliban consented to a political agreement with the Afghan government. Blinken argued that the United States might even want to gamble and stay longer if the Taliban rejected the offer.

For nearly two decades, Tony Blinken and Joe Biden had thought in tandem about the war. As the staff director of the Senate Foreign Relations Committee that Biden chaired, Blinken had traveled to Afghanistan with him and jointly interrogated officials in Washington about what they saw. They worked well together, because they agreed about so much, including the need to end the war.

Even with all that shared history, Blinken didn't think he had much chance of prevailing when he made the case to Biden in the Oval, with Jake Sullivan and Ron Klain watching. Indeed, he was met with arguments he had heard repeated many times over the decades. Biden told him that withdrawal was a hard thing that needed to be done. He didn't want to get caught in the trap of giving the war one more try. Blinken's proposal would simply keep the US in Afghanistan with no real exit. When he left the meeting, Blinken was sure he had failed to persuade.

A few days later, however, Biden surprised him. "I thought about this," he told him. "We need to leave, but let's give this a try. Press the Taliban. See if you can get somewhere." Biden couldn't help appending his skepticism about the plan's chance of success. But it was important, he said, to show the Europeans how seriously he took their concerns.

Blinken's conduit to the Taliban was Zalmay Khalilzad, who had played the same role in the Trump administration. In fact, he was the diplomat who had crafted the withdrawal that Biden now felt forced to implement. Even though Khalilzad was a partisan Republican, a veteran of the George W. Bush administration, Blinken left him in place as the special representative for Afghanistan reconciliation. Khalilzad had a trusting relationship with the Taliban, which would be hard to replace. Besides, Biden had known Khalilzad forever—they were roommates on Biden's first trip to Afghanistan. He liked the guy.

When Khalilzad went to Doha to meet with the Taliban on Blinken's behalf, he tried to cajole them one last time. After his arguments flopped, he told them, "I have to report this to the president. When we withdraw and there's no political agreement, we see the risk of escalation and continuing conflict. Would you rather see war than an agreement?" The Taliban told him that if the US stayed past the deadline, then the deal was null and void.

And that was that. Khalilzad didn't push any harder. The Biden administration made no further attempt to leverage the presence of its remaining 2,500 troops in the country to cut a better deal. Trump's deal was the deal.

As BIDEN PREPARED his final decision, Jake Sullivan had the NSC generate two documents for the president's nightly reading. One outlined the best case for staying in Afghanistan; the other made the best case for leaving.

This reflected Biden's deep-seated belief that he faced a binary choice. He felt like the foreign policy elite hadn't appreciated what staying in Afghanistan would entail. If Biden abandoned the Doha Agreement, attacks on US troops would resume. Only, during the yearlong cessation of hostilities, the Taliban had recharged their batteries. They had spent the year growing stronger, forging new alliances, sharpening their plans.

Thanks to Donald Trump's drawdown of troops, the United States no longer had a robust enough force to fight a surging foe. So if the United States committed to staying, it was really committing to escalating a war that no longer made any sense.

In early April, Biden gathered his top aides for one last meeting, before he formally made his decision. Toward the end of the session, he asked Sullivan, Blinken, and Director of National Intelligence Avril Haines to leave the room. He wanted to talk to Austin and Milley, the retired general and the current one, alone. It made sense to think of the generals as a package. Their relationship traced back decades. Milley had served under Austin in Afghanistan and Iraq. He once led Austin on a nighttime tour of forward operating bases outside of Baghdad—what Milley promised was a "a quiet sector"—but an improvised explosive device shredded their Humvee. As smoke filled the vehicle, Milley worried that Austin, travelling in a back seat, hadn't survived. He began furiously screaming Austin's code name. There was a beat of terrifying silence until Austin shouted, "Really smooth, Milley. A real quiet sector." When the Biden transition called Milley to gauge his reaction to Austin's nomination, he couldn't believe he might be partnered with his old comrade.

Milley was a realist about Afghanistan. When the deliberations over withdrawal began, he knew that Biden wasn't going to be budged from his deeply held positions. During the Obama administration, Milley had worked for the Joint Chiefs, helping prepare the options presented to the president.

Now he was the one charged with providing the military's best advice to the president. And the president thanked him profusely for it. They had bonded over their shared Irishness. Biden told him, "I'm seventy-eight, but we could have grown up in the same neighborhood drinking beers."

Instead of revealing his final decision to Milley and Austin, he made it sound as if it were still a work in progress. "This is hard," he told them. "I want to go to Camp David this weekend and think about it."

Milley knew that this was likely disingenuous, and he didn't especially care. In fact, as a student of military history, he even respected the tactic. All along, it was clear to Milley that Biden was fighting the last bureaucratic war. Even as Biden carefully and respectfully absorbed his advice, Milley knew that he was being managed. He knew that Biden was trying to bring him along to support a precooked decision.

Biden didn't know it, but Milley actually shared his analysis of the Obama years. A younger Mark Milley had sat in meetings in the basement of the Pentagon, listening to top generals boast about how Obama was a young president that they could manipulate. And he didn't like it. Now that Milley was in charge, he didn't want to repeat that mistake.

America had given up on the forever wars—a term that Milley hated. Still, Milley knew that his preferred path for Afghanistan wasn't shared by the nation he protected. Having just survived Donald Trump and a wave of speculation about how the military might figure in a coup, Milley wanted to demonstrate his fidelity to civilian rule of the military. If Biden wanted to shape the process to get his preferred result, well, that's how a democracy should work.

ON APRIL 14, Joe Biden announced his decision to the nation in the Treaty Room of the White House, the very same spot where, in the late fall of 2001, George W. Bush had informed the public of the first American strikes against the Taliban.

Biden delivered the speech at two thirty in the afternoon, hardly prime time, which would have arguably better suited the occasion. Then again, Afghanistan had long ago receded from the forefront of the national conscience. It hardly featured in the previous year's presidential debates. The conflict had become background noise.

"I'm now the fourth United States President to preside over American troop presence in Afghanistan: two Republicans, two Democrats." Pushing his finger into the podium, he intoned, "I will not pass this responsibility on to a fifth."

As he walked through his thinking, he invariably turned to the military rank and file. Thinking about them, he could not help but project an image of Beau Biden: "Throughout this process, my North Star has been remembering what it was like when my late son, Beau, was deployed to Iraq—how proud he was to serve his country; how insistent he was to deploy with his unit; and the impact it had on him and all of us at home."

The speech contained a hole that few noted at the time. There was scant mention of the Afghan people, not even an expression of best wishes for the nation that the United States would soon be leaving behind. The Afghan people were only incidental to his thinking. (Biden hadn't even spoken with the country's president, Ashraf Ghani, until he informed him of his decision on the eve of its announcement.) Scranton Joe's infinite reserves of compassion were directed at people with whom he felt a connection; his visceral ties were with the American soldier.

Biden announced that the withdrawal would be completed on September 11, the twentieth anniversary of the attack that drew the United States into war. The symbolism was polemical. Mark Milley loathed it. How did it honor the dead to admit defeat in the conflict that had been waged on their behalf? Eventually, the Biden administration pushed the withdrawal date forward to August 31, an implicit concession that it had erred.

But the choice of September 11 was telling. Biden took pride in ending an unhappy chapter in American history. The war on terror may have been a just cause—and Democrats might have once referred to Afghanistan as the "good war"—but it had metastasized into a fruitless fight, wasteful and excessive, mindlessly cruel. It had deflected the United States from the policies that might preserve the nation's economic and geostrategic dominance. By leaving Afghanistan, Biden believed he was redirecting the nation's gaze to the future.

11

Hug Bibi Tight

JOE BIDEN didn't know all the ways that the world might conspire to derail his presidency, but he was intimately familiar with one. On May 10, rockets launched from the Gaza Strip descended on the skylines of Tel Aviv and Jerusalem. The Iron Dome, Israel's protective canopy of countermeasures, detonated most of the munitions. But a few slipped through the system's cracks. Furious retribution followed.

This is how it always began—a sequence of events that ran on a loop, playing in the background of Biden's career—except this time the cache of rockets in Gaza, produced with Iranian assistance, was vaster than in past skirmishes; thus, the possibilities for sustained warfare were greater, too.

Two days after the first rocket attack, Biden national security aides gathered in the Oval Office. Across the room from Biden sat Brett McGurk, his primary Middle East adviser on the National Security Council, square jawed, hair tightly cropped, with a name and appearance that evoked a sergeant in a World War II movie. Not so long ago, he was a wunderkind, nurtured by the conservative legal establishment, a clerk for the late William Rehnquist. At the height of the Iraq War, the Bush administration dispatched him into the thick of the quagmire, where he advised ambassadors and negotiated with prime ministers.

That youthful experience—and the many failures he witnessed—left him humbled. As Obama retained him in his inner circle of diplomats, Mc-Gurk acquired a quiet respect for the limits of American foreign policy. The nation kept making big promises about how it would revolutionize the Middle East. But instead of fulfilling those promises, it repeated a cycle where it would inflate expectations for change, only to violently disappoint. Even Obama, who preached restraint, had issued a series of rousing-but-hollow threats against Syria's Bashar al-Assad.

McGurk liked to say that if he could reduce Biden's Middle East policy to a bumper sticker, it would read "No New Projects." That meant no peace processes, no grand plans for strategic realignment, no grandiose objectives. His job was to minimize the prospects of a crisis—to keep the Middle East off the president's desk as much as possible.

Biden came from a different generation than his foreign policy team; he was old enough to have met with Golda Meir, on the eve of the Yom Kippur War in 1973. He grew up in a world where most Americans, especially liberals, regarded Israel as both a historical miracle and a sympathetic underdog. At the dinner table, Biden's father would tell him, "If Israel didn't exist, we'd have to create it." When he first met Nancy Pelosi in the 1970s, she was helping a San Francisco neighbor organize a fundraiser for Israel. Biden was the keynote speaker. Pelosi loaned her Jeep, for the sake of squiring Biden around town so that he could extol the case for Zionism.

Over the past decade, mainstream Democrats had begun to drift from their elders on the subject of Israel. They didn't regard it as quite the same sacred commitment. Jake Sullivan, for one, had spent his career during the long, intermittent premiership of Benjamin Netanyahu. From afar, he saw how Netanyahu undermined Barack Obama. Up close, he watched how Netanyahu sought to foil the nuclear treaty that Sullivan had negotiated with Iran. Bibi then proceeded to openly root for the political victory of his autocratic American cousin, Donald Trump.

But if any of Bibi's chicanery bothered Biden, he never let it show. As vice president, Biden visited Israel in 2010, only to be sucker punched by an incendiary announcement that the government had approved the construction of new housing in East Jerusalem, against the wishes of the Obama administration. According to most pundits, Bibi deliberately humiliated him. Biden's colleagues in the White House wanted him to skip a dinner with Bibi and bolt the country in protest. Biden rejected that advice. Instead of delivering a tongue-lashing, he embraced Netanyahu that evening, then gently prodded him. "This is a mess. How do we make it better?" He later sent Netanyahu a photograph, inscribed "Bibi, I don't agree with a damn thing you say, but I love ya."

In the first months of the Biden administration, it looked as if those warm feelings had faded. The Israeli press wrote fretful stories theorizing that the new administration wanted retribution against Bibi for his support of Trump. For weeks, Biden failed to return Netanyahu's congratulatory phone call. A headline in *Haaretz* exclaimed, "No Phone Call from Biden Is a Wake-Up Call."

But that headline was merely a projection of anxieties. When he finally connected with Netanyahu, the president launched into a nostalgia trip. He reminded Netanyahu how they had met in the eighties, when Bibi worked in the Israeli embassy in Washington: "Did you ever imagine we'd be sitting where we are today?"

Now, as Netanyahu engaged in the opening skirmishes of war, Biden told his advisers in the Oval to scrap the old playbook. Historically, an American president would call for a cease-fire and urge restraint. The secretary of state would be dispatched to the region. But that wasn't how Biden wanted to approach this crisis.

For starters, he didn't see this as a conflict with two sides equally at fault. No nation would tolerate rockets raining down upon its cities. In his view, Israel had a clear right to defend itself—and he would defend their right to assert that right. But more than that, he said, he knew how Bibi's mind worked, after decades of meetings. He explained that criticism would merely push Bibi away.

In his view, the quickest way to end the conflict was to stand squarely with Israel, to smother Netanyahu with love. Then, at the right moment,

Biden said that he would take advantage of the trust he had deposited in the bank. Only then would he tell Bibi to wind the war down. But in the meantime, he was going to hug Bibi tight.

BRETT McGURK and Jake Sullivan saw the risk in the strategy that Biden outlined. Biden wanted to hug Bibi at the moment in his political career when Netanyahu had every personal incentive to fight a prolonged war.

Israel had just finished its fourth election in two years. And Netanyahu was dangling in a precarious position. Thanks to Israel's madcap parliamentary politics, his opponents had won the right to organize a governing coalition, but that was a Herculean task. They had twenty-eight days to cajole a raft of ideologically disparate small parties into an alliance. If they failed, the nation would head to the polls yet again.

In the meantime, Netanyahu remained in office as the national caretaker, and the war he led complicated his opponents' task. As Israelis rallied around the flag—or cowered in bomb shelters—the horse trading required to build a parliamentary majority seemed crass. Worse, the opposition needed to entice Israel's only Islamist party into its coalition, which carried obvious political risks, given that the Islamists who ruled Gaza were the ones lobbing rockets. In a late-night address to the nation, Bibi intoned, "This campaign will take time."

That sounded ominous to McGurk. Biden had told him that he didn't want to repeat the Gaza war of 2014, which lasted nearly three months and preoccupied John Kerry, then the secretary of state, who decamped to the region for endless shuttle diplomacy.

Yet everything the White House heard from Israeli officials suggested that Netanyahu wasn't blustering about a prolonged campaign. The head of the Israeli military, Aviv Kochavi, kept intimating to Mark Milley that his army was preparing for a ground invasion of Gaza, which would entail close combat and risked substantial casualties. Preventing such an invasion became a primary goal of the White House.

But hugging Bibi also exposed Biden to criticism from his own party. After the Black Lives Matter protests, a new cohort on the Left conflated the Palestinian cause with the deaths of George Floyd and Breonna Taylor. Bernie Sanders, who had more vestigial sympathy for Zionism than that, wrote an op-ed in *The New York Times* with the headline "The U.S. Must Stop Being an Apologist for the Netanyahu Government." Even Gregory Meeks, the chairman of the House Foreign Affairs Committee, who normally stood squarely with the Jewish state, asked the Biden administration to delay a sale of precision-guided missiles to Israel. Suddenly, the Middle East stood to alienate allies Biden badly needed on the Hill.

Israeli carelessness in the war exacerbated the ire of progressives. Four days into the conflict, the Israeli Air Force destroyed a tower in Gaza City that housed offices belonging to the Associated Press and Al Jazeera. Israel claimed (without evidence) that the building was a sanctuary for militants, but critics alleged that it was a spiteful attack against media critical of Israeli aggression.

When Biden called Netanyahu after the strike on the AP building, he declined to chastise him. Instead, he led Bibi through a long Socratic exercise: "Help me understand your strategy," he pleaded. Biden spent more than an hour conducting his inquiry in the spirit of friendship. But he was also trying to expose the shortcomings in Bibi's thinking.

He asked, "How will this end?"

"When we restore deterrence," Bibi explained.

"And how will you know when you've restored deterrence?"

"We'll know."

Bibi inadvertently admitted he had no defined objective. But Biden held his tongue.

DEALING WITH THE ISRAELIS was an adventure. The nature of coalitional politics is that some of Bibi's sworn enemies served in his cabinet. They passed along information that occasionally undermined their boss. One of the men that Netanyahu defeated in a past election, Benny Gantz, was now the defense minister. Where Bibi seemingly wanted the campaign against Hamas to continue indefinitely—which conveniently kept him in the politically popular post of wartime commander—Gantz quietly let the White House know that he had a different opinion. Even though Gantz had enthusiastically supported the bombardment of Hamas, he told the Biden administration that Israel had started to run out of targets it felt compelled to strike.

On May 19, Biden placed his fourth call of the war to Netanyahu from his residence. In each successive call, Biden tried to intimate incrementally greater skepticism about the need to continue the assault on Gaza. Now he wanted Netanyahu to know that he was out of time.

"We need to accomplish more," Bibi told Biden.

Although the intervals kept shifting—two days, fifty-two hours, an indefinite extension—he kept begging for time. But he struggled to justify his request, because he couldn't point to fresh targets that needed striking.

"Hey, man, we're out of runway here," the president replied. "It's over."

And then, like that, it was. By the time the call ended, Netanyahu reluctantly agreed to a cease-fire that the Egyptians would broker.

ON THE AFTERNOON of May 21, Brett McGurk took a call from Abbas Kamel, the director of Egypt's intelligence directorate—and a primary back channel through which the United States and Israel conveyed messages to Hamas. There was a note of panic in his voice. A cease-fire was scheduled to begin in three hours. Both sides agreed that they would refrain from any aggression in the lead-up to the official start of the agreement, a test of the other's fidelity to the deal.

But Kamel was beginning to lose his cool. According to Hamas, the Israelis had warned the residents of three buildings in Gaza to evacuate, the standard Israeli prelude to an air strike. If that happened, Kamel told Mc-

Gurk, the whole deal was off. The war would resume, and that could only lead to an unruly escalation.

When Kamel called, McGurk was sitting outside Jake Sullivan's office. He knew that Sullivan was on the phone with the Israeli national security adviser, Meir Ben-Shabbat. So he sent a note to Sullivan explaining the Egyptian fears. He wanted Sullivan to relay them to the Israelis.

Sullivan asked his Israeli counterpart, "What the hell is this about? Did you really just do this?"

"No, no, no, no," Ben-Shabbat replied. "We wanted people out of those buildings. Because if Hamas attacks us, we'll destroy them. But we're not going to do it unless they fire at us first."

McGurk thought, *What a very Israeli explanation*—and he passed it along to Kamel. Neither man could be sure that it would prove persuasive to Hamas. After he hung up the phone, McGurk began to watch the clock, hoping that the silencing of guns would hold until the deadline.

As he waited, he and Sullivan were told to come to the Oval Office. Netanyahu had called Biden, and they listened to the conversation. After a morning of panic, Netanyahu wanted to assure the American president that he wasn't about to scuttle the imminent arrival of peace. "Joe," he said jovially, "We have a cease-fire."

12

Rabbit Ears

WHEN JOE BIDEN watched Kamala Harris tank an interview with NBC News anchor Lester Holt on June 8, he must have felt a pang of familiar discomfort. She was sitting in Guatemala City, at the tail end of a successful trip to Central America. Yet she seemed utterly unprepared for a predictable question. Having traveled to the region for talks that intended to help address the root causes of migration, Holt wanted to know, "Do you have any plans to visit the border?"

Harris replied, "At some point you—we are going to the border. We've been to the border. So this whole thing about the border. We've been to the border. We've been to the border."

The answer caused Holt to scrunch his face in incredulity. "You haven't been to the border."

Harris began to sink into a crouch, where she could do nothing but kick out in self-defense. "And I haven't been to Europe," she replied. "And, I mean, I don't understand the point that you're making. I'm not discounting the importance of the border."

This wasn't how Symone Sanders, her communications adviser, had prepped her. It was a display of logical acrobatics—as if *Saturday Night Live* writers had scripted the moment for parodic purposes—and it made Harris the butt of unending criticism, from all quarters.

When Joe Biden learned about her performance, he professed concern for Harris. During his eight years as Obama's deputy, he had his share of verbal misadventures. He seemed to feel genuine empathy. Over the next two days, he kept calling to check in with her. "Don't let them get to you," he told her. As he described his reaction to his senior staff, he told them, "Make sure you have her back." She had a tough job, worthy of their empathy.

THE IMPOTENCE of the vice presidency is a comic premise—a job that suggests power but doesn't have much of it. But what's harder than being a vice president is being the vice president to a former vice president.

On the one hand, Biden wanted to treat Harris with the respect that he felt Barack Obama hadn't accorded him. He made a point of referring to her as *the* vice president, as opposed to *my* vice president. He was a stickler for asking her opinion in meetings—and making sure that her office was kept in the loop.

But while he treated her with impeccable respect, he simply didn't hand her the substantive role that he played in the Obama administration. Biden had helped plug the gaps in Obama's résumé. Obama didn't have the legislative or foreign policy experience that Biden possessed. Where Obama was a relative novice in Washington, Biden had relationships in the Senate (and in foreign capitals) that extended back decades.

Biden didn't need Harris in the same way Obama needed Biden.

Ron Klain assumed the role of Harris's guide. He thought of himself as the building's resident expert on the vice presidency, having worked for both Al Gore and Joe Biden as they sat in the second chair. But he struggled to productively help her. He felt Harris kept making life excessively difficult by imposing all sorts of constraints on herself. She told him that she didn't want to work on women's issues or anything to do with race. She wanted her office to be majority female—and to have a Black woman as chief of staff. To Klain's ear, she was creating too many rules, and they made it hard for her to find her footing. He told her, "This is baseball, you need to start getting out of the dugout and scoring some runs. You can't score runs if you're not on the field."

Constantly in search of a portfolio but reluctant to accept them when they were suggested to her, she asked to be placed in charge of relations with Scandinavia—away from the spotlight. But then when she finally asked for a meaty assignment, to be placed in charge of the administration's response to the assault on voting rights, Klain initially balked—hardly the vote of confidence she needed.

Instead of carving out an independent role, she stuck by the president's side—an omnipresence at nearly every Oval Office meeting. In part, that was just life in the time of COVID, which limited her ability to travel the world. In part, she needed to cultivate a relationship with a boss she didn't know especially well.

In meetings, Biden and Harris adopted uncannily similar styles. What they craved from aides was deeply practical. They wanted to know how everyday folks out there would interact with a policy. How would they find out about it? Would they have an easy time accessing a program? These were earthy questions, but also usually neglected by high officials.

Harris's contributions in meetings were regarded as incisive. As a former prosecutor, she took pride in asking piercing questions. Even as she didn't want to be defined by race, she asked questions about equity that tended to be neglected, inquiring about how policies might resonate with, say, Native Americans or people with disabilities. She impressed Mark Milley with how she sharply interjected herself into national security discussions.

But she was being guided by staff whom she didn't know and didn't especially trust. And given the circumstances, Biden didn't feel especially obliged to coach her along. At the beginning, he said that they would have weekly lunches. But those began to fall off the schedule.

THE WORLD DESCRIBED Central America as a terrible assignment for her. Even some of the president's own aides wondered to themselves if there wasn't something sadistic about Biden giving her a task that Obama once assigned to him—a hazing ritual. It wasn't hard to see the downsides: immigration is the most contentious issue in American politics, and while she was not in charge of it, she would be invariably associated with it.

But that wasn't how Harris thought about the task, at least at first. She had never conducted high-stakes diplomacy before. According to her aides, it excited her. When a new assignment came her way, she prepared for it as if it were a trial. She inhaled briefing materials. If her national security aides recommended a book—like when they mentioned Patrick Radden Keefe's *Say Nothing* in advance of a meeting on Northern Ireland—she read it, even if it were only tangential to the mission at hand. Harris prided herself on her discipline: how she ate carefully, how she exercised regularly, how she consumed her daily intelligence briefing the night before, how she left herself time for a full night's sleep.

Her disciplined quest for mastery of policy often struck advisers as a bit much. Harris didn't want to just master the details; she was always in the mode of cross-examination. For those sitting with her, it could be an inspiring experience, but also a profoundly exhausting one. When she brought in her top national security aides, Nancy McEldowney and Phil Gordon, she would encourage them to take opposing sides and stage debates for her. She enjoyed watching staff engage in intellectual combat. Getting dragged into a briefing with Harris meant that the day's schedule was about to unwind. In her disciplined desire to prepare, she would become undisciplined about her own calendar.

Harris's obsession with prep was the product of both intellectual fascination and understandable insecurity. She explained to aides that she understood her place in history as the first Black woman to hold her job. And she felt as if she would be unfairly punished by the press corps if she ever faltered—and that her slipups might make it difficult for every Black woman who followed in her path. So the ultimate goal of all that intensive preparation was to move through her public appearances without any missteps.

She was surely right about how large parts of Washington relished her screwups, never extending her any grace. Still, she was holding herself to an impossible standard. And in her obsessive desire to avoid making mistakes, the pressure she applied in her internal monologue almost doomed her to make them.

HARRIS POSSESSED what one of her colleagues described as "rabbit ears." Whenever there was a hint of criticism of her—either in the West Wing or in the press—she seemed instantly aware of it. Rather than brushing it aside, she wanted to know who was speaking ill of her and what they were saying. When she read a devastating story on CNN's website about her mismanagement of her team, she responded by briefly freezing out an aide whom she suspected of cooperating with reporters.

She let the criticism guide her. Instead of diligently sticking to the Central America assignment, she seemed to accept the conventional wisdom about it. It was a futile gig, so she let it fall to the side, missing an opportunity to grind her way to a meaningful achievement.

13

Go Left, Young Man

ONCE UPON A TIME, it seemed significant that the headquarters of the AFL-CIO, a midcentury temple clad in marble, sat a block away from Lafayette Square, in view of the White House. In 1955, when the world unironically referred to Big Labor, Dwight Eisenhower laid the cornerstone of the edifice, an act of obeisance that any sensible politician would have paid, given the movement's ability to deliver a decisive share of the electorate. From a broad window on the top floor of the new building, the head of the American labor movement could stare at monumental Washington, as if he were himself a fixture of the landscape.

For most of his long tenure occupying that office as president of the federation, Richard Trumka didn't experience any similar sense of grandeur. He felt belittled by the lip service of past Democratic administrations. Clinton and Obama seemed to choke on their words when they paid the requisite tribute to the once mighty pillar of their party's coalition.

But, in early spring, as Trumka joined a virtual meeting with the head of the National Economic Council, Brian Deese, he felt briefly transported to that bygone era of labor's might. Deese had assembled important figures in the labor movement. He told them, "We've gathered you because business keeps showing up in the White House. They come here to ask for our help. Sometimes they offer donations. But we want to change the conversation.

We wanted to know what you want us to ask of business on behalf of labor."
No administration had asked Trumka that before. In fact, it was quite moving to hear it.

Like Biden, Trumka ascended to high office at an early age. Biden was
elected senator at twenty-eight; Trumka became the president of United
Mine Workers at thirty-three. A coal miner—and the son of a coal miner, a
descendant of Polish and Italian immigrants—with a plush mustache and
meatloaf fingers, Trumka had worked his way up from the underground
shaft, first becoming a union lawyer. It was in that capacity that he met the
young senator from Delaware in 1974, at the height of a strike.

From the start, Trumka felt a sense of cultural kinship, a shared sense of
class identity. It was the way Biden talked, how he treated him so warmly,
unlike so many of the boomer meritocrats who had begun to populate the
new Democratic elite. "He's a blue collar guy and I'm a blue collar guy,"
Trumka would enthuse. When Biden contemplated yet another run at the
presidency in 2019, he paid a visit to Trumka's office, where he told him
that the balance of power in the economy needed to shift from corporations
toward workers. He told Trumka that collective bargaining was the only
true solution to the problem.

During the early days of the Biden presidency, Trumka kept asking fa-
vors of the new administration and the president kept doing them. Historically, the secretary of labor was a potential candidate for designated survivor,
an afterthought in the cabinet. But Trumka tried to imagine a figure who
might be able to revive the department. He came up with the name Marty
Walsh, the mayor of Boston. Before his foray into politics, Walsh had been
the president of Local 223 of the Laborers' International Union of North
America, a loyal son of the movement. Trumka began to mount a furious
campaign on Walsh's behalf. When he prevailed, he felt as if he had one of
his own in the position he cared about most.

Then in early February, the Retail, Wholesale and Department Store
Union was waging a campaign to unionize Amazon's warehouse, with a
largely Black workforce, in Bessemer, Alabama, on the outskirts of Birming-

ham. The union managed to force a vote on the proposition, scheduled for March. Trumka decided to push his luck, to see how far Biden might go on labor's behalf.

Rather, Trumka knew better than to push Biden directly, so he went through a denizen of his inner circle, Steve Ricchetti. Although Ricchetti hardly had the résumé of Walter Reuther—he spent years as a lobbyist on behalf of General Motors, Pfizer, and the American Hospital Association—Trumka liked that Ricchetti came from the Midwest. During the campaign, Ricchetti gathered a handful of union chiefs on Zoom and gave them his cell phone number.

Now Trumka was calling. He wanted the White House to shoot a flare of solidarity into the ether, to let the workers know that a force even more powerful than Amazon was on their side. What he heard back made him skeptical that he'd get his wish. The White House counsel's office, with its corporate lawyers and technical objections, questioned the legality of the president using his power to influence a union election.

Yet, in the end, Biden pressed ahead. The president filmed a short video. Taking into account the qualms of his lawyers, he carefully avoided mentioning Amazon. Sitting in front of a blue background, he stared at the camera and pointed his finger. "I made it clear when I was running that my administration's policy would be to support union organizing and the right to collectively bargain." He continued, "Let me be really clear: it's not up to me to decide whether anyone should join a union. Let me be even more clear: it's not up to an employer to decide that either." Given the timing of the video—and reference to workers organizing in Alabama—his message was unmistakable.

And it wasn't nearly enough. The union lost the vote in Bessemer—and some of Trumka's colleagues in the movement regretted enlisting Biden in a doomed struggle. But the moment energized Trumka.

For decades, labor had been starved, but Biden kept feeding it agenda items. As part of the American Rescue Plan, he included a big boost in the minimum wage, although the Senate parliamentarian stripped that provision from the bill. He stood in front of Congress, in an address to a joint session, and made the case for the Protecting the Right to Organize Act—or, since every piece of modern legislation is titled with an acronym in mind, the PRO Act—which would give the government new powers to punish corporations that stifle unions. But all these agenda items were just agenda items, not accomplishments—and Bessemer showed the limits of a supportive president's powers.

Still, at the tail end of his career, Trumka felt almost ecstatic. He crowed that he could feel the zeitgeist shifting. Even in defeat, he felt as if the wind was at his back.

WHEN CONGRESSWOMAN Alexandria Ocasio-Cortez, the face of the rising social democratic left, talked about Joe Biden, she did so with a whiff of disdain. "In any other country, Joe Biden and I would not be in the same party," she once quipped. That wasn't Bernie Sanders's view. During the primaries, one of his informal advisers, Zephyr Teachout, published an op-ed accusing Biden of corruption. When his campaign manager, Faiz Shakir, mentioned the piece to him, Sanders erupted. A nasty attack had been launched against his opponent, and it looked as if it had his blessing. Later that day, Biden and Sanders were scheduled to cross paths backstage at a candidates' forum in Iowa. When Sanders caught sight of Biden, he made his way over to him. "I apologize for that. That's not the way I feel about you."

When Sanders ran his campaign against Hillary Clinton in 2016, a large part of the Democratic establishment dismissed him as either a crank or a party crasher. But Sanders always noted that Biden never joined the attacks. He sensed that Biden broadly agreed with his depiction of the American economy. Sure, Biden didn't like to call out bankers or CEOs by name like Sanders did. But throughout the primary, Sanders would watch Biden at labor rallies, where they often followed each other on the program, and he noted that Biden consistently showed empathy for those without college degrees, a group he considered the most neglected in American politics.

Where Sanders looked at Biden, he saw the possibilities for symbiosis. During the transition, Shakir began to push the idea that his old boss should be secretary of labor. When he pitched the idea to Ron Klain and Anita Dunn, they were surprisingly open to it, which might have been empty enthusiasm for an idea that would never travel. But when Biden called to turn Sanders down, he did so with affection. "Man, I really would have liked to work with you, Bernie, in this capacity. It really kind of would have been huge," he told him. But he told him that he couldn't afford to elevate any senators to the cabinet, with the margins in that chamber so tight.

Some members of Sanders's inner circle would have liked to see him continue to shake his fist at power, but he decided to play against type. Rather than rushing to the microphone to voice his criticisms—and he had plenty of them—he would push the administration in meetings and phone calls. He told his staff, "I'm going to fight these fights internally. We'll go sit in the White House. We'll challenge him on this and that and the other thing. But then once he says no, I want to keep it together." He added, "This could be historic and far be it from me to be quibbling on the margins."

Despite himself, Sanders found that he trusted not only Biden but also Ron Klain. Sanders has a temperamental aversion to career staffers; he considers them innately conservative, more concerned with their careers than political transformation. They tended to obfuscate to avoid conflict rather than talk straight. But he began talking to Klain once a week, and he liked that the White House chief of staff didn't tap-dance when he had bad news to deliver. Rather than regarding Sanders as a nuisance, Klain gave the impression that he enjoyed their conversations.

As Biden began to prepare his big package of social spending, Sanders privately urged him to go bigger, to expand Medicare, to control the prices of prescription drugs. Instead of dismissing Sanders, Biden told him, "Hey, Bernie, if you can get there, if you can work with Pelosi and your progressive friends to push a little more, that's great with me."

After he would return from the Oval Office, Sanders would tell his advisers, especially the ones who wanted him to revert to his old adversarial self: this was his once-in-a-lifetime opportunity to realize his dreams, maybe not fully, but meaningfully. In their hearts, they knew that given his age, it would likely be his last.

THE CONVERGENCE between Sanders and Biden was, in part, the product of a generational saga. Many of the fortysomething aides who ran Biden's policy apparatus had grown up working for men whom Bernie Sanders would have considered his enemies—the likes of Treasury secretary Larry Summers and Steve Rattner, the financier who orchestrated Obama's bailout of the auto industry. But the younger wonks left the Obama administration with a nagging sense of disenchantment, which led them on an ideological odyssey.

During the Trump years, the out-of-power wonks had an unofficial spokesman and leading theorist. He also was the primary architect of the Biden domestic agenda. While Jake Sullivan ended up running foreign policy in the administration, during the campaign, he orchestrated the construction of the Build Back Better agenda—$6 trillion of spending on expanding the social safety net, combating climate change, and bolstering American manufacturing.

Sullivan was an earnest Minnesotan with carefully parted blond hair who vigorously defended the artistry of Billy Joel to his friends. When he would describe himself as the type of kid everyone hated for having memorized world capitals, he also evinced the sort of self-deprecation that disarmed skeptics. His mother, a guidance counselor at a public high school in Minneapolis, burned with ambition for her children, four of whom went to Yale. Tony Blinken hired one of them, Sullivan's younger brother, Tom, to be his deputy chief of staff for policy.

After starring on the high school debate team, Sullivan embarked on the long march through the Institutions: after Yale, a Rhodes Scholarship, followed by a Supreme Court clerkship for Stephen Breyer and a seat at the State Department. He was a favorite of Hillary Clinton, who kept handing him portfolios of ever greater importance. Richard Holbrooke once hailed him as a future secretary of state.

When Hillary prepared to run for president in 2015, she asked Sullivan to help her get back up to speed on domestic policy. During her time as the nation's top diplomat, she had lost touch with the parts of the world that didn't require a passport. Like anyone with a newspaper, Clinton could see the anger lurking across the country. Occupy Wall Street (on the Left) followed the rise of the Tea Party (on the Right). Thomas Piketty's *Capital in the Twenty-First Century* bestrode the *New York Times* bestseller list. Clinton's instruction to Sullivan was to understand the ire that stoked the rising political fortunes of the Left. This wasn't an academic mission, because she anticipated Senator Elizabeth Warren, who was far more in sync with the rising populist tide, would be her most dangerous primary opponent.

Within Hillary Clinton's factionalized world, Sullivan was viewed with suspicion by other top aides, one of whom sniffed that he was a Rockefeller Republican. As a product of the old establishment, Sullivan certainly wasn't predisposed to railing against finance. Like his boss, however, Sullivan was also returning to domestic policy after seven years in the national security apparatus—after the State Department, he served as Vice President Biden's national security adviser. As he surveyed the changed landscape, he belatedly began to absorb the full reality of the financial crisis and its trail of suffering. He felt as if he hadn't paid nearly careful enough attention to the seismic shifts in American life.

During his absence, the crisis propelled a term of analysis into the mainstream. For decades, *neoliberalism* was a piece of left-wing academic jargon, a sneering Marxian description of the prevailing economics. Suddenly, the sneer felt deserved, at least partially, since it contained important truths. After the fall of the Berlin Wall, a mania for markets had swept through the Western world. Elites had embraced the fashion of austerity, starving nations of public investment. As the government sat on its hands, power and wealth dangerously concentrated in a new oligarchy.

As he pondered these criticisms, Sullivan found the arguments far more persuasive than he had anticipated. And, in introspective moments, he admitted that he felt the sting of these criticisms. He had worked to craft and steward free trade agreements. Yet, he began to wonder if he had neglected what the deals might mean back in Minnesota. While he wasn't prepared to propose that Hillary Clinton adopt Elizabeth Warren's policies, he pushed in that direction. On the whiteboard in his office during the Clinton campaign, he scrawled the word *rents* and left it there, as a token of his growing hostility to monopoly.

Having devoted a good portion of his adult life to Hillary Clinton's presidential aspirations, he experienced her defeat to Donald Trump as a personal rebuke. Perhaps he hadn't gone far enough in pushing her policies and rhetoric to meet the anger of the moment. "I have the humility of the defeated," he would say. A *Washington Post* reporter followed him around Yale, where he was teaching for the semester. As Sullivan shared a greasy pizza with law students, he waxed philosophical, almost painfully so. "How do we solve for this basic and growing division in our society that gets to issues like dignity and alienation and identity? . . . How do we even ask the question without becoming the disconnected, condescending elite that we are talking about?"

An entire generation of young Democratic wonks, with a similar establishment pedigree, found itself in the same brooding mood, tinged with fear. They didn't worry about just Trump. They fretted about what would become of the Democratic Party. It seemed as though the party was fracturing, just like the nation. At Hillary Clinton's nominating convention, they saw the rage of Bernie Sanders's supporters—and it was directed at the wing of the party that had nurtured their careers.

Their elders were denizens of an old Democratic establishment that made a virtue of picking fights with the Left. To battle with Jesse Jackson or Robert Reich was regarded as evidence of political savvy and intelligence, since it required resisting the impulse of bighearted compassion and required consideration of the unintended consequences of social policy.

But Sullivan and his cohort broke with their mentors and attempted to cultivate the rising Left. One of Sullivan's close collaborators on the Clinton campaign, the economist Heather Boushey, organized a reconciliation tour. Along with Mike Pyle, who left the Obama White House to work in finance, she put together a series of dinners in Washington, New York, and San Francisco. Young establishment wonks broke bread with Elizabeth Warren disciples, labor union officials, and intellectuals from left-leaning think tanks. At these meals, the establishment found itself gravitating toward an alliance—or rather a confluence.

In the face of rising inequality, the establishment wonks agreed with the Left far more than their twenty-five-year-old selves could have ever imagined. And much of the Left was strangely moving in the establishment's direction. Under the tutelage of Elizabeth Warren, progressives in Washington had grown more interested in wielding power than in carping for the sake of carping. Just because some of the establishment types worked at investment banks didn't inherently disqualify them as allies. Factions that had once eyed each other wearily learned to comfortably coexist.

When Sullivan put together his revised ideas in an essay, he called it "The New Old Democrats." He extolled his skepticism of neoliberalism while rejecting socialism. Given that he was an old person's idea of a young man, it wasn't surprising that his rallying call was wrapped in nostalgia. His vision amounted to a resurrection of the ideas that prevailed before neoliberalism appeared on the scene. He wanted to go back to the tenets of the liberalism of the postwar years, a return to public investment, aggressive regulation, and pervasive unionism. Without consciously intending it, his manifesto echoed the latent instincts of his old boss Joe Biden.

From afar, and sometimes even up close, Joe Biden didn't look like a tribune of a new economic order. During his years in the Senate, he followed the currents of his party and voted to reform the welfare system and to repeal financial regulation. He loved to deliver a stem-winder in a union hall, where he proclaimed himself a proud "union man," but was hardly a robust presence on the picket lines. His fidelity to Delaware's credit companies earned him the derisive moniker the "senator from MBNA."

Spiritually, however, he wasn't aligned with the centrist consensus. When he would exclaim that he was a "union man," he wasn't pandering for votes as much as he was expressing his class allegiance. It wasn't just his penchant for muscle cars and his proud self-identity as a son of Scranton—or how he bragged about having attended a state college.

In private, Biden would rail against those he perceived as the idle rich, who extracted wealth without creating jobs. He resented the presence of trust-fund kids who showed up in Washington as interns. Fundraising was an activity he didn't enjoy—and his campaign balance sheets showed it—since it required pandering to the rich. So even as he cast his vote for neoliberalism, he had the temperamental makings of a populist. And in the White House, his aides began to turn his instincts into policy.

NEARLY EVERY DEMOCRATIC ADMINISTRATION is riven by ideological division. And Bruce Reed has been present for most of them. A Rhodes Scholar from Idaho, he captained the Oxford hockey team in the early eighties, which is a deceptive biographical fact. He is lanky and speaks in careful sentences, wrapped in self-effacing barbs, incapable of a rousing locker-room peroration.

Reed came of age in the Clinton administration, at the height of the third way, when a rising faction of the Democratic party agreed that the old nostrums of liberalism were softheaded; wisdom and victory lay close to the center, it believed. When he left government in 2001, he became CEO of the third way's flagship think tank, the Democratic Leadership Council, an organization that Jesse Jackson memorably denounced as the "Democratic Leisure Class."

When rumors circulated that Biden might appoint Reed to head the Office of Management and Budget, the organized Left conspired to thwart that development. Progressive columnists pointed to the fact that Obama had named Reed to be the lead staffer on the Simpson-Bowles commission for deficit reduction. Reed was depicted as the skinflint who would clutch the purse strings and prevent the social safety net from blossoming. But, for all its venom, the Left hadn't kept careful tabs on Reed's career.

Reed once wrote a short humorous essay for the *Washington Monthly* about how the nation's capital could be divided into two tribes, hacks and wonks. You were either a political animal or a policy nerd. "Hacks come to Washington because anywhere else they'd be bored to death. Wonks come here because nowhere else could we bore so many to death." In the essay, Reed described himself as a "wonk working among hacks." Despite having worked for a think tank with an ideological bent, he didn't have the zealous temperament of an ideologue. He prided himself on being open-minded and responsive to evidence, a wonk to the core.

Unlike the vast majority of his colleagues in the Biden administration, Reed was the rare former staffer to resist the lure of the private sector. Leaving the Obama White House, he worked for Common Sense Media, an advocacy group that aimed to protect kids from the predatory elements of the entertainment industry. The group had just started to turn its attention to the evils of Big Tech. With little fanfare, Reed helped negotiate a California law protecting privacy, the first of its kind, an experience that brought him into contact with Silicon Valley giants. The more he saw these companies up close, the more he worried about their influence and intentions.

The Democratic Leadership Council cultivated an alliance with business. But Reed had begun to read about the history of the anti-monopoly tradition in America, which stretched back to Thomas Jefferson and provided a focal point for the New Deal. He began to wonder if the nation had strayed too far from that tradition. For decades, the nation had undergone a frenzy of consolidation, in nearly every industry. Sectors once rife with competition—aviation, banking, pharmaceuticals, defense contracting—were suddenly dominated by a handful of behemoth firms.

Even as Reed consulted for Common Sense, he kept traveling with Joe

Biden. In the darkest days of the campaign, when nobody thought Biden would win his party's nomination, Reed trudged alongside Biden through the icy Main Streets of Iowa. Along the way, he saw how Biden instinctively recoiled from monopoly, in his own way. What radicalized Biden was a story he had heard about how the Jimmy John's sandwich franchise required employees, even the workers who slapped cold cuts onto bread, to sign agreements preventing them from working for its competitors. To Biden this was an egregious example of corporate bullying. For Reed, it was a symptom of the problem of economic concentration. Because such a small number of companies were competing for workers, those firms had leverage over their employees, the ability to force them to consent to absurdly restrictive conditions.

The tight-knit nature of Biden's inner circle can be claustrophobic, but it also permits ideas to percolate with minimal bureaucratic friction. Both Reed and Klain were enthusiastic about curbing the growing power of monopolies. It wasn't what the outside world expected, exactly. Longtime servants of Big Tech were scattered across the administration.

But over the spring, Biden appointed two of the most important public intellectuals of a resurgent anti-monopoly movement. At the Federal Trade Commission, he installed a thirty-two-year old Columbia Law professor named Lina Khan as the chair. In her twenties, she published one of the most-read law review articles of all-time, which dissected Amazon's monopolistic practices. On the National Economic Council, Brian Deese installed Khan's colleague at Columbia, Tim Wu. Like Khan, Wu styled himself a modern-day heir to the early twentieth-century Supreme Court justice Louis Brandeis. Wu titled one of his treatises *The Curse of Bigness*, which he borrowed from a book Brandeis wrote in 1914. Placing the pair in the administration signaled an intent to return to the robust trust-busting of a past era.

Through the spring, Wu, with Reed's support, worked to put together an executive order translating the spirit of that past into the twenty-first century. By July 4, he had a draft of an executive order to show the president. It tied together disparate policies—seventy-two in total—under the banner of antitrust. Where antitrust had lived in a government backwater for decades, the order created a council chaired by the president, to regularly convene cabinet secretaries and agency heads, so that the whole of government could begin thinking in tandem about promoting competition.

The order promised to break up the heavily concentrated market for hearing aids, by allowing devices to be sold over the counter for the first time. It limited the ability of airlines to exact outrageous fees from customers. It protected farmers against equipment manufacturers that made it impossible to bring broken equipment into independent repair shops. All these might seem small bore, but they added up to a portrait of an economy. And it came with a top-line mandate: The Federal Trade Commission was instructed to more vigorously enforce the antitrust laws. That's a grandiose promise, and it came without detailed instructions. But it gave Lina Khan the backing of the president as she sought to inject new life into old laws.

Biden styles himself a stickler about executive orders. He calls himself an "Article 1 guy," a creature of the Senate, who (theoretically) prefers Congress set the course. Government by presidential fiat irks him. So with a pen in hand, he read the draft that Wu supplied him, searching for passages that he worried overstepped his constitutional bounds.

But Reed had spent so many years working over Biden's shoulder that he knew how to shape policy to avoid his peeves and how to calm his anxieties, by reminding Biden of the specifics that mattered to him most. Reed highlighted a provision that outlawed the sort of noncompete agreements that Jimmy John's abused. The specifics in the order, like lowering the costs of hearing aids, appealed to Biden's political instincts. That made for a good narrative. Everyday folks could relate to that.

On July 9, Biden signed the order, with Lina Khan hovering beside him. Biden explained its importance by using a sweeping abstraction that could have easily come from Elizabeth Warren's mouth. "Capitalism without competition isn't capitalism; it's exploitation," he said. He also uttered a line that Reed had pushed to include in the speech, a piece of rhetoric that might have felt esoteric but carried great personal and ideological significance. "Forty years ago, we chose the wrong path, in my view, following the misguided philosophy of people like Robert Bork." This was a reference to the late conversative law professor whose arguments persuaded presidents of both parties to hardly ever enforce the antitrust laws.

When he delivered this line, Biden didn't mention his personal history with Bork. Back when he was chair of the Senate Judiciary Committee, in 1987, Biden derailed Robert Bork's nomination to the Supreme Court, building a bipartisan coalition to oppose the ascent of the right-wing jurist. It was a defining moment in Biden's biography, when he began to redeem himself from a humiliating plagiarism scandal.

Having stymied Bork's career, he was now attacking his legacy. To his critics, Bork was the theorist who ushered in an era of unrestrained capitalism, whose arguments justified scaling back the government's role in the economy, permitting the unchallenged reign of large corporations. It was that era that Biden announced he was now bringing to a close.

14

Face to Face

FOR THE ENTIRE WORLD, COVID was an isolating event. That was true even in the White House. Back in the campaign, Kate Bedingfield and Jen O'Malley Dillon were two of the highest ranking aides, the communications director and campaign manager. Yet, they had never experienced the bond of a road trip, with the trust-building exercises of closing the hotel bar, sharing plates of fried food, and endless waits in holding rooms.

When they finally traveled together, it was the fifth month of the administration, the first presidential trip abroad. COVID had scrambled that ritual, too. The White House hadn't begun to plan for its maiden European jaunt until February. And because of the late start, the Biden team couldn't secure prime accommodations.

The row houses they rented in Cornwall, England, for a meeting of the G7 were at the very end of a cul-de-sac. Bedingfield and O'Malley Dillon shared a bathroom with five other colleagues. Every morning, they received a pot of porridge and a ration of instant coffee, which the staff divided among themselves. Joe and Jill Biden occupied their own home, but its living room looked out onto a shared green space. When Bedingfield helped Biden prepare for a press conference, she had to draw the shades so that the media couldn't peer through the window.

The aesthetic echoes of the austere late forties were unintentional;

however, the thematic resonances were carefully planned. Biden wanted his trip to pay homage to the great institutions that emerged from the ruins of World War II, to help restore them to their pre-Trump sense of themselves. After stopping at the G7 summit, he would travel to the headquarters of the European Union and NATO, followed by a summit with an adversary of these alliances, Vladimir Putin.

Whatever the cuisine and the housing, this was Joe Biden's idea of heaven. In preparation for meeting a global leader, Biden liked to hold court with his advisers. He loved analyzing his interlocutors—their psychological tendencies, their domestic political considerations. They made for the subjects of great stories. Over the years, he had come to know Turkey's president Recep Tayyip Erdoğan. When dealing with a head of state like Erdoğan, he tried to connect with him personally, but also politician to politician. Working through a knotty issue, he would tell him, "Go out, do your press conference, criticize me, say whatever it is you need to say. And then come back, and let's get this done."

As a global leader with his own share of insecurities, Biden was acutely aware of their presence in his peers. He knew that leaders are sensitive to perceived slights, and he was conscious of the fact that he might unintentionally make a head of state feel small. So he instructed his press operation to say as little as possible in advance of a meeting with Putin. He said that he didn't want Putin to feel attacked in public, as if he were ambling into an ambush.

Area experts from the State Department and the National Security Council would descend to brief him. While Biden loved expounding, he couldn't stand to have bureaucrats imposing the shackles of protocol on him. He sometimes felt like the experts lectured him as if he were a newly elected member of the House. When an official from the State Department tried to suggest talking points for a press conference, Biden called him a "horse's tail."

Most of the press corps hadn't ever joined Biden on a foreign trip. They weren't accustomed to his rhythms. After meeting Erdoğan in Brussels, Biden was scheduled to talk with reporters. But the media sat waiting for hours, notebooks open, speculating about the myriad reasons for a delay—a health incident, a crisis. Really, he was sitting in a meeting room at NATO's headquarters, recounting his session to Tony Blinken and Lloyd Austin, enjoying the hell out of being the Leader of the Free World.

BACK AT the very beginning of his administration, Biden had kicked around the idea of appending a summit meeting with Putin to his European voyage. As aides stress tested the idea with Biden, he listened to their objections: "Wouldn't a summit merely serve to enhance Putin's global standing?" Biden responded, "Where have you been? This isn't Kim Jong Un. This is the president of a nuclear power, a permanent member of the UN Security Council."

When Biden called Putin to extend the invitation in April, the Russian leader could be forgiven for confusion. Biden had just described him as a "killer" in an interview with ABC News. Putin inevitably complained about that description, but Biden told him that he hadn't intended to attack him. He was just trying to honestly answer a question that a reporter posed to him.

After describing a new set of sanctions that he intended to impose on Russia, Biden told him, "We should meet face to face; there's a lot of ground to cover." He suggested that they hold a summit in Geneva. Biden thought hard about the proposed setting. He didn't want to huddle on the sidelines of a meeting with other global leaders. By engaging with Putin one on one at a distinct stop on his itinerary, he tried to tell the Russian leader, *I get that you're the big man on campus.*

Although Putin didn't accept on the spot, he didn't disparage the idea, either. A month later, a meeting was set for Geneva.

AT THE FIRST STOPS of his European trip, Biden found himself basking in the warm glow of historic allies, who craved a taste of that old-time transatlanticism. The format of the G7 suited him. In an intimate setting, he could have a free-flowing conversation, which permitted jovial asides. And it yielded results. The Europeans signed on to statements striking a harder line against China, despite initial reluctance. Even Emmanuel Macron suspended his Gaullist instincts and affirmed, "America is back."

Geneva, however, felt like a far different setting. When Air Force One landed, staff were told to keep their personal devices on the plane. Aides kept the shades of their hotel rooms closed.

The site for the meeting was an eighteenth-century mansion, Villa la Grange, on the banks of Lake Geneva, tucked in a municipal park. To secure the space, the Swiss had to persuade a couple to move their wedding to a different venue, to sacrifice their special day for the sake of global stability.

As the meeting began, the leaders posed for the requisite photo session, along with Tony Blinken and foreign minister Sergei Lavrov. They sat in the library surrounded by leather-bound volumes, a globe separating the pair, as if harkening back to the day when the world was divided into spheres of influence. Putin posed in the disaffected slouch that he reserved for occasions like this, a technique to distract from his own diminutive stature. Biden once described the pose to a friend as that of an "asshole schoolkid."

When the press left the room, Putin's body language changed. He suddenly seemed less diffident. The Russian press had spent months portraying Biden as a fragile old man, a piece of spin that Putin internalized. But when he greeted Biden, he seemed taken aback by his appearance. "You look good," he exclaimed. It was an observation that he kept repeating. When Putin called Angela Merkel to deliver his postmortem of the meeting, he told her, "President Biden is very fit."

Biden wanted to disarm Putin with his straightforwardness, which occasionally careened into playful banter. The message he intended to convey was that America had higher priorities than conflict with Russia. His administration was too busy investing in its own future and revitalizing its alliances.

Where Putin expected Biden to give him the hard sell on how Russia should work with the United States to contain China, Biden surprised him with his restraint. "We have a long border with Canada and Mexico that has challenges. You've got thousands of miles with China. I wouldn't want to be in your position."

Their tour of the horizon stopped at Afghanistan. Putin asked, "Why did you leave Afghanistan?"

"Why did you leave?" Biden snapped back, a reference to the Soviet Union's withdrawal from the country in 1989, after ten years of occupation.

Biden told him a story about how he had visited Afghanistan in 2009, along with John Kerry and Chuck Hagel. Because Kerry wanted to visit the spot where Osama bin Laden had eluded American troops in the Himalayas, the trio took a helicopter ride into the mountains. A snowstorm forced them to land on a rocky outcropping. As they stood and surveyed the valley, Biden could see what he believed to be Taliban in the distance. A sniper accompanying the group pulled out his rifle, but Biden began frantically waving at him to put it away. "I just wanted to gauge the distance," the sniper told him.

Biden related this story to Putin, intending to point out that Afghanistan was a sprawling country that couldn't be effectively governed by a central authority. Or as he told Putin, "It's the 'Graveyard of Empires.'"

But Putin had fixated on the presence of the sniper. The Russian president mimed taking out his own rifle. "I would have killed them all," he said.

Biden thought bantering with Putin might help create a necessary sense of ease, but he also needed to warn him not to cross certain lines. Biden needed to let Putin know that he would respond forcefully to further ransomware attacks against critical infrastructure in the United States.

"Put yourself in my shoes. I mean, with the attacks on our infrastructure. Imagine if something happened to your oil infrastructure . . ." He let the thought hang in the air.

As Biden rehashed the conversation with his aides, he felt he'd performed

well, but he said that he didn't have any illusions about what he had accom-
plished. "This is going to be hard," he said. Rather than rushing to any judgment about the future of the relationship, he told Sullivan that he wanted to
spend time absorbing the meeting.

Still, he did little to disguise his exuberance. On the plane back—after
days of endless meetings—he wanted to keep on talking. Tony Blinken,
who had a better sense than anyone of what it's like to be subjected to
Biden's airplane monologues, once quipped, "If I didn't fall asleep in front
of him, I'd never get any sleep." Biden prowled Air Force One in search of
aides whom he could assail with his stories.

15

Independence Day

IT FELT as if the nation was emerging from its dark winter. An article in *The Atlantic* predicted that the coming summer would be a twenty-first-century version of the Roaring Twenties, an explosion of pent-up joy as people escaped the confines of quarantine. American youth would party with abandon. The economy would kick into overdrive as restaurants reopened and travel resumed.

The vaccinated were getting antsy. Having been told that two weeks after their second shots their immune systems would offer robust protection against the virus, they wanted to escape their masks.

When the head of the Centers for Disease Control and Prevention, Rochelle Walensky, went to testify in the Senate on May 11, her interlocutors flayed her for continuing to recommend masking, despite all the evidence that the vaccines worked impeccably. Susan Collins exclaimed in her most disappointed voice, "I used to consider the CDC the gold standard. I don't anymore."

Walensky, a celebrated infectious disease specialist, had accepted one of the hardest jobs in America. She inherited an agency that carried deep psychological scars. Its burned-out workforce suffered from years of disrespect. The last CDC chief, the Trump-appointed Robert Redfield, failed to

adequately defend his agency from critics. All this needed fixing as the battered agency battled a pandemic.

Everyone in the administration found Walensky personally engaging.
They considered her smart, polished, and deeply committed. But they also
came to appreciate the fact that she had only limited managerial chops and
even less political experience. Anthony Fauci had lobbied to get her the job,
which plucked her from leading a division of Massachusetts General Hospital. But she had never run a sprawling bureaucracy before, hobbled by the
fact that she largely interacted with staff via Zoom in those early months of
the administration.

Walensky didn't like how Washington operatives relished talking to the
press about closed-door debates. It caused her to move defensively through
her day, holding information tightly, worried that her collaborators might
run their mouths.

Even as she absorbed the anger of Congress, she didn't hint at the possibilities of a change in policy. Not even the White House had an inkling of
her imminent change of mind. But the day after her testimony, she told the
secretary of Health and Human Services, Xavier Becerra, that the CDC
would be issuing new guidelines that declared the vaccinated no longer
needed to wear masks in stores and public spaces. The announcement
would come the next day.

She planned on rolling out a massive change in policy, a policy that would
transform behavior in every grocery store and gym, without seemingly consulting anyone outside the CDC. As officials at HHS began to absorb her
plan, they couldn't overrule her, lest they trample her independence—and
mimic the sins of the Trump administration.

They had a few hours to help her prepare her announcement, though.
As they combed through her remarks, they stumbled on a line she included:
At the same time she said the vaccinated could take off their masks, she
wanted to warn, "Don't throw it away yet. Keep it in a drawer." They convinced her that the line would merely confuse her audience. Even as they
attempted to simplify her message, they knew that the suddenness of the

change—and the limited time that the administration had to prepare for its rollout—would leave the nation spun around.

KATE BEDINGFIELD, the White House communications director, learned about Walensky's recommendation a few hours before it was announced, as she listened to a conference call on her walk to work. As she strolled down Sixteenth Street, with earbuds implanted, she muttered to herself in shock and then began to let her mind enjoy the news.

After she arrived at work, the White House operations team sent an email instructing staff that they no longer needed to wear masks in the building. Bedingfield stepped out of her office, ripped the mask from her face, and blurted, "Ta-da." She walked down the hall to Ron Klain's office and joked, "If I had known this was coming, I would have worn makeup today."

That the announcement came without warning made it feel like a gift. For months, Bedingfield had worked with the president to craft cautious responses to questions about when life might return to normal. He sweated any clause that might give false hope. But here in a flash, it looked as if normality was spontaneously returning. In the Rose Garden, she stood with her colleagues and watched the president deliver quickly composed remarks cheering the CDC's decision. She saw Jeff Zients beaming with an unobstructed smile.

But that smile was, in effect, a mask. Zients had quiet misgivings. He had expected that science—and the administration's fidelity to it—would force uncomfortable decisions, and it might require new restrictions. But he hadn't anticipated that the scientists would tilt in the other direction, that they would so quickly undo restrictions.

In the seclusion of the office, Zients and Andy Slavitt complained that Walensky had put the White House in a tough position. For starters, how were they going to communicate her decision? What about the unvaccinated? Wouldn't they hear her guidelines and assume that they didn't have to wear masks? What about kids, who weren't eligible for the vaccine? This might have felt like liberation, but it had the hallmarks of a public health nightmare.

Although de-masking wasn't Zients's decision, he absorbed blame for it. In a weekly phone call with governors, he found himself on the receiving end of a bipartisan drubbing. Having finally persuaded their citizens to wear masks, the governors complained that they were being undermined by the administration. Vaccinations were once seen as the ticket to freedom from masks. But if everyone exploited the new rules to unmask, then Walensky had inadvertently removed the most powerful incentive to get the shot.

STILL, the numbers looked good, and for a moment in June, David Kessler permitted himself to revel in a state of optimism. New cases of COVID plummeted below 10,000 per day. It was a thrilling dip. To celebrate the progress, and to claim a bit of credit for itself, the White House planned an event on July 4, on the South Lawn, where it would host a barbecue and proclaim the nation's independence from the tyranny of the virus. That wasn't Kessler's idea, but he could understand the spirit of it.

Then, after the briefest bout of good feelings, Kessler reverted to dour thinking and remembered that a new delta variant of COVID had ripped through India, with a speed and deadliness that surpassed anything witnessed in the pandemic. On a single day, May 7, Delta infected 414,188 Indians. Delta had begun to ravage pockets of the American South, causing him to fear a wave that would outstrip the horrors of the previous year.

As Kessler watched cases begin to rise toward the end of June, he called Vivek Murthy, his old student, to see whether they couldn't get the White House to tone down its Fourth of July hoopla. The last thing the country needed was a sense of complacency, a false sense that the virus was in the rearview.

Murthy passed along their shared anxieties to the White House. While aides weren't prepared to scrap the celebration, they agreed to ratchet back the rhetoric in the president's July 4 speech, to cut some language from the president's remarks that might have reeked of a premature declaration of victory—and to pepper the speech with clauses that implored the unvaccinated to seek the jab.

Still, in the spirit of a victory party, with a volleyball net planted on the lawn and a bouncy house installed in the shadow of the portico, Biden couldn't resist a bit of crowing. "We are emerging from the darkness," he said. This was the false hope that Biden claimed to strenuously resist.

Only 67 percent of Americans had received their first dose, falling short of a goal that the president had publicly set for his administration. It wasn't a spectacular fail, just an omen of how hard it would prove to conquer vaccine hesitancy. And the delta surge might only have been in its earliest days, but it was unmistakably beginning. As Kessler watched the emergency rooms fill in places like Missouri and Alabama, he thought, *I signed up to fight one pandemic, not two.*

16

The Highway to Bipartisanship

JOE BIDEN believed in the gospel of unity with his whole heart. In the Oval Office, in the presence of a delegation of Republican senators, he wanted to make good on his high-minded sermons. But Roger Wicker of Mississippi, the ranking Republican on the Commerce Committee, was making it difficult.

The quick passage of the American Rescue Plan reinforced Biden's faith in his own legislative prowess. He told aides that conditions would likely never be so ripe for him to cut a deal with Republicans. On May 13, he brought Wicker and his fellow Republicans, a group of senior senators who arrived with the blessing of Mitch McConnell, to the White House to discuss the prospects of a bipartisan bill to spend on what the White House branded "hard" infrastructure—the roads and bridges and transit and electrical grids that politicians always claim to want to deliver.

In Biden's mind, the terms of a deal were screamingly obvious. But he also told aides that he wasn't sure that anyone in the modern-day Republican Party fathomed their own political interests.

Before these talks went anywhere, Wicker, who first arrived in Congress as a member of Newt Gingrich's revolutionary vanguardist crew, wanted to make one thing perfectly clear. The tax cuts for the rich that Donald Trump signed into law in 2017 were sacrosanct. "My crowning achievement of thirty years in the United States Senate," Wicker told the room, his voice cracking. "We are not taking that away from me."

But Wicker didn't leave it at that. He launched into a lengthy explanation of how the Trump tax cuts had fueled unprecedented growth, a boom cut short by the untimely arrival of COVID. To Gina Raimondo and Pete Buttigieg, the cabinet secretaries watching from the periphery of the discussion, it didn't feel like an opening bid in a negotiation—more like a political speech, delivered to a captive audience. The pair did their best to politely keep their annoyance to themselves.

Kamala Harris, however, didn't want to leave Wicker's argument unrefuted.

"No, Senator," she retorted, "the economy wasn't doing great in 2019. We had epic levels of inequality. That wasn't nearly good enough."

As the cabinet secretaries watched, they felt like pumping their fists but also covering their eyes. The room turned to Biden. However much he might have disliked Wicker's monologue, he prided himself on his ability to achieve a state of detachment in the course of back-and-forth with Republicans.

"I hear you," he told Wicker. "We can't find common ground there. Let's get back to work."

After the Republicans left the room, the cabinet secretaries and aides kept listing the reasons why they would never be able to persuade specific senators to deal. But the president waved off the objections. Some of these Republicans were old colleagues. "Good guys," he called them. More than that, he said, "Don't be dismissive. Don't be disrespectful. You might find it painful. It's important to try."

THE PRESIDENT KEPT checking in with Republicans. In the aftermath of the American Rescue Plan, when the bipartisan negotiations over that bill quickly fizzled, there were hard feelings in need of soothing. Republicans who came to the White House in a spirit of compromise fumed that the

administration had just paraded them into the Oval Office as a public-
ity stunt. But, notably, they largely directed blame in the direction of Ron
Klain—casting him as the president's progressive puppeteer—and not at
Biden.

Without giving her a heads-up, Biden dialed Susan Collins on Super
Bowl Sunday. There wasn't an agenda, but he didn't want her feeling neglected, even when she might be nursing a sense of disappointment.

In the course of Biden's calls, he came away convinced that a faction of
the GOP was willing to deal on infrastructure. Trump had endlessly promised to invest in infrastructure and never pursued it. But by floating the
idea so vociferously, Trump had provided Republicans a measure of cover
to move forward with Biden.

The possibility of a deal helped clarify Biden's grand strategy. He wanted
to propose spending roughly $6 trillion on his Build Back Better agenda,
which encompassed infrastructure, funding to combat climate change, and
the expansion of the social safety net. Biden knew that he could never pass
one piece of legislation that large, especially just having signed a $1.9 tril-
lion bill. Optics demanded that he split his program into two less frightening chunks.

There was an obvious dividing line in the agenda that permitted the
administration to halve it. Anita Dunn gave the separate pieces simple, declarative names. The infrastructure investments—in electric vehicles, in
broadband, in ports and transit—she called the Jobs Plan. She dubbed the
social spending part the Families Plan. Since the Families Plan would need
to pass on a party line vote through the reconciliation process, the administration jammed its climate change agenda into that bill. Even though it didn't
really fit, the administration knew that there was no chance of building a
bipartisan agreement around those provisions.

Biden liked to extol the fine art of sequencing. And there was no doubt
in his mind that the Jobs Plan would come first. Although there were powerful Democrats on the Hill who argued that the prospects for an infrastructure deal with Republicans were dim, Biden disagreed—and at least

he needed to get caught trying. Joe Manchin had signaled that he wouldn't vote for another massive social spending bill passed using reconciliation, without Biden pursuing bipartisan legislation.

Progressives didn't love the strategy. Engaging in a protracted negotiation with Republicans over repairing bridges and roads terrified them. It would consume Biden's political capital, chew up dwindling days on the calendar, and prevent him from ever turning to the agenda embedded in his Families Plan, the thing they truly wanted.

Infrastructure might not have thrilled the Left, but it thrilled Biden. When he was Obama's sideman, he felt frustrated with the stimulus package passed in 2009. It didn't have enough sweep or grandeur. This time around, Biden could rebuild his beloved Amtrak. As a self-styled car guy, he could hasten the transition to electric vehicles. Just as the New Deal electrified rural America, this bill would extend broadband to remote parts of the country with no access to the Internet. Infrastructure was government that people could see and touch and experience. While the Left might not regard it as ideologically enticing, it would help keep the United States in the economic race with China.

But the White House understood that its sequencing would require a little sleight of hand. If the administration pursued the Jobs Plan first, progressives would worry that their considerations were being stuffed into a second-class bill. So the administration decided to top off its infrastructure bill with a package to spend $400 billion on senior care—a provision that unions promoted and Nancy Pelosi loved.

Still, for progressives to realize their dreams, they would have to patiently wait for Biden to live out his phase of bipartisan experimentation.

As JOE BIDEN embarked on his negotiation, he kept Pete Buttigieg by his side. Biden said the young transportation secretary reminded him of his late son Beau. And this was his apprenticeship in dealmaking.

The officially sanctioned Republican negotiations were conducted by

West Virginia senator Shelley Moore Capito, whom Biden personally liked. But he also knew that she was in a tough spot. Her desire for a deal was far greater than Mitch McConnell's appetite for one—and she privately signaled that to the White House.

For weeks, Capito arrived with offers, outlining how much her party was willing to spend on infrastructure. And the White House reciprocated with counteroffers. During his back-and-forth with Republicans, Biden had shaved the American Jobs Plan to a fraction of the original proposal, agreeing to reduce its price tag by $1 trillion. It irked him that Republicans had barely budged in his direction. They had agreed to boost their proposal by $150 billion, not remotely enough.

What Buttigieg appreciated about Biden was his pattern recognition, which allowed him to make a flash judgment about every number that slid across his desk. He instantly knew if a proposal contained promise—and when it was a dead end. And in early June, Biden called Capito and told her that it was time for them to move on. It was important to Biden that Capito left the conversation with warm feelings. He knew that her opinion of him could shape the next phase of talks. The first round of negotiation was ultimately a performance. He wanted to persuade an audience of moderate Senate Republicans that he was, in fact, a good-faith partner.

THE NEGOTIATIONS with Capito broke down just as Biden left for Europe for eight days. In the press, the collapse of talks was seen as an ominous sign, a prelude to Biden's shifting his attention to a reconciliation bill. But Louisa Terrell, the White House's top lobbyist, stayed in quiet touch with a group of moderates in the Senate, a club within the club, that was hungry to assert itself. In the strange parlance of Congress, they were a "gang": five Republicans, five Democrats. Many of them had worked together in the dying days of the Trump presidency to pass a bipartisan COVID relief bill, which proved their theory of the case. By hanging out in the middle, they represented the balance of power in the Senate. In their self-estimation, there was no reason they couldn't run the place.

Rob Portman, the Republican senator from Ohio, had cobbled together this group in the hopes of finishing the job that Capito had begun. In some ways, Portman was acting out a personal psychodrama. He should have been the archetypal Never Trump Republican. During the Bush administration, he served as the US trade representative, a true believer in globalization, and then ran the Office of Management and Budget. Yet he was also a politician. And stuck with Trump, whatever his private misgivings. But he could clearly see his party drifting away from him. In January, he had announced that he wouldn't run for reelection. Cutting a bipartisan deal on infrastructure would provide him with both a legacy and some conscience-salving sense that, in the end, he resisted the antidemocratic forces in his party.

For his primary negotiating partner from the other side of the aisle, Portman worked with Kyrsten Sinema of Arizona. Even among the small group of moderate Democrats in the gang, there was a sense that Portman outfoxed them with his choice. Sinema could generously be described as mercurial. When she first ran for Senate in Arizona in 2018, she faced accusations that she exaggerated her up-from-poverty biography for dramatic effect. In a short time, she went from being an activist affiliated with the Green Party to the sort of politician that activists hounded. Yes, she transgressed the unspoken sartorial rules of the stodgy chamber with adventurous fashion choices. But she also zealously raised money from business interests, and her voting record reflected that alliance.

Portman and Sinema were fellow moderates, but profoundly different creatures. Portman had spent years preparing budgets and negotiating with foreign governments on behalf of the United States. He fixated on details. His colleagues complained about how tight he held the purse strings. Where Portman traveled with a small army of wonks—he usually brought a war room full of staffers with him to negotiations—Sinema would show up in his office with just her chief of staff. It was asymmetrical warfare, and the Democrats knew it.

When the talks included the larger group of moderates, they tended to take place in the evening in Portman's hideaway office in the Capitol. Mark Warner, the Virginia Democrat, an oenophile, liked to supply bottles that lubricated the discussions. (Mitt Romney declined to partake on religious grounds; Bill Cassidy, Republican from Louisiana, didn't touch the stuff; everyone else imbibed.) After Biden dispatched Steve Ricchetti to join the discussions, he walked around the room pouring, as if he were the sommelier of the Senate.

Following the collapse of the Capito negotiations, the gang could no longer keep word of its talks quiet. Media began to stalk its gatherings. Even when the senators tried to secretly hustle Ricchetti and Terrell into the Capitol, reporters tended to catch wind of meetings. The senators would agree in advance that nobody would engage on the way out the door. Yet, Joe Manchin and Jon Tester would invariably stride straight to the gaggle of journalists and deliver their sense of the proceedings. The gang had wanted to keep the negotiations quiet to insulate them from outside pressure, the condition necessary for making tough concessions—a desire for solitude that couldn't withstand the senatorial ego.

IN THE grand Washington tradition, the gang announced a deal before it actually had a deal. Rather, it had agreed to the broad contours of an agreement. It had a price tag, a collective sense of how much to spend, and how it would pay for it. Much of the heavy lifting had been done in the Capito negotiations, which provided a skeletal structure for the moderates to work with. Now only the details were left to be haggled over, and those details could easily prove to be the shoals on which the whole agreement crashed. Still, a framework was something to crow about.

On June 24, the group traveled to the White House to meet with the president. And he received them in a euphoric mood. After the meeting ended, he took them to a bank of microphones in the White House driveway and bellowed his endorsement: "Neither side got everything they wanted in this deal; that's what it means to compromise."

For nearly five months, the old Joe Biden with loose lips and excessive faith in his own improvisational talents had barely made an appearance on the presidential stage. The weight of the presidency was like the belated implant of a superego in his psyche. But with the prospects of a bipartisan victory within reach, he slipped.

Jittery Democrats were worried that Biden was going to celebrate his bipartisan accomplishment and then neglect to pursue his Families Plan with any rigor. Speaking in the East Room, he wanted to allay those concerns. His goal was to explain to progressives that the bills were part of a coherent legislative strategy.

Biden needed a bipartisan bill to pass so that the moderates in his own party would have an accomplishment to trumpet. With their infrastructure bill, the moderates had a chance to show that the Senate worked and its traditions didn't need to be blown to smithereens by progressive Jacobins. Having done their centrist business, moderate Democrats would return the favor and join a party line vote in support of the president's reconciliation bill.

Meanwhile, progressives needed to be persuaded that the infrastructure bill, which didn't truly address the climate crisis or combat social inequities, wasn't the end of Biden's legislative agenda. Even Nancy Pelosi believed this critique. She told the president that the infrastructure bill wasn't a worthy achievement unto itself, which caused him to snap back at her, "It does great green things." She told him that her members would cast an indifferent vote for the infrastructure bill only if they knew that it guaranteed the passage of a larger social spending bill.

The bills were joined at the hip. Everyone knew it, even the Republicans who had just visited the Oval Office. But in his zeal to reassure, Biden went further than he intended. One hour after appearing in the White House driveway with the moderates, he told reporters, "If this is the only thing that comes to me, I'm not signing it."

As soon as the threat emerged from Biden's mouth, the Republican members of the gang whipped themselves into a state of collective freak-out. They were prodded by their colleagues. Lindsey Graham said that Biden had made the Republicans look like "fucking idiots."

Mark Warner was visiting friends on an island in Maine with poor cell reception. He found a hill where he had decent enough coverage to begin damage control. Jon Tester was working on his farm in Montana but left to gather with the rest of the gang on a call. The group spent an hour and a half griping about Biden.

When Warner passed along the complaints, it was hardly necessary. The White House understood that it needed to apologize with abandon. Biden called Portman and backtracked, and then issued a public retraction: "My comments also created the impression that I was issuing a veto threat on the very plan I had just agreed to, which was certainly not my intent."

The White House felt grateful that Portman brushed the gaffe aside, salvaging the deal. Yet the misstep had an unintended benefit. It did help assuage the anxieties on the Left, which assumed that Biden had committed what's known as a Kinsley gaffe, after the journalist Michael Kinsley, who coined the term. He hadn't lied or jumbled his words, but merely revealed a truth that he didn't intend to admit.

A FRAMEWORK is just that. The bipartisan group had rallied behind a vision, but the details were the gritty part of the negotiation, where everything suddenly felt tenuous again. Because Republicans had less to lose from a deal falling apart, they could afford to drive harder for what they wanted. Mitt Romney had an aversion to investing in mass transit. He became singularly focused on ratcheting down spending on buses and subway systems. Even when the group arrived at a consensus on funding for transit and the matter seemed settled, Romney wouldn't relent. He was an implacable noodge.

To iron out details—and to stop the likes of Romney from hijacking the process—the group decided to cull its numbers. Instead of negotiating as a scrum, it agreed to let Sinema and Portman finalize the bill on the group's behalf. But every time the Democrats sent Sinema into a room with Portman, they worried that she would fold. They would urge her to hold firm. Each time she emerged, Democratic agenda items had fallen from the bill. Portman wasn't splitting the difference. He was imposing his will. The Democrats agreed that they needed Steve Ricchetti to take over as their primary negotiator, to bring the painful haggling to a merciful end.

When the process began, the question was, Would ten Republicans have the courage to join their Democratic colleagues and overcome the filibuster? After all, the five Republicans who negotiated the deal were the chamber's five most moderate. Which Republicans would supply the next five votes?

Donald Trump sensed an exploitable opportunity. Twitter and Facebook had removed him from their platforms, but he still issued press releases and called in to right-wing television shows. Even though the bill did nothing to erode his tax cuts—and even though he purported to want infrastructure spending—he denounced the Republican members of the gang: "Who are these RINO Republicans that are so dedicated to giving the Radical Left Democrats a big and beautiful win on Infrastructure? Republican voters will never forget their name, nor will the people of our Country!"

Normally, this sort of rhetoric terrified Republicans into submission. But Trump's argument was so patently hypocritical—and the parochial reasons for supporting spending on crumbling bridges so compelling—that his party experienced a rare moment of independence. In the end, Mitch McConnell, an obstructionist to his core, couldn't resist the chance to repair an ancient, ailing bridge connecting commuters in Kentucky to the economic opportunities of Cincinnati. He announced that he would support the bill, and eighteen Republicans followed his lead, handing Biden his second legislative triumph.

All of which Joe Biden trumpeted as evidence that democracy still worked. The nation was still capable of consensus, of doing the basic work of paving potholes, preventing bridges from collapsing, and ensuring clean water—the biggest investments in its infrastructure, in fact, since the 1950s. But the bill did more than that. It subsidized a network of charging stations for electric vehicles; it contained the most money spent on rail since Amtrak's creation in 1971. This was a profoundly unsexy bill, but it modernized the nation, helping to forestall a tumble into the ranks of the economically uncompetitive.

In his triumphant mood, Biden placed a congratulatory call to Chuck Schumer. "You're a magician," he told him. But Schumer couldn't help but think that this was the easy stuff. Everything to come would be a painful slog—the infrastructure bill still needed to clear the House, and moderates and progressives were girding to fight over the scale and scope of the president's social agenda.

"Thank you, Mr. President," Schumer told him, "But the rabbit still has one foot in the hat."

PART THREE

LEAVING

June–August 2021

17

Gut Check

B Y MID-JUNE, doubts started to invade Jake Sullivan's mind. Plans to withdraw American troops from Afghanistan were storming ahead. When the military wanted to move, it moved with staggering efficiency. But when Sullivan thought hard about the military's speed, he did so with both admiration and a touch of worry.

Each week, Secretary of Defense Austin and chairman of the Joint Chiefs Mark Milley trekked across the Potomac to update Biden on the state of the withdrawal. Their presentations were often stuffed with reports of Taliban victories. Governmentally, Afghanistan is subdivided into 419 districts. In February, the Taliban controlled approximately 78 districts. By the end of June, the number surpassed 100.

None of this sat comfortably with Sullivan, but it didn't necessarily suggest anything imminently catastrophic to him, either. If the Taliban captured a border crossing with Tajikistan, did that really portend disaster for the American withdrawal?

Still, Sullivan worried that the pace of the military's drawdown might leave the United States exposed. So Sullivan arranged a set of meetings, what he called a "gut check." He wanted Milley and Austin to help answer the questions that bothered him: Was it worth slowing down the military's exit? Should it remain stationed at Bagram Airfield—the largest American base in the country—just a little longer?

These weren't innocent questions. In early May, in the basement of the Pentagon, the administration's top national security officials gathered for what's called a rehearsal of concept drill, or ROC. Ever since Donald Trump began musing about leaving Afghanistan, the generals had been refining intricate plans for getting out. Lloyd Austin had visited Kabul in March, a month before President Biden made his decision to exit. General Scott Miller, the lead commander in Afghanistan, presented him with a step-by-step, week-by-week blueprint for shutting down bases and heading for the doors. The ROC was the first time that the military had a chance to share these blueprints with civilians.

At the core of the plan was a belief that speed meant safety. The military would be most vulnerable in retreat. Therefore, haste was the greatest imperative. Because Biden had already announced that withdrawal was happening, the time to begin pulling out was now.

The generals wanted to impart that same sense of urgency to the State Department. They wanted to begin reducing the size of its embassy in Kabul, to speed up the processing of visa applications for any Afghans who had helped the US over the course of the war. General Frank McKenzie, the head of Central Command, warned that conditions in the country would deteriorate quickly as soon as forces began to leave. Therefore, it was dangerous for foreign service officers or American citizens to stay any longer than necessary.

That warning sat badly. While the military might have wanted to bolt for the exits, the State Department felt strongly that it should keep a robust diplomatic presence in Kabul. Brian McKeon, the deputy secretary of state for management and resources, told the general, "We at State have a higher tolerance of risk than you do." It was a quip that the generals never forgave.

Over the course of the spring, the military certainty about its timeline only grew. So when Austin and Milley answered Sullivan's questions about Bagram, they did so with such conviction that his own doubts began to recede. Austin spoke with authority. Years earlier, he had overseen the base, and he could describe the difficulties of defending it with details gleaned from experience. In the end, Sullivan concluded there was no universe in which staying at Bagram made sense. It would have required asking hundreds of departed troops to return to the facility.

Austin and Milley recommended that the military complete its drawdown by July 1, nearly two months ahead of the president's deadline for departing the country, leaving only 650 service members, the bulk of whom would be stationed at Hamid Karzai International Airport on the outskirts of Kabul so that they could evacuate the embassy and its staff if it were ever overrun.

When Austin and Milley showed Biden their plans, he gave them his blessing. After having imposed the withdrawal on the Pentagon, he allowed it to plan for it free of his micromanagement. After all, his commanders knew logistics best, not him.

ON JUNE 24, two days after Biden gave the military the green light to shutter Bagram, Ashraf Ghani arrived in Washington for talks with the president. Not so long ago, Ghani had been a creature of the city himself. For years, he served as a functionary at the World Bank. (His experience at the bank culminated in a coauthored book, *Fixing Failed States*, a work that wasn't remotely autobiographical.) Ghani described himself as master of the capital's byways of power. He once bragged, in Trumpian fashion, that nobody understood Trump better than him.

Although Biden had announced his plans for leaving Afghanistan—and affirmed them, over and over—Ghani didn't believe that they would come to pass. Rather, he believed Biden could be budged, his position softened. Ghani seemed to cling to every mention of the fact that the Biden administration wanted to continue to cooperate with his government on counterterrorism as wishful evidence that a meaningful US presence might remain.

On the eve of his visit to the White House in late June, Ghani hosted a dinner at the Willard hotel, one of the grandest old edifices in the city, where Lincoln had stayed on the eve of his inauguration. In a gilded room, Ghani assembled a gilded party of foreign policy eminences—an A-list set of allies. There was former general David Petraeus, who once commanded the war, and former secretary of state Madeleine Albright. Retired ambassadors and think tank big shots, all great believers in the project of transforming Afghanistan, lined the table.

Having gathered his venerable audience, Ghani posed a question to them: "What should I ask of the president tomorrow?"

It was a late hour to begin strategizing for the next day's meeting. Then again, without fully appreciating it, Ghani had become almost incidental to his own demise. After all, the Trump administration hadn't even bothered to include him in negotiations of the Doha Agreement that determined the fate of the nation he ruled.

Ghani, with his bald head and carefully trimmed beard, cut a depressive figure, a mood that infused the room. Most of Ghani's guests had sunk a good part of their lives into the project of building a new Afghanistan. Petraeus, for one, had funded a scholarship for a woman attending the American University of Afghanistan. He stayed in touch with friends in Kabul. Now, he felt as if the nation were about to be handed over to the enemy he had fought so hard against, and all the gains of twenty years would disappear in a flash.

After the meal, Ghani walked along the table, shaking the hand of each of his guests, pausing and having a moment with each.

As Petraeus said his farewell, he wondered to himself, *Will I ever see Ghani again?* And an even more extreme thought occurred to him: *Will any Afghan president ever visit the White House again?*

WHEN BIDEN met with Ghani, the night after the dinner in the Willard, he wanted to give him a good shake so that he would take his own perilous position seriously. Maybe it was a long shot to think that Ghani would enter into a unity government that minimized his own role. But if he didn't, he at least needed to prepare to defend his nation against the Taliban onslaught.

Biden kept pressing him hard: You need to stop changing generals so damn often! Stop assigning important tasks to your inexperienced pals. You need to learn to trust the professionals in your military, the ones that we trained.

As Jake Sullivan watched Ghani navigate the meeting, he marveled at his effortless elusiveness. Ghani couldn't even be bothered to defend himself in the face of Biden's criticism. He just nodded his head in empty agreement. "Oh yes, of course," he told Biden, every time he was asked to make a tough decision.

This guy isn't ever going to follow through, Sullivan thought.

THE AGREEMENT that Mike Pompeo signed with the Taliban in February 2020 set a course for ending America's involvement in the Afghan war. But it didn't end the war. The Taliban kept on fighting to reclaim control of the government from which they were ousted in 2001.

On paper, the Ghani government possessed advantages. Its armed forces were massive, some one hundred eighty-six thousand strong. Even if there were reasons to worry about how this army would perform without the presence and support of its benefactor, experts in the US government had confidence in a small but solid core of the Afghan military, especially its special operations forces.

Yet the Taliban, with a significantly smaller force—somewhere between seventy thousand and eighty thousand men—were unmistakably advancing and had been ever since Pompeo's agreement. Perhaps the reasons should have been perfectly evident. Pompeo's deal had freed five thousand of the Taliban's best, most motivated fighters from prison. Meanwhile, corrupt government commanders kept skimming money earmarked for the salaries of the rank and file. Without the prospect of Americans fighting alongside them, the unpaid grunts on the front line concluded that they didn't want to die on behalf of a doomed cause. Tribal leaders and local politicians arrived at the same dim assessment. Across the country, they cut deals to hand over power to the Taliban, or at least not get in their way.

In Washington, there was a dawning realization that the Pentagon no longer had a good handle on the state of the crumbling Afghan army. Part of the problem was COVID. During the pandemic, US military advisers stopped visiting frontline troops. Instead, they began conducting virtual sessions with their Afghan protégés, a poor substitute. That deafness and blindness was compounded by the withdrawal. The United States simply lost the vivid picture it once had when thirteen thousand of its troops mingled on the front lines.

Still, the United States had plenty of plausible ideas about how to stanch the deterioration of the Afghan army. It wanted Ghani to consolidate the army around Kabul for a last-ditch defense. It wanted Ghani to bring back the likes of Hamid Karzai so that experienced leaders could rally the nation.

Biden kept trying to puncture Ghani's bubble, to find some way to goad him from his bizarre complacency. A month after their face-to-face meeting, he called him in Kabul. "I am not a military man any more than you are," Biden told him. But he permitted himself a politician's judgment of Ghani's predicament. "I need not tell you the perception around the world and in parts of Afghanistan, I believe, is that things aren't going well in terms of the fight against the Taliban."

While importuning Ghani, Biden kept returning to "perceptions" of the army's success, in the hopes that this might move Ghani, who was so clearly sensitive to his own image.

Again, Ghani did little to disagree with the president. But he could have easily pointed the finger in his direction. If there was a perception that the Afghan government would lose, it was because its patron was abandoning the fight.

It wasn't just the US military abandoning Afghanistan, but a raft of American-funded contractors, too. There were a slew of them on the ground.

These contractors maintained the Afghan air force, all the fighter jets and helicopters that had provided a decisive tactical advantage over the Taliban.

But the contractors didn't want to stay in Afghanistan, knowing their well-being and safety would depend on the Afghan army. Besides, the Pentagon had notified them that the money for their contracts would now flow through the Afghan government. And like any serious profit-seeking venture, they assumed that corrupt officials in the Afghan government would skim their fees.

As contractors began to leave, Congressman Tom Malinowski, a Democrat from New Jersey and one of the few full-throated critics of Biden's withdrawal decision in the party, began asking questions of them. In late spring, he heard a story that horrified him. A contractor told him his men were obligated to rip the avionic systems out of Afghan helicopters. They were destroying the early-warning systems that enabled a pilot to avoid getting blown to bits by a rocket.

Was the US mindlessly exposing allies to unnecessary risk? It seemed so. After two decades of fighting side by side with Afghans, the United States was acting with callousness that shocked Malinowski. Because he had served as the assistant secretary of state for democracy, human rights, and labor in the Obama administration—and he was friends with the likes of Tony Blinken and Jake Sullivan—he began to ask around about the contractor's complaint.

His friendships yielded a quick response. But what he learned only further horrified him. A contract with the manufacturer of the early-warning systems specified that they were to be used by the US government. The Pentagon read these contracts literally: The fact that there were no longer Americans plausibly to protect meant that there was no choice but to destroy these systems. By ripping out the equipment, contractors were rendering the helicopters effectively useless. They were destroying the army's air cover, its most important battlefield advantage. The Afghan soldier on the front line could be forgiven for fearing that he was now on his own.

18

The Kill List

IN MID-JULY, a fax arrived in Hillary Clinton's home office in Chappaqua, New York. Given her history as the world's most famous victim of hacking, email posed an intolerable risk. The sender worried that if the document that unfurled from Clinton's machine fell into the wrong hands, it might result in the murder of dozens.

The document contained the names of 125 Afghan women—prominent in politics, in media, in civil society—who would likely be targeted for assassination by the Taliban if the group returned to power. After Clinton scanned the fax, she began to refer to it as the Kill List.

Among the many sensitivities of the Kill List was its source. She received it from a government official, worried by the failure of the Biden administration to plan for an impending catastrophe. The official was part of a group spread across the government, but mostly clustered at the State Department, which felt as if the White House was leaving the women to a terrible fate, not taking the most basic steps to prevent it. Without official approval, the group had begun to work with activists to collect the names of the most vulnerable Afghan women, in the hopes that the list might prod the administration to take action on their behalf.

Appealing to Hillary Clinton seemed an obvious choice. The Taliban were her longtime adversary. Just after the group came to power in the nineties, the State Department flirted with recognizing the new theocratic regime. That's what the oil companies wanted and what some of the geo-strategists in Foggy Bottom advised. But human rights groups turned to the then First Lady for help preempting the Taliban's campaign for legitimacy. They told her stories about the Taliban beating women who accidentally flashed their ankles from beneath their burqas, which enraged her. She is-sued a public condemnation and invited the activists to meet with her hus-band, stymieing the effort to mainstream the Taliban.

Clinton felt bonded to the women of Afghanistan. By speaking out against the Taliban, she found a sense of purpose in a difficult period, amid her husband's scandals. After she left the White House, her relationship with the women of Afghanistan deepened. She created NGOs that sup-ported them. As secretary of state, she would meet with prominent activists when they came through town—and would ask after them when they left. Quietly, and with her own money, she funded a fellowship for a young Af-ghan woman.

Even before Clinton received the Kill List, she had become a clearing-house for complaints about Biden's Afghanistan plan. She heard from jour-nalists fretting about the fate of colleagues in Kabul, from foreign leaders who couldn't quite believe that the United States was leaving so quickly and with so little forethought for what might come after. Because of her stature—and because her protégé was Jake Sullivan, the national security adviser—they assumed that she stood a chance at importuning the admin-istration to change course. And even if she couldn't roll back the decision to leave, then perhaps she could persuade the administration to, at least, pre-emptively evacuate the Afghans that the Taliban would inevitably target.

Clinton began to call the White House and State Department to explain her worries. She knew her calls annoyed her old friends, but she didn't care. She hoped her questions might sharpen their plans.

"Okay," she would ask, "tell me who I'm going to talk to about this. Who is the one-star, or the national security person, or the deputy secre-tary?" She kept hearing about the endless meetings about issuing visas to

Afghans, but she didn't know who ran the process. That lack of leadership confirmed her fears.

Worse, the administration was focusing all of its planning on extracting Afghans who had worked with the US military and the embassy. But they simply weren't preparing to evacuate the Afghans who were inspired by the rhetoric of the Bush and Obama administrations and had risked their lives to build a civil society with liberal values. Those Afghans were going to be left behind, forced to suffer whatever retribution the Taliban might inflict upon them. When she pressed on this point, she felt as if the administration dismissed her. One of her old friends scoffed. "If they want to leave, they can leave."

THE ARRIVAL of the Kill List focused Clinton's mind. It gave her lobbying a tangible, achievable objective: rescuing 125 specific women. When she called the likes of Jake Sullivan and Tony Blinken, she told them, "I know the list exists. I take it seriously and so should you."

She knew her best chance was to show some empathy for their thinking. She wanted to convey that she respected their decision to prioritize the evacuation of American citizens and Afghans who worked directly with the US. But she pressed them, "Widen the aperture." Part of the reason that the women on the Kill List were in danger is that first ladies, secretaries of state, and ambassadors had elevated their work, had called attention to their example.

But sometimes it seemed as if Clinton's involvement hindered more than it helped. The NSC began referring to "Hillary's List," a less ominous name, which made it sound like Clinton was asking for a personal favor. When the list was shown to one NSC official, it was dismissed. "These are fancy people. They'll get out no matter what." But that missed the point entirely. The prominence of these women is what made them such obvious targets for the Taliban.

After all her deflating calls with administration officials, Clinton concluded that the US government wasn't going to save the women on the Kill List, so she would have to try to do it herself.

In the intimate circle of humanitarian organizations in Washington, the name Hillary Clinton didn't just refer to a person, but a network of groups that she helped to found to promote the human rights of women. Her network of NGOs began collecting the cell phone numbers of the women on the Kill List and urging the women to get their documents in order to prepare for a hasty departure. Most of the women didn't want to consider such a possibility. They believed that their prominence offered them protection. They were fixtures on television, they were friends of the powerful. It was a perfectly human impulse, to shield oneself from the consideration of the darkest scenario. The Clinton groups told the women to get in touch if ever the time to flee arrived. Clinton felt sure it would come quickly.

19

Withdrawal

August

"August is your month," Ron Klain told Neera Tanden. He had asked his friend, whose nomination to lead the Office of Management and Budget had faltered in the Senate, to coordinate the White House's efforts to rally support for the crown jewel of Joe Biden's first year, and possibly his first term: a $3.5 trillion piece of legislation that went under several different names. First branded "the American Families Plan" and then remarketed as "the Build Back Better bill," it was known to Washington insiders as the reconciliation bill, since it could only plausibly succeed on a party line vote, using a parliamentary maneuver.

For months, the White House had delayed a big push on behalf of the reconciliation bill, waiting for the president to finish a bipartisan deal to spend hundreds of billions on infrastructure. With the Senate's passage of that bill, the time had arrived for the administration to push hardest on behalf of the legislation that carried its hopes for truly transforming the nation.

Granted, August was still, well, August—when the invasion of oppressive humidity forced the mass evacuation of official Washington. Anticipating a sun-drenched hole in the calendar, Jen Psaki piled her family into the car for a week at the beach. Tony Blinken headed off to the Hamptons. The president escaped to Camp David for a breather.

While it wasn't the White House's primary focal point, there was an important date circled at the end of the month. On August 31, the United States would officially complete its withdrawal from Afghanistan, the end of the longest war in American history, an event that demanded a moment of solemn commemoration.

At the State Department, a team was working hard to generate the substance to go with the symbolism. The administration's envoy for Afghanistan, Zalmay Khalilzad, flew off to Doha with his deputies to meet with representatives of the Taliban.

The State Department didn't expect to solve Afghanistan's problems in a few weeks. But if everything went well, there was a chance to wheedle the two sides into some sort of agreement that would culminate in Ghani's agreeing to resign from office, beginning an orderly transfer of power to a governing coalition that included the Taliban. There was even a provisional plan to have Tony Blinken fly out (most likely to Qatar) at the end of the month to preside over the signing of an accord.

It was an ending, but not the end. Within the State Department, there was a strongly held belief: Even after August 31, the embassy in Kabul would remain open. It wouldn't be as robustly staffed as before, but some aid programs would continue apace; visas would continue to be issued, especially to the translators and clerks who worked for the United States during the war. A few thousand employees of the embassy and aid organizations would leave. But the United States, at least not the State Department, wasn't going to fully abandon the country in which it had invested so much money, so many lives.

Of course, there were plans on the shelf for catastrophic scenarios—and they had been practiced in "tabletop" simulations—but it wasn't expected that they would be needed. Every intelligence assessment said that the Afghan military would be able to hold off the Taliban for months—albeit the number of months kept dwindling as the summer progressed, as the Taliban kept conquering terrain more quickly than the analysts predicted. But as August began, the grim future of Afghanistan seemed to exist in the hazy distance, beyond the end of the month, not on America's watch.

August 6–10

On Friday, August 6, a very different reality confronted Jake Sullivan. He had begun to anticipate a Taliban surge. But it was happening awfully quickly. A provincial capital, called Zaranj, in the remote southwest of the country, fell to the Taliban, a victory that was effortless—and an omen.

Sullivan asked one of his top aides, Liz Sherwood-Randall, to convene a deputies meeting for Sunday with her counterparts across the government. Contingency plans for August contained a switch to flip in an emergency. To avoid a reprise of the fall of Saigon, with desperate hands clinging to the last choppers out of Vietnam, the government had designed what it called a noncombatant evacuation operation—a NEO, for short. In those plans, the embassy would shut down and relocate to the airport. Troops, which were prepositioned in the Persian Gulf and waiting at Fort Bragg, would descend on Kabul to further protect the airport. Military transport planes would haul American citizens and visa holders out of the country in a sprint.

Even before Sherwood-Randall had a chance to assemble her meeting, the most pessimistic expectations were exceeded. By Sunday, the Taliban captured four more provincial capitals, and General Frank McKenzie, the head of Centcom, filed a commander's estimate warning that Kabul could be encircled in thirty days. That was a rattling assessment, a far faster collapse than predicted in the intelligence reports that the White House had been consuming since January.

Strangely, McKenzie's dire prediction did little to alter plans. Sherwood-Randall's group unanimously agreed that it was too soon to declare a NEO. The embassy in Kabul was particularly forceful on this point. All along, the acting ambassador on the ground, Ross Wilson, wanted to avoid cultivating a sense of panic in Kabul that would collapse the army and the state. Even the intel agencies seconded this line of thinking.

When Sherwood-Randall's group returned its verdict, Sullivan wasn't totally satisfied, especially after having read McKenzie's grim estimate. On Monday, he kicked the question of the NEO higher up the bureaucratic chain, posing it to a principals meeting, which included the likes of Lloyd Austin, Mark Milley, and Tony Blinken. And again, the group unanimously agreed it was premature to call a NEO.

At the end of the meeting, Sullivan told them, "Guys, I don't want to be here in thirty days and to say, 'What the hell were we thinking?' I want specific granular metrics for what would make you say yes. Write them down now."

August 12

At 2:00 a.m., Jake Sullivan's phone rang. It was Mark Milley. He called at a late hour because he feared that a worst-case scenario was coming to pass. The military had received reports that the Taliban had entered the city of Ghazni, less than a day's march from Kabul.

The intelligence community always assumed that the Taliban wouldn't want to storm Kabul until after the United States left and the Ghani government crumbled. According to the analysis, the Taliban wanted to avoid a block-by-block battle for the city, a lesson the group had learned from the last time it messily conquered the nation.

But the proximity of the Taliban to the US embassy and Hamid Karzai International Airport (or HKIA, as everyone called it) was terrifying. It necessitated the decisive action that the administration had thus far resisted. Milley wanted Sullivan to set the wheels of a NEO in motion. If the State Department wasn't going to move quickly, the president needed to order it to. At very least, it was time to light a fire under the State Department's ass, he said.

"I've got it," Sullivan told him.

THE GROUP that set foreign policy prided itself on its collegiality. No shouters, no raging bulls in the mix. Lloyd Austin has the booming voice of an authoritative dad, but he is also somewhat shy. For all the years he spent issuing orders, his bureaucratic style relied on soft power. He tried to win battles with friendly persuasion, not force.

But Austin shared Milley's sense of urgency. Later Thursday morning, he took a crack at nudging along the evacuation. In an 8:00 a.m. video conference with the inner circle of national security advisers—Sullivan, Blinken, CIA director Bill Burns, and USAID administrator Samantha Power—he asked, "Should we remove our people from the embassy and close it down?"

"There will be limited warning if the army and government collapse," Austin told the group.

He directed his question about the embassy to the acting ambassador, Ross Wilson, who joined the meeting from Kabul. Wilson, who for months had resisted the idea of abandoning the diplomatic post, was a figure who annoyed the Pentagon. The generals felt he didn't grasp the possibilities for a calamity.

Instead of directly answering Austin's question, he assured the group that he was relocating the embassy to the airport. And there were plans to send four hundred employees out of the country and to destroy sensitive material. Granted, they were largely just plans. Then again, nobody in the meeting ordered him to move faster.

August 13

With the passage of each hour, however, Jake Sullivan's anxieties kept growing. Sullivan called Austin and told him, "I think you need to send someone with bars on his arm to Doha to talk to the Taliban so that they understand not to mess with an evacuation." Austin agreed to dispatch General McKenzie, the Centcom commander.

That morning, Austin hosted a video conference with the top civilian and military officials in Kabul. He wanted updates from them before he headed to the White House to brief the president.

Ross Wilson told him, "I need seventy-two hours before I can begin destroying sensitive documents."

"You have to be done in seventy-two hours," Austin retorted.

The Taliban had advanced at such a rapid clip. They were now perched outside Kabul. Delaying the evacuation of the embassy compound posed a danger that Austin couldn't abide. Thousands of troops were about to arrive to protect the new makeshift facility at the airport, and the moment had come to head there.

Abandoning an embassy has its own protocols—and they are rituals of panic. The diplomats had a weekend, more or less, to purge the place, to fill its incinerators, disintegrators, and burn bins with documents and hard drives. A cache of American flags needed destroying so they couldn't ever be used by the enemy for propaganda purposes.

Wisps of smoke would soon begin to blow from the building's chimneys— a plume of what had been classified cables and personnel files. Chinooks would be available to shuttle personnel to the airport. Even for those Afghans who didn't have access to the Internet, the narrative would be legible in the sky.

August 14

On Saturday night, Tony Blinken placed a call to Ghani. He wanted to make sure that Ghani remained committed to negotiations in Doha. The Taliban delegation there was prepared to agree to a unity government, which they would run—and would allocate a dozen cabinet slots to ministers from the Ghani government.

That notion had broad support from the Afghan political elite. Former Afghan president Hamid Karzai was scheduled to fly to Qatar the next day to join the discussions. Everyone, even Ghani, agreed that he would need to resign by the end of the month. But Blinken wanted to make sure that he wasn't wavering from his commitments.

While Ghani said that he would comply, he began musing aloud about what might happen if the Taliban invaded Kabul before August 30. Before hanging up, he told Blinken, "I'd rather die than surrender."

August 15

On Sunday, Ashraf Ghani's social media team posted a video on Facebook of the president talking to his ministers on the phone. As Ghani sat at his imposing wooden desk, which once belonged to King Amanullah, who fled an Islamist uprising a century earlier, his aides hoped to project a sense of his calm.

During those early hours of the day, a small number of the Taliban eased their way to the gates of the city, and then into the capital itself. The Taliban leadership didn't want to invade Kabul until after the American departure. But conquering territory happened without soldiers even having to fire shots. In their path, police simply laid down their arms; soldiers walked away from checkpoints. As if propelled by the tides, Taliban units kept drifting in the direction of the presidential palace.

Rumors traveled even more quickly than the invaders. Ghani said that he wasn't terribly worried—at least he tried not to betray his own sense of panic to his minions. But panic kept creeping ever closer to his own doors. A crowd formed outside a bank. Nervous customers were rushing to empty their accounts, but they encountered chaos. A guard fired into the air to disperse the melee. The noise of gunshots reverberated through the nearby palace, which had largely emptied for lunch. Ghani's closest advisers pressed him to flee, since the Taliban were surely getting closer. "It will be either your palace guards or the Taliban," one adviser told him, "but if you stay, you'll be killed."

This was a fear rooted in recent history. In 1996, when the Taliban invaded Kabul, they took the tortured body of the former president and hung it from a traffic light outside the presidential palace.

Instead of testing his fate, Ghani hustled onto one of three Mi-17 helicopters waiting inside his compound, bound for Uzbekistan. The helicopters were instructed to fly low to the terrain, in the hopes that they might evade detection by the US military. From Uzbekistan, he would fly to the United Arab Emirates, and an ignominious exile. Without time to pack, he fled in plastic sandals, accompanied by his wife and closest advisers. On the tarmac, aides and guards grappled over the last seat.

When his staff returned from lunch, they moved through the palace searching for the president, unaware of how he had abandoned them, and their country.

AT APPROXIMATELY 1:45 P.M., Ambassador Wilson went to the lobby of the empty embassy for the ceremonial lowering of the flag. Exhausted and emotionally shattered by the work of clearing the building, he prepared to leave behind a concrete monument to his nation's defeat. Only a few military officers remained to complete a final sweep. One from the 10th Mountain Division went room to room, pressing the last occupants to leave. He found some embassy employees going about their jobs without any seeming recognition of the threat outside the compound's gates. Others he encountered, according to testimony he later provided investigators, were cowering in a corner.

Wilson made his way to the helicopter pad so that he could be carried to his new outpost in the airport. As he prepared to leave, a pilot told him that fifteen minutes earlier he had witnessed a trio of choppers leaving the presidential palace. Wilson didn't need the pilot to extrapolate. He was sure that Ghani had fled. By the time he relayed his suspicions to Washington, officials there already possessed intelligence that confirmed Wilson's circumstantial evidence.

It fell to Jake Sullivan to relay the news to the president, who was ensconced at Camp David for the start of a theoretical vacation. Biden exploded in frustration. "Give me a break," he exclaimed.

LATER THAT AFTERNOON, General McKenzie made his way to the Ritz-Carlton on the marina in Doha. Well before Ghani's departure from power, the wizened marine had scheduled a meeting with an old adversary of the United States, Mullah Abdul Ghani Baradar.

Baradar wasn't just any Taliban leader. He had cofounded the group, with Mullah Omar, whose sister Baradar later married. His initial legend was built on a reputation as a daring military tactician. (Baradar, was, in fact, his nom de guerre, which translated as "brother.") In 2010, Pakistani intelligence serendipitously captured Baradar in a raid in Karachi, only belatedly realizing it had nabbed such a famous prisoner. For eight years, he languished in a Pakistani prison.

Despite his battlefield ferocity, Baradar had an inclination for diplomacy, especially relative to his militant comrades. Hamid Karzai considered him his best potential partner for peace. When the Trump administration had wanted to cut a deal with the Taliban, the State Department pressured the Pakistanis to release Baradar from prison so that it would have a viable interlocutor.

Afghanistan is one of the poorest nations on the planet—and the Taliban are among the most fanatical religious political parties in the world—but Baradar and a delegation of the Taliban took up residence at a well-appointed resort on the Persian Gulf. From the window in Baradar's room, it was possible to stare at a pool with bikini-clad women. When the American envoy Zalmay Khalilzad first visited his digs, he quipped, "This must be the closest you have come to heaven," a tease that Baradar took as an accusation, quickly drawing his curtains closed. Over many months, Khalilzad and Baradar sat across a table in Doha. A relationship formed as they negotiated a deal to end the US presence in Afghanistan.

McKenzie was far less trusting, and he had arrived with the intention of delivering a stern warning to Baradar. But events had galloped ahead with rapidity that he hadn't anticipated. He barely had time to tweak his agenda for the meeting, after learning about Ghani's exit.

An Alabaman whose speech betrays his origins, McKenzie unfolded a map of Afghanistan translated into Pashto, which he had brought along to the meeting. There was a circle drawn around Kabul—a radius of thirty kilometers—and he pointed to it. When he talked about it with the Pentagon, he referred to it as the "ring of death."

"If you operate inside the thirty kilometers, we'll assume hostile intent and we'll strike hard."

McKenzie tried to bolster his threat with logic. "We don't want to end up in a firefight with you. That's a lot less likely to happen if you're not in the city."

Baradar not only understood, he agreed. He also wanted the United States military to leave by the end of the month with little fuss. As the Taliban's leading pragmatist, he wanted to transform his group's inhospitable image. He wanted foreign embassies, even the American one, to remain in Kabul. "We'll protect it," he promised. Baradar didn't want a Taliban government to become a pariah state, starved of foreign assistance that it badly needed.

But there was an elemental problem with the McKenzie plan. It was too late. Taliban fighters, a hundred or so on motorcycles, had already drifted into the outskirts of the city. They faced no resistance, so kept moving forward. The invasion wasn't designed, it was just what the collapse of the Ghani government permitted.

Kabul was on the brink of anarchy. It wouldn't be long until armed gangs started to roam the streets. Baradar told the general, "We have two options to deal with it: you take responsibility for securing Kabul, or you have to allow us to do it."

McKenzie replied, "I'm telling you that my order is to run an evacuation. Whatever happens to the security in Kabul, don't mess with the evacuation, or there will be hell to pay." It was an evasive answer. The United States didn't have the troops or the will to secure Kabul. McKenzie had no choice but to implicitly cede that job to the Taliban.

Baradar walked toward a window. Because he didn't speak English, he wanted to press his comrades to make sure that he fully understood. "Do you understand what McKenzie is saying? Is he saying that he won't attack us if we go in?" His adviser told him that he had heard him correctly.

As the meeting wrapped up, McKenzie realized that the United States would need to be in constant communication with the Taliban. They were about to be rubbing shoulders with one another in a dense city, in a tense situation. Misunderstandings were inevitable; so was the need to coordinate. Both sides agreed that they would designate a representative in Kabul to talk through the many complexities so that the old enemies could muddle together toward a common purpose.

Soon after McKenzie and Baradar ended their meeting, Al Jazeera carried a live feed from the presidential palace, capturing the Taliban wending their way into the seat of Afghan power. They went from room to room, in awe of the building, seemingly bemused by their own accomplishment.

They gathered in Ghani's old office, where a book of poems remained on his imposing wooden desk, across from a box of Kleenex. A Talib sat in the president's Herman Miller chair. His comrades stood behind him in a tableau, cloth draped over the shoulders of their tunics, guns resting in the crooks of their arms, as if posing for their own official portrait. A fighter recited a verse from the Koran: "Indeed, we have granted you a clear triumph, O Prophet."

August 16

As the US embassy relocated to the airport, it became a magnet for humanity. The extent of Afghan desperation shocked officials back in Washington. Only in the thick of the crisis did top officials at the State Department realize that hundreds of thousands of Afghans, perhaps three hundred thousand, had fled their homes as the civil war swept through the countryside—and made their way to the capital. Long before the collapse of the Ghani government, the streets of Kabul were thick with refugees, some of them homeless, nearly all of them desperate. Now, with rumors of evacuation flights leaving the airport, these refugees choked the road leading to its main entrance.

The runway at Hamid Karzai International Airport divided the facility into halves. A northern sector served as a military outpost—and after the relocation of the embassy, a consular office—the last remaining vestige of the United States and its promise of liberation. A commercial airport stared at these barracks, offices, and hangars from across the strip of asphalt. A concrete blast wall wrapped around the whole of it, with a serpentine road leading to the terminal, designed to slow the approach of a suicide bomber.

In the chaos of August 16, the civilian airport was abandoned by Afghans who worked there. The night shift of air traffic controllers simply never came. Meanwhile, the US troops, which Austin ordered to support the evacuation, were only just arriving. And there weren't enough of them on the ground yet. So the terminal was overwhelmed. Afghans began to spill onto the tarmac itself.

The crowds arrived in waves. On the Sunday afternoon, a crowd gathered late in the day and dissipated of its own accord, since it was clear that no flights would depart that evening. But the next morning, the compound still wasn't secure, so it refilled with Afghans. As Ross Wilson watched from his new office, he thought that the airport was easier to enter than a movie theater. He began to worry for his own safety as the crowd moved in the direction of his headquarters. Would the military have to fend them off with guns? He considered it a real possibility. The normally unflappable military commanders were palpably panicked. Fortunately, the mob moved past the American building, and then remnants of the Afghan army steered the crowd in a different direction.

In the chaos, it wasn't entirely clear to Wilson who controlled the compound. The Taliban began freely roaming the facility, wielding bludgeons, trying to secure the crowd. Apparently, they were working alongside soldiers from the old Afghan army. Wilson received worrying reports of tensions between the two forces. Even though both armies wanted to clear the mob from the airport, they had been at war for nearly twenty years.

The imperative was to begin landing transports with equipment and troops. A C-17, a bulky transport plane, a warehouse with wings, filled with supplies to support the arriving troops, managed to land. The crew of the plane—call sign REACH885—lowered a ramp to unload the contents of the jet's belly, but those pallets were rushed by a surge of civilians.

The American crew was no less anxious than the Afghans who greeted them, fearful for their own safety. Almost as quickly as the plane's back ramp lowered, the panicked crew reboarded and resealed the jet's entrances. The crew received permission to fly out of Kabul, to flee the uncontrolled scene.

But there was no escaping the crowd on the ground, for whom the jet was a last chance to avoid the Taliban and the suffering to come. The plane began to taxi slowly enough that some Afghans climbed onto its wing. Others sought to stow away in the oversize wheel wells that housed its bulging landing gear. To clear the runway of human traffic, Humvees began rushing alongside the plane. Two Apache helicopters flew just above the ground, to give the Afghans a good scare and to gust the civilians from the plane with rotor wash.

But only after the plane had lifted into the air did the crew discover its traumatic place in history. When the pilot couldn't fully retract the landing gear, a member of the crew went to investigate the issue, staring out a small porthole for monitoring such problems. Through the window, it was possible to see the blood and guts—scattered remains of human beings.

Videos taken from the tarmac went instantly viral. They showed, in the distance, a twenty-four-year-old dentist from Kabul plunging to the ground from the elevating jet. The images harkened back to the photo of a man floating to his death from an upper story of the World Trade Center, plummeting bodies that seemed to sum up an era.

THE WHITE HOUSE woke to the images of Afghans falling from the sky. Jen Psaki knew that she would be leaving her family on the beach and returning to Washington. Right-wing media were already feasting on the fact that she wasn't standing in front of the podium. Psaki wrote to Ron Klain, "I'm contemplating coming back." With characteristic efficiency, Klain responded instantaneously, "I'm sorry. I think you need to."

Jake Sullivan watched the president learn about the C-17 and sadness overcome his face. Over the next months, Sullivan kept replaying the sequence of events in his head. *If only . . . if only the pilot hadn't made the decision to leave Kabul so quickly . . . if only the troops had cleared the runway.* Sullivan knew that this was the moment that defined everything. Already, there were some in the press who said it would define his own career. He worried that the image was so terrible, that it inspired such visceral emotions, there would be nothing that the administration could do to mitigate it.

20

The White Scarves

EVER SINCE Hillary Clinton received a copy of the Kill List, her aides had begun to prepare for the moment that the Taliban assumed power. Her network of NGOs procured access to safe houses across Kabul, many of them shelters for victims of spousal abuse, which they would use as gathering points for the women they hoped to evacuate.

The Georgetown Institute for Women, Peace and Security, an NGO run by Clinton's old chief of staff and close friend Melanne Verveer, had compiled a list of the 1,500 Afghan women and their families that the Taliban would most likely target, expanding the Kill List that Clinton had received. But now that the moment of maximum peril had arrived, Clinton's groups had to make agonizing choices. Who among the 1,500 would they try to evacuate first? They had only a handful of safe houses and a handful of seats on airplanes out of Kabul. Having to decide whom to extricate felt like a thought experiment in a college ethics seminar, except it wasn't an intellectual exercise at all.

On August 16, the day after Ghani fled Kabul, the Clinton groups began making their first phone calls. They gave sixty women the addresses for safe houses and told them that they needed to arrive in twelve hours. Although the Clinton advisers in Washington and New York had scant experience organizing an evacuation, they passed along specific instructions. The fleeing women couldn't call their mothers and fathers to tell them about their impending departure. They shouldn't bring luggage or stash jewelry under their clothes or dress themselves in any way that suggests travel. If they had kids coming with them, they should bring extra diapers. An extra battery for their phones, if easily obtained, was a good idea.

Hillary Clinton had called Lloyd Austin, who said that he would put the names of the sixty women on a list at the airport so that marines would let them through. The women needed to wear an article of clothing that would make them easy to pick out from the crowd. Clinton's aides told the women to wear white scarves.

Cars, driven by private security forces, were sent to the safe house to pick up the White Scarves—as the women were now known. They departed for the airport in groups of six, driving through a city without police, without any authority imposing order.

Outside the airport, marines struggled to hold a perimeter. Crowds clogged the streets, preventing the cars carrying the White Scarves from traveling farther. The women began to walk on foot, attempting to carve their way through the block of humanity. One woman in the group put down her two-year-old daughter, only to watch the crowd surge in her direction, trampling her little girl.

When overwhelmed marines briefly lost control of a gate to the airport, several of the White Scarves were propelled by the surging crowd into the terminal, as if bodysurfing a wave of their desperate compatriots.

Clinton's aides followed events together in a Zoom room, which they left perpetually open on their computers for weeks. They created the shared forum after a mayor, hiding in a closet, failed in repeated attempts to reach the group. The mayor had left a message with Huma Abedin, Clinton's long-time adviser: "I'm not afraid to die, but please tell my family I love them." Whenever anyone in the group had a problem that needed solving or a piece of intelligence worth sharing, they would unmute themselves.

The aides on the Zoom were one step removed from the White Scarves, who were in touch with a Dari-speaking woman working for one of the

Clinton NGOs. But occasionally it felt as if they were right there with them. A call arrived from Kabul, placed on speaker so that everyone in the Zoom could listen. They heard a woman standing outside the airport. As she spoke, a fusillade of gunshots echoed through the Zoom, followed by a terrible shriek. The call went quiet, and the Clinton advisers believed that they had just eavesdropped on an atrocity. After a long silence, the voice in Kabul returned. She told them that gunshots were an attempt to control the increasingly unruly crowd.

When the first groups made it to the airport gate, they showed the marines their scarves and told them that their names were on the Hillary Clinton list, expecting that they would be able to step into safety. "There's not a list," the marines told them—and in retrospect, as the troops tried to hold their ground, were they really expected to phone their superiors to check?

After the gunshots, after dehydration and hunger, the stranded White Scarves stood in the dust and August sun, worried that the Taliban might murder them if they returned home. One woman retreated to a gas station. The group on Zoom followed reports of how she locked herself in a bathroom stall. Through a WhatsApp chain, they told her to spend the night there so that she could try to enter the airport again the next morning. But as she settled in for the night, she saw the Taliban pass in front of the gas station. She sent a panicked message, asking whether she should go in search of a new hiding place. But the Clinton aides told her to stay in place, not sure whether they might be putting her in even greater danger.

The members of the Clinton group felt as if they had grown entangled in a dangerous business far beyond their capacities. They knew that the White Scarves had potentially lost faith in them and that they had begun to lose faith in themselves.

21

John Bass Stands at the Gates of Despair

August 17

It was hard for John Bass to keep his mind on the task at hand. For just over two years, from 2017 to 2020, he had served as Washington's ambassador to Kabul. Afghanistan was perhaps the most stressful posting in the foreign service, but a career of hardship assignments had conditioned Bass not to let the job drag him down.

During that tour, like any earnest foreign service officer, Bass did his best to absorb the country and meet its people. He planted a garden with a group of Girl and Boy Scouts and hosted roundtables with the country's coterie of brassy journalists. When his term as ambassador ended, he left behind friends, colleagues, and hundreds of acquaintances.

Now, as word of the shocking events in Kabul arrived with dizzying velocity, Bass kept his face pressed to his phone, consuming any shard of news, checking for any word from his old Afghan network. He felt sadness and anger, moving through his days beset by worry and a sense of dread about what might come next.

Yet, he also had a job that required his attention. The State Department had assigned him to train future ambassadors, a group of appointees that had not yet been sent abroad. In a seminar room in suburban Virginia, he did his best to focus himself on passing along wisdom to these soon-to-be emissaries of the United States.

As he prepared to start a session, one of his colleagues noticed his muted phone light up. Bass stared over and saw a call from the State Department Operations Center, not a number that regularly flashed on his phone. He apologized to his students and stepped into the humidity to take the call.

"Are you available to talk to Deputy Secretary Sherman?"

The familiar voice of Wendy Sherman, the number two at the department, came on the line. "I have a mission for you. You must take it and you need to leave today." With the crisis, she said that she would have to be terse. "I'm calling to ask you to go back to Kabul to lead the evacuation effort."

The ambassador to Kabul, Ross Wilson, was shattered by the experience of the past week. Even Wilson admitted that he was exhausted and wasn't in a frame of mind to complete the job. Sherman needed Bass to manage the exodus.

It wasn't a request that Bass expected. In his flummoxed state, he struggled to pose the questions he thought he might regret not asking later.

"How much time do we have?" Bass wanted to know.

"Probably about two weeks, a little less than two weeks."

"I've been away from this for, you know, eighteen months or so."

"Yep, we know, but we think you're the right person for this."

Bass returned to class and scooped up his belongings. "With apologies, I'm going to have to take my leave. I've just been asked to go back to Kabul and support the evacuations. So I've got to say goodbye and wish you all the best, and you're all going to be great ambassadors."

As Bass went in search of his rental car, he tried to ground himself in the practical. Because he wasn't living in Washington, he didn't have any of his stuff with him. He googled the nearest REI and drove straight there in search of hiking pants, rugged boots, and a few boxes of Clif Bars. Because he didn't have a laptop, he would need to pick one up from the IT department in Foggy Bottom. Without knowing much more than what was in the news, Bass rushed to board a plane taking him to the worst crisis in the recent history of American foreign policy.

August 19

Less than thirty hours later—3:30 a.m., Kabul time—John Bass touched down at Hamid Karzai International Airport, as he had dozens of times before. In his bleariness, Bass began touring the compound. At the American headquarters, he ran into the military heads of the operation, familiar faces whom he had worked with before. There was Rear Admiral Peter Vasely. Over the summer, he assumed command of the small remnant of US forces in Afghanistan. There was Major General Chris Donahue, the head of the 82nd Airborne, out of Fort Bragg, a decorated soldier who had a habit for landing at the center of big moments. On September 11, he was the aide-de-camp for the vice chairman of the Joint Chiefs, Richard Meyer, standing next to him on Capitol Hill when the first plane struck the World Trade Center. He later served as a squadron commander in northern Afghanistan and then led special forces in the country.

The military men sat Bass down and presented him with the state of play. There was no denying that the situation was bizarre. The success of the American operation now depended largely on the cooperation of the Taliban—an army the United States had been striking a week earlier.

Mullah Baradar's delegation in Doha had passed along the name of a Taliban commander in Kabul—Mawlawi Hamdullah Mukhlis. It was Donahue's job to coordinate with him, but the logistics of their meetings were themselves the subject of prolonged negotiations. The United States didn't want Donahue to leave the airport—and the Taliban wanted to make sure that Hamdullah didn't walk into an ambush. Eventually, both sides agreed that daily meetings would take place in the departures building on the commercial side of the airport,

Hamdullah and Donahue developed a relationship that felt all consuming. In addition to their daily meetings, sometimes twice daily, they texted on their phones. Donahue needed the Taliban to help control the crowds that had formed outside the airport—and to implement systems that would allow passport and visa holders to pass through the throngs.

But the Taliban were imperfect allies at best. Taliban checkpoints were run by literal-minded warriors from the countryside, who didn't know how to deal with the array of documents being waved in their faces. What was an authentic visa? What about families, where the father had a US passport, but his wife and children didn't?

Every day, a new set of Taliban soldiers tended to arrive at checkpoints, unschooled in the nuances of travel documents, unaware of the previous day's orders. Which meant that checkpoints grew crowded, until Donahue managed to reach Hamdullah, who cleared up the confusion. But by then buses were enmeshed in hopeless jams.

Frustrated with the unruliness, the Taliban would sometimes simply stop letting anyone through, suspending cooperation for a day or two, until Donahue managed to repair the rift.

Donahue's requests were often garbled in translation. He would ask Hamdullah for help cutting a path through a crowd. Then he would have to clarify that he didn't want the crowds cleared with truncheons, which caused Hamdullah to vent about the confusing demands of his erstwhile enemy.

Even though Donahue gritted his teeth as he dealt with Hamdullah, the Taliban commander seemed to feel a camaraderie with his fellow soldier. Their exchanges simulated a human relationship. Hamdullah began to open up and seemed to crave the general's sympathy. He confided to Donahue about his worry that Afghanistan would suffer a devastating brain drain, as American airplanes evacuated so many of his talented compatriots.

In a video conference with General Milley, back at the Pentagon, Donahue recounted Hamdullah's fears. And his description caused the chairman of the Joint Chiefs to laugh.

"Don't be going local on me, Donahue," Milley quipped.

"Don't worry about me, sir," he responded. "I'm not buying what they are selling."

———

By the time Bass left his meeting with Donahue and Vasely, the early morning sun had broken through. Bass asked to tour the gates to the airport where Afghans amassed. Having flown through the night, he was bolted awake by the smell of feces and urine, by the sound of gunshots and bullhorns blaring instructions in Dari and Pashto. Dust assaulted his eyes and nose. He felt the heat that emanated from human bodies crowded into narrow spaces, with slender shade.

As Bass approached the gates, the atmosphere grew palpably tenser. Marines and consular officers, some who had flown into Kabul from other embassies, were trying to pull passport and visa holders from the crowd. But every time they waded into it, they seemed to provoke a furious reaction. To get plucked from the street by the Americans was to win life's lottery—and that smacked of cosmic unfairness to those left behind. Sometimes the anger swelled beyond control, so the troops shut down entrances to allow frustrations to subside.

The most chaotic of the entrances was Abbey Gate. It stood on the other side of a canal, knee-deep with fetid water. Afghans would jump into the muck and needed to be hoisted over a wall, just taller than the height of a full-grown man. In a rampage, trampled bodies drowned in the river of shit.

John Bass was staring at despair in its rawest, saddest, most seething form. As he studied the humanity encircling the airport and then turned back to the building that became his makeshift office, he wondered if he could ever make any of this a bit less terrible.

Bass cadged a room in barracks belonging to the Turkish army, which had offered to operate and protect the airport after the Americans finally departed. Every morning, his alarm blared at four thirty. He would splash water on his face and walk 150 meters to his office. As soon as he left the door, he would listen for gunfire. If it was ubiquitous, he knew it would be an

especially challenging day. It meant that the Taliban were already attempting to frighten restive crowds into submission.

His days tended to follow a pattern. They would begin with the Taliban's grudging assistance. Then, as lunchtime approached, the Talibs would
get hot and hungry. Abruptly, they would stop processing evacuees through
their checkpoints. Then, just as suddenly at six or seven, as the sun began
to set, they would begin to cooperate again.

Each day, he needed to devote his tired brain to crafting fresh schemes
to satisfy the Taliban's fickle demands. One day, the Taliban would let
buses through without question; the next, they would demand to see pas-
senger manifests in advance. Bass's staff created a system of official-looking
placards to place in bus windows. The Taliban would wave them through
for a few hours, then declare that system unreliable.

Bass kept studying the map for new routes to guide evacuees through
the dense, impassable crowds. The Taliban agreed to let Afghan employees
of the embassy amass at a gas station and then travel through an unused
entrance on the northwest side of the compound, dubbed Glory Gate. But
access to Glory came and went quickly.

Over his day, Bass would drop everything and join video conferences
with Washington. He became a fixture in the Situation Room. Biden would
pepper him with ideas for squeezing more evacuees through the gates.
"Why don't we have them meet in parking lots?" "Can't we leave the airport and pick them up?" Bass would kick around Biden's questions with
colleagues to determine their plausibility, which was usually low. Still, he
appreciated Biden's applying pressure, making sure that he didn't overlook
the obvious.

Above all, Biden wanted to know if it was possible to push back the August 31 deadline for leaving the airport. In a television interview, Biden had
promised that the United States wouldn't leave until it had extricated every
American citizen from the country. There was little chance of fulfilling his
promise, given that the embassy was still struggling to get in touch with a
small handful of citizens.

Bass, however, couldn't be more adamant about the necessity of leaving on schedule. Maybe Khalilzad could get the Taliban leadership to agree to a delay. But Bass knew the Taliban soldiers who manned the checkpoints had a date for the American departure in their head. If the US stayed longer than originally promised, there would be Talibs who treated the US contingent at the airport as hostile invaders. And he wanted to make sure that the planners back in DC didn't ever forget that American soldiers and diplomats were surrounded by an old enemy, in a compound that couldn't be less defensible. Staying was a risk that couldn't be justified. It wasn't even a close call.

THE BUSY WEEKS in Hamid Karzai International Airport crowded out nightmares. Despite everything, Bass kept pushing through, even as many of his colleagues were struggling. Some simply couldn't tolerate the hardheartedness required by the job, constantly denying families, with fathers in tears and children fainting from fear. Bass had imported consular officers from around the world. Many of them found the work too emotionally grueling to bear. In the course of a day, he would empathetically thank them for their hard work, and then board them on departing planes.

At the end of his first day at the airport, he went through his email. A State Department spokesman had announced his arrival in Kabul. Suddenly, friends and colleagues deluged him with requests to save Afghans. He began to scrawl the names he excavated from his inbox on a whiteboard in his office. By the time he finished, he filled every crevice of the six-foot-by-four-foot surface. He stood back and looked at the collection of individuals assembled. Even though he would pass along these names to be processed, he knew there was exceedingly little chance that he could help. The orders from Washington couldn't have been clearer. The primary object was to load planes with US citizens, visa holders, and passport holders from partner nations, mostly European.

In his mind, he kept another running list of Afghans—those he had come to know personally during his time as ambassador. Some would be subjected to the tyranny of the Taliban, beyond his ability to rescue them. Their faces and voices were etched in his memory, and he could be sure that, at some point when he wasn't rushing to fill C-17s, they would haunt his sleep.

22

Sullivan's Choice

SOMEONE ON THE BUS is dying."

Jake Sullivan was flummoxed. What to do with such a dire message sent by a friend he trusted? It described a caravan of five blue-and-white buses, stuck one hundred yards outside of the south gate of the airport, carrying a dying human being. If Sullivan forwarded this problem to an aide, would it get resolved in time?

The message came with the number for a bus driver. Sullivan picked up his phone and called. In the middle of everything—as he was running the Situation Room, briefing the president, and generally coordinating the operation—the national security adviser tried to have a calm conversation with a frantic Afghan bus driver. "Where are you?" He needed to know the location of the bus so that he could relay it to a commander in Kabul, so that troops could come and guide it into the airport, where doctors could treat the evacuee.

Over twenty years of war, Americans acquired an intimate relationship with Afghanistan. Journalists worked with translators and fixers. NGOs built schools for girls. Watching the desperate scenes on the news—and knowing the brutality of the Taliban—these Americans were frantically trying to help the friends and acquaintances they had accumulated over the decades.

Jake Sullivan sometimes felt as if every member of the American elite were simultaneously asking for his help.

When he left secure rooms, he would grab his phone and check personal email accounts, which overflowed with urgent pleas. *This person just had the Taliban threaten them. They will be shot in fifteen hours if you don't get them out.* Sometimes the senders tried to shame him into action. They attempted to move him with accusations of moral indifference. *If you don't do something, their death is on your hands.*

To his colleagues in the Situation Room, it seemed as if the spirit had been yanked from his tired body. Sullivan usually moved through the world with a lightness; paragraphs flowed from his mouth, as if he had woken up ready for a television hit. But now, he was withdrawn, exhausted, and un-characteristically terse.

It wasn't just pleas for help from outside the building. The president kept hearing from his own friends and members of Congress about stranded Afghans. Biden would become emotionally invested in their cases. There were three buses of women at the Serena Hotel that kept running into logistical obstacles. He told Sullivan, "I want to know what happens to them. I want to know when they make it to the airport." When the president learned about these cases, he would become engrossed in trying to solve the practical challenge of getting them to the airport, mapping routes through the city.

Foreign policy is usually conducted in the abstract—it's about grand strategy, great power relations, bilateral meetings, aid programs—but Biden and Sullivan found themselves staring hard at the consequences of their decision. A process run from the sanitized distance of the Situation Room felt uncomfortably intimate; the ethical dimension of policy had become achingly personal.

AFGHANISTAN WAS a collective trauma for the administration, especially the State Department. When Wendy Sherman, the deputy secretary of state, went to check in with members of a task force working on the evacuation, she found grizzled diplomats in tears. She estimated that a quarter of the State Department's personnel had served in Afghanistan, at one point or another. They felt a connection with the country, an emotional entanglement. Fielding an overwhelming volume of emails describing hardship cases, they had an easy time imaging the faces of refugees. Even in the seat of American power, they felt the shame and anger that comes with the inability to help. To deal with trauma, the State Department brought a therapy dog into the building with the hope that it might help ease the staff's pain.

In the crisis, the State Department redirected the attention of its sprawling apparatus to Afghanistan. Embassies in Mexico City and New Delhi became call centers. Staff in those distant capitals assumed the role of caseworkers, assigned to stay in touch with the remaining American citizens in Afghanistan. They tracked their flights and helped counsel them through the terrifying weeks.

Sherman sent her Afghan-born chief of staff, Mustafa Popal, to Hamid Karzai International Airport to support John Bass. All day long, she responded to pleas for help: from foreign governments, who joined a daily video conference she hosted; from Yo-Yo Ma, who kept writing on behalf of an orchestra; from members of Congress. There was a moment in the midst of the crush when Sherman felt compelled to travel down to the first floor, to spend fifteen escapist minutes cuddling with the therapy dog.

Government is a clinical word. It doesn't connote anguish and suffering. But the situation at State was so palpably rough that Veterans Affairs volunteered to send over caseworkers trained to counsel sufferers of post-traumatic stress disorder.

ON SUNDAY, August 22, Joe Biden turned away from Afghanistan to twist arms on behalf of his congressional agenda. That evening, he placed a call to Stephanie Murphy, a congresswoman from Florida. Murphy didn't like the direction of the Build Back Better bill. It cost too much, and it put her in a bad position. She hailed from one of the last congressional districts in the country that remained vigorously contested. Along with a small handful of other Democrats with such vulnerable seats, she wanted the White House to have a little sensitivity to her plight.

Biden wasn't in a sensitive mode. He was quite grumpy. "I've been dealing with these people all day," he told Murphy.

Biden wasn't clear what he meant when he referred to *these people*.

But Murphy quietly seethed at the term. She was emerging as a critic of the president's Afghanistan withdrawal—and for deeply personal reasons. At the age of six months, her family emigrated from Vietnam. When the United States withdrew in 1975, her family was left behind, even though they had served as loyal allies of the Americans. Her mom had worked on an air base; her dad served in the South Vietnamese government. They felt abandoned.

As Murphy watched the throngs at HKIA she couldn't help but think of her own origin story, her own family. And after the unintentionally inflammatory start to the call, Biden realized that he was treading on sensitive ground.

"When did your family leave Vietnam?" he asked.

"Nineteen seventy-nine," she told him. Because she was fuming, and worried that she might say something disrespectful, she left it at that.

The president was happy to pivot to the real reason for his call. He wanted to pass his legislative agenda. And he told Murphy that the polling showed the immense popularity of the provisions contained in the two bills.

But Murphy knew that he didn't have the votes. Kyrsten Sinema was one of her closest friends, and Murphy knew that she would never accept the $3.5 trillion price tag of Build Back Better. And as the cochair of the Blue Dog caucus, Murphy knew the mind of the moderates in the House.

What's more, Sinema and the moderates had made a pledge to the Republicans who supported the infrastructure bill. They assured them that there would be a pause between the passage of the two pieces of legislation. Republicans didn't want to be seen as accomplices of a grand progressive plan to remake American life. They needed a little plausible deniability about their role in passing the Biden agenda.

"We must be as bold as the votes will bear," she told him. She wanted Biden to know that he wasn't on the path to victory unless he scaled back the legislation. Her warning triggered the president.

"If you're not with me, you're the opposition," he told her.

Murphy couldn't believe that the call was sliding into rancor.

"Sir, I'm not the opposition," she pleaded. "I'm trying to help you achieve your agenda."

"You are the opposition."

"I think we're going to just have to live with a difference of opinion then. Have a good evening."

With that, Biden was left alone on the line.

The call was supposed to be the beginning of a charm offensive. Biden was going to call a slew of wavering moderates in the House. But his aides decided to postpone that initiative, waiting for a moment when he was in a better frame of mind.

23

Lily Pads

THE BIDEN administration hadn't ever intended to conduct a full-blown humanitarian evacuation of Afghanistan, and it certainly hadn't planned for one. It anticipated an orderly departure, unfolding over months. In the worst scenario that the administration pondered, it planned on transporting between fifteen thousand and forty thousand people from Kabul.

What changed were the images from the airport. Refugees plunging from the sky had the rare effect of unifying Washington in denouncing the inadequacy of the evacuation. Suddenly, Republicans were shaming the administration for not airlifting refugees. The denunciations were humiliating and politically catastrophic, but perversely liberating. Under this cloud of outrage, the administration could afford to be more generous without fear of being accused of opening the borders to strangers.

After Kabul fell to the Taliban, the president told the Situation Room that he wanted to immediately revise policy. He wanted all the planes flying thousands of troops into Hamid Karzai International Airport to leave filled with evacuees. Pilots should, of course, pile American citizens and Afghans with visas into those planes. But there was a category of evacuees that he now especially wanted to help, what the government called Afghans at risk. These were the newspaper reporters, schoolteachers, filmmakers, and lawyers, and the members of a girls' robotics team who didn't have paperwork but did have every reason to fear for their well-being in a Taliban-controlled country. The president said that he didn't want any excess capacity on the outgoing flights.

This was a very different sort of mission. The State Department hadn't vetted the Afghans at risk. It didn't know if they were genuinely endangered or simply strivers looking for a better life; it didn't know if they were petty criminals or university professors. But if they were in the right place at the right time, they were herded up the ramp of C-17s.

With the shift in policy, Milley asked aides to print out the copy of Emma Lazarus's poem about huddled masses yearning to breathe free, so that he could tape it into his notebook.

In anticipation of an evacuation, the United States had built housing at Camp As Sayliyah, a US Army base in the suburbs of Doha, Qatar. It had the capacity to hold eight thousand Afghans, housing them as the Department of Homeland Security collected their biometric data and began to vet them for immigration. Within twenty-four hours, however, it was clear that the United States would hustle far more than eight thousand Afghans to Qatar.

As the numbers swelled, the United States set up dormitories and tents at Al Udeid Air Base, a bus ride away from As Sayliyah. Nearly fifteen thousand Afghans took up residence there, but their quarters were poorly planned. There weren't nearly enough toilets or showers. Procuring lunch meant standing for three or four hours in a line. Evacuees were crammed into tight spaces in the middle of the desert, in the thick of summer, without air-conditioning. Single men slept in cots opposite married women, a transgression of every customary standard of traditional Afghan society.

The Qataris didn't have the best reputation for how they treated foreign labor imported to their country. But they were also determined to use the crisis to burnish their reputation. To solve the humanitarian catastrophe on the American bases, the Qataris erected a small city of air-conditioned wedding tents and began to cater meals for the refugees. Every other day in late

August, Secretary Austin called the Qatari minister of defense to check in, mainly just to profusely thank him again for his generosity.

From the moment that Biden changed policy, the administration knew that the number of evacuees would quickly exceed Qatar's capacity. It needed to erect a network of camps. What it created was something like the hub-and-spoke system used by commercial airlines. Refugees would fly into Al Udeid and then would be redirected to bases across Europe, what the administration termed "lily pads."

Erecting this network required a massive amount of quick diplomacy, not all of which succeeded. Tony Blinken spent forty-eight hours pressing the Kuwaitis to house evacuees but couldn't land a deal. European allies, like Germany and Spain, wanted to lend a hand, but they didn't want to permanently take refugees, fearing that such generosity would ignite a populist backlash. State Department lawyers were dispatched to craft agreements that provided legal assurance that the Afghans would stay for fifteen days and would be flown to the US. Within a week, the State Department had secured the use of ten bases across Europe and the Middle East.

Just as the Biden administration began to marvel at its improvised creation—and just as refugees were beginning to flow from the lily pads to a welcome center at Dulles International Airport, outside Washington— four Afghan evacuees fell victim to measles. All the refugees in Qatar and Europe needed vaccinations, and the CDC instructed that it would take twenty-one days for immunity to take hold. To keep disease from potentially flying into the United States, the State Department needed to call around the world, asking if Afghans could stay on bases for three extra weeks.

In the end, the US government housed sixty thousand Afghans in facilities, many of which didn't exist before the fall of Kabul. It flew 387 sorties from HKIA. At the height of the operation, an aircraft took off every forty-five minutes. It was a terrible failure of planning that necessitated a mad scramble—a mad scramble that was an impressive display of creative determination.

———

EVEN AS THE ADMINISTRATION pulled off this improvised feat of logistics, an impression took hold, stoked by the emotions of the moment, that it was reacting slowly and ham-fistedly. What stung is that the toughest criticism emerged not from the trolls in conservative media but from the columnists and venerable reporters that Biden's inner circle respected and tended to heed. Early in the crisis, the *New York Times*'s veteran national security correspondent David Sanger wrote, "After seven months in which his administration seemed to exude much-needed competence—getting more than 70 percent of the country's adults vaccinated, engineering surging job growth and making progress toward a bipartisan infrastructure bill—everything about America's last days in Afghanistan shattered the imagery."

In the thick of the crisis, Biden didn't have time to voraciously consume the news, but he was well aware of the tough coverage. "We're getting killed," he would admit. It frustrated him to no end.

But it was also striking, however, how little it changed his mind. In the caricature version of Joe Biden that persisted for decades, he was barometrically sensitive to shifts in opinion, especially when it emerged from columnists in the pages of the *Post* or *Times*. But the criticism of the withdrawal caused him to stubbornly defend his own logic. Through the whole last decade of the Afghan war, he had detested the conventional wisdom of the foreign policy elites. They were willing to stay forever, no matter the cost. After defying their delusional predictions of progress for so long, he wasn't going to back down now. In fact, everything he witnessed from his seat in the Situation Room confirmed his faith in exiting a war without hope.

So much of the commentary just felt overheated to him. He wondered aloud to an aide, "Either the press is losing its mind, or I am."

24

The Red Dot

O N AUGUST 24, Hillary Clinton placed a call to the emir of Qatar—a last-ditch appeal on behalf of the women on her list. Her aides had hatched a revised plan. The White Scarves would furtively gather at the Serena Hotel, not far from the airport but away from the scrum, and board buses that would collectively carry them through the airport gates. To execute this plan, the buses would need to pass through checkpoints that the Taliban had erected throughout the city. She needed the help of the emir, because the Qataris had the trust of the Taliban. Unlike any other foreign government in Kabul, Qatari officials could move through the city with relative ease.

The emir agreed that representatives from his embassy in Kabul would accompany buses carrying the White Scarves to the airport, running a series of motorcades that would help ease their way through the Taliban checkpoints.

Aides in Washington and New York tracked the buses using GPS, red dots on a map slowly meandering through the streets of Kabul. For hours, they sat and started at a single stationary object. They knew one bus carried a pregnant woman—and according to reports from the bus, she felt sharp pains in her belly. When the Taliban boarded the bus to check documents, the woman couldn't stand the sense of danger. Despite the presence of the Qatari, she clamored to leave the bus. She said that she didn't want to risk losing her baby. The woman and her husband disembarked and disappeared into the crowd.

The Clinton aides knew all of this as it unfolded. But more than forty-eight hours after the buses left the Serena Hotel, they also watched the red dots cross into Hamid Karzai International Airport.

ONCE THE BUSES entered the airport, planes were needed to carry the women away. Clinton called an aide to Ukraine's president, Volodymyr Zelensky, asking if she could board refugees on a military transport plane destined for Kyiv. Her efforts earned her a reprimand. "What are you doing calling the Ukrainian government?" Jake Sullivan asked her. "Well," she responded, "I wouldn't have to call, if you guys would."

Although Clinton assured him that she would coordinate with the administration, she had already made contact with heads of state across the globe. She knew that her conversation with Canadian prime minister Justin Trudeau was a bit impetuous. He had every reason to turn down her request to house the White Scarves, because she wasn't advocating on behalf of the US government. By the time he hung up the phone, however, he volunteered to accept five thousand of her refugees.

But before the White Scarves could be resettled in Canada, they needed temporary housing in another country while they waited for the processing of their paperwork. Clinton knew the prime minister of Albania, Edi Rama. Her husband had achieved mythical status in his country, after the bombing campaign he initiated in 1999 to protect ethnic Albanians, just over the border in Kosovo. Rama liked to joke about a generation of children in his country born with the first name Bill Clinton. She told him that her organizations would vet the women and would pay for them to stay in Albania, no matter how long. "I couldn't possibly turn you down," Rama replied,

Like so much in the chaos of Taliban-controlled Kabul, it worked until it didn't. Buses filled with White Scarves wound their way to the airport, where they boarded charter flights that carried them to a refueling stop in the Republic of Georgia—where Clinton had negotiated a layover agreement—and on to Albania.

But then suddenly, the Taliban boarded a bus and began demanding that the Albania-bound women unveil so that their faces could more thoroughly be checked against their passport photos. For the first time, the Taliban said that the women couldn't leave without an Albanian visa—but that document had never been issued to them.

A member of the staff of Vital Voices, one of the NGOs that Clinton had cofounded, was already in Tirana, the Albanian capital, to begin securing housing for the White Scarves. She went to the foreign ministry and spent the night creating an electronic visa that could be sent to the White Scarves on their phones. The Albanians felt that a QR code would make the email look more official. Since there was a bag of potato chips sitting around, they took a photo of the QR code on the side of the packaging and appended it to the improvised visa.

When the White Scarves showed the Taliban the visa on their phones, it was good enough. The women on the bus escaped to Albania—and so did more than one thousand other Afghan women and their families who Hillary Clinton and her groups managed to rescue.

25

The Bitter End

August 26

That morning, Jen Psaki made her way to the Situation Room. Along with White House communications director Kate Bedingfield, she had become a regular presence there. It was more efficient to have Psaki and Bedingfield directly absorb information for themselves, rather than wait for Jake Sullivan and his deputies to debrief.

As she entered the room, she stopped to chat with Jon Finer, the deputy national security adviser.

"The press is starting to understand that the ISIS-K threat is real," she told him.

He stopped her before she went further. "I think we're getting reports of an attack."

Every intelligence official watching Afghanistan was obsessed with the possibility of an attack by ISIS-Khorasan or ISIS-K, the Afghan offshoot of the Islamic State group, which imagined creating a new emirate in central Asia. As the Taliban stormed across Afghanistan, they unlocked a prison on Bagram Airfield base, freeing hardened adherents of ISIS-K. These were veterans of the Taliban who had broken with the group, on the grounds that it had gone soft and needed to be replaced by an even more militant Islamist vanguard. The intelligence community was sorting through a roaring

river of unmistakable warnings about an imminent attack, exquisitely detailed in everything but the actual specifics of the plans.

Finer and Psaki slipped into their seats as Sullivan got the meeting un-
derway. As they watched, they kept noticing General Frank McKenzie on
the screen in Tampa at Centcom headquarters. He kept receiving notes
from aides and then muted himself as he conversed out of earshot.

When he unmuted, he told the group of an attack outside the perimeter
of the airport. Fortunately, he said there weren't any reports of US casualties. But that was just the foggy aftermath of an explosion, when intelligence is at its most imprecise. Everyone wanted to believe that the US had
escaped unscathed, but everyone had too much experience to believe that.
McKenzie kept muting and then returning with updates as he confirmed
the room's suspicions of American deaths.

Biden hung his head and quietly absorbed the reports. As the nature of
the catastrophe became clearer, he urged his generals to exact retribution.
"You have all the authority you need," he told them.

THE EXPLOSION RATTLED John Bass's office, and then the whole building went quiet. It was not hard for him to imagine what had happened.
Despite the warnings about ISIS-K, he and his colleagues kept the gates to
the airport open to an ally. The British had been screening their evacuees at
the Baron Hotel, just down the road. They had a group moving through a
Taliban checkpoint, but American troops needed to clear a path through
the crowd at the Abbey Gate. As the soldiers frisked a group hoping to enter
the airport, a suicide bomber detonated himself. Thirteen Americans perished; so did nearly two hundred Afghans.

Bass and his military counterparts had spent long portions of their careers working amid violence. They wore the armor of experience. And they
felt the tyranny of the clock. Mourning would distract from the task at hand.
Afghan employees of the embassy were scheduled to arrive soon. Bass sti-

fled his anger, stuffed his sadness deep inside, and immediately turned to the logistical question, *We can't use Abbey Gate any longer, so how are we going to compensate for its absence?*

THE BODIES of the dead troops were flown to Dover Air Force Base for a ritual known as the dignified transfer: flag-draped caskets are marched down the gangway of a transport plane and then driven to the base's mortuary and prepared for burial.

So much about the withdrawal in Afghanistan had slipped beyond Joe Biden's control. But grieving was his expertise. If there was one thing that everyone agreed Biden did more adroitly than any other public official, it was comforting survivors. The Irish journalist Fintan O'Toole labeled him "the Designated Mourner."

Accompanied by Mark Milley, Tony Blinken, Lloyd Austin, and his wife, Jill, Biden arrived clad in black. They made their way to a private room, where grieving families gathered. Even before Biden began to offer condolences, he knew he would be standing face to face with raw anger. A father had already turned his back on Lloyd Austin and angrily shouted at Milley, who held up his hands in the posture of surrender.

When Biden entered, he shook the hand of Mark Schmitz of Missouri, who lost his twenty-year-old son, Jared. In his sorrow, Schmitz couldn't decide whether he wanted to sit in the presence of the president. According to a report in *The Washington Post*, the night before, he had told a military officer that he didn't want to speak to the man he blamed for his son's death. In the morning, he changed his mind.

Schmitz couldn't help but cast spiteful glares in Biden's direction. When Biden approached, he held out a photo of Jared. "Don't you ever forget that name. Don't you ever forget that face. Don't you ever forget the names of the other twelve. And take some time to learn their stories.'"

"I do know those stories," Biden retorted.

After the dignified transfer, the families piled onto a bus. A sister of one of the dead screamed across the tarmac in Biden's direction. "I hope you burn in hell. That was my brother."

Of all the moments in August, this was the one that caused the president to second-guess himself. It was the one time that he kept reanalyzing his actions. He asked Jen Psaki, "Did I do something wrong? Maybe I should have handled that differently." It was a thought that he repeated through the day.

As Biden left, Milley saw the pain on the president's face. He tried to lift him up. "You made a decision that had to be made. War is a brutal, vicious undertaking. We're moving forward to the next step."

THAT AFTERNOON, Biden returned to the Situation Room. There was pressure, from the Hill and from reporters, to push back the August 31 deadline. But everyone in the room knew the intelligence assessments about ISIS-K. If the US stayed, it risked the arrival of more caskets at Dover.

As Biden discussed the state of the evacuation, he received a note, which he passed along to Milley, who chuckled. The general read the note to the room: "If you want to catch the five thirty mass, you have to leave now." He turned to the president. "My mother always said it's okay to miss mass, if you're doing something important. And I would argue that this is important." He paused, realizing that the president might need a moment after his bruising day and his bruising month. "This is probably also a time when we need prayers."

Biden gathered himself to leave. As he stood from his chair, he told the group, "I will be praying for all of you."

August 29–30

Leaving was arguably the most dangerous part of the mission. All along, military planners had expressed agita about the United States' final hours in Afghanistan. As the American presence was quickly reduced to its final planeloads of personnel, the airport would become uniquely vulnerable. There would no longer be marines stationed along the perimeter. Scant helicopters to provide cover.

To protect against the prospect of a last-minute attack, the military kept details of the departure under the tightest of wraps. Departure would occur in the middle of the night, shrouded by darkness.

But a right-wing pundit had tweeted the hour of scheduled departure, somehow naming the precise details. The fact that the timing had been announced on social media caused the Pentagon to feel as if operational security was compromised, and it changed its plans. The tweet forced a slightly earlier departure than intended.

On the evening of the twenty-ninth, at seven thirty, John Bass was cleaning out his office and preparing to leave. An alarm sounded and he rushed to take cover. A rocket flew over the airport from the west, and a second crashed into the compound but without inflicting damage.

Bass, ever the stoic, turned to a colleague. "Well, that's about the only thing that hasn't happened so far. So, of course, that's going to happen before we go." He was genuinely worried, however, that the rockets weren't a parting gift, but a prelude to an attack.

Despite that fear, Bass kept imploring General Donahue to delay departure a bit longer. He wanted his military colleagues to remain at the outer access points, since there were reports of American citizens making their way to them.

Donahue was willing to give Bass a few extra hours. And at 3:00 a.m., sixty more American passport holders arrived at the airport. Then, as if anticipating a final burst of American generosity, the Taliban opened their checkpoints. A flood of Afghans rushed toward the airport. Bass sent his most experienced consular officers to stand at the edge of the concertina wire, next to the paratroopers, scanning for passports, green cards, visas, any official-looking documents.

A consular officer caught a glimpse of an Afghan woman in her twenties waving a printout showing that she had just won a slot in a program called the Diversity Visa Program. "Wow. You won the lottery twice," he told her. "You're the visa lottery winner and you've made it here in time." She was one of the final evacuees admitted into the airport.

The remaining State Department officials in Kabul posed for a photo and then walked up the ramp of a C-17. About four hundred marines followed.

As Bass prepared for takeoff, he thought about two numbers. In total, the United States had evacuated 124,000 people from Hamid Karzai International Airport, which the White House liked to tout as the most successful airlift in history. Staring into the darkness, Bass also thought about the number of Afghans he had failed to get out. He thought about the friends whom he couldn't manage to extricate. He thought about the last time he flew out of Kabul, eighteen months earlier, and how he had harbored a sense of optimism for the country then. A hopefulness that now felt as remote as the Hindu Kush.

LLOYD AUSTIN and Mark Milley watched General Donahue board a C-17, the impending departure of the last American boots on the ground. They followed along on screens in the secretary of defense's commander center in the basement of the Pentagon. A drone streamed video in real time, filtered through the hazy green of a night vision lens. A few hours earlier, the Pentagon learned about the rocket attacks on the airport. Austin and Milley were nervous that it might be reprised, with more devastating effect.

The last five C-17s sat on the runway—carrying "chalk," as the military refers to the cargo of troops. An officer in the command center narrated the procession on the runway for them. "Chalk one loaded . . . chalk two taxiing." With the last of the planes taking off, he bellowed, "Chalk five rolling."

Milley felt a rising sadness and anger. While he was proud of the professionalism of the forces, he mourned the deaths of the thirteen troops and loss of the war. He couldn't stand the way the country was talking about the evacuation. There were so many ad hominem attacks launched by the president's political opponents. He felt embarrassed for the nation by the shouting and the yelling, and worried for its future.

As the planes flew away to safety, there was no applause, no hand shaking. A murmur returned to the room. Austin and Milley watched the great military project of their generation—a war that cost the lives of comrades, that took them away from their families—end without remark. They stood without ceremony and returned to their offices.

Across the river, Biden sat in the Oval with Sullivan and Blinken, working through his edits for a speech he would deliver the next day, commemorating the end of the war. One of Sullivan's aides passed him a note, which he read to the group. "At 3:20 ET, Chalk one in the air." A few minutes later, the aide returned with an update. The planes were safely away.

Biden asked Blinken and Sullivan to join him in the private dining room, next to the Oval Office. He wanted to call Austin to thank him. The secretary of defense hadn't agreed with the decision to leave Afghanistan, but he implemented the withdrawal plans in the spirit of a good soldier.

The war was now finally and officially over. Each of them looked exhausted. Sullivan hadn't slept for more than three hours over the course of the evacuation. Biden didn't talk about his own sleep patterns, but his aides sensed that he hadn't rested much better. Before returning to the Oval, they spent a moment together, lingering in the melancholy.

PART FOUR

THE BOG

September–December 2021

26

Mr. Zelensky Comes
to Washington

September 1

In his dispirited mindset, the president needed to take an overdue meeting with a head of state.

For two years, Volodymyr Zelensky had desperately craved this moment: an opportunity to sit in a plush chair across from the American leader, in the White House, with cameras clicking. It was evidence that Ukraine's primary benefactor, its most powerful protector against the looming Russian menace, still had its back.

During the Donald Trump presidency, Zelensky kept trying to wrangle this invitation. Trump, of course, wouldn't extend him that courtesy. Or rather, he offered Zelensky an invitation on a corrupt condition: Zelensky would have to investigate the dodgy Ukrainian business dealings of Joe Biden's son Hunter.

To Zelensky's credit, he never acceded to Trump's request. But his lingering resentments from the episode, which embroiled the first year of his unlikely presidency, radiated in strange directions. At least, subconsciously, he seemed to blame the head of the Biden family for the humiliation he suffered, for the political awkwardness he endured.

Even before he arrived in Washington, he told aides that he regarded Biden as weak. Rather than cultivating a relationship with the new American president, he kept poking him. Back in May, to restore a fractured relationship with Germany, the Biden administration had lifted Trump-era sanctions against the company building Nord Stream 2, a pipeline bringing Russian natural gas to Germany.

Zelensky felt as if Biden had undermined the Ukrainian economy—and crushed Ukraine's security. By allowing Germany to complete Nord Stream 2, Biden was risking Ukraine's historic role in the natural gas business. For decades, Russian gas had traversed pipelines that ran through Ukraine, which allowed Ukraine's government to collect a hefty transit fee.

To obstruct the Biden administration's decision, Zelensky looked for allies wherever he could find them. He made common cause with Ted Cruz, which the White House interpreted as a sign of Zelensky's unseriousness. Cruz vowed to use his senatorial prerogative to single-handedly block the confirmation of Biden State Department appointees. Whether he understood this or not, Zelensky was complicit with this stunt. It reeked of what the administration considered amateurism.

To be fair, Biden didn't think much of his Ukraine counterpart, either. It was a strange fact: Biden had been deeply involved in Ukrainian politics longer than Zelensky. Barack Obama had dispatched him to Kyiv, after the revolution of 2014. He knew the nation's political class and considered some of its members his friends. The very fact that Zelensky was an outsider might have been the source of his political appeal, but it seemed to alienate him from Biden. Zelensky was a slapstick comedian, when it was backslapping pols who tended to command Biden's instant respect, since he could see himself in them.

As Zelensky sat down with Biden in the Oval Office, the gravelly-voiced actor seemed oblivious to Biden's doubts. He also seemed almost willfully unaware of Biden's moral code. Where Biden tended to expect Zelensky to open with expressions of gratitude for American support, Zelensky crammed his conversations with a long list of demands, as if he might not ever again get a chance to talk to an American president. It seemed as if he didn't have time for niceties, since he skipped right past them.

Zelensky cut straight to it: he needed to join NATO.

The age difference—Biden is more than thirty years older—felt screamingly apparent. Biden tried his best to pass along some wisdom that might temper the younger man's zeal. Whatever the merits of Ukraine's case for joining the alliance, most of western Europe didn't support it. Ukraine didn't have the votes, so this wasn't the moment to force the issue.

Biden's tepid response agitated Zelensky. And in his agitated state, Zelensky's frustration occluded his capacity for logic. After begging to join NATO, he began to lecture that the organization is, in fact, a historic relic, with waning significance. He told Biden that France and Germany were going to exit NATO.

It was an absurd analysis—and a blatant contradiction. And it pissed Biden off.

Even Zelensky's most ardent sympathizers in the administration agreed that he had bombed. And it suggested more difficult conversations to come, although neither man yet had an inkling of how difficult.

27

Manchinema

Two days after John Bass and Chris Donahue boarded the last flights out of Kabul, the president woke up to the domestic reverberations of the disastrous withdrawal. On September 2, Joe Manchin wrote an op-ed in *The Wall Street Journal* that suggested it was time for Biden to shelve his pursuit of Build Back Better. Manchin recommended what he called a "strategic pause."

This statement was what linguists call a performative. By stating the need for delaying the legislation, he was making it so. His vote was the one that the White House felt least sure about receiving.

What did Joe Manchin want? The answer was slippery. He clearly didn't like the size of the Build Back Better proposal, which now totaled $3.5 trillion. There was evidence of rising inflation, and Manchin didn't want a fresh injection of government spending compounding the problem. But was he bargaining in good faith to create a bill that allayed his substantive concerns? Or was he preparing to grind Biden down with an endless negotiation on behalf of his friends in the fossil fuel industry back in West Virginia?

The thing about Manchin is that he is like a Faulkner novel, a stream of consciousness monologue that could be painfully difficult to read, since the point of view kept shifting. But there was one consistent sentiment that he mouthed in nearly every meeting and that reassured Ron Klain. Even as he expressed his doubts, he kept telling Biden, "Don't worry, Mr. President, we're going to get this done." So instead of constantly reinterpreting Manchin, the White House assumed that most of his outbursts were just noise, which could be largely ignored.

IT WOULD have been easier if Biden were dealing with just Manchin, but he wasn't. He needed to bring Kyrsten Sinema along, and dealing with both of them was a maddening exercise. It was as if they were strategically out of sync. They kept pushing in opposite directions. Sinema didn't want to raise taxes but was less skittish about spending money; Manchin was happy to raise taxes but didn't want to spend too much. Pleasing one of the holdouts made it harder to cut a deal with the other.

On September 22, Biden decided to confront the problem head on. Rather than conduct separate negotiations with Manchin and Kyrsten Sinema and six centrist House Democrats, he pulled them together for a meeting in the Oval Office.

When senators entered the Oval Office to negotiate with Biden, they were surprised by his collegiality. He treated them as his equal. It was as if he were still Joe Biden (D-Del.), a legislative dealmaker, not a president imposing his will on them. Meetings with legislators were sometimes scheduled for two-and-a-half-hour blocks. And they were endless. Sinema came to the White House ten times over the summer and early fall. He was solicitous and patient, trying to edge them to consensus, for the most part.

But Biden found it hard to negotiate with the centrists assembled in the room. Their visions for how the bill should be tempered were divergent. By assembling them together, he was hoping to force them to harmonize their disparate opinions.

"What are the things that you hope to have in this bill?" he asked.

It was a question that ignited a free-for-all. Everyone supported spending on climate; some pushed for expanded childcare, while others considered housing to be most important. But the cacophony is what Biden intended.

"Each of you are saying 'do fewer things and do them bigger,' but you're all saying different things," he said. "And if you add up all your different things, it's actually a pretty big number. If you add all this up, it's well over $2 trillion. Is there anyone who has a ceiling for what they would be willing to accept?"

The room went silent. Biden felt like the teacher waiting for his class to answer a question. After a beat of waiting, he decided to call on a student.

He turned to Kyrsten Sinema. Over the weeks, she and Biden had plenty of conversations on the phone.

"Your real number is 1.1 trillion," he told the group.

The room turned to Sinema and watched her stare at the president. Another moment of painful silence.

"That number was meant to be private," she said. "And now you've just made it public. If that number gets out, I'll know it's one of you."

Biden began to haltingly apologize. "I didn't know it was a secret."

As he tried to make amends, Sinema stood up. "Well, it sounds like if I'm not willing to go up to an infinite number, then I should just leave the room."

And for a brief moment, the president seemed torn over whether to argue with Sinema or to placate her. But Sinema couldn't contain herself. She snapped, "You asked if anyone has a cap. Of course I have a cap. So I should just leave."

"No, no, no, no," Biden told her. "You shouldn't leave the room."

She returned to her seat, but the awkwardness lingered both in the meeting and beyond. When Biden aides tried to call Sinema, she simply didn't answer. At the moment the White House needed to nail down her support, she went AWOL. They desperately wanted a deal but had no choice but to hope that her anger would eventually subside.

WITH EACH passing day, Nancy Pelosi found herself growing more agitated that chances for legislative victories were slipping away. In August, she cut a deal with the moderates in her caucus. They wanted her to guarantee a vote on the infrastructure bill, and she promised them one by September 27. But that deadline slipped because she couldn't deliver enough votes.

The problem was that the progressives in her flock didn't trust the moderates, not the ones in the House, not Manchin or Sinema. They worried that if the moderates passed their beloved infrastructure bill, the progressives would be deprived of their primary bargaining chip. The moderates might grudgingly support the progressives' grand plans to expand the safety net, but would seek to edit them down to a fraction of the proposed size— or perhaps kill them altogether.

Pelosi didn't especially care for the infrastructure bill, at least not as a standalone piece of legislation. But her mission was to keep the wins coming, and she had a promise to her moderates to keep. Her best hope was to press to make it happen all at once, if she could, advancing both bills. If she needed to be the one to pressure Manchin into compliance, well, she would play that role. She'd placed a call to him, left a message to have him call, and then went to glad-hand at a sacred ritual.

SINCE 1909, the annual congressional baseball game has been legislative warfare by other means. The event sounds quaint, but it isn't. It takes place at the major league ballpark, not much more than a mile south of the Capitol, where the Washington Nationals play. Each party fields a competent team in uniforms worthy of professionals.

Among the mascots for the Washington Nationals are dead presidents, caricatures of George Washington, Thomas Jefferson, and Abe Lincoln. In the middle of the inning, they asked the crowd to get to its feet. And from behind home plate, they led Joe Biden out onto the field, a surprise visit from a leader who desperately needed the goodwill of the backbenchers on the field and in the dugout. The president loved it. He trotted onto the field in a frenzy of schmoozing, taking selfies, signing baseballs, handing out ice-cream bars emblazoned with the presidential seal.

Nancy Pelosi trailed the president as he circled the ballpark, then perched herself in the stands. As she watched Biden enjoy himself with abandon, her phone rang. It was Joe Manchin. Despite the noise of the crowd—and the fact there were cameras all around her—she went to work.

"We have got to get this done, Joe."

Manchin wasn't having it. "I don't believe in entitlements," he told her.

Pelosi started to grow aggravated, but this wasn't the time or place for either having a philosophical debate about the role of government or brokering a deal. She was shouting to make herself heard. To all the world, it looked as if she were chewing out whoever was on the other side of the conversation.

"I'm having a hard time hearing you," she said. "Why don't you write some of this down. I want to make sure that I have this right. Then text it to me."

A text arrived, a document that she had never seen before. She struggled to make sense of it. In a memo dated July 28, Manchin outlined the spending that he'd accept in a final reconciliation bill. He said that he could accept $1.5 trillion—and, with specificity, described the tax hikes he favored and the clean energy programs he preferred. What surprised Pelosi, shocked her, really, was that Manchin affixed his signature to the bottom of the document—and Chuck Schumer had signed it, too.

In her state of shock and anger, she phoned Schumer. "What's this? He just sent me this thing and it kinda has your name on it."

Schumer fumbled for an answer. "That was my acknowledging that I saw what he was doing."

But Pelosi had every reason to be furious. The House had already passed a budget resolution authorizing $3.5 trillion in spending. And Pelosi was driving House committees to furiously finish the donkey work required to create a fully realized bill. But Schumer knew that all that work was futile, and he hadn't bothered telling her. They were producing language for a bill that Joe Manchin was never going to support.

Why hadn't he bothered telling Pelosi about that? The best Schumer could muster was that his agreement with Manchin wasn't binding.

In truth, Schumer was engaged in the very same process as Pelosi. He just wanted to press forward. When Manchin arrived in his office with the "contract," Schumer agreed to sign it because it was the path of least resistance. Schumer needed Manchin's support for a procedural vote advancing Build Back Better—and this contract was the condition of his support. If Manchin voted against the procedural vote, the whole bill would be stalled, if not effectively dead. So rather than attempting to negotiate with Manchin, he did what it took to move forward, even if it left him with a future mess. He could deal with the mess when the moment arrived. In the meantime, he just signed the damn thing. But he also handwrote an addendum onto the document that supplied him with cover. It read, "Will try to dissuade Joe on many of these."

28

Mark Milley's Map

IN EARLY October, young intelligence officers would emerge from the basement of the Pentagon and assemble around the round table in Mark Milley's office. They would splay a map of Ukraine across it—and each time they returned, the map was filled with new markings, red lines, arrows, and circles.

Back in April, five months earlier, military intelligence had watched the Russians amass troops on the Ukrainian border. They saw how a Russian military exercise could provide the pretext for assembling an invading army. But the Russians ultimately sent their troops back to their bases, after European leaders called Putin and voiced their concerns. That was, in retrospect, a trial—a test of how the West might respond to a large Russian assemblage on the fringe of Ukraine.

As Milley looked at the map—and combed through the intelligence—it was clear that this time was different. The intelligence officers had an intercepted copy of Russian war plans—and they could sketch those plans out on the map, with stunning clarity. And it wasn't just a theoretical worry; they could see how the plan was materializing on the ground. The Russian military was starting to build field hospitals and line up tanks and helicopters. If this was just an exercise, why were they bringing such large supplies of plasma to the border?

Milley showed the map to Lloyd Austin, and he agreed. They needed to brief the president on the Russian war plans that his intelligence officers had pieced together. For Milley, who loved reading military history, it was hard to fathom that he was about to warn the president that the Russians were months away from launching the largest land war in Europe since 1945.

On a Sunday in mid-October, Milley took his map to the Oval Office and stood it on an easel. There was a good-size audience assembled for the presentation—not just the president, but the vice president, the secretary of state, the secretary of defense, the national security adviser, the director of national intelligence, and the director of the Central Intelligence Agency.

Milley began with what sounded like an encyclopedia entry on Ukraine. He used his map to explain the country's topography and talked about its weather. Then he began to give a tour of the periphery of the country—and pointed to the forward positions, where the Russians had moved troops. At each point, he described the composition of the Russian units and described their capabilities.

When Milley began to gather a rhythm, with his Boston accent, he didn't bellow, but he burned with a frightening intensity, like a hockey player who had removed his gloves but not yet thrown a punch. He began to show how the troops on the border would eventually descend on Kyiv. Troops would flow down from the north and wrap themselves around the city, leaving it isolated.

"The Russians estimate that they can take Kyiv in seventy-two hours," he told the group.

At the same time, the Russians would launch an amphibious assault on Odesa from the Black Sea.

On another axis, troops would march westward from the swaths of Donetsk and Luhansk that the Russians already occupied. According to the intercepted intelligence, the Russians believed that it would take six weeks for these troops to cross the Dnipro River. They would briefly rest there, before sweeping toward the Polish border, stopping at a red line that Milley had drawn on the map. The Russians were going to conquer nearly the whole of Ukraine, but they weren't going to cross the Carpathian Mountains. They would leave a small rump of territory that could remain as Ukraine. Historically, that terrain had never actually belonged to the Russian empire. Before World War I, it was an Austro-Hungarian possession. By stopping at the red line, the Russians would position themselves ominously close to NATO-protected territory, but not quite rubbing against it.

"They hope to reach the red line by May 8," Milley said. That was V-E Day, the anniversary of the date that the Allies vanquished the Nazis.

It was an immensely detailed presentation, with estimates of the number of tanks and the varieties of artillery that the Russian army would use.

Biden wanted to know, "Can you make that public?"

"It's probably not a good idea for me to stand behind the podium and do that," he said. "But Avril has the ability to declassify this," he said, shooting a glance in the direction of the director of national intelligence, Avril Haines.

"We need to do that," Biden told him.

"Okay, we can dumb this down and make it unclassified. That can inform the media."

That seemed to satisfy Biden, who paused. It was clear that the president was trying to absorb the magnitude of the presentation.

"What's at stake?" he wanted to know.

It seemed an obvious question. But Milley needed a beat to consider his answer.

"This is all about the end of the World War II rules-based order. Russia doesn't like it. Russia has never liked it. They can't stand that Ukraine wants to be part of NATO."

Biden soaked it in. "We can't let them win." But he also wanted to make it very clear that he wasn't prepared to bear any burden in pursuit of victory. "We need to avoid war with Russia, while imposing severe costs."

Milley tried to turn the president's dictum into a baseball metaphor.

"You mean we need to hit line drive singles right down the middle." Biden wanted him to focus hard on managing the risks. It was important to get weapons to Ukraine, but it was more important to avoid getting drawn into World War III.

He scribbled down the president's thoughts—and kept them tucked in a pocket in his notebook.

THE TIMING of Milley's presentation was serendipitous. Biden already had imminent plans to meet with Europe's most powerful leaders at the G20 in Rome a few days later, on October 30. Biden gathered his closest allies in a room in the conference center that hosted the event, so that he could present a sanitized version of the evidence of the impending Russian invasion—and to get their support for a devastating set of sanctions that he hoped might deter Putin.

"This is the real deal," Biden told the group.

As he made his case, nobody questioned the credibility of his assessment. But it wasn't hard to sense their skepticism. Even though nearly twenty years had passed since the Iraq War, the American intelligence agencies still suffered from the taint of that debacle. And perhaps that skepticism colored the tepid response in the room.

His toughest audience was his oldest friend in the room. The German chancellor, Angela Merkel, had a long, complicated relationship with Vladimir Putin. Because she speaks Russian, Putin latched on to her. Brutishly intimidating her at times and attempting to charm her at others, Putin once exclaimed, "I trust her. She's a very open person."

But the decision for how her government would handle Russia was not really hers to make. Merkel was about to retire, and she brought her likely successor, Olaf Scholz, with her into the room.

To inflict serious pain on Russia, Biden needed the Germans to, at least, threaten to abandon the Nord Stream 2 pipeline, which was on the cusp of completion and would have the capacity to ship fifty-five billion cubic meters of natural gas each year. This was a big ask. Biden outsourced the job of pressing them to Jake Sullivan, who tag teamed with Boris Johnson.

But Merkel and Scholz were maddeningly evasive. They both kept saying, "We hear what you're saying. We have to stop this catastrophe from happening." But what did that even mean?

Sullivan believed the only hope of deterring Putin—and it was a thin one—required presenting him with specific instances of the severe economic consequences of invasion. But with the German hedging, that felt far away. Sullivan had tried to implore that it was time to rush to the battle stations, but other than the Brits, the allies were dawdling.

THE INTELLIGENCE about the Russian invasion was so stark that Sullivan decided there wasn't time to spare. Meeting with Blinken, Austin, and the rest of the national security hierarchy, the group agreed that the administration would dispatch CIA director Bill Burns to Moscow. It was time to let Putin know that the US knew that he was about to invade Ukraine. It might not be possible to dislodge him from his plans, but they needed to try.

Burns described his assignment as the "short straw." A small part of what made it unattractive was that he needed to fly into Moscow on November 2, at the beginning of the Russian winter. Approaching the city, his plane circled for hours, as storms prevented him from landing. His flight was diverted to Latvia, where he would spend two and a half hours sleeping in Riga, waiting for the weather to clear.

This was a climate that Burns knew well. For three years, he served as ambassador to Russia. More than any member of the administration, he was a close student of Putin and could even claim to have had a personal relationship with him. He understood the Russian leader's psyche—which he described as "cocky, cranky, aggrieved and insecure"—and had more experience delivering tough news to him than any other American.

The other reason he drew the short straw was his low profile. He traveled light. Compared with Tony Blinken or Lloyd Austin, his journeys abroad didn't require massive advance work—and his trips never attracted much attention, since his schedule wasn't public—at least in theory.

That's why he found himself taken aback by the presence of cameras at the first of his scheduled meetings, with Nikolai Patrushev, the head of the Kremlin's national security council. Patrushev was a cocky figure, a product of the Russian security service, part of his boss's longtime cabal. He relished the art of trolling and feats of guerilla diplomacy, like ambushing Burns with media. Burns, who had the demeanor of a family doctor, knew to smile and shake hands, as if the whole event had been stage-managed in advance.

But after the cameras disappeared, Burns felt as if he were the one who caught his counterpart off guard. Patrushev told Burns that he expected the meeting to cover the agenda for the next Biden-Putin summit. He seemed genuinely blindsided by the fact that Burns wanted to talk about Ukraine.

Burns expected Patrushev to deflect and dissemble in the face of the evidence. It seemed remarkable, therefore, that he didn't spend much time pushing back.

"We may still be catching up economically, but our military is modernized," Patrushev quipped, which struck Burns as a terrifying nondenial.

As Burns travelled across the city, he noted how strange Moscow seemed. The streets were devoid of pedestrians; traffic felt unseasonably light. He had arrived at the height of the country's fourth and worst wave of COVID.

To insulate himself from the virus, Putin had sequestered himself in his ornate Italianate palace on the Black Sea. Burns theorized that COVID was a bracing experience for Putin. In a time of mass death, the isolated autocrat began to ponder what the actuarial tables suggested about his own longevity.

As Putin lounged in his lonely splendor, he made his way through Russian history books. Throughout his life, he claimed to feel a strong sense of personal destiny. But with time on his hands, and with biographies of czars on his nightstand, he realized he hadn't really measured up, especially not to the truly great Russian leaders. What had he done to reverse Russia's imperial decline? There were no conquests to show for his decades in the job. Next to Peter the Great, his achievements looked paltry, at best.

Over decades, Burns had observed, sometimes with his own eyes, as officials questioned Putin—and how he listened to their skepticism with interest. But Burns knew that such conversations were now improbable, if not impossible. Even before COVID, Putin's inner circle had atrophied. Now, it barely existed, which meant that his delusions of grandeur were accepted as policy.

The culmination of Burns's visit to Moscow was a scheduled conversation with Putin himself. In truth, he could have just as easily spoken with Putin from the confines of his office in Langley, since Putin wasn't taking face-to-face meetings. When he finally had his scheduled appointment with the Russia leader, Burns was led to a room in the Kremlin with a telephone.

Burns's placid diplomatic style made him like an open window that sucked the hot air out of the room. He calmly walked through the intelligence of an impending invasion—and sketched out the severity of the sanctions that the West would impose, so that Putin could precisely account for the costs of his actions.

As Putin internalized Burns's message, he responded without reverting to his litany of historical grievances or pounding the table about the threat of NATO.

Rather than denying his intentions of invasion, it was as if Putin wanted to provide Burns with a glimpse of his own strategic thinking. He explained that conditions had never been more ripe for him to conquer Ukraine.

For starters, there was Volodymyr Zelensky. Putin said he was the feeble leader of a hopelessly divided polity. Putin did not deign to describe Ukraine as a nation, since it wasn't in his view. He said that he would be able to score a quick military victory, at a low cost.

In the past, Putin had resisted the temptation to invade Ukraine, because he worried about the European reaction. But he figured that he didn't have much to worry about on the Continent. Angela Merkel had vacated the scene, replaced by a relative novice. He said that recent elections in France exposed Emmanuel Macron's political fragility. And even though the West blustered about the strength of sanctions, Putin bragged that he'd built his economy to withstand the blow. He had stockpiled an impressive reserve of foreign currency.

Putin hadn't quite delivered a point-blank confirmation of the intelligence, but he talked as if the decision to invade were a fait accompli. Burns felt that it was his mission to barrage Putin with the questions that his advisers lacked the courage to ask: How is this going to end? How are you going to occupy a country with forty million people who are bound to resist? "I know we live in a glass house," Burns told him, "but we know how an occupation can start off successfully and then end badly." But this was a Socratic exercise in futility, and Burns had no illusions about that.

As he flew back to Washington, Burns wrote a quick memo for Biden. He had arrived in Moscow deeply pessimistic and he left even more so. The worst was very likely going to come to pass.

29

The Big Ask

October 24

Joe Biden was rushing, but there were some things that couldn't be rushed. They required a personal touch. On October 24, he invited Manchin and Schumer out to his house in Wilmington for Sunday breakfast.

Scranton Joe loved his real estate. For much of his adulthood, he kept stretching his credit and surpassing his bank account to build familial estates, a series of white elephant projects that consumed him. His house was the incarnation of his pride, a sprawling rebuke to his doubters, material proof of how far Joey had come. When he took Manchin around the place, he didn't bother tempering his boastful self. It was a tour in service of a mission, the sort of intimate gesture that he thought might mean something to Manchin.

For three hours, they sat and went through all the hard choices that would edit down a $3.5 trillion piece of legislation into a bill nearly half that size. For Biden, this wasn't a sentimental exercise. He knew that Manchin held all the leverage and that he had no choice but to surrender programs. But he also felt obliged to try one last time, to take one final stab at getting Manchin to accept a more robust extension of the child tax credit and a plan that would penalize utilities for using dirty energy. Schumer pushed hard on funding for public housing. But there was no budging the senator. That meant precious priorities fell to the side, but it also allowed for a sense of closure.

Biden felt as if they had worked through their differences in the spirit of genuine compromise. The bill landed at $2.3 trillion. It wasn't a deal, since so many details needed to be worked out, but it was close.

And when Joe Manchin shook the president's hand, he told him, "I will get this done." That was enough for Biden—a big thing to say in his house, with a shake of the hand, two men of the old school, dealing in the spirit of yore. At last, the president believed that he could look skeptical progressives in the eyes and assure them that he would be able to deliver Manchin. It would just take a little more time.

October 27

Nancy Pelosi felt that Joe Biden needed to be more assertive. Sometimes he would begin a sentence by apologizing to her: "I don't mean to bother you . . ." And she would think, *Oh, please, you're the president of the United States.* Nor could she understand his dithering. Of all people, he should know that legislation doesn't just drift into place. It needs to be forcefully squeezed into existence, with deadlines, with charm offensives, with the hint of menace and occasional bullying. Above all, Pelosi believed in the Big Ask. There comes a moment when the president explicitly, unambiguously, tells members of Congress that they must vote for his agenda. That moment had arrived.

The next day, October 28, the president was flying to Europe to attend a climate conference in Glasgow, where he promised to rally the world in defense of the planet. But what did he have to show for his own country, for his own efforts? All his most serious solutions were contained in the two pieces of legislation yet to clear the House. Passing his agenda, showing that his administration wasn't all talk, was his best claim to legitimacy in the world's eyes.

That evening, from her office in the Capitol, Pelosi called Biden. She told him, It's time; you need to come to the Hill before you leave the country and tell House Democrats that they need to vote for the infrastructure

bill, that they must vote for it that very day. Biden's presidency was starting to slip away. With endless legislative haggling, he was beginning to look
weak, as if he couldn't even corral his own party.

Joe Biden said that he agreed with Pelosi. On his way to Europe, he
would come to the Hill. It was time for him to seize control, to notch a win.

SOON AFTER PELOSI hung up, Pramila Jayapal caught wind of the president's imminent visit. And she knew what that meant. If the president came
and personally implored House Democrats to vote for the infrastructure
bill, her entire bargaining strategy was ruined. Holding up the infrastructure bill was her only source of leverage in negotiations with the moderates.
They wanted it badly, and she was relatively indifferent to its fate. What
she cared about was protecting Build Back Better from Joe Manchin and
Kyrsten Sinema, who wanted to whittle it down to an uninspired nub.

In her panic, Jayapal placed her own call to Ron Klain. She told him,
Don't do it; if the president comes to the Hill tomorrow, he'll be humiliated;
if he asks Democrats to support the infrastructure bill, he'll lose. Pelosi
doesn't have the votes.

Klain tried to cast aside her doubts, but, through the months, he came to
consider her a loyal ally of the White House. He passed along her whispered concerns. Jayapal had managed to implant an element of doubt about
Pelosi's tactics.

October 28

That morning, when the president arrived at the Capitol and entered
the crowded meeting room, he stepped into a standing ovation. As the applause died down, he deadpanned, "I'm here for the buffet."

Biden takes an almost romantic pleasure in winning over a crowd that he
desperately needs, and he ratcheted up the charm. "I want to speak to you
from the heart," he told the more than two hundred Democrats assembled.

"I don't think it's hyperbole to say that the House and Senate majorities and my presidency will be determined by what happens in the next week."

He came bearing flowers. After months of haggling with Manchin and Sinema, he had the outlines of a deal for Build Back Better. The bill would spend $1.7 trillion on climate, extend the Child Tax Credit for a year, create universal pre-K, and fund childcare and in-home care. He promised that it could garner fifty votes in the Senate, which implied that he was sure that he could deliver Sinema and Manchin, although neither senator had publicly confirmed their support for the framework.

As he made the case for the legislation, he told the Democrats that the combined weight of the bills was greater than the combined accomplishments of FDR and LBJ. Now, Biden existed in a state of flow. He was building to his climax, the moment that Pelosi so desperately wanted. "I need you to help me. I need your votes."

Upon hearing the word, a vast swath of the hall began chanting, "Vote, vote, vote."

But after having worked the room into a frenzy, Biden immediately tamped down that frenzy. He held up two fingers and stage-whispered, "Both."

His gesture required little extrapolation. He not only failed to explicitly make the Big Ask, his fingers seemed to tacitly endorse Jayapal's strategy of keeping the bills linked.

As the president finished his speech to another ovation, Pelosi made little effort to suppress her frustration. She approached the podium and stood next to Biden. Taking his place at the microphone, she brazenly attempted to reinterpret his remarks so that they accorded more closely with her wishes. "The president has asked for our vote today." Her emphasis was on *today*. And she kept repeating the word. "In order for us to have success, we must succeed *today*." This wasn't just about repairing bridges and filling potholes. It was a vote of confidence in the president.

The chants began to resound again: *"Vote, vote, vote."*

On his way out the door, the president encountered a teenager who happened to be in the meeting. He wrapped his arm around him and joked, "Let me tell you something, young man. You're doing great already, and if you follow in my footsteps, if you ever go into politics, just remember this advice. If someone tells you you could be president of the United States or Speaker of the House, choose Speaker of the House."

IMMEDIATELY AFTER BIDEN left the room, Jayapal and her contingent of progressives quickly departed, too. Anticipating the president's arrival—and the complications it might pose for her strategy—Jayapal had called an emergency meeting of the Congressional Progressive Caucus in an auditorium nearby in the Capitol Visitor Center. When the progressives hastily hustled into their meeting, they knew that they were rushing toward an uncomfortable debate. By refusing to vote for the infrastructure bill, they were now openly defying Pelosi. They risked being accused of tanking the Biden presidency.

As Jayapal presided over the meeting, her members were given the chance to stand up and argue how the faction should handle its strategic conundrum.

Mark Takano, a congressman from Southern California, started to deliver a speech urging militancy in the face of pressure from leadership. As he began speaking, Pelosi entered the room, a shock to everyone in attendance. Pelosi would later note that she was a longtime member of the Progressive Caucus, who just wanted to listen to speeches, although it was impossible to remember the last time she attended one of its meetings.

With Pelosi unexpectedly watching, Takano seemed to melt. He began peppering his speech with effusive praise of her. His remarks began to awkwardly meander. Colleagues swore that they saw tears in his eyes.

This was likely Pelosi's last term as Speaker. For most members of the House, she was the only leader they ever knew. Her strength was the stuff of legend. She was revered and feared—and her disapproving presence was rattling.

Under her breath she muttered, "They say they love me, but they won't trust me."

After twelve minutes of listening to the speechifying, she left the meeting. She didn't need to stay any longer. A message had been sent.

PELOSI HAD RESORTED to the tactic, however, out of desperation. She knew that the progressives had read Biden's speech with Talmudic care, and they hadn't heard the magic words. When Jayapal finally emerged from the Progressive Caucus meeting, she told the cameras, "He did not ask for a vote on [infrastructure] today. The speaker did, but he did not."

As Pelosi sat in her office with Steny Hoyer and Jim Clyburn, her deputies, the troika kept on whipping, although the futility of their vote grubbing was painfully clear. And it was maddening. Jayapal had undermined her. For the coming weeks, Pelosi would give Jayapal the silent treatment, no longer responding to texts or calls.

And when Pelosi thought about the White House, she struggled to understand Biden's behavior. He flat-out whiffed. Why wasn't Biden pressing harder for victory? Why was he so afraid to demand the loyalty of his party in his time of need? She remained convinced that he could have prevailed that day if he had only asked for it.

The trio of old pros knew that they had no choice but to accept a humiliating retreat. They sent out a notice informing their members that there would be no further votes that evening.

30

Pressure Drop

PELOSI WAS STUCK, and everything seemed to be imploding around the president. The next day, Virginians were going to vote for governor in an off-year election—and she already anticipated that the Democrat, Terry McAuliffe, was going to lose his bid to reclaim the job. His loss would surely precipitate a fresh round of recriminations, where moderates and progressives pointed the accusatory finger at each other, initiating a bout of wailing about how the Democrats had lost their way.

While the White House kept professing that it would get a deal with Manchin—and said that they were yards away from finalizing one—the senator's public language suggested otherwise. On November 1, Manchin held a press conference where he seemed to, yet again, express his willingness to sink Build Back Better. "I'm open to supporting a final bill that helps move our country forward, but I'm equally open to voting against a bill that hurts our country."

Hearing Manchin say that he might vote against Build Back Better hurt Pelosi's ears. And it fueled her determination to quickly burrow her way out of the legislative morass. Despite having just failed—and despite the reigning mood of pessimism—Pelosi set herself another audacious goal. This week she would jam them both through. She would march the two massive pieces of legislation in tandem. It was a matter of grit, resilience, and whipping as if her legacy and the future of the party depended on it.

By Friday, November 5, Pelosi was achingly close to passing both bills—which still felt unbearably far. Out of her 222 members, there were only 6 centrist holdouts, pitching a late fit. And at 9:00 a.m. Pelosi assembled them into her conference room to drag them into compliance with her will.

The angriest of the recalcitrants was Stephanie Murphy, a head of the moderate faction of the Blue Dog Democrats. A night earlier the group published a letter saying that they couldn't support Build Back Better without a score from the Congressional Budget Office, providing an independent accounting of the bill's ultimate cost.

Murphy described her obstreperousness as a matter of principle. She said that she couldn't vote for the bill without knowing its genuine price tag. "When did it become revolutionary," she liked to argue, "to know how much money you're voting to spend?" But it was also emotional. She felt as if Pelosi had betrayed the moderates. She kept promising a vote on the infrastructure bill before the House turned to the reconciliation bill. Now, Murphy was finally going to force Pelosi to fulfill that promise.

As Murphy walked into the room, she headed toward a spread of bagels and doughnuts. One of her fellow holdouts whispered to her, "Should we have brought a taster?"

It was a suspicion that Jim Clyburn seemed to confirm. The seventy-eight-year-old whip was in no mood to coddle the holdouts. "This is a historic moment and you're letting it slip away," he told them. It was communities of color that would suffer from further delay. That description was received as an accusation, which made Murphy even less likely to be pliant.

Once Clyburn simmered down, Pelosi handed the meeting over to Brian Deese. She imported him from the White House in the hopes that his calming demeanor and command of the numbers might allay the holdouts' concerns. He walked them through charts and tried to drown their objections in data.

"Is this enough information for you to feel comfortable?" Pelosi wanted to know.

But Murphy was still in a combative mood. She snapped, "I don't work off a White House estimate, I'm a member of Congress."

A buzzer summoned the group to vote on the floor, prematurely ending the meeting.

"Feel free to come back and use this office to talk things over," Pelosi told her.

An offer that Murphy rejected.

AFTER THE VOTE, Pelosi returned to her office with Clyburn and Hoyer so that they could spitball ideas that might snap the holdouts into submission. It felt as if they were going round and round, when she received a text from Joyce Beatty, the chair of the Congressional Black Caucus. "Can we come talk?"

The text felt like yet another omen of disaster. Beatty was bringing the leadership of the CBC to her office—some of the most senior members of Congress—so that they could collectively complain about how Pelosi was taking the group for granted, by spending all her time assuaging the progressive and moderates.

But the more Pelosi listened to the CBC, the more she sensed an opportunity. They shared her upset with the holier-than-thou progressives who claimed to speak on behalf of communities of color. Finally, she felt she was in the presence of a group that shared her urgency to win. Instead of ushering them from her office, she asked them to stay and help her find a route out of the morass.

Brenda Lawrence, a congresswoman from Michigan who spent the first thirty years of her career working for the Postal Service, suggested that Pelosi narrow her horizons slightly. She should hold a vote on the infrastructure bill that evening, immediately followed by a vote on a rule that would set the terms of debate for Build Back Better, scheduling a vote on it in two weeks. That would give time for the CBO estimate that the holdouts wanted, but it would also set a firm date for passing Build Back Better.

Pelosi loved it. It wasn't that she cared so much about the substance of the proposal. The genius of it was the source. She thought the progressives would have an impossible time rejecting a strategy that carried the imprimatur of the Black Caucus.

Despite the frostiness of her relationship with Jayapal, Pelosi called her to test her resolve. Pelosi knew that the CBC proposal essentially required Jayapal's capitulation—and that it would take a little more time to wear her down.

"I have thirty-five votes against it," she told Pelosi.

"That's bullshit," Pelosi said.

Jayapal allowed that her calculation might be slightly off and began to revise her estimate downward.

But Pelosi didn't believe Jayapal could control her faction. Pelosi said that she planned to press forward with Lawrence's plan. She was going to put it to a vote, daring the progressives to reject her.

At 4:00 P.M. Jayapal called an emergency meeting of the Progressive Caucus. She wanted to gauge how her ninety members would respond to Pelosi's pressure, but that pressure kept mounting.

As the progressives filed into the room, Pelosi called a procedural vote, initiating the process that would culminate in the chamber voting on the infrastructure bill later that evening. The vote itself was a technicality, but its defeat carried consequences. If Pelosi lost the vote, the rules required her to temporarily hand control of the House to the Republicans. It was a vote her party couldn't afford to lose.

But instead of rushing to vote on the measure, the progressives stayed in their meeting, essentially thumbing their nose at Pelosi, the legislative equivalent of a wildcat strike.

Jayapal had required the members to leave their phones outside the caucus meeting. As the devices sat on a table, they filled with vituperative texts and voicemails from Pelosi and her staff. In one message, she fumed, "I wish you could show the respect for our institution and your leadership to come to the floor and cast this vote. By not doing that, you are yielding control of the floor to the Republicans and the insurrectionists."

Pelosi was no longer politely asking for votes. Her staff got in touch with Jared Huffman, a progressive stalwart from California and a passionate environmentalist. Huffman was supposed to travel as part of Pelosi's delegation to the climate summit in Glasgow. But Pelosi's staffer had left a message telling him that his place in the delegation was no longer secure.

The pressure from Pelosi materialized at the door of the meeting room in the Longworth House Office Building. Joyce Beatty asked to speak with the progressives so that she could make the case for moving ahead with the infrastructure bill. But Jayapal wouldn't let her into the room—a gesture that embarrassed and frustrated many of the progressives.

After a month of sparring with the progressives, Pelosi felt as if she was finally about to break their resistance. Pelosi placed her second call of the day to Biden. She told him it was time to finish the job. It was time for him to ask the progressives for their votes—only it needed to be done in unambiguous, irresistible language. This time, he couldn't whiff.

A few minutes later, Jayapal received word that the president would be calling, and she brought her cell phone into the room. Biden asked to speak with everyone in the room. Members left their chairs and crowded around a small table, covered with pizza boxes, where Jayapal laid her phone and put it on speaker.

For weeks, Biden kept saying that his presidency was hanging in the balance. But now he wanted to convey that he was at his wit's end. There was a bracing weariness in his voice. He said, "If we don't do this today, I'm not sure any of this is going to happen." The future of his entire domestic agenda was in their hands.

But Biden wanted them to know that he wasn't abandoning Build Back Better. He floated an idea, which Pelosi had been kicking around with her leadership team and quietly testing with her rank and file. What if he could get a commitment from the Stephanie Murphy group that they would vote for Build Back Better in two weeks' time, if the CBO score roughly matched the White House's estimates?

There was distress in the president's voice—and many of the members in the room considered it embarrassing that he was groveling for their votes. Jamie Raskin, congressman from Maryland, stood to address the group. As the leader of the team of House managers that had presented the case for impeaching Donald Trump, after January 6, Raskin acquired an almost prophetic authority within the party. He told them, "Yes, we're progressives. But we're also Democrats. This nation is facing the threat of authoritarianism. I'm a proud progressive, but I'm also a proud Democrat. I see the bigger picture. We can't fail here."

AFTER THE PRESIDENT'S SPEECH, the thirty-seven-year-old congressman from Colorado, Joe Neguse, went to the front of the room to have a quiet word with Jayapal. After four years in Congress, Neguse had achieved a unique stature with his Democratic colleagues. Pelosi installed him on her leadership team, stamping him for bigger things. Although he was a stalwart of the Progressive Caucus, he was close with moderates like Josh Gottheimer. The child of Eritrean immigrants, he was considered a rising star in the CBC.

Neguse told Jayapal that he wanted to begin working with the moderates on the draft of a deal along the lines of the one that the president had proposed, in case the progressives decided to pursue that path. She gave him permission to launch an exploratory mission.

When Neguse texted Josh Gottheimer, they agreed to meet in Stephanie

Murphy's office. What Neguse didn't announce was that he was bringing along a handful of other progressives, whom Jayapal also wanted in the room, including Mark Pocan, a congressman from Wisconsin and former head of the Progressive Caucus. It was a profoundly awkward choice. Pocan once denounced the Problem Solvers Caucus, the group that Gottheimer headed, as the "the Child Abuse Caucus," because he abhorred its reluctance to challenge Trump-era immigration enforcement. For years, Pocan and Gottheimer couldn't stand the sight of each other.

Yet there they were, sitting in front of Gottheimer's laptop, editing an agreement in the hopes of rescuing the Biden presidency. As they haggled over phrases, Gottheimer kept stepping into the hallway to take calls from Steve Ricchetti. It was perfectly clear that the president was sitting next to Ricchetti, desperately trying to push the process forward. He could hear Biden asking questions in the background as Ricchetti barked at Gottheimer, "What's taking so fucking long?"

When Neguse showed Jayapal the final draft of the deal, she couldn't quite bring herself to agree. The fact was that she just didn't trust Pelosi, and she trusted moderates like Murphy and Gottheimer even less. What would happen if she voted for the infrastructure bill and the moderates then broke their word and voted against the rule? What would happen, two weeks from now, if the CBO estimates about the bill were higher than the White House predicted? Would the moderates bail on the bill then?

Jayapal took the elevator up to Stephanie Murphy's office to talk through her reservations with Neguse and Gottheimer. Despite her differences with Josh Gottheimer, they were friends. They entered the House in the same terrible year, 2017, and would occasionally break bread together.

Jayapal asked to step into the receptionist's room in Murphy's office so that she could talk to Gottheimer without any prying eyes. "I don't know if I can get the progressives to support this," she told him. "How can I trust you?"

"Do you want to look them in the eye? Would that help?"

"It would," Jayapal replied.

Gottheimer left to gather the moderates and told them that they would have to make personal promises to Jayapal. They were furious that she was forcing them to act like schoolchildren promising never to throw paper airplanes in class. But for a moment, they held their tongues.

"Guys you have to honor your word. Do I have your word?"

She stared at each of them individually, pausing to hear their assent.

When she finished, Gottheimer left the room and phoned Pelosi. He told her, "Call the vote."

BEFORE SHE ANNOUNCED the deal, Jayapal wanted to speak with the president one more time. A few days earlier, Neguse and Jayapal had quietly met with Kyrsten Sinema. She didn't want to publicly announce that she would vote for both bills, but told them privately she would. Her negotiations with the White House were very nearly complete. That meant there was one final obstacle: Jayapal wanted Biden's personal assurance that he would deliver Joe Manchin.

Biden had assiduously courted Jayapal. He had her over to the White House for breakfast; he led a rendition of "Happy Birthday" for her in the Oval Office; he called her after her appearances on cable TV. After one of her visits, he asked for the number of Jayapal's mother in Bangalore, India.

After she told the president that the progressives would deliver the infrastructure bill for him—and he promised that he would deliver Build Back Better—she joked that he definitely had to call her mother now.

On the other side of the world, a phone rang. "Please hold for the president of the United States."

ALL AFTERNOON, the senior staff of the White House worked the phones, rounding up votes, checking in with members. They gathered in the residence for what they assumed would be a triumphant moment. Everyone was there, except for Kamala Harris. She had packed up her bag and left for the day. And when her adviser Symone Sanders learned about the gathering in the residence, she knew that she needed to get Harris back to the office. Having traveled to the vice presidential mansion, Harris returned to work. It was the humiliation of the vice presidency in microcosm.

But at least she was there for the victory. Biden could finally sign his infrastructure bill into law, more than seven months after he began pursuing it. And on November 19, Build Back Better cleared the House on a party line vote. The moderates remained true to their word. Pelosi delivered, as she almost always did. Now, it was time for the president to deliver. All that separated the president from the pantheon of Democratic presidents he aspired to join was one reluctant man.

31

Variant of Concern

A WEEK BEFORE THANKSGIVING, David Kessler told Jeff Zients that he was ready to leave his job. This was Kessler's third attempt at extricating himself from the forever war on COVID. When he signed up for the job, he thought he would be long gone by this point in the year. But each time he tried to exit, Zients talked him out of it. One day, we'll leave together, he told Kessler. It just didn't feel as if that day would come very soon.

Thanksgiving was a brief respite that Kessler excitedly anticipated. His ten-month-old grandchild was coming to dinner. But just after breakfast, reports began to emerge from South Africa about a new variant, B.1.1.529—a mutation that seemed to defy most expectations for how the virus would evolve, with an especially unusual geometry that scientists hadn't ever seen. There were reports of a spike of cases in the province of Gauteng, not a slow build, but a peak that shot up like a straight line. Transmissibility was always a defining characteristic of the coronavirus, but the rate of spread witnessed in South Africa was of a different order of magnitude.

That morning, Natalie Quillian assembled the administration's doctors and pressed them for information. All during the fall, the administration had braced for the arrival of new variants. It kept waiting for a new strain that would render the vaccine useless. A variant called mu filled the White House with anxiety. Thankfully, it came and went without the grimmest scenario ever materializing. But perhaps this time it might. Quillian asked the doctors to work the phones to see if they could learn anything more concrete.

Because of the infant, Kessler's dinner would be early, leaving him the evening to sit in his office. From the AIDS crisis of the nineties, Kessler knew scientists across Africa. One of the best was Glenda Gray, the head of the South African Medical Research Council. "Any intelligence you can share?" he wrote.

At 11:39 p.m., he received a reply. "Dear David, it's looking bad. Our test positivity has increased over just a few days. Seems to be replacing delta, it's a dominant strain, also reinfection in people who had delta as well." He forwarded her note to Zients and Fauci, realizing that there was a chance that he might have just agreed to stay for the worst phase of the pandemic.

THE NEXT DAY, just after lunch, Jeff Zients, Natalie Quillian, and Anthony Fauci gave the president his first thorough briefing on the variant. Quillian was at her parents' house, working in a guest room, grateful that the president had scheduled a conference call, not a Zoom, since it meant that she didn't have to bother with work clothes.

Given how little they knew about the variant, they agreed to restrict travel from South Africa. It would at least help buy some time to get a handle on the basic scientific questions.

Biden, understandably, kept pressing on one question: "Will the vaccine offer any protection against the new variant?"

Fauci told him that they didn't know.

"When will you know?"

"Not for another two weeks or so," Fauci replied. The NIH was already scouring the globe for a sample, which it could use to sequence the strain. But there was no avoiding the fact that they were in for a painful period of ignorance, unsure of whether the virus had defeated the vaccine, unsure of the new strain's severity, unsure of whether the existing stockpile of tests could even detect its presence.

THE NEW VARIANT received an official name from the World Health Organization, the next available letter in the Greek alphabet: omicron. It had arrived at the worst moment in the calendar, coinciding with the holiday season, a time when much of the nation sat in crammed tubes that flew from city to city so that families could unite and disregard any semblance of social distancing.

In anticipation of visiting with family members—and not wanting to unwittingly inflict COVID on elderly parents and grandparents—Americans rushed to test themselves. Lines formed outside clinics. The shelves at Walmart and CVS were emptied of home tests.

On December 6, NPR's Mara Liasson posed the obvious question to Jen Psaki at one of her briefings: "Last week, obviously, the President explained some ramp-up in testing, but there are still a lot of countries, like Germany and the UK and South Korea, that basically have massive testing, free of charge or for a nominal fee. Why can't that be done in the United States?"

Psaki explained that testing had ramped up—and that made it possible for insurers to reimburse the purchase of any test.

Liasson kept going: "That's kind of complicated though. Why not just make them free and give them out . . . and have them available everywhere?"

"Should we just send one to every American?" Psaki said it so derisively that her answer became a headline.

On his first day in office, Biden had promised that he would make testing ubiquitous. At this moment of need, it was palpably not. On television, pundits decried the shortage as evidence of rank incompetence.

To be fair, the administration had invested significantly in testing. When Biden came to office, there wasn't a single domestic test for home use on the market. With money from the American Rescue Plan—and by wielding the Defense Production Act on the industries' behalf—the administration helped increase the number of factories that could churn out tests.

But the Biden administration simply treated testing as a lower priority than vaccines. It believed that an inoculated country wouldn't need to constantly test itself. An assumption that the virus's constant mutation invalidated.

But it's hardly clear that a robust testing regimen would have yielded a healthier nation. The United Kingdom spent billions on free testing. But that program ate up 20 percent of the National Health Service's total budget. And even with that expenditure, testing didn't measurably dent the spread of disease. In fact, Parliament eventually opened an investigation trying to answer the question, Why did that massive expenditure accomplish so little?

And until the omicron crunch, it seemed as if Americans had little interest in home testing. During the summer, the pharmaceutical giant Abbott destroyed millions of tests that it believed it wouldn't be able to sell.

Of course, the White House had witnessed enough variants to know that another surge of the pandemic was likely—and in the event of that surge, Americans would be anxious to know whether they had contracted the disease; that testing would be essential to making everyday decisions, like whether it was wise to send a kid with a runny nose to school.

The president would eventually admit that he wished he had ordered the government to buy more tests. And the fact that the White House scrambled to recover from its failure, eventually setting up a system where it was possible to order free tests and implementing exactly what Psaki ridiculed, was a tacit admission of its error.

As KESSLER sat waiting for the inevitable spike in omicron cases, which he knew would tear across the unvaccinated, causing tens of thousands of preventable deaths, he was increasingly in a fatalistic mood. What else could the administration do to stanch the spread of the virus? When he thought back on everything that the White House had done, he felt as if it had executed as skillfully as possible in the middle of a once-in-a-century pandemic. Sure, there was some fumbling along the line. The CDC was a broken institution, and it struggled to communicate to the nation with any clarity about how to navigate everyday life.

The vaccine was the way out of the mess; the administration had bet everything on it, had run every play in the public health playbook to persuade the reluctant to accept the vaccine, but the political maladies of modern American life were ruining its chances. It was as if a large chunk of the nation had joined a death cult, oblivious to their own well-being and without any feeling of solidarity for their neighbors. It made him despair, to use a phrase borrowed from Biden, for the soul of America.

32

The Eruption

December 9

Ever since the fall of Kabul, Joe Manchin couldn't have been clearer. He didn't want to be rushed into passing Build Back Better. At first, he spoke of the need for a "strategic pause." Then he told friends that he preferred waiting until the next spring, when the nation would have a better sense of whether inflation was a fleeting condition or more nettlesome than that. His arguments were substantive, but it was hard not to project his subconscious reasons for wanting more time. A delay would avert his own hard choice about whether he would cast a vote for a bill filled with provisions that he didn't especially like.

But as Christmas approached, Joe Biden was running low on patience. Steve Ricchetti was Manchin's jovial handler, impossible to dislike and eager to please. But when Ricchetti spoke with the senator, he channeled his boss's anxiety. "We've got to get going on this," he told Manchin. For months, Ricchetti had tried to nudge Manchin to yes; now he was trying to shove him in that direction.

The West Virginian didn't want to pick up the pace. "We've got inflation problems," he shot back. "There are a lot of issues. I'm just not there yet."

The White House couldn't afford to remain in a state of suspension for much longer. A large swath of the party wanted Biden to turn his attention to voting rights. If Manchin got his way, there would be another three or four months of legislative haggling, which would be terrible for Biden's approval ratings. It would keep the president stuck in the unattractive pose of a legislative supplicant. And there was no way to know if Manchin's objections would melt with time. There was, in fact, a good chance that he might grow ever more obstreperous.

Ricchetti was on a mission. He exuded more willfulness than Manchin was used to seeing. "We've got to push," Ricchetti told him.

"Well, call a vote," Manchin snapped. "Call up a vote. Let's see how it goes . . ."

December 14

Manchin's mind was hardly set. His emotions were a swirl, really. He was happy to kick the bill into the next year, but also eager to be done with the haggling, to relieve himself of all the pressure. What he wanted varied with the days of the week.

That evening, he had a meeting with the president. Like so many of his visits to the White House, it wasn't announced on the public schedule. Since his conversation with Ricchetti, Manchin had apparently taken another swerve. He brought along a document that he hoped might put the whole Build Back Better saga behind him. It was a version of the bill that he could support—$1.8 trillion on climate, on universal pre-K, on expanding Obamacare.

Ever since September, Manchin had despised the fact that the Democrats hadn't made any hard choices about the composition of the bill. In fact, Pelosi had added items back into the House bill that Manchin had already negotiated out of it. It was, in his view, the height of fiscal irresponsibility. In his proposal, Manchin believed that he made the painful decisions that Democrats resisted.

Biden knew he couldn't agree on the spot. In fact, he could see a bundle of complications. By agreeing to Manchin's plan, he would need to persuade Sinema to agree to tax provisions that she had already rejected. Because Manchin stripped the Child Tax Credit from his proposal, Biden would need to convince the Left that it would have to live without its beloved program.

And when Klain looked closely at the document, he felt as if its accounting didn't add up. The proposal wasn't close to the final product, since the amount Manchin wanted to spend didn't line up with the price tag. He wanted a ten-year commitment to childcare and universal pre-K, but he hadn't allocated enough funding to make that possible.

Still, Biden was pleased with the thrust of Manchin's thinking. It was arguably more intentionally composed than the hodgepodge version of Build Back Better that passed the House. It felt close.

"We can't get this done quickly," Biden told him. "Let's pick up the conversation after Christmas."

December 15

But when Manchin heard the leadership on the Hill the next day, it was as if they weren't apprised of his conversation with Biden. Schumer and Pelosi kept trumpeting their hope that the bill would pass the Senate before Christmas. To tamp down Democratic expectations, the White House wanted to put out a statement, explaining that there wasn't going to be any imminent progress on Build Back Better.

Manchin hadn't expected to see a draft of a White House statement, but he was appreciative that they told him that he could look it over before its release. That sort of courtesy mattered to him. He considered himself a man of chivalry. And the thing he liked about his relationship with the president is that they adhered to a set of respectful rules. Manchin privately trumpeted the fact that he and Biden had agreed to never attack each other in public. One of the reasons that he kept negotiations alive is that Biden had faithfully abided by that code of honor.

Being Joe Manchin was both thrilling and exhausting. Even among the

extroverts attracted to politics, he stood out. When he encountered a reporter in the hall, he stopped to answer their question. If a junior member
of congress texted him, he responded. Being the center of attention filled
him with joy, even as it ground him down.

When lefty protesters paddled up to his houseboat in kayaks and heck-
led him as he dressed for work, Manchin put on a brave face. He tried to
treat them with civility, even as he considered their angry presence menacing. Really, what was the world becoming? Kyrsten Sinema couldn't even go
to the bathroom without a protester yelling at her, recording the whole terrifying incident so that it could be played a million times on social media.
There were other, darker incidents that he didn't like to discuss. Protesters
showed up at the homes of his children. There was an incident with his wife,
when she was at home alone in West Virginia.

That's why the draft of the White House's press release pushed him
over the edge. Most of the language was innocuous and accurate. But he
hated that his name was the only one included in the document. He was
already vulnerable—and it was like they were casting the presidential spotlight on him. *Look over here, this guy is the obstacle to realizing the progressive
agenda. Feel free to bully him into submission for us.*

Perhaps the White House didn't get it, so he tried to make his position
clear. Manchin's chief of staff, Lance West, sent revisions in tracked changes
and told Louisa Terrell, the head of the Office of Legislative Affairs, that
Manchin didn't want to be named in the statement. Or perhaps if he were
named in the statement, the White House could mention that it was still
negotiating with Sinema, too. Naming them both would take some of the
heat off Manchin. West emphasized that the current draft was a bad idea. It
would raise tensions, he warned—and potentially knock negotiations off a
constructive course.

As the White House looked at the revisions, it accepted many of Manchin's edits to the document. But it couldn't quite understand the problem with how it mentioned him by name. The statement hadn't included
Sinema, because they were done negotiating with her. She was, more or

less, supportive of the existing package. So the White House didn't make the change he wanted. It left his name in the release.

The document read, "My team and I are having ongoing discussions with Senator Manchin; that work will continue next week. It takes time to finalize these agreements, prepare the legislative changes, and finish all the parliamentary and procedural steps needed to enable a Senate vote." Really, what could be remotely bothersome about that?

December 16

When the world saw the release, it reacted with a shrug. The delay of Build Back Better had become so familiar that it was becoming cliché. Democrats were thoroughly conditioned to the endlessness of the process.

The one person, however, who didn't have a blasé reaction was the individual who mattered most. The fact that the White House solicited his opinion and ignored it, well, that filled him with rage. His inclusion in the press release felt intentional and spiteful.

All along, Manchin had been a good sport about Build Back Better. He didn't like that he was being railroaded into supporting a bill that he didn't especially like. But he was a loyal soldier—and he really wanted Biden to succeed. For months, Manchin sublimated his anger. Now, it came pouring out in a volcanic rage. He texted Ricchetti and told him that the release was "unconscionable" because it endangered his family. It was a betrayal—and Manchin said that he was "done" negotiating with the White House.

December 17

When Steve Ricchetti called Manchin the next day, he did his best to assure him. He wanted him to know that the White House hadn't intended to attack him, and he was truly sorry that he felt undermined. Ricchetti tried to convey what he considered to be the obvious truth: the White House needed Manchin's vote; it had zero interest in alienating him.

But Ricchetti wasn't too worried about Manchin. When a member of Congress told him that they were "done" negotiating, Ricchetti never panicked. That's what they all said. With all his experience, he knew not to take such threats too seriously. Ron Klain wasn't worried, either. He described Manchin's exasperation as a "hot text." After the steam evaporated, Manchin would surely revert to gregarious form.

Joe Manchin asked his staff to prepare two press releases. One asserted that negotiations were on course. The other announced that he could no longer support Build Back Better; he was bailing on the president. He told his staff to have both ready for his forthcoming appearance on *Fox News Sunday*. Although he had a good sense of which of the releases he would need, he wanted to preserve his options.

Given how cordial his call with the president had been on Tuesday, he couldn't understand why everything had exploded. Why did they publish the press release? Why hadn't they come groveling back to him? Did the president even know that his staff had failed him so badly?

Perhaps it was a sign of his mental exhaustion, but Manchin's anger remained volcanic. But he wanted to keep that anger out of public view. Even if the White House hadn't abided by the rules of engagement, he wanted to stay true to his chivalric code.

December 19

Thirty minutes before his appearance on *Fox News Sunday*, Lance West placed a call to Steve Ricchetti letting him know what was about to land. Manchin was going onto the network that Democrats considered enemy territory and would announce that he wouldn't support Build Back Better.

Like Manchin, Biden considered himself a man of honor. And this was the height of dishonor. Biden kept fuming to his aides that Manchin was walking away from a handshake deal—one sealed in his own home—the height of betrayal.

From their disparate homes, Ron Klain, Jen Psaki, and Joe Biden sat down at their televisions knowing that they were about to watch Joe Manchin destroy the legislation that they considered the central, lasting achievement of the administration. As Biden waited, his anger kept growing. It posed a dilemma for the staff as they pondered how to respond. Should they find a way to calm Biden and steer him toward the high road? Or should they just embrace his fury, since they felt it themselves?

Every aspect of Manchin's betrayal stung. It was hard to think strategically under the circumstances. But the group focused on one question: How would Manchin's fellow Democrats in the Senate respond? The White House couldn't afford for its own party to turn its rage against the president. They didn't want members of Congress to jump to the conclusion that Biden had bungled negotiations. Democrats, the Biden aides concluded, deserved to hear a detailed explanation of how Manchin had betrayed them.

WHEN MANCHIN APPEARED on the screen with the show's host, Bret Baier, he seemed as if he had a cup of chamomile tea and practiced his breathing. He intended a more-in-sorrow-than-in-anger performance. And he wasn't going to jump straight to the punch line. He felt like he needed to deliver a preface to his decision—to talk about his underlying reasons for opposing Build Back Better: inflation and the debt, concerns that he'd aired dozens of times before.

Then he took his turns toward the declarative. "I've always said this, Bret, if I can't go home and explain it to the people of West Virginia, I can't vote for it. And I cannot vote to continue with this piece of legislation. I just can't."

Baier seemed surprised by the admission and pressed for a clarification. "You're done? Is this a no?"

"This is a no on this legislation."

Because he was Joe Manchin, who hated to be hated, he couldn't help but add, "I've tried. I mean, I really did."

WHEN THE WHITE HOUSE staff reconvened, they agreed upon a course: they would quickly publish a long rebuttal, recounting how Manchin had stabbed them in the back.

Psaki agreed to put it out under her own name. The statement would self-consciously deviate from the White House's preferred tone. Where the White House tended to abhor process stories, this would be filled with nitty gritty that exposed what she described as "breach of his commitments to the president." The group assembled its account quickly and then presented the draft to the president for approval.

The president absorbed the language. It was intended to wallop: "[Manchin] will have to explain to the nearly two million women who would get the affordable day care they need to return to work why he opposes a plan to get them the help they need." Even as he approved the release of the statement, Biden appreciated that it could create a spiral of bad feelings.

Indeed, when Manchin read it, he considered the Psaki statement a confirmation of all the reasons that he had abandoned the White House. The statement was the ultimate calumny.

That afternoon, Biden tried call to Manchin, but the senator had turned off his phone and the president's call went straight to voicemail. "Joe," he said, his anger unmistakable, "how can you do this to me—and at Christmastime?" It took the president several hours before he finally reached him, a short call in which both men suppressed their anger, refrained from recriminations, and agreed to take a breath. But after he hung up the phone, Manchin couldn't contain himself. He began to reach out to friends and colleagues on the Hill to complain about Ron Klain and the rest of the White House staff. "They're so smug," he griped. Anyone who heard him rant could see that his scars weren't going to heal quickly. It wasn't clear that they ever would.

PART FIVE

NEVER-ENDING
WINTER

January–February 2022

33

Where Have the
Better Angels Gone?

J UST BEFORE the New Year, when Biden called his friend Jon Meacham, he plastered on a resolute face. By any objective measure, he was in a terrible place. For months, he had invested his precious presidential time into the pursuit of Build Back Better, only to look like a fool when Joe Manchin sideswiped him on Fox News. Despite the attention he devoted to Vladimir Putin, Russian troops were rolling toward the Ukrainian border. Not so many months earlier, Biden had told aides that his presidency would be defined by his response to COVID, yet omicron was surging through households and schools and workplaces, a triggering reminder of the early days of the pandemic.

The primary agenda item for the call with Meacham was hardly more uplifting. The president was looking ahead to a grim milestone. He wanted to discuss a speech commemorating the first anniversary of January 6 that Meacham was helping write.

Part of why Biden felt simpatico with Meacham was the sentiment in the subtitle of the historian's most recent book, *The Soul of America: The Battle for Our Better Angels*. Biden was among the truest believers in the power of the better angels. They might advance only a few yards at a time, but they kept on advancing.

That faith, however, had begun to wobble. The past year had chastened him. He began it hopeful that the nation would embrace the blessing of the vaccine. But moral suasion and logic failed to move red America to protect itself. The power of right-wing propaganda inoculated a large portion of the country against reason.

By the end of September, the nation had exhausted Biden's faith in the better angels. Because so many Americans resisted the collective efforts to smash the virus, he tried to force their compliance by mandating the vaccination of the military, the federal bureaucracy, health care workers, and employees of large companies. And he was done politely asking. When he announced the mandates, he bellowed, "We are patient, but our patience is wearing thin. And your refusal has cost all of us."

Working through drafts of the January 6 speech with Meacham and Mike Donilon, Biden kept pushing them to toughen the language, to harden the speech's critique of Donald Trump. That, too, represented a shift in his thinking. When he came into office, he felt as if he could destroy Donald Trump by ignoring him. He worried that by going near the fire, he would feed it. So he rarely mentioned him by name. When the former president held a rally or issued a menacing statement, Biden resisted the impulse to respond.

As he edited the speech, it was as if he were permitting himself to fully process the horror of January 6. The more he paused to think hard about it, the angrier he became. Even after rioters went in search of Mike Pence's neck, even after congressional leaders feared for their own lives, the Republican Party remained staunchly loyal to Trump. The party was enthusiastically complicit in Trump's plot to short-circuit the next election.

He said he was done dancing around the subject of Trump. This was the occasion to deliver the indictment of Trump that history demanded and the man deserved.

In the final draft, Biden stuck to the literary conceit of omitting Trump's name. But he now did so derisively. "He's not just a former president. He's a defeated former president" was a statement intended to wound what he described as Trump's "bruised ego."

Even before his writers began working on the speech, Biden knew that he wanted to deliver it in Statuary Hall, where insurrectionists had literally defecated on Congress. Standing on the site of the riot, he wanted to re-count history without euphemism, to provide a rejoinder to the right-wing revisionists who sought to soften memories of the day. The threats against democracy were ominous, and he believed that they needed to be described with graphic imagery: "I will allow no one to place a dagger at the throat of our democracy."

Meacham had worked on Biden's inaugural, a speech that celebrated the resilience of institutions. As he watched the evolution of this speech, he thought to himself that his friend had journeyed from Locke to Hobbes, to a darker, more realistic view of human nature. At the age of seventy-nine, Biden was confronting his teetering faith in better angels.

As MEACHAM AND DONILON finished the January 6 speech, he wanted them to draft a companion address. A week later, on January 11, he intended to fly to Atlanta, to the cradle of the civil rights movement, to lay out his prescription for the crisis of American democracy. He wanted the pair to write a rhetorical case urging the Senate to scrap the filibuster so that it could pass a pair of bills protecting the right to vote.

Scuppering the filibuster wasn't a position that came easily to Biden, an institutionalist to the core who abhorred tampering with the rituals of the institution he loved most. After the death of his first wife and daughter, the Senate lifted him from his depression and provided meaning to his exis-tence. He has always extolled it as a utopia of pragmatism, a community where adversaries could peaceably coexist.

But he'd also reached a breaking point. As recently as 2006, the Senate had reauthorized the Voting Rights Act of 1965. In his day, the legislation wasn't partisan or remotely controversial. Even a reformed segregationist like Strom Thurmond could support it, as did Mitch McConnell. The fact that Republicans senators he knew and liked had reversed themselves and were now blocking bills to protect basic voting rights illustrated how the Senate of his memory no longer existed.

Not everyone in Bidenland was thrilled with the prospect of this second speech. Nearly a year earlier, Anita Dunn had begun to worry about the administration's approach to voting rights. More than any other member of the Biden inner circle, she lived with the issue. For decades, her husband, Bob Bauer, served as the Democratic Party's premier election lawyer. Bauer had organized the Biden campaign's legal team and carefully studied the weaknesses in the legal superstructure of American democracy.

A month after the Biden team arrived in the White House, Dunn had urged her colleagues to craft their own approach to voting rights so that they didn't blindly follow the strategy of progressive groups. Dunn felt that some of the groups, intent on fundraising off the issue, were stoking fears— and not paying sufficient attention to the gravest threats to democracy.

It was true that a raft of new restrictive laws had been passed by Republican state legislatures. These bills undid reforms enacted in the pandemic. They made it somewhat harder to vote by mail. While Dunn regarded these Republican bills as malicious and anti-democratic, she didn't consider them catastrophic. And as an objective matter, she was correct: If states limited early voting to fourteen days, as opposed to seventeen, was that really the end of democracy? If volunteers could hand water to voters in line 101 feet from a polling place, as opposed to 100 feet, would that really alter the results of an election?

It was as if the Republicans were trolling and Democrats kept taking the bait. To combat these new laws, the Democrats were pushing sweeping legislation—that had little to do with the immediate crisis—and had exceedingly little hope of ever prevailing in the Senate. Joe Manchin and Kyrsten Sinema couldn't have been clearer about their unwillingness to scrap the filibuster. Why invest so much energy on a strategy that was such a long shot—and that came wrapped in such overheated rhetoric? If they failed to pass legislation described as necessary for saving democracy, wouldn't that just unwittingly undermine faith in elections and discourage electoral participation?

Democrats weren't focusing nearly enough attention on the immediate problem of electoral subversion. If Trump loyalists wanted to exploit their control of state legislators to invalidate the results of elections, they could.

But Dunn's suggestion that the White House develop its own strategy for formulating a voting rights bill that might pass the Senate went nowhere. With every other issue, the Domestic Policy Council conducted a rigorous review of the administration's options. But voting rights were never subjected to the standard processes for evaluating policy so that the White House might develop its own opinions about the underlying merits of provisions in the bills. The president simply accepted the claim that the bills were necessary for the political survival of the Democratic Party, because that's what activists and Nancy Pelosi told him.

Dunn wasn't the only dissenter. There were others who quietly worried that the White House was headed down a fruitless path. But they didn't raise their voices for fear of the antipathy their opposition might provoke. They didn't want to be seen as apologizing for voter suppression.

But Dunn had anticipated how the issue would play out. There was no budging Manchin and Sinema. Despite presidential lobbying and the pressure of their fellow senators, they remained committed to preserving the filibuster in its current form. Activist groups grew so frustrated with the White House's inability to push forward voting rights legislation that they vowed not to attend Biden's speech in Atlanta.

As Biden prepared to give his speech, the White House understood that he was making the case for legislation that was unlikely to pass. He was about to give a full-throated oration in defense of doomed bills. He was setting himself up for an embarrassing loss—and he would have to swallow the blame for the failure. It was an entirely foreseeable debacle.

EVEN THOUGH HE KNEW he had little hope, Biden engaged in one last stab at moral suasion. He thought of civil rights as his issue; the cause had pro-pelled him into politics in the first place. It was a claim that some activists initially viewed with skepticism. When Reverend Al Sharpton first met him in the nineties, he confronted Biden about his support for a crime bill that ratcheted up punishments. Instead of engaging with Sharpton, Biden tried to cut him down to size. "You're starting to get a national reputation that you don't want to get out there." Sharpton snapped back that at least his reputation would rest on his principles. But over time, Sharpton came to see Biden as his ally. In the Obama White House, Sharpton marveled at the fact that Biden was the most vocal proponent of police reform in meetings. He sometimes wondered if Biden was atoning for having authored the crime bill back in the nineties. After meetings, Biden would put his hands on Sharpton's shoulders and tell him, "Al, you've got to push them on this."

Now, Biden wanted to make a final impassioned appeal to the better angels, an argument that would shake senators by their lapels and make them consider their place in history:

> So, I ask every elected official in America: How do you want to be remembered?
>
> At consequential moments in history, they present a choice: Do you want to be on the side of Dr. King or George Wallace? Do you want to be on the side of John Lewis or Bull Connor? Do you want to be on the side of Abraham Lincoln or Jefferson Davis?

In the course of working on the speech, none of his advisers argued against the inclusion of the passage. But its implications were clear enough. He was arguably accusing Joe Manchin and Kyrsten Sinema of siding with the man who had fired water cannons at Black children.

Joe Biden didn't relish making enemies. That polemical passage represented a deviation from form. In his feisty mood, he was leveling the harshest historic verdict on the two senators he still needed most, if he had any hopes of reviving the core of his domestic agenda, not to mention reforming the filibuster.

ON JANUARY 13, two days after his speech, Biden paid yet another visit to the Capitol. He wanted to make a final plea to Senate Democrats in person. But an hour before he arrived, Sinema gave a speech on the floor declaring that she would never support a change to Senate rules, undercutting Biden before he even had a chance to persuade her.

While he was in the Capitol, Biden made his way across the building to Mitch McConnell's office for an impromptu visit with his old adversary and friend. His speech in Atlanta had irked McConnell, who didn't especially like being lumped in with Bull Connor and Jefferson Davis. A day earlier, McConnell denounced Biden's speech as "profoundly—profoundly—unpresidential." Then, in his most disappointed voice, he moaned, "I've known, liked, and personally respected Joe Biden for many years. I did not recognize the man at the podium yesterday."

Rather than accepting the fact of McConnell's enmity, Biden wanted to patch things up with him. He needed McConnell to know that he hadn't actually intended to compare him with one of the great villains in American history. But when Biden arrived at McConnell's door, the minority leader wasn't there. The possibility for a cathartic moment evaporated. As he turned around, Biden found himself walking the halls he had haunted as a senator, a president futilely wandering.

34

Get Caught Trying

WITH EACH BRIEFING, Biden could see Russia's war plan clicking into place. And the firm assessment of his intelligence community was that Russia would likely make its move in January, since it needed its tanks and trucks to traverse frozen ground before the onset of the spring mud, which would clog machinery and bog down convoys.

Over the past months, the Biden administration had tried to fortify the Ukrainian defenses against the coming onslaught. But those steps were self-consciously tentative. If Biden advertised the onrush of American arms shipments, he worried that he might supply a pretext for the Russians to launch their attack.

Even as the Pentagon flowed Stingers into Ukraine, it carefully avoided using their name in public statements. The Pentagon surmised that in the Russian mind, the missile launchers were the piece of weaponry that humiliatingly ended the Soviet occupation of invasion of Afghanistan in the late seventies. To even mention that they were going to be sitting on the shoulders of Ukrainians grunts risked a massive overreaction. So Pentagon briefers resorted to euphemistically describing the substance of American shipments.

Since everyone in the US government assessed that the Russians would quickly trounce the Ukrainians, the Biden administration began making plans for how it would buck up a Ukrainian insurgency, a partisan army that would fight the occupiers from within. The State Department explored creating a Ukrainian capital in exile in Poland; the Pentagon designed logistical systems for transporting arms into rebel hands.

Even though Biden didn't have much hope in diplomacy, he wanted to keep rigorously pursuing it. His overriding goal was to avoid anything that might let Putin claim the moral high ground, to make sure that the world recognized his lone culpability for the looming catastrophe. If Russia said that it had security concerns, he wanted to make a good-faith effort to address them—even if it required him to sit through painful conversations with Vladimir Putin.

Russia understood this calculus. And in some sense, it was engaged in the very same exercise. On December 17, the Russian foreign ministry published the drafts of two treaties, which it said would allay the Kremlin's anxieties. These were maximalist proposals. Not only did the Russians want to legally prevent Ukraine from ever joining NATO, it wanted NATO troops and weapons removed from every nation that had joined the alliance since 1997. That meant that countries like Poland and Estonia would be left essentially unprotected by NATO. What Russia proposed was nothing less than the dismantling of the security architecture of the post–Cold War era.

Rather than rejecting Putin's gambit outright, Biden wanted to force his hand. On December 30, Biden called Putin to suggest a process for negotiating the security deal that Putin said he craved.

In the course of explaining his plan, Biden couldn't help but slip in a warning about Ukraine. He told Putin: "Look, we know from hard-won experience that military campaigns give way to a long slog. Trying to take and occupy territory in another country is another proposition, as you know from your long history. You should give that some thought. On top of sanctions and the support that we'll give to the Ukrainians, there's a basic law of historical physics that you're going to be up against. And you're going to have to factor that in."

Biden's use of the word *occupy* provoked Putin to erupt. "We've been occupied; we've been occupied by the Nazis; we've been occupied by the French!"

Even when Putin pounded the table, reciting his litany of historic grievances, he rarely displayed emotions this raw.

When he settled down, Putin grudgingly responded to Biden's proposed framework for negotiating. "I'm going to give this one, maybe two rounds."

When Biden hung up, Jake Sullivan thought that Putin was barely going through the motions.

To MARK his first year in office, Biden wanted to hold a press conference that put to bed all the swirling speculation about his age and diminishing mental powers. He believed that he was capable of a tour de force, where he dazzled with his command of the intricacies of policy. Since Ukraine would be among the primary topics, he could flash the world a glimpse of his statesmanship.

The primary problem with such appearances, however, wasn't Biden's age or acuity. It was his indiscipline and imprecision, traits that stalked the entirety of his career. And when he worked his way through the reporters' questions, demonstrating his stamina, he couldn't help himself. Asked how he would hold Russia accountable for an invasion, he replied, "It depends on what it does." He continued, "It's one thing if it's a minor incursion, and then we end up having a fight about what to do and not do."

In his mind, he knew exactly what it meant—and it had an impeccable logic. He knew from intelligence that there were scenarios, however unlikely, that didn't feature a massive land invasion of Ukraine. Russia might launch a paralyzing cyberattack or merely escalate the existing conflict in the Donbas.

But Biden's phrasing muddied his message. Just as he intended to send Putin an unambiguous message, he added an unnecessary hint of ambiguity.

When the president finished, aides showed him the sentence and the problems that it might introduce. Straightaway, Biden agreed that the press office needed to clean up his gaffe. While trying to dazzle, he had tripped, confirming the very thing his critics alleged about him.

Even before his aides had a chance to issue a clarification, Volodymyr Zelensky zinged him for his mistake. He tweeted, "We want to remind the great powers that there are no minor incursions and small nations. Just as there are no minor casualties and little grief from the loss of loved ones. I say this as the President of a great power."

Biden had erred, but so had Zelensky. In the White House, the tweet confirmed the impression that Zelensky was unserious. Who tweets sarcastically, when they are about to be conquered by an authoritarian foe? Why was he estranging himself from his best source of protection?

ON JANUARY 21, Tony Blinken returned to the shores of Lake Geneva, the site of the previous summer's Biden-Putin summit, back when it seemed as if the rivalry between the countries could be diplomatically managed.

Where meetings with Putin were always uncomfortable, time spent with Sergei Lavrov was different. Rather, there were usually two different versions of himself that Lavrov presented to the world. There was the mouthpiece of the regime, who blustered in official meetings. "Mr. Nyet," they called him. The other Lavrov was a cartoonish version of a European diplomat from the old school—a chain-smoking ironist, a fop who liked to issue urbane asides over whiskey.

For ninety minutes of scheduled dialogue, Lavrov mouthed Putin's talking points with conviction. He insisted that there was no invasion in the works. He thundered about NATO's threats to his country.

Blinken, whose father and uncle were diplomats, understood the game. He told Lavrov that the United States would issue a formal reply that would address Russia's concerns.

But as Lavrov made his way out the door, Blinken asked if he could speak to him alone. He ushered him into a conference room, while their aides waited outside. He hoped that he could have a moment of honest conversation, where Lavrov broke from his official persona and reverted to his alter ego.

"Sergei, tell me what it is that you're really trying to do?"

Blinken was posing a question that flummoxed the Biden administration. Did the Russians really believe that they would be able to govern the forty million people of Ukraine, who had their own strong sense of national identity and thirty years of experience living in an independent democracy?

But Lavrov brusquely ignored the question. He left the room and walked away.

If Biden couldn't stop Russia, then he at least needed to prepare Ukraine. And bizarrely, that exercise felt only slightly less excruciating.

Joe Biden didn't especially enjoy his conversations with Volodymyr Zelensky. To describe them as conversations wasn't quite right. They often began as litanies. When the actor-cum-politician got on the phone, he tended to launch into a list of demands, transmitted without ever really pausing for a response.

On January 27, the leaders connected again, and Zelensky straightaway began one of his diatribes. But Biden stopped him.

"Come on, man," Biden told him. "We're going to support you. But there's got to be give-and-take here. We've got to talk about the strategy here. We've got to talk about the things that you're doing."

Back in early November, it was Tony Blinken who first pulled Zelensky aside at the United Nations climate summit in Glasgow and told him about the imminent Russian invasion of Ukraine. He watched as Zelensky struggled to absorb the warning that his neighbor wanted to erase his country from existence. Then, in early January, Bill Burns visited him in Kyiv to repeat the warnings, to press him to act in the face of the coming onslaught.

Burns felt sympathy for Zelensky. Nobody would want to believe that something so terrible could happen to their country, and what the Americans were describing was the worst nightmare.

But what made Zelensky such a confusing interlocutor is that he kept pushing for more—for more weapons, for a place within NATO—even as he denied the intelligence about the invasion.

And Biden felt as if he needed to dramatize the predicament. He told the far younger Ukrainian leader, "Let's press pause on everything we can do for you. Let's just focus. They are coming for Kyiv. They are coming for Kyiv."

Over the course of January, the US had shared intelligence with Zelensky about Russian plans to decapitate the Ukrainian government and replace it with a puppet regime, subservient to Moscow. Biden was, in effect, pleading with Zelensky to take his own self-preservation more seriously.

But Zelensky refused to believe that the Russians were about to launch a strike on Kyiv.

"No they aren't," Zelensky replied. Whatever the intelligence claimed, it was simply illogical for Putin to attack Kyiv. This was most likely an exercise in coercive diplomacy, not an omen of total invasion.

By denying reality, Zelensky was failing to take important steps needed to defend Ukraine. His country didn't have advanced plans for continuity of government that would help guide the country if the Russians managed to kill him. With so much foreknowledge of the Russian battle plans, he could foil the invasion—or at least slow it down. In the face of the looming attack, the Ukrainian military had conducted exercises in the north of the country. Instead of leaving the troops in place as a buffer against invasion, they returned the battalions to their bases. The decision perplexed officials in the Pentagon, who considered the dispersal to be utterly negligent.

That he didn't appear to be taking any of these steps was a data point that informed the military's assessment of Ukraine's capacity for survival. Russia had begun modernizing its military in 2008, reforming its command structure, spending billions on advanced weapons. It had been preparing its battle plans for months. If the Ukrainians weren't preparing to fend off the overwhelming force amassing on its border, then the war would be a rout. Mark Milley told congressional intelligence that he expected Kyiv to fall within seventy-two hours, and nobody in the administration saw any reason to question that prophecy.

35

Vacancy

ON JANUARY 27, Stephen Breyer announced to the world that he would be leaving the Supreme Court, after nearly twenty-eight years on the bench. For a floundering presidency, his retirement represented a gift, a chance to accomplish something conventionally regarded as worthy of the history books.

Back in the primaries, in his quest to win the endorsement of South Carolina congressman Jim Clyburn, Biden promised to name the first ever Black woman to the highest court, if he ever had a vacancy to fill. It was a vow that earned Clyburn's endorsement—which delivered Biden the primary victory that salvaged his campaign.

If you asked Joe Biden, and he'd probably tell you even if you didn't, there wasn't anyone in Washington who had confirmed more Supreme Court justices than he had. He presented himself to aides, and to the wider world, as the master of the process, who knew all the blind corners that usually wrecked nominations. But whatever the merits of his historical claims to acumen, he was also in a position of weakness. His choice wasn't entirely his own.

Joe Manchin—and to some unknown extent Kyrsten Sinema—hovered as a menace to the Biden presidency. All through his first year in office, Biden would tell his friends and supporters, "Joe Manchin has never voted against me anytime I asked." Then, with the collapse of Build Back Better, Manchin abandoned him. And in Manchin's bitter mood, who knew how he might set out to further wound Biden? The senator, in effect, had veto power over Biden's pick.

And then illness further scrambled Biden's calculus. Just as Breyer retired, the White House received word that New Mexico senator Ben Luján had checked himself into the hospital feeling dizzy. He had suffered a stroke, at the age of forty-nine. His condition would keep him out of the Senate for weeks, if not longer. In the worst-case scenario, Biden didn't need just Manchin, he also needed the support of a Republican defector.

Within the White House, this felt as if the moment the entire presidency might topple. Having failed to pass his signature piece of legislation, he couldn't afford the humiliation of the failure to confirm his preferred nominee. In his self-conception, he would nominate someone who might go down in history as a great justice, as the second coming of William Brennan or Thurgood Marshall, but what he really needed was the win.

Ron Klain, who served as Biden's chief counsel on the Senate Judiciary Committee back in the late eighties and early nineties, had his own passionate theories about how to best manage the process, and he had his own candidate for the job. Through his involvement with Harvard, Klain became friendly with Ketanji Brown Jackson, who served on the university's board of overseers. Jackson had clerked for Breyer, and it wasn't hard to imagine that the sentimentalist in Biden would like that poetic symmetry of her occupying her mentor's chair.

Jackson had an elite résumé—all the finest degrees, all the right clerkships—and a reserved yet self-confident demeanor that presented as the textbook definition of a judicious temperament. She could also write rigorous opinions with fists, including a memorable excoriation of Trump, when the ex-president asserted a ridiculously expansive view of executive privilege. "Stated simply," she wrote, "the primary takeaway from the past 250 years of recorded American history is that Presidents are not kings." That line suggested the characteristics of an effective liberal justice for the times, who really only had the power to eloquently howl in dissent.

Less than a year earlier, Biden had elevated Jackson to the District Court of Appeals, taking the seat that Merrick Garland vacated when he became Attorney General. Biden and Klain quickly credentialled her, which made a next promotion possible. For all appearances, she seemed the chosen one.

A line in her résumé, however, kept tripping the White House. She had spent two and a half years as a public defender, where she defended accused terrorists detained in the military prison at Guantánamo, among other unsavory clients. During her nomination to the court of appeals, Republicans raked her for these cases.

And even if there weren't a cause for hesitation, Biden wasn't going to simply settle on a front-runner. When former senator Doug Jones joined the White House to help manage the confirmation process, he was given a briefing book with dossiers on twenty leading candidates. But he eventually realized that there were only a handful in serious contention.

Jackson's primary competition was district court judge J. Michelle Childs. Months earlier, nobody would have considered her a leading contender, but she had a powerful patron in Jim Clyburn. Ever since the Clinton administration, the South Carolina congressman had championed her career, touting the fact that her résumé broke the template that Democrats tended to use to tap judges. She had attended the University of South Carolina School of Law, which meant that she wasn't part of an Ivy League clique. The Supreme Court was already packed full of meritocrats. What it needed was someone who could speak for the people in Clyburn's rural district.

In the House, Clyburn's job was the whip. His expertise was rounding up votes, and he managed to wrangle influential endorsements of his candidate. Lindsey Graham said he would happily support Childs, a matter of home-state fidelity. Joe Manchin kept extolling her candidacy, since she was a relative centrist. For an embattled president, Childs became the great temptation, the sure thing, at a moment when he couldn't afford anything else.

BIDEN WANTED to test how moderate Republicans might respond to Jackson, since Manchin was never going to volunteer his support for Jackson and surrender whatever leverage he had over the process. But perhaps Biden could box him in.

Over the course of early February, Biden began placing calls to Susan Collins and Lisa Murkowski. Biden would never get them to fully commit to a nominee, but he felt he could get a truthful sense of their openness to her nomination—and he trusted that they wouldn't leak their conversation. While Biden was exploring their interest, Steve Ricchetti heard from Mitt Romney. They had a relationship that went back years. After the Obama administration, Ricchetti accompanied Biden on a quiet visit to Romney in Utah to talk about their shared interest in cancer research. It was a visit that conveyed respect, and that apparently left an impression on Romney.

Where Collins and Murkowski had voted to place Jackson on the appellate court a year earlier, Romney hadn't. But he told Ricchetti that he was in a different place now. While he couldn't guarantee his support for Jackson, he wanted to convey his openness to her nomination. Collins and Murkowski told Biden the same.

This made for a strange calculus. The administration had three likely Republican votes for Jackson. But it couldn't be sure that they would still be there if Manchin publicly rejected her. And there was no way to know that Manchin wouldn't announce his opposition before the Republicans could announce their support.

With lingering uncertainty, Biden reconsidered Childs, and seemed to be leaning toward her. But then he heard from Cedric Richmond, who ran the White House Office of Public Engagement. A former congressman from Louisiana, Richmond was Jim Clyburn's protégé. They dined together regularly at the National Democratic Club on Capitol Hill. Now he felt the need to forcefully interject. "Look, this is the first Black female. They have to pass academic muster as well as everything else. She wasn't even on law review."

Biden asked his aides to prepare rollout strategies for each of the leading candidates, including California Supreme Court justice Leondra Kruger, a compromise candidate who impressed in her presidential interview. His aides were genuinely unsure where he might land. The next day, Biden said that he had made up his mind. He was going with Jackson. For someone who considered himself an expert on the judiciary, Biden felt as if he needed to nominate the woman with the greatest likelihood of becoming a great justice. It was worth the risk.

36

The Way to
Joe Manchin's Heart

M ORE THAN A MONTH had passed since the untimely death of Build
Back Better, but Joe Manchin was still raging. Manchin trained his
anger on Biden's chief of staff. When he said the name, he almost always
spewed, Ron *fucking* Klain. In his inflamed imagination, Klain played the
role of Rasputin, who kept pushing Biden away from his centrist moorings.

But there was one member of the administration that Manchin considered a kindred spirit, and he wanted to keep her close. When he spoke with
commerce secretary Gina Raimondo, he told her, "You're not one of them."
By which he meant, her political frame of reference wasn't San Francisco or
Brooklyn. She had friendships with CEOs, just like he did. And he knew
that Raimondo had her own issues with Klain. She once called the chief of
staff to warn him about what she perceived as the administration's leftward
drift: "You know they didn't elect Elizabeth Warren president."

In early February, Manchin called Raimondo. He wanted to invite her
and her husband to watch the Super Bowl on the houseboat. It would be a
small gathering. Only one other couple—and no agenda.

After she accepted, Raimondo called Steve Ricchetti to ask him about
the protocol for visiting with Manchin. "Is there anything you want me to
convey?"

Ricchetti told Raimondo that she didn't need to persuade Manchin of anything. "Just keep him talking," he instructed.

Even after the events of December, Biden still held out hope that he could revive talks with Manchin. Biden kept scouring Washington in search of a new envoy to Manchin, who could prod him back to the table. "I need a broker," he kept saying. By which he meant someone Manchin could trust as a neutral arbiter.

Manchin, an old quarterback and enthusiastic fan, took his football seriously. The Super Bowl was a social occasion, but in his mind, far more than that. Raimondo felt as if an ill-timed intervention might explode in her face. She waited until halftime to make her move.

An energetic talker, warm, and not averse to shamelessness when the moment demanded it, Raimondo spoke to Manchin as if she had license to lay it on thick. "Come on, man," she pleaded, "you've got to talk to us. It's too important."

But Manchin did want to hear it. He began to rehearse all the reasons that he felt betrayed by the White House's press release. Raimondo wanted to drag Manchin forward, but he was marooned in his grievances about the past.

Raimondo put on an empathetic face, but she knew that she needed to keep pushing. "You cannot *not* talk. What if we have dinner at my house, just you, me, and Ron Klain. Totally casual. Not staff. No nothing."

Manchin said he needed to think it over. A few days later, Manchin's friend the journalist Steve Clemons called Raimondo. Whenever relations between Manchin and the White House frayed, Clemons played the role of peacemaker. He was adept at explaining the West Virginian's thinking with a calm clarity. Now he was stepping in to broker the summit that would bring the two sides together. He told Raimondo, "OK, the senator is in."

OVER THE YEARS, especially when they both served as governors and bumped into each at confabs, Manchin and Raimondo bonded over their shared Italian heritage. And Raimondo didn't care if she was behaving like a cliché; she was going to win him over with her eggplant Parm, roasted pork, and cannoli.

As she finished her work in the kitchen, the doorbell rang. Both Manchin and Klain arrived precisely on time. They stood awkwardly together in the entryway of her townhouse. Welcoming the pair was painful, since they only grudgingly acknowledged each other's existence.

Before she could usher them inside, her husband and their fifteen-year-old son, Tommy, returned from an errand. She had dispatched them to buy a bottle of Manchin's favorite scotch. Tommy presented it to him. "Senator, look what we've got you. Can I get you a glass?" Manchin exploded in laughter. Raimondo smiled appreciatively, hoping that her son might have dispelled the heavy mood.

When Raimondo sat Klain and Manchin at the table, she felt the moment demanded a small speech.

"Listen, I love you both. I have known Ron for a long time. He himself is a successful businessman." Klain had worked as a top executive at a venture capital firm run by AOL founder Steve Case.

"I didn't know that," Manchin interrupted. Since Manchin seemed to constantly imply that Klain was a socialist, Raimondo knew that subtly mentioning Klain's capitalist past would help bolster his standing.

She continued, "Joe, I love you. I share a lot of your politics. But I need you to like each other and work together. I did the cooking. Now you talk. I need you to bury the hatchet now."

Klain knew this evening was about swallowing pride. He didn't even say anything about the pork, which wasn't exactly a meal fit for the only man in the White House to have been inducted into the Indiana Jewish Hall of Fame.

Despite the anger he felt toward Manchin, Klain knew what he needed us to do for the sake of the Biden presidency.

"I'm sorry. This was my mistake," he told Manchin. "The country needs us to get this done."

Raimondo admired how Klain had sublimated his ego. Now it was Manchin's turn. She glanced over at him.

"I accept your apology," he said. "Let's move forward."

But Manchin couldn't help but add, "You're never going to agree to what I want." He said that the White House was going to reject his energy proposals.

To which Klain could only really reply, "Try me."

CHUCK SCHUMER had his own repair work to complete. Manchin liked to say, "We argue like brothers." But a contentious phone call on New Year's Eve, where they traded blame for the collapse of Build Back Better, felt more like fratricide. Months of Schumer's suppressed frustration with Manchin came rushing out in the form of invective. In the moment, it felt cathartic to scream. But their relationship was a wreck. Now, Schumer needed to issue his own apology, to find a path forward. He wouldn't be much of a majority leader if he wasn't on a speaking terms with his fiftieth vote.

On February 15, Schumer invited Manchin to dinner at an Italian restaurant on Capitol Hill, a meal his staff dubbed the Pasta Summit. One of Manchin's winning qualities was his openness. He always took the meeting. And he received Schumer as if he were reuniting with a friend he hadn't seen for ages.

Manchin was an expert at preserving his options. He wasn't sure he wanted a deal, but he wanted to keep the prospects of a deal alive. This time, he would set the terms. If they wanted him to vote for a bill, it was going to be his bill. It wasn't going to be a warmed-over version of Build Back Better. That was a sprawling mess, an incoherent, badly designed piece of policy that he didn't want revived. To get anything done, they would have to start from scratch.

When Manchin described this, Schumer didn't have any choice but to accept. There was a tinge of retribution to Manchin's plan. He wanted to force progressives to accept energy provisions that he knew they would hate. While Manchin wanted clean energy, he couldn't abide legislation that would penalize the fossil fuel industry.

"We can figure it out," Schumer told him.

There was another condition: Manchin didn't want to deal with the White House. He wanted to negotiate with Schumer, and Schumer alone.

"I can work with you," Manchin said.

They agreed to have their top aides meet, in private, with the aim of getting a bill done by Memorial Day. Without the president hovering over them, they could talk in a more relaxed setting. Manchin made it clear that he wasn't promising anything. He wanted to keep an eye on inflation, which could sink a deal if it kept galloping upward. But he said that he was ready to struggle his way to yes.

AFTER HE LEFT the dinner, Manchin phoned Steve Ricchetti to tell him all about it. They had a funny relationship. It sometimes seemed that Manchin forgot that Ricchetti worked at the White House—and treated him more like a fishing buddy.

Ricchetti knew that Manchin was in a precarious state. He could either come to Biden's rescue or do irreparable harm to the White House.

While Manchin seemed to be edging back to the negotiating table, he would also muse aloud about how he had composed a farewell letter in his head, an official resignation from the Democrats, his ancestral party.

After all the attacks leveled against him, he just didn't feel part of the team anymore. Members of the Senate, who wore the same blue jersey, denounced him as a corrupt tool of the coal industry. They were questioning his integrity and that just wasn't right.

Then, after feeling sorry for himself, he would begin to self-aggrandize. Each time the Democrats attacked him, his poll numbers in West Virginia ticked upward. When he went down to Palm Beach for the weekend, America's greatest entrepreneurs hailed him as a true hero. Some whispered to him that he ought to consider running for president himself, and they would even back him.

Why wouldn't he become an independent?

When he began to bluster about these grand plans, Ricchetti would try to gently redirect him. "You don't want to be that person."

He told Manchin that he was getting bad advice. The Senate wasn't going to be evenly split forever. There would come a moment when he would no longer be the most sought-after man in Washington. It was even possible to name the date on the calendar when his relevance would dissipate. On Labor Day, campaign season would begin—and the Senate would turn from legislating to stumping. After the election, Manchin wasn't likely going to be the decisive senator. Which meant he had only a few months to make his move, to inscribe his name in the history books.

PART SIX

EASTERN FRONTS

February–April 2022

37

"I Know What You're Doing"

THERE WAS NO DOUBT that the intelligence community had its blind spots, but Russia wasn't one of them. The White House possessed a molecular understanding of the Russian military and its operations. Most of the time, it felt as if the White House strangely understood the machinations of its foe Russia better than its ally Ukraine.

But there was one piece of intelligence that the administration didn't possess. It never had the precise date for when Russia would launch its invasion.

Initially, the intel suggested that the Russians would invade on January 20. But Jake Sullivan felt sure that the administration had foiled those plans by engaging Russia diplomatically. When Blinken met with Lavrov in Geneva, the secretary of state promised that the White House would submit a proposal that would allay Russia's security concerns. Russia, Sullivan theorized, couldn't afford to invade while it was awaiting that document.

Once Russia postponed its initial invasion date, it suddenly contended with the fact of the Winter Olympics in Beijing, which began on February 4. Nearly everyone in the intelligence community agreed the Russians wouldn't dare risk storming across the border while its most important ally was hosting an event it considered such a profound source of international prestige. That meant the invasion would start soon after the snuffing of the Olympic flame on the twentieth of the month.

The Russian playbook, deployed in places like Syria and Chechnya, suggested that the invasion would follow a provocation, either real or invented. And there were ample examples of false flag schemes that the Russians were hatching. Russia, it seemed, intended to stage an attack, which it would attempt to blame on the Ukrainians, thus supplying the Kremlin with a casus belli.

There was an almost comic quality to these plots—as if they were kitschy homage to the tradition of subterfuge that traced back to the Potemkin village. In early February, the American intelligence community uncovered a scheme that involved Russia filming the scenes from the aftermath of a faked explosion, replete with faux corpses.

Sullivan set up a group assigned to quickly determine whether exposing such schemes might plausibly delay the Russian invasion. If the US could illustrate the phoniness of a pretextual scheme, then the Russians would surely need to devise another. The intelligence community, which could be painfully slow, trained itself to quickly decide whether exposing the schemes risked betraying a source.

The White House took satisfaction in its gamesmanship. Like Sullivan, many aides were veterans of the Hillary Clinton campaign. They remembered how Russian information warfare had damaged Clinton's candidacy. Now, they were beating the Russians at their own game. And intel reports showed that Putin was supremely annoyed at the White House's ability to deny him the narrative he felt he needed.

On February 10, the intelligence community uncovered an elaborate Russian plot—plans for a staged car bombing in eastern Ukraine—which they were convinced was the proximate justification for an invasion. What surprised the Biden administration was the timing of the plans. It looked as if Russia wanted to push forward while China was still hosting the Winter Olympics. The Russians were apparently trying to claw back the element of surprise.

At 5:15 p.m., Jake Sullivan called a principals meeting for 6:00 p.m. The leadership of Biden's national security team hurriedly assembled in the Situation Room. After months of anticipation and preparation, they were suddenly going through the paces of their own plan. Sanctions against Russia were ready to roll, but not quite. The Treasury needed to finalize an agreement with the Europeans coordinating the freezing of Russian accounts.

Afghanistan hung over the group. Collectively, they were determined not to repeat the mistakes of that debacle. In that instance, the White House moved too slowly to close its embassy. Not this time. Even if the Europeans kept their consulates open, the US had already made the decision to shutter its outpost in Kyiv. There might be a political cost to being the first to bolt from Ukraine—and the Ukrainians would surely hate that news. But Austin and Milley persuasively argued that it was unnecessarily risky to leave a diplomatic presence on the ground. They couldn't abide the risk that Russia might shell an occupied American embassy, even unintentionally, which might necessitate the sort of reprisal they dreaded. As the group worked through its list of decisions, it agreed that the time had come to tell Americans in Ukraine to leave the country immediately.

The president entered the meeting forty-five minutes after it started. He said that he wanted the declassification of the intelligence about Russia's plans to begin immediately so that the administration could share the evidence of an impending invasion as widely as possible. Once the White House exposed the plot, it might even delay Russia's plans again.

As the White House barreled through its to-do list, it reached the point where all it could do was hunker down, study the satellite imagery, cull the incoming intelligence, and wait for the signs of war.

EVERY HOUR THAT the Russians didn't roll over the border was an opportunity to forestall it. Sullivan wanted to take one last stab at diplomacy. Sergei Lavrov was a dead channel. The State Department was increasingly convinced that Putin had shut him out of his inner circle. Putin probably hadn't even revealed the scale of the planned invasion to his own foreign minister.

Sullivan believed that his best hope was to connect with one of the small handful of aides within the Kremlin that Putin still consulted. He asked to meet with Yuri Ushakov, one of Putin's closest foreign policy advisers, in Scandinavia—and to his surprise the Russians agreed. Sullivan quietly told the Ukrainians and Europeans of his plans. But just as he made preparations for the trip, he received a message from the Kremlin. It simply said that the occasion needed to be rescheduled for a later date.

February 18

Lloyd Austin was finishing a visit to an air base in central Poland. A month earlier, he had ordered thousands of additional troops deployed to NATO's eastern front, to both reassure the alliance's members in the region and to counteract whatever delusional thoughts might enter Putin's mind about launching an even wider war.

On his way to the airplane carrying him home, he called Sergei Shoigu, the Russian defense minister. Over the last year, they had touched base occasionally. But Austin wanted to take his own stab at warning the Russians off their plans.

"I know what you're doing," he told his counterpart.

"We're just exercising," the Russian replied. "They'll be leaving soon."

That felt ominous to Austin. *Leaving soon* was not the same as *coming home*. And when Austin kept pushing Shoigu to cite an end date for the exercises, the Russian wouldn't supply him with one.

Austin carefully modulated his emotions, in most cases. But he simply couldn't in the face of such blatant dissimulation. "You can't fool me. I know what you're doing. You can't do this. You will face significant economic consequences."

But Shoigu was blowing him off. And Austin, who intellectually had assimilated the fact of the invasion, now felt it personally.

CONVENTIONAL WISDOM IN WASHINGTON held that Joe Biden gave Kamala Harris the worst assignments. But the Munich Security Conference was different. Biden considered the confab the ingathering of *his* people. As a senator and vice president, Biden wasn't going to let anyone tear him away from Munich, where he could do the glorious business of Atlanticism with the great and good. For Biden to dispatch Harris to Munich at this moment in history was a public vote of confidence.

The Biden administration was less sure that it wanted Volodymyr Zelensky in attendance. State Department officials kept prodding their counterparts in Kyiv: "Are you sure that you want him to come?" But Zelensky kept insisting that he needed to make the trip, despite all the warnings that the Russians might invade in his absence.

Harris booked time with him at the Commerzbank building, across the street from the conference hotel. Sitting at the table with him and a retinue of aides, she walked through the latest intelligence, while Zelensky scribbled notes.

"Study what we're sharing very carefully," she urged him. "It sure looks like the makings of an invasion."

"I'm not convinced," he told her.

"All I can do is share the facts," she replied.

"Okay, if you're right, what should I do? What's your advice?"

Harris pleaded with him: "Accept it. This is real. Denial is not helpful. Even if we're wrong, you need to be prepared. Take steps for your own safety. Plan for the continuity of government. You need to believe this is going to happen."

It was hard to know if she was making any progress, since he didn't really have anything substantive to say in response to her plea.

As she left the meeting, she put her hand on her chest, unsure whether she would see Zelensky again.

February 22

"When the fuck is this going to happen?" Sullivan asked Mark Milley. Nearly two weeks had passed since the administration publicly declared that an invasion was imminent. But they still didn't have hard evidence that Putin had issued orders to unleash the massive army sitting on Ukraine's border.

"We're telling you what we know at the time we know it," Milley replied.

That morning, Milley and Austin meet with the Ukrainian foreign minister Dmytro Kuleba at the Pentagon. The Ukrainian was the son of a diplomat, a wunderkind who rose through the ranks, an efficient operator—who seemed far more worldly than Zelensky or the aides around him. But Austin and Milley wanted to pierce his polished exterior and give him a good shake so that he might acknowledge the imminence of catastrophe.

Since Austin was the preternaturally calm one, he went first. He walked Kuleba through the latest evidence that his country was about to be overrun.

But Kuleba deflected it. He said that Putin's true target was Lithuania, although he allowed that the Russians might try to capture more of eastern Ukraine.

In his unfailingly polite way, Kuleba said that he appreciated the value of the intelligence that the US kept making public, but hinted that it was also inducing panic in his country. "It comes at a cost to us," he said.

Now, it was Milley's turn. Where Austin practiced restraint, Milley was worked up. His months of frustration with the Ukrainians came out in a machine gun spray of dismaying facts.

"This is what you can expect. Seventy battalions will attack. . . . It's coming. There will be an attack in the next twenty-four to forty-eight hours. . . . You haven't seen anything like this since World War II. . . . They are coming lock, stock, and barrel. . . . It's going to be massive movements along multiple axes."

Milley's colleagues chuckled to themselves about watching him in emotional overdrive, struggling to contain himself. If it didn't terrify you, it was a good laugh.

Across the table, Milley stared at Kuleba. His face was the shade of snow. None of the Americans could be sure if it was the substance of the presentation or the style of it that left Kuleba looking so wan.

February 23

When Bill Burns woke up that morning, he felt nagged by doubts. Maybe Russia's buildup was a big bluff. For weeks, he had waited for the invasion to happen. Every day, it felt imminent. And every day, the Russian troops sat in their bases in Belarus. Was it possible to look at the aggregation of data points, which formed such a clear pattern, and then impose the wrong interpretation on them?

That morning he spoke with Bruno Kahl, his German counterpart, who was in Kyiv. "It's not going to happen," he told Burns. Tony Blinken heard the same thing from foreign minister Annalena Baerbock. She told him she thought the Americans had overstated the Russian plans. To which Blinken replied, "Call me in a few hours."

There was nothing more irritating than Europeans smugly chastising the United States for its overconfidence. But given the way that events were unfolding, it felt annoyingly possible that they might be right.

At eleven in the evening, all doubts melted away. Vladimir Putin released a twenty-eight-minute video. He sat at a clean desk, intersecting it at an off-kilter angle, with his hands resting motionless in front of him. "Citizens of Russia, friends, I consider it necessary today to speak about the tragic event in Donbas and the key aspects of ensuring the security of Russia." His style was strangely academic. And before he reached his inevitable conclusion, he spent nearly fifteen minutes lecturing about the history of

American power. Occasionally, he lifted one of his hands to emphasize a point, then returned it to its place. The moments he exhaled before beginning a sentence were the only sign that an authentic being was delivering the remarks.

Then he landed on the sentence that everyone in the administration had so long anticipated. He declared war, but dared not call it that. It was a special military operation:

> The purpose of this operation is to protect people who, for eight years now, have been facing humiliation and genocide perpetrated by the Kiev regime. To this end, we will seek to demilitarize and denazify Ukraine, as well as bring to trial those who perpetrated numerous bloody crimes against civilians, including against citizens of the Russian Federation.

JAKE SULLIVAN WAS in his office when he picked up the phone and heard Mark Milley barking at him, "It's starting."

Milley was calling from a command center in the basement of the Pentagon, and he was having two simultaneous conversations, one with Sullivan, the other with aides tracking the movement of Russian troops.

He spoke to Sullivan in clipped sentences. "Twenty-four missiles in the air, no confirmed hits."

Days earlier, Russian troops had left their bases and moved to forward operating positions. Now, they were rolling toward the border. Planes, loaded with bombs and missiles, were airborne. It wasn't quite unfolding like Milley predicted. The Russians hadn't launched a cyberattack in advance of its military operation. But the military operation was roughly playing out as Milley presaged when he whipped out his map with red lines in October. The Russians were pouring into the country from every plausible direction—from Crimea in the south, from Belarus in the north, from Russian-occupied areas of Ukraine in the east.

Sullivan went to brief the president on the beginning of the war that he expected for months, yet that also felt like the dawn of a terrifying new age.

WHEN HE FINISHED with the president, Sullivan connected with Andriy Yermak, Zelensky's chief of staff. They weren't friends. But he was a human being whom Sullivan knew and liked. Only a few days earlier, Sullivan had met with him in Brussels to talk through the administration's plans. Now, as they spoke on the phone, Sullivan struggled to think of anything other than the fact that Yermak might not survive another night.

Sullivan knew that Yermak was somewhere in a bunker beneath Kyiv—and that Russian troops were on the outskirts of the city and that assassins might be in pursuit of Zelensky. And if they tried to capture or kill Zelensky, Yermak would likely suffer his boss's fate.

Even though it was hardly his specialty, Sullivan couldn't help but provide Yermak with survival instructions. "I hope you're somewhere protected. . . . Don't tell me where you are. . . . Keep moving around. . . . Be mindful of his comms." This was trite advice, Sullivan knew, but he struggled to convey the depth of his feelings.

"We're going to be okay," Yermak replied.

Yermak said that he wanted to put Zelensky on the phone so that he could speak with Biden. Sullivan called up to the White House residence so that Biden could take the call in his study. When the White House operator patched Zelensky through, he pleaded with the president. "Do whatever you can to make this stop," Zelensky told him. He asked him to call Putin and tell him to "turn this off."

Zelensky's gravelly voice was so raw, his sense of urgency so palpable, that it felt, for a flicker, as if Biden were in the bunker himself.

38

The End of the Dream

FROM THE SEATS in the Situation Room, the invasion of Ukraine unfolded as dramatic irony. The Biden administration, more or less, knew each of the significant Russian moves before they transpired. And there was a locale on the map where the generals, spymasters, and foreign policy hands collectively turned their attention.

Antonov Airport was the home to a proud achievement of Ukrainian avionics, the world's largest airplane, a hulking cargo jet nicknamed Mriya, the "Dream." But the Russians envied the facility for an entirely different reason. It sat on the edge of the suburb of Hostomel, six miles from Kyiv, with a wide runway running through the middle of the facility.

In Putin's war plan, Antonov was the crucial target. Once paratroopers seized Antonov, the Russians could quickly land troops. Successfully taking the airport would allow Russia to position its most skilled soldiers on the outskirts of the enemy capital, without having to bother with slogging through the muck of the countryside. Since Kyiv would be dazed by its initial assault, Russia figured the forces it placed at Antonov could saunter into the capital and install a puppet regime.

More than a month before the war began, Bill Burns flew to Kyiv to secretly meet with Zelensky. He implored him to mount an aggressive defense of the Hostomel airport, to shift air defenses to the facility, whatever it took to stop the Russians from gaining a bridgehead so proximate to Kyiv.

But the Americans could never tell if the Ukrainians were heeding their advice. The Ukrainians shared exceedingly little information. Milley kept pressing his counterpart, General Valerii Zaluzhnyi, for a copy of his war plan—he wanted a sense of his stockpiles and how he planned on using them. The fact that Milley never received a copy was utterly perplexing. The Ukrainians kept begging for more weapons, without giving the least hint of what they intended to do with them.

Then, in February, Zaluzhnyi finally agreed to share a one-page summary of his plan with the Pentagon's attaché at the embassy in Kyiv. He would only let her take handwritten notes, summarizing the document. It was strange behavior that hardly suggested confidence, competence, or trust.

But the American intelligence had precisely anticipated the Russians' opening move. Early in the morning on the twenty-fourth, Russian Ka-52 Alligator attack helicopters banked toward Hostomel, after flying along the Dnipro River, close to the ground to evade radar. At the air base, the civilian employees who worked in cargo transport heard the unexpected roar of rotors, the sound of gunfire strafing their workplace. Some huddled in a bunker beneath the airport's cafeteria; others dove to take cover in a sewer.

It wasn't that the Ukrainians had ignored Burns's warning. In fact, they had moved air defenses to Hostomel. But Ukrainian paranoia was also justified. The Russians had recruited the son of an airport employee, who revealed the location of the air defenses, allowing the Russians to knock them out and begin landing troops.

And they hadn't truly taken Burns's warning to heart. A few weeks earlier, the Ukrainians had shifted experienced soldiers away from Hostomel to the eastern front. The remaining three hundred fighters in the airport were a collection of inexperienced conscripts and guardsmen, not enough to fend off Russian special forces. When one of them ran out of ammunition, he jumped into his car and used it to plow into Russians. In the end, there was no possibility of resisting, only jumping over fences and clambering into fleeing vehicles.

Matthew Chance, a CNN correspondent, approached the air base because a source told him that the Ukrainian army had quickly retaken it. He stopped at a checkpoint, which he assumed the Ukrainian army had set up, and asked the soldier, "Who's in control of this region?"

The soldier answered, "It's the Russians that are in control."

"Well, where are the Russians then?"

"We are the Russians."

KYIV WAS FILLED with Russian sleeper agents, some of whom spent the months before the war driving taxis through the capital; others lived in apartments a short walk from Volodymyr Zelensky's office. With the onset of war, these assassins and saboteurs were unleashed.

To fend off the threat from within, state radio instructed civilians on the most effective techniques for assembling a Molotov cocktail. The government began distributing tens of thousands of guns to civilians.

Jake Sullivan knew that the Russians might try to kill Zelensky, but there was no hard intelligence about any of the particular plots. He learned of them only after the fact from the Ukrainians.

Around the world, rumors began to swirl, some of them presumably planted by the Russians, that Zelensky had gone missing. His voice quivering, the Italian prime minister Mario Draghi told his parliament that Zelensky had failed to show for a phone appointment.

This was just panic—and the fog of war. But it highlighted the fact that the Ukrainians were fighting two wars: One of them would take place in villages like Hostomel. The other was an information war, a war for hearts and minds. It became quickly apparent that the latter was Zelensky's specialty. His résumé hardly suggested that of a wartime leader, but he was ready to play the role of a lifetime.

In response to Draghi's premature premonition, Zelensky tweeted, "Next time I'll try to move the war schedule to talk to #MarioDraghi at a specific time. Meanwhile, Ukraine continues to fight for its people."

The next day, the Associated Press ran a story that quoted an exchange between Zelensky and an unnamed American official. In the account, the American official asked Zelensky if he wanted to evacuate Kyiv. To which Zelensky replied, "The fight is here; I need ammunition, not a ride."

It was one of history's great retorts, a line that screenwriters might conjure as they imagine their next blockbuster, and according to the administration it was apocrypha, a bit of lore traveling through the wire service of record. And it went instantly viral, affixing itself in the popular imagination, cultivating the image of a Churchillian leader willing to risk his life for the sake of his nation.

Jake Sullivan's advisers considered asking for a correction, but never bothered. A good story that came at their expense was understandable in the circumstances. If anybody deserved a little slack, it was Volodymyr Zelensky.

Until the moment of the invasion, the White House had experienced its Ukraine policy as a slog, where it kept pushing allies to pursue policies that they resented. The Europeans weren't enthusiastic about cutting economic ties with Russia. The Germans kept wobbling about their plans for Nord Stream 2. Even the Biden administration's own Treasury department resisted the idea of kicking big Russian banks off Swift—the international system that allows banks to communicate with one another across borders—because it would threaten financial stability.

But then, the images of Ukrainians huddled on subways and crowded into trains evacuating embattled cities roused the publics in Europe and America into a rare state of fervent solidarity. *The New York Times* ran a story about the struggle of a flag maker in Cincinnati to keep up with demand for the Ukrainian standard. Blue and yellow flags began to fly from apartment buildings in places like Seattle and San Francisco. European nations, where populist politicians won robust followings by railing against immigration, threw open their doors to Ukrainian refugees.

Policies that the administration struggled to achieve through patient diplomacy suddenly materialized on their own. The Germans announced that they were no longer pursuing Nord Stream 2. Europeans agreed that Russia should be removed from Swift.

When Jake Sullivan woke up in the morning, he found himself surprised by the new sanctions that the Europeans and British announced while he slept. It felt as if the Western world had entered into a global bidding war, each nation racing to show their leadership by slapping ever-more-punitive measures against Russian oligarchs. This was pleasing, but also wild. The allies weren't coordinating with one another—and they were implementing sanctions with the goal of showing up one another. The White House prodded the allies to move in sync. But, in reality, the rush to pile sanctions on Russia was a function of helplessness. There was little the governments could do to tilt the battlefield in the Ukrainians' favor.

IN HIS PESSIMISTIC STATE, Sullivan asked Matt Miller, a communications specialist who temporarily joined the NSC to help manage the crisis, "What's our plan for preparing the nation for Kyiv falling?" The president's speechwriters began to write an address that Biden could deliver if the Russians captured the Ukrainian capital.

To prevent that from happening, on the second day of the war, the president authorized a fresh shipment of arms. The administration announced it would send $350 million worth of Stingers, Javelins, and small arms, some of them stockpiled in Poland. In a forty-eight-hour period, the United States doubled its spending on the Ukrainian military.

As trucks carrying the weapons began streaming across the Polish border, Sullivan watched nervously. There was no doubting the morality of arming the Ukrainians, but he worried that the Russians might suddenly regard the United States as cobelligerent and target the shipments or the airfields in Poland, where the arms were being warehoused. It wasn't that he considered this an overwhelming possibility. But the consequences of an attack would be so dramatic that it could draw the US into a war with Russia.

ON SUNDAY EVENING, two days after the delivery of the weapons began, Vladimir Putin took to state television to announce that he was putting his nuclear forces on high alert, a posture he described as "special combat readiness." He seemed to be amplifying a message he had delivered on the eve of the invasion: interfere in Ukraine, he warned the West, and suffer "consequences you have never seen in history."

It sounded ominous, but what exactly did he mean? Bill Burns considered it within the realm of possibility that Russia might use a tactical nuclear weapon—not a bomb that would destroy a city, but something that could devastate thousands of soldiers in one attack, spreading radiation ever farther.

Before the war started, Sullivan had commissioned a group, called the Tiger Team, to ponder how the US should respond to Russia's use of a nuclear weapon. As the Tiger Team pondered scenarios from hell, it would run exercises where members of the National Security Council would role-play—with the hopes that the exercises might yield strategic insights. But Putin's speech had thrown them for a loop.

In the early days of the war, the Russians ghosted their American counterparts. Lloyd Austin's line of communication to Sergei Shoigu went cold. Milley used to talk with Valery Gerasimov, his equivalent at the apex of the Russian military, but he hadn't heard from him in weeks. These were textbook circumstances for misunderstanding and miscalculation.

When Biden's military commanders briefed him on Putin's speech, they admitted their befuddlement. None of the Russia hands had ever encountered the phrase *special combat readiness* in all their studies of their adversary's military doctrine. It was a curious description. If the United States were to change its nuclear posture, it would trigger a series of actions—movements at silos, bombers loaded at bases. But as the American military scanned imagery from Russia, it didn't see anything of note.

Biden's commanders told him that Putin was likely bluffing. He was engaged in a provocative rhetorical gambit to spook the US and its allies from taking more aggressive steps on Ukraine's behalf. Milley advised him not to raise the stakes any further. The greatest dangers would be reciprocating Putin's bluster with an actual shift in America's own nuclear posture.

"It's a helluva bluff," Biden said.

If there was genuinely nothing to the Russian rhetoric, Biden went on, let's tell the world that we're not elevating our threat level. If we have a chance to reassure the world—not false assurance, but the real deal—let's do it publicly.

Even still, Putin was messing with nuclear kindling. Worried about the next Russian escalation, the administration reached out to the Kremlin to create a military-to-military channel that could be used to work through any confusion that might inadvertently lead to nuclear Armageddon. The governments needed a line of communication—not for the sake of dialogue, that wasn't possible, but to let the other side understand their concerns, to have a chance to step back from catastrophe.

ZELENSKY HAD HIS own fears of calamity. On March 3, the Russian army launched an attack on the nuclear power plant in Zaporizhzhya, the largest in Europe. The Ukrainian president called Biden and told him that he had good reason to believe that the Russians had booby-trapped the facility, with the intention of causing a meltdown. Having survived Chernobyl, Ukrainians intimately understood and deeply feared the consequences of a reprise of that disaster. If Zelensky's information was correct, he was describing an act of terrorism that would reverberate through the generations.

Sullivan began to assemble nuclear experts from across the government, to see if there weren't steps that the administration could take to avert a meltdown. He gravitated to an engineer, Jill Hruby, who ran the National Nuclear Security Administration and who became his primary source of counsel. Working with Andriy Yermak—and American diplomats in Poland— they helped to procure backup generators and the diesel to fuel them, and then placed them within a short train ride of the facility. Sullivan gave the Ukrainians the names of American experts who could help iron out issues with the sensors that detected radiation levels at the plant. For forty-eight hours, the Situation Room believed that Ukraine was standing on the precipice of a disaster that would draw the United States deeper into the conflict. Only over the course of days did it become clear that the worst wouldn't unfold—and even if it did, the Ukrainians now stood a good chance of managing it.

But there was no doubt that they were dangling over the brink.

39

The Battle of Kyiv

THE RUSSIAN PARATROOPERS moved beyond the fence encircling the Antonov air base and began to snake through the forest outside Kyiv and into the surrounding villages. This was how Vladimir Putin's plan for taking Ukraine was supposed to unfold. The arrival of elite Russian units, on the edges of the city, intended to stagger Kyiv's defenders. It would allow Russian troops to rush to capture the capital, an almost effortless victory.

At first, this plan looked like a masterstroke. But with the Russians a quick drive from the office of the presidential administration, it began to break down. For months, Ukraine's top commander, General Valerii Zaluzhnyi, had failed to fully internalize the American warnings about the centrality of the Antonov air base to the Russians' ambitions. Now that he could see the evidence of the mistake, he quickly corrected it.

On the first evening of the war, he ordered bombers to fly over Antonov's runway—and to crater it. He dispatched the 72nd Mechanized Brigade, an elite unit, far more skilled than the conscripts who retreated from the airport in the first hours of the war, to retake the facility.

That wasn't possible, at least not yet. But the Ukrainians held a position close enough to Antonov to fire on the Russian helicopters as they approached the airfield with reinforcements. Some three hundred Russian soldiers were shot from the air, according to the Pentagon's estimates. The next wave of Russian Il-76 that approached Antonov turned around to avoid meeting that fate.

By adjusting their strategy, the Ukrainians set the terms for what would come to be known as the Battle of Kyiv. Russian soldiers were implanted in the near suburbs of Kyiv, places with names like Irpin and Bucha and Hostomel. They occupied homes in the villages, requisitioned the vodka in their cabinets, looted their living rooms, and raped women.

But the Russians faced the same obstacles that always hobbled invading armies. They stumbled through foreign terrain while battling an opponent with a will to fight that they could never match. The Ukrainians destroyed local infrastructure to save the nation. Troops detonated roads, bridges, and railway tracks—anything to impede the Russians' advance. After Ukrainians blew up the dam that held back the Irpin River, Russian paratroopers threw off their tactical gear and swam for their lives. Zaluzhnyi's men managed to eliminate most byways into Kyiv—and fought the Russians ferociously at the remaining entry points.

This was the razor-thin margin of Ukraine's independent existence, the ability to hold back the Russians at the barricades of steel and sandbags that constituted the new gates of Kyiv.

With each passing day, the improbable thought of a Ukrainian victory became slightly more probable. A new Ukrainian identity solidified itself: a nation of plucky underdogs, whose guile allowed them to survive Goliath's assault. After a week of war, they had blocked the Russian advance into Kyiv. But that felt like a mere respite.

THE IMPULSE TO DISPLAY solidarity was a human impulse, a political imperative, and an excruciating conundrum for the Biden administration. And it was exacerbated by the European Union's foreign policy chief, Josep Borrell. On February 27, he offered to finance the purchase of MiG-29 fighter jets that could be sent to Ukraine. It was an option that European ministers were considering, but just an option. And Borrell's public tendering of that offer caught them by surprise.

During those first days of the war, Ukrainian fighter pilots were central characters in the nation's emerging narrative: they were daredevils who couldn't lose a dogfight. This was, largely, a conceit of the propagandists, the sort of tall tale that sprouts in war. One pilot, dubbed the Ghost of Kyiv, was said to have shot down forty planes.

These pilots weren't flying state-of-the-art jets. They were trained to master the MiG-29, a twin-engine artifact of Soviet times. Ukraine's allies possessed a limited stockpile of these planes, mostly housed on Polish Air Force bases.

In the heat of battle, Ukraine couldn't rationally assess its needs. But it knew that it needed more firepower—and if Borrell wanted to give Ukraine more, then it was going to pressure the Western alliance to make good on his offer. Zelensky zealously lobbied to make it happen, importuning his allies, telling them, "This is not ping-pong! This is about human lives! We ask once again: Solve it faster. Do not shift responsibility, send us planes."

Thanks to this pressure campaign, it became increasingly difficult for governments in the West to back away from Borrell's promise. The Poles and the Biden administration began negotiating to make good on it. Poland would give Ukraine the MiGs—and the United States would give Poland F-16s, replenishing the Polish Air Force with a sufficiently robust fleet to fend off the Russians, if it ever came to that.

But within the Biden administration—and within Biden's head—there were competing voices, pushing in different directions. Tony Blinken argued passionately for facilitating the delivery of the MiGs. He felt more deeply attached to the Ukrainian cause than anyone in the administration. On his father's side, his family traced its roots back to the country. His great-grandfather Meir was an acclaimed Yiddish poet in Kyiv; his grandfather was born there. Over his years as a diplomat, Blinken kept finding himself drawn, perhaps subconsciously, to his ancestral land.

Blinken represented the moralistic lobe of Biden's foreign policy brain. As a young aide in the Clinton administration, he worked on the American response to the Balkan War and believed passionately in deploying American power to stop a genocide in motion. That moralistic impulse within Blinken led him to argue that the US should deliver the Ukrainians the weapons they said they needed.

Another part of Biden's brain worried incessantly about the dangers of escalation—and his administration still didn't have a theory of what might trigger Russian escalation. It was relying on instinct to avoid what Russia might consider an unacceptable provocation. In nearly every discussion about arms destined for Ukraine, Biden would pose the question: "Does this increase the risk of nuclear war?" It was the Cold War fear that he carried into the Situation Room, the concern he felt most obligated to repeat.

Mark Milley appealed to Biden's sense of caution. He didn't think the Ukrainians actually needed the MiGs. The fate of the war wasn't being decided in the air; it was being determined on the ground. Milley pointed out that the Ukrainians were flying only five sorties a day. And if the Ukrainians already had fifty planes, why did they need more?

LIKE DONALD TRUMP, Joe Biden is a voracious consumer of television. That's not to say that they share the same taste in programming. As befits a vestige of another era, Biden cares deeply about *Meet the Press* and the other Sunday shows. He watched these programs to see what the pundits were saying about his presidency.

In the first week of March, such shows were filled with complaints that he wasn't doing enough to help the Ukrainians, despite the hundreds of millions of dollars in weapons that he had already shipped. And pundits began to hammer him on the question of the MiGs. In a video conference with members of Congress, Zelensky begged for their help. He told them delivering the jets was the single most important thing the United States could do for Ukraine.

As Biden pondered his decision about the transfer of the jets, his aides began to flip-flop. Jake Sullivan had initially opposed the transfer. But in the face of the public pressure, his position softened. Over at the State Department, Sullivan's evolution was regarded as an omen, a sign that Biden was done getting pummeled on the issue.

But when Biden gathered his advisers, he said, in essence, that his head, not his heart, would guide the decision. The delivery of the planes simply wasn't worth the risk. Even if he was getting clobbered on television, he wasn't going to let the pundits push him to make a decision that he regarded as a relatively empty gesture of solidarity, especially when it was so unclear how the Russians might react.

The whole episode was a fiasco. Instead of closely consulting with the Poles, the Biden administration seemed to be negotiating with their ally through press releases. And the fiasco didn't fade. Rather than letting the issue die, the Poles ambushed the White House with an unworkable proposal: Poland would fly twenty-eight planes to Ramstein Air Base in Germany, an American outpost, where Ukrainian pilots would receive them. This meant that no fighter jets would fly directly from Polish soil. It was a stunt—since it shifted the onus back to the United States to be the ultimate naysayer.

John Kirby, the Pentagon chief spokesman, rejected the Polish proposal, which meant that criticism would continue to dog the administration.

As the Russian army began to stall outside Kyiv, top officials within the national security apparatus asked a question of themselves: Why did their prewar assessments overstate the prowess of the Russian army? One theory held that the problem was mirror imaging. Pentagon officials genuinely believed that if the US military had assembled more than one hundred thousand troops, using Russia's modernized weapons against an unprepared enemy like Ukraine, it would have prevailed in a rout.

But the Russian tactics were a mess. Lloyd Austin had organized Thunder Run, the spear tip of the assault on Baghdad during the Iraq War. He knew how to run a convoy—and the Russians were committing every error in the book. A forty-mile line of vehicles stalled in the mud, with trucks that hadn't been properly prepared or maintained. Their supply line became a turkey shoot. Ukrainians on motorbikes could furtively move through the forest and position themselves to pick off the tanks at the front of the convoy, creating detritus in the road that further mired the advancing vehicles.

Bill Burns, for his part, couldn't understand why the Russians had failed to take out the air defenses around Kyiv in the first hours of the war, when they had the element of surprise. It was an omission that allowed the Ukrainians to maintain a protective canopy around the epicenter of their government. It was a mistake, he speculated, born of arrogance.

After it recovered from the staggering first punch that the Russians threw, the Ukrainian army began to benefit from a decade of deep cooperation with the American military. The Americans had instructed the Ukrainians to develop a decentralized command-and-control structure, where well-trained officers had the flexibility to maneuver without waiting around for approval. It was nearly the opposite of the sclerotic hierarchy that Russia imposed on its soldiers, who never understood their tasks until they were ordered to implement them. If Ukraine represented democracy—and Russia its opposite—then their armies were a fair reflection of the contrasting virtues of those systems.

BEFORE THE WAR BEGAN, the dominant concern was how an emboldened Russia would behave after a quick military victory. Now, the administration pondered a far different question. With Russia's campaign stalling, what would it do to reverse course? How would it respond to its battlefield humiliation?

In early March, the intelligence community learned that Russia had asked China to supply it with a fresh cache of weapons. And to the White House's surprise, China seemed inclined to oblige.

Jake Sullivan worried this would change the course of the war, for the Ukrainians, of course, but also for the US. It was one thing to fight a proxy war against Russia. There was, at least, a history of that. But it was quite another to be locked in a battlefield struggle against both Russia and China. If China granted Russia's request, then the administration would have to forcefully respond. It would set America's relationship with China on a far more hostile course.

All through the winter, Sullivan had tried to prevent this from ever happening. Starting in November, he dispatched his aides Laura Rosenberger and Kurt Campbell to share intelligence of Russia's invasion with Qin Gang, China's ambassador to Washington. The information they presented to him wasn't classified, and carried no risk of betraying sources or methods. But the details of the invasion plan hardly mattered. What they wanted to convey was how war would harm China's interests. It would wreck the global economy, just as it recovered from COVID. It would upset the stability of the global system, which China claimed to value.

Perhaps unsurprisingly, China absorbed every word from these meetings, said little substantive in response, and then relayed what it heard to the Kremlin. And US intelligence quickly learned that China had betrayed these conversations. China's behavior hardly suggested a country studiously guarding its neutrality.

Serendipitously, the evidence of China's willingness to arm Russia arrived as Sullivan prepared for a long-scheduled meeting in Rome, on March 14, with his Chinese counterpart, Yang Jiechi.

Under less contentious circumstances, Sullivan would have given the Chinese a preview of an agenda item like this. But Sullivan chose to blindside Yang with the evidence. Yang had no idea that the United States had caught wind of China's decision to supply Russia. Sullivan took advantage of Yang's stunned state to deliver a tough warning: "The bottom is going to fall out of the relationship if you move forward."

Sullivan told Yang that this issue needed to be addressed quickly—and at the highest level. He suggested that they set up a conversation between

Biden and Xi. Normally, such calls were the subject of endless negotiations over picayune details. But four days after Sullivan's meeting in Rome, Biden and Xi connected in a video conference.

Despite the rising tensions, Biden and Xi maintained the pretense that they were old friends. Biden knew better than to quickly press Xi. He tried to build slowly, walking him through the state of the war. Russia, he seemed to be suggesting, was desperately struggling, bogged down in a war that it couldn't win.

Then he pivoted to the intercepted intelligence and his warning: "I'm not threatening you. But if Chinese weapons are killing Ukrainians—or China is trying to unravel sanctions, the consequences for your relations with us, and the Europeans, not just with governments but with the private sector, are going to be profound. You don't want to do this."

Biden pointed out that without his even asking or directing them to, hundreds of companies up and left Russia after the outbreak of war. And he predicted the same fate would befall China: "The pressure on companies to change their relationship with China, if you become a cobelligerent with Russia, is going to be overwhelming, and you need to understand that dynamic."

Xi had nothing to say about the charge.

But Xi said that he wanted to address America's own dangerous behavior in Ukraine. He said that he was disturbed that the United States was operating labs in Ukraine, where it was developing biological and chemical weapons. This was one of the most cartoonish pieces of Russian propaganda—and it was beyond disturbing to hear it emanating from the mouth of China's leader.

Biden struggled to keep his cool. "You know better than that, this is crap. Stop mouthing nonsense Russian talking points: I know you know that, so give me a break."

Xi, however, wouldn't drop the argument.

It was probably the tensest exchange that Biden had ever had with Xi. And it was unclear if his stern warning would dissuade Xi or provoke him to stubbornly persist with his plans, to demonstrate how he would never cave to American demands.

By the middle of March, it was increasingly clear that the government in Kyiv would survive—and so would the transatlantic alliance supporting it. The administration felt it was time to consolidate its achievement and soak up some praise.

A presidential trip abroad is a venture that typically requires months of careful preparation. But the White House saw that there was a European Union meeting on the schedule—and it suggested to Brussels that Biden would be happy to crash it so that the president could stand shoulder to shoulder with the rest of the coalition, a projection of strength.

The culmination of the trip would be a stop in Warsaw, which was about as close to Ukraine as he could plausibly get. Although Zelensky couldn't risk the trip across the border to Poland, his foreign minister and defense minister would take the long, halting train ride, for the sake of face time with the American president.

Biden began working on a speech worthy of the moment. As Biden sat in the Oval Office, dictating lines to Mike Donilon, Mark Milley watched and egged the president on. "This is your 'Mr. Gorbachev, tear down this wall' speech," the chairman of the Joint Chiefs told him.

On the afternoon of the speech, Biden visited with Ukrainian refugees outside Poland's national soccer stadium, which had come to serve as a massive social service center, a showcase for that nation's beneficence. As he made his way through the crowd, he met with women and children who had survived weeks living in basements as Russian shells fell on their cities. Now they were lost souls, far from home, worried that they might never see their fathers and husbands again, because they were fighting on the front lines.

It was overwhelming for Biden. When a woman broke down in tears as she recounted her plight, he hugged her. He dropped the N95 mask from his face and picked up her daughter, a little girl in a pink coat and white beanie, her hand clutching the lapel of his navy blazer.

"I don't speak Ukrainian," he said, "but tell her I want to take her home."

The visit with the refugees had put him in a passionate frame of mind. He never doubted the righteousness of the cause, but he was feeling it with zeal. A few hours later, he stepped in front of Warsaw's Royal Castle, addressing a crowd of Poles and Ukrainians.

At this late stage in his career, he had largely stopped giving speeches with cadences and imagery that aspired to be described as Kennedyesque. With his age and his stutter, he seemed to accept that he would have to settle for workmanlike oratory, a folksiness that mimicked his colloquial patterns of speech. But, here in his moment, he strove for loftiness and built his speech to culminate in a grand exhortation about the moral imperative of thwarting authoritarianism.

Speaking at an excited clip, he bellowed, "A dictator bent on rebuilding an empire will never erase a people's love for liberty. Brutality will never grind down their will to be free. Ukraine will never be a victory for Russia— for free people refuse to live in a world of hopelessness and darkness. We will have a different future—a brighter future rooted in democracy and principle, hope and light, of decency and dignity, of freedom and possibilities."

Then, for a final flourish, with the power of the occasion propelling him forward, he deviated from his text. "For God's sake, this man cannot remain in power."

After delivering the speech that might have earned him the credit he deserved and craved, his improvisation became the headline. It sounded as if he were calling for regime change in Russia. It was exactly the sort of needless provocation that he abhorred, especially since it had no basis in policy. It was a potential propaganda coup for the Kremlin, which always tried to portray the United States as an imperialist meddler.

When Biden left the stage, Jake Sullivan had the thankless task of reading back the president's words to the president. Biden instantly knew that the White House would have to clarify his mistake. By the time Biden piled into the motorcade, leaving the Royal Castle, his aides had released a statement walking back his sentence. Suddenly, the press wasn't marveling at his rhetoric or his diplomatic triumphs; it was back to describing him as a blowhard lacking in self-control. *The Washington Post* reminded its readers that Biden had once described himself as a "gaffe machine."

Biden left for home, ending his triumphalist tour, feeling sorry for himself. He knew that he had erred, but then resented his aides for creating the impression that they had cleaned up his mess. Rather than owning his failure, he fumed to his friends about how he was treated like a toddler. Was John Kennedy ever babied like that?

40

Bankova

THEN, in a press conference, the Battle of Kyiv was over. On March 25, an apparatchik, Colonel General Sergei Rudskoi, told a group of assembled reporters that his country was abandoning its campaign to capture the Ukrainian capital so that it could concentrate on what he called "the main thing," the "complete liberation of the Donbas."

It was hard to know if this was a genuine concession of defeat or a feint, since Russian statements so often failed to correspond to reality. But over the next week, the occupying army began to recede from the villages northwest of Kyiv, ebbing back to the Belarusan border, leaving behind the flotsam of Russian occupation: charred tanks obstructing the roadways, department stores in rubble, once productive home gardens burned to the ground, bullet-ridden apartments with washing machines dangling by electrical cords from facades that no longer exist, and corpses.

Putin had justified his invasion with rhetoric that dehumanized. Ukraine, he proclaimed, wasn't a country. It was a province of Russia under the control of a Nazi clique. But it was the occupiers who behaved like Nazis. In the town of Bucha, an old railroad stop in the country that grew into a leafy middle-class suburb, the Russians hog-tied men and summarily executed them, 419 dead bodies in all. One of the weapons of choice in Bucha was the fléchette: steel darts crammed into artillery. It exploded in all directions, implanting darts in chests and heads to deadly effect. To make room for the bodies in the overcapacity morgue, the village priest dug a grave in the yard of his church, packed so densely that elbows protruded from the clay.

Atrocities weren't isolated incidents. In nearly every sizable town that the Russians occupied, there were torture chambers and reports of rape. Such accounts made it impossible to celebrate Russia's defeat in the Battle of Kyiv. And they fundamentally changed the moral calculus of the war. How could the Zelensky government persuade the Ukrainians to accept a peace deal, when an agreement would inevitably surrender his compatriots to life under the same murderous regime that savaged Bucha?

Even if the Ukrainians didn't feel the exhilaration of victory, the Battle of Kyiv was one of the great upsets in modern military history. And it was the United States that supplied the weapons that made it possible. Javelins stalled the convoy descending on Kyiv, and Stingers shot planes from the sky over Hostomel.

When the Biden administration described its emerging plan for arming Ukraine, it used a slogan from World War II. It called it a "lend-lease," the same name that Franklin Roosevelt used for his policy of arming Great Britain. Congress gave the Biden administration vast powers to pass along whatever weapons from the American arsenal it deemed the Ukrainians needed.

In the course of weeks, the US military created a sprawling network for transporting arms into Ukraine. It pulled weapons from caches in Europe and the Middle East, shipping much of it to a terminal in Alexandroupoli in northeast Greece and then hauling it to a central depot in eastern Poland. Because Biden promised that there would be no American boots on the ground in the war zone, the military relied on Ukrainian truckers to pick up pallets of guns and ammunition and then drive them across the border. It was like an Amazon warehouse in the holiday season, with trucks leaving at all hours, in rapid succession. Logistics were the bane of the Russian military. By contrast, moving things around, quickly and in challenging circumstances, was the thing the US military did best. Some of the very same flight crews that evacuated Afghans were now transporting weapons.

Before the war started, the United States sent weapons that hardly required any training, like Javelins. But with Ukrainian success, the sophistication of the systems loaded onto the trucks increased. That meant that the military needed to create a center in Germany for training Ukrainians to use the more advanced systems—and a tele-help center so that Ukrainians could call for assistance if there was a feature on a weapon that failed.

Experts in the Pentagon tried to anticipate the weapons that Ukraine would need next, and then pre-positioned them in Europe so that they were ready to be loaded on trucks as soon as the Ukrainians asked for them.

By April, the Pentagon began to embed Ukrainian intelligence officers directly within its operation, to eliminate any inefficiencies in the transmission of information. It created what it called a fusion cell in Poland, so that the US didn't need to pick up the phone and track down the Ukrainian who could make best use of the intel. Ukrainian officers were sitting right alongside their American counterparts, ready to relay intelligence to the correct destination, for immediate use. There were rules for the sharing of sensitive information, of course. The US wouldn't pass along information that might be used to assassinate Russian officers. Nor did it share intel about targets inside Russia. Still, the frictionless transfer of information became a battlefield strength.

Among the pieces of intelligence that the United States had intercepted was fresh evidence of China's intentions. After Biden's strident warning, China decided that it wasn't going to send arms to Russia, at least for the time being. This was an enormous diplomatic victory, which shaped the course of the war, although the administration couldn't trumpet its success.

Having lost the Battle of Kyiv, Russia said that it was regrouping and recharging, but it wouldn't have a fresh infusion of arms from its most important ally. While China continued to rhetorically supply the Kremlin, Russia was left militarily isolated. The puppet government in Belarus was its only partner. While it still didn't feel like a war that Ukraine would win, it increasingly felt like a war that it would not lose.

JOE BIDEN ENVIED Boris Johnson. He never said so, but some aides in the White House suspected it. The British prime minister had visited Kyiv on April 9, and strolled the empty city streets with Volodymyr Zelensky by his side. Biden had botched his chance to deliver a Kennedyesque speech in Warsaw, but now Johnson got to prance around Ukraine, living his Churchillian fantasies. Biden desperately wanted to take the trip himself. He asked if it was possible, but the US military wouldn't tolerate the risk.

The city might not have been a wise destination for a presidential visit, but Kyiv no longer endured regular attacks. It began to emerge from its bunkers, both literal and metaphorical. The time had come for the United States to show the flag in the city and to begin the process of reestablishing a diplomatic presence there. The first American visit needed to have some heft. Biden decided to dispatch Lloyd Austin and Tony Blinken, a buddy trip to the fringe of a war zone.

Although the battle for Kyiv was over, the mission still felt risky and required total secrecy. Within the State Department, the details were kept from all but a few close aides. A quick reaction team prepared for the possibility of extracting Blinken and Austin if they came under attack. The military would monitor the long train ride from a makeshift command center in eastern Poland.

The Ukrainian railroad, unloved before the war, had acquired a heroic reputation at the moment of crisis. It transported millions to safety, as it kept running in the most dangerous of circumstances. On April 24, it carried Blinken and Austin, traveling in separate railcars, decorated in the frilly style of a 1970s disco.

As the trains made their way down the tracks, they kept stopping. Back in the command center in Poland, these pauses sparked moments of panic. The Russians had proven themselves to be terrible at what the military calls dynamic targeting. That is, they couldn't hit an object in motion. But they were plenty adept at blowing up stationary objects.

After eleven hours of halting progress, and occasional moments of anxiety, the pair pulled into the station in Kyiv. They piled into a motorcade, which wended its way up a hill, past checkpoints, to the Bankova, the office of the presidential administration. Austin stared out the window. He knew war zones—and this didn't look like one. He could see outdoor cafés, with smiling young people sipping cappuccinos. Families strolled wide boulevards, carrying shopping bags.

But then they entered a different world. The Bankova was shrouded in darkness. Sandbags covered each window; plywood pallets remained as makeshift barricades, jamming doorways. They were led through the building by flashlight into a formal meeting room.

After months of talking to the Ukrainian leadership over the phone, they saw them assembled in the flesh. General Valerii Zaluzhnyi, chief of staff Andriy Yermak, foreign minister Dmytro Kuleba, and, of course, Zelensky himself. Despite the formality of the occasion, the meeting began with the good cheer of comrades.

But the message that Blinken and Austin wanted to deliver had the edge of tough love. They would supply Ukraine with more arms, but Zelensky needed to show more gratitude for the support. Austin told him that it grew harder to give Zelensky what he needed when members of Congress opened the newspaper and saw him excoriating the US for its insufficient support.

Through social media, Zelensky had managed to talk over the heads of governments to communicate directly with publics in the West. He became the political leader that many Americans and Europeans most admired in the world. This was threatening to global leaders. It meant that Zelensky could effectively pressure them to become more directly entangled in a conflict, which they worried could spin dangerously beyond their control.

Zelensky's pressure tactics were undeniably effective—and more than justified—but they were also wearing thin. In their calls, Biden kept boxing Zelensky on the ears for trying to drag him deeper into the fight. "You'd love nothing more than to draw us into World War III," he told the Ukrainian president in a call.

Austin and Blinken mentioned that they were hearing complaints from multiple foreign leaders who disliked how Zelensky portrayed them as uncaring when they were extending him a helping hand.

This wasn't the first time that an American official had been dragooned into giving Zelensky relationship-management tips. Bill Burns had tried to gently supply him with instructions for more productively conversing with Joe Biden so that he didn't sound so abrasive and insensitive to the president's domestic considerations. Zelensky had failed to abide by the moral code of Scranton, where gifts are followed by thank-yous.

The fact was that sanctions against Russia were causing gas prices to spike—even if they weren't especially high by historic standards, they were the metric that most Americans used to judge the state of the economy. And over the six weeks of war, they were already up a dollar per gallon. This was the sort of hike that traditionally doomed the political future of presidents.

When Blinken and Austin later recounted their meeting to aides, they felt as if Zelensky seemed taken aback by the criticism, by the fact that they had journeyed all the way to Kyiv to tell him to be nicer to his patrons or the supply of weapons might not be endless.

By the time the pair arrived back in Poland, Zelensky had already tweeted, "Grateful to @POTUS and the American people for the leadership in supporting Ukraine in our fight against Russian aggression. We defend common values—democracy and freedom. We appreciate [his] help. Today it is needed more than ever!"

41

The Gorge

THE BONFIRE BURNED intensely in the March night. From across the way, Brian Deese could see the illuminated visage of Joe Manchin. Deese had journeyed deep into West Virginia, one of the wildest parts of the state, in search of a moment of bonding with Manchin—the sort of gesture of intimacy and respect that mattered to the senator. Now, in the light of the flames, Deese felt as if he were going native, staying up late with Manchin and his minions, as if he had been thrust into an elaborate trust exercise.

When Deese left for the trip, he had the president's advice ringing in his ears: "Keep this all at a low key."

If there was a lesson that Biden extracted from the first year of his presidency, it was that he had spent too much time trapped in senatorial minutiae. Of course, he loved it. Ron Klain once felt compelled to chide him, "You're not prime minister," in his quest to extract Biden from the legislative weeds. But Biden painfully arrived at the realization that his deep involvement was time consuming and, worse, counterproductive. By taking the lead in negotiations, the president elevated the stakes. He pressurized the conversations, when they actually needed space to breathe. And there was no way that he was risking deep involvement in another round of negotiation that could go sour and make him look like a chump.

There was a pretext for Deese's jaunt. The president of West Virginia University had pulled together a group to discuss the economic development of the state. The journey culminated in a visit to New River Gorge, a newly minted national park, where the group had planned on spending the night at a lodge. Manchin suggested that Deese join him in zip-lining over the craggy terrain—and the pair posed for photos in their helmets and harnesses.

But really this was just a bit of theater. Manchin knew exactly why Deese had joined him. Before he departed for West Virginia, Deese sent Manchin a document, which he hoped would provide a bit of structure for their conversations. He copied out the climate and energy provisions from the House version of Build Back Better—and then stripped away everything that Manchin had announced he opposed. The whole point of spending time with Manchin was to get a sense of what he actually wanted—or, more to the point, what he actually disliked.

When Manchin expressed his disagreements, there was sometimes a trollish edge. He kept testing Deese to see if he was as left wing as he suspected. And he had a long list of items that he couldn't stand. He hated that rich families would receive tax credits to buy fancy electric cars. (Biden, in fact, agreed with him about that.) He also despised a program called the Civilian Climate Corps. This was a left-wing pipe dream and a spectacular waste of money. And Manchin wasn't going to be the one to make it real.

Much of Washington assumed that Manchin, with his frat boy demeanor, struggled with the details of policy. No doubt, he bluffed his way through certain hearings on issues beyond his ambit. But energy was his thing. A senator from West Virginia couldn't really survive without a deep understanding of it. He might not have an Ivy League degree like the fancy experts in the White House, but he prided himself on his ability to match them with his granular grasp of EPA regulations and tax credits.

As Deese stayed up with the senator and his staff, he began to internalize the lesson of his day with Manchin: The White House couldn't preserve the architecture of Build Back Better. If there was going to be a climate bill, it would be a bill that Manchin would craft—on his terms, not theirs. And the White House was likely going to be a bit player in the process.

JUST AFTER DEESE'S TRIP to West Virginia, Lance West grabbed a drink with Chuck Schumer's anointed negotiator, Gerry Petrella, at a bar on Pennsylvania Avenue. The pair had a rapport. While Petrella came from the south shore of Long Island and West hailed from Huntington, West Virginia, they bonded as fellow outliers in a world of elites.

As they drank, they began to work out a plan for finally cracking the substantive differences that separated their bosses. Several weeks earlier, in an interview with *Politico*, Manchin had signaled his willingness to explore common ground in a troika of areas: lowering the price of prescription drugs, remaking the tax code, and investing in clean energy. That would serve as the broad outline for a bill. To give themselves a chance of success, West and Petrella agreed to start with prescription drugs, the issue that would yield the quickest agreement, and then move on from there. Since energy was going to be the trickiest negotiation, they would leave that for last. The gap between Manchin and Schumer manifested itself in the language they used to describe the issue. Where Manchin framed the goal as energy security, Schumer talked about reducing carbon emissions.

To have any prayer of progress, they knew that they needed to shield their conversations from the outside world. Twice a week they would furtively meet in an unused conference room in the basement of the Capitol rather than in either of their offices, where colleagues would notice. They worried about keeping the White House in the loop, since word might spread from there. So they vowed to hold any word of progress as tightly as they could.

The Capitol Hill press corps had a rote question for Manchin: "Are you negotiating with the White House yet?" He could, in good faith, say that he wasn't.

NEGOTIATIONS, WEST AND PETRELLA agreed, would ramp up as soon as the Senate confirmed Ketanji Brown Jackson to the Supreme Court. That happened on April 7. Mitt Romney, Lisa Murkowski, Susan Collins, and Manchin all rallied around her, in the end. When the Senate approved Jackson, Biden stepped into the dining room off the Oval Office to place a call to Joe Manchin.

"Thank you for your help," he told him. Biden knew that if he pushed Manchin on reviving Build Back Better it would backfire, so he didn't mention the subject.

But Manchin surprised him by bringing it up himself. "I'm going to keep working at it," he told Biden. There wasn't a hint of tension in the conversation. For the first time in months, it seemed as if Manchin might have worked through his anger.

PART SEVEN

THE
COUNTEROFFENSIVE

May–November 2022

42

The Spring of Self-Pity

I N MAY, Ron Klain attended a graduation at Tufts. The whole atmosphere was exuberant. Speaker after speaker extolled the class of 2022 for gritting its way through pandemic; they marveled at the fact that the university community could finally assemble in person, after years of Zoom and incessant disruption.

As Klain watched the explosion of joy, he thought, *Why aren't we receiving any credit for making this possible?* The whole nation could rush to see *Top Gun: Maverick* in theaters thanks to the White House, because of the steps it took to disseminate vaccines, and its guidance for safely reopening the economy. The public wanted a return to normal; well, this was normal.

Yet the public seemed to think that Joe Biden had almost nothing to do with this feat. Judging by the polling, the public had little regard for his presidency. Only 38 percent of the nation approved of his performance— roughly the same response that Donald Trump consistently mustered.

Klain saw something darkly humorous about the White House's inability to move that number. Each time the public grew exercised about a problem— the lack of COVID tests, a shortage of baby formula, container ships unable to unload in ports—the administration would drop everything to solve it. These were the practical details of life, where the government touched the quotidian, and Biden obsessed over them, spending hours, say, sorting through the logistics of using the air force to import baby formula from abroad. But each time the Biden administration made progress fixing an issue, it suddenly disappeared from the public's list of top concerns. The public only lashed the administration, never rewarded it. There was no glory in technocratic troubleshooting.

Biden considered his poor approval rating a failure of the media, which somehow neglected to note all the ways in which his administration was superior to Trump's. It was also a failure of his own White House to effectively communicate. He complained that there weren't enough surrogates on television defending him. One of his fixations was David Axelrod's appearances on CNN. He was part of the Obama in crowd, and Biden complained to a friend that he still didn't get a fair shake from the guy.

Frustrated that his achievements weren't being credited, he summoned Anita Dunn back to the building. She had initially joined the White House because the president had personally insisted. Everyone knew that she would be a short-timer, and she left in August, just before the Afghanistan withdrawal—when everything started to go wrong for him. Now, he wanted her back, to help correct the course, to help bring him back to the highs of those first months in office, which now felt so remote.

SHORTAGES OF COVID TESTS came and went, shipping containers stuck at sea were unloaded, but inflation was a fug of misery that economic winds couldn't blow away. Not that the Biden administration really understood what it was confronting. At first it described the phenomenon as "transitory," which, to be fair, is what the Federal Reserve chair thought, too. It seemed like the pandemic had deprived consumers of the ability to dine and drink so they spent that cash buying stuff, but that stuff wasn't quite plentiful enough. Supply and demand were out of whack. The administration's economists kept predicting that equilibrium would eventually return. Except it didn't.

Then Biden tried to brand inflation as "Putin's price hike," which never took root, even though the Russian war had spiked energy prices.

Inflation is one of those abstractions that convey complexity and mystery, that deprive institutions and individuals, even the president of the United States, of agency. When inflation is on the rise, it spins beyond control. That is the very definition of the problem, and it frustrated Joe Biden to no end.

Biden obsessed over gas prices. It sometimes seemed that Biden couldn't go through a meeting without asking about the price at the pump. He asked that a report on gas prices be included in the binder that he took home with him every evening to peruse.

He was convinced that the fossil fuel industry was using the war in Russia as a pretext for profiteering—and because the oil companies had every incentive to restore Republican majorities in Congress, some of his aides were convinced that they were going to screw Biden by keeping prices high.

Even if his energy policy intended to wean America from fossil fuels, he wasn't going to let that policy objective get in the way of his party's political survival, or of blunting inflation's toll on the consumer. He kept ordering oil released from the government's Strategic Petroleum Reserve to drive down prices. Indeed, each time he added a fresh batch of oil to the world's supply, the cost of the commodity dropped. Over the months, after he released 180 million barrels of oil, the reserve dwindled to its lowest levels since the 1980s.

BRIAN DEESE was one of the officials charged with combating the rise in prices. As he absorbed criticism, he would console himself by staring at a chart, which he shared only reluctantly with reporters, as he didn't want to seem insensitive to the human toll of inflation. But he liked to look at it to remind himself of the underlying logic of Biden's economic policy.

The chart was a retort to the charges that the administration's frenemy

Larry Summers kept hurling at it. Summers blamed inflation, in part, on the American Rescue Plan, which injected far too much cash into the economy. The policy was perilous. It had run the economy too hot and led to employers chasing too few workers. To curb inflation, Summers argued that the unemployment rate needed to drift upward, to around 6 percent.

Deese's chart was a reminder of Biden's theory of the case. While inflation was unnerving, jobs brought stability. And all the metrics measuring economic stability were sky-high. More workers were employed, which meant that they had health insurance. Credit card delinquency and bankruptcy were way down. Household net worth was 20 percent higher than in 2019—which meant Americans were wealthier than they had been before the pandemic struck. These numbers reflected the economic principles that Biden waxed lyrical about.

But Deese conceded that this was a terrible political argument. It did nothing to refute the fact that prices in the grocery store were rising at a painful rate. He didn't consider the argument worth selling to the public. The task—of preparing for the midterm elections—was thankless, and it largely fell to Mike Donilon.

BY MAY, Donilon needed to face down the stirrings of internal revolt. Political reporters began quoting anonymous Democratic strategists, accusing the administration of rank incompetence, since it had no clear plan for the coming midterm elections. An article on CNN's website reported that the White House was "unprepared and unresponsive even to basic requests for help or information." Anger toward Ron Klain, long submerged, came rushing into public view. Anonymous sources alleged that he wasted precious time tweeting—so focused on the controversy of the moment that he wasn't looking ahead, he wasn't thinking strategically.

The early planning for the midterms had been outsourced. When Anita Dunn left the White House in August, she began working with the political arm of the Center for American Progress (CAP) on what it called the "GOP Branding Project," really a six-month search for a panacea.

Several elections back, Republicans had found the perfect smear for Democrats. They denounced them as *socialists*, no matter how moderate they might be. But what was the all-purpose epithet that Democrats could hurl back in Republicans' faces? It was an exercise that the CAP group approached with scientific precision, a ream of polling and endless focus groups. After all that deliberation, the group emerged with an answer: MAGA. It took Trump's original slogan—Make America Great Again—and repurposed it in its abbreviated form, which reeked of extremism and carried unsavory tones. According to the research, voters were two times less likely to vote for someone branded with the label. It was also, the report proclaimed, "a potential dog-whistle for our base."

When Donilon passed along these findings to the president, Biden thought the attack needed tweaking. The phrase didn't quite capture how far the Trump wing of the party had strayed from the Republican Party of yore. He suggested "ultra-MAGA," which became the new tagline.

The term suited Biden's sense of how he wanted his party to run in November. He needed to go on the attack. If he sat back and let the Republicans turn the election into a referendum on his presidency, he would lose. His best hope was to replay the 2020 election: The Democrats needed to relentlessly remind voters that Donald Trump—and the lunatics who imitated him—were on the ballot, too. Biden liked to incessantly quote of one his father's sayings, "Joey, don't compare me to the Almighty, compare me to the alternative."

Having identified the foundation of his midterm strategy, he wrung his hands about deploying it. He still held out hope that a bipartisan coalition might deliver him the CHIPS bill, which subsidized the growth of the American semiconductor industry. Biden didn't want to spar with Republicans when it might interfere with legislative success.

On the other hand, he heard the warnings about how his low approval ratings would drag his party toward electoral disaster. He couldn't wait around forever—and when he attacked the ultra-MAGA, he would stay true to himself, making sure to praise the sane Republicans whom he still believed might be game for legislative collaboration.

When Biden debuted the attack in early May, in a speech at the White House, he used it to lambaste the Republican economic agenda—which was indeed extreme, but also happened to be the most traditional part of the right-wing program. George W. Bush, whom nobody would describe as ultra-MAGA, had peddled variations of the same agenda of privatizing social security and cutting taxes for the rich. Still, there was a logic to this branding. This economic agenda also happened to be most at odds with the populist pretensions of the new-look Republican party, and deeply unpopular.

Ultra-MAGA sounded a little clunky, a little cringe. No strategists or talking heads hailed the strategy as evidence of newfound savvy. In fact, Republicans seemed to mock it as ineffectual, by embracing the term of abuse as a badge of honor. The congresswoman Elise Stefanik tweeted, "I'm ultra-MAGA. And I'm proud of it." And the new line of attack did nothing to stop Democrats from continuing to quietly moan about the administration. Catastrophe in November still felt inevitable.

43

Dobbs v. Biden

FOR NEARLY A YEAR, it was possible to forecast the day that would trouble Joe Biden's conscience. In the fourth month of his presidency, the Supreme Court agreed to hear the case of *Dobbs v. Jackson*—testing the constitutionality of a Mississippi law banning abortions after the fifteenth week of pregnancy, with no exceptions for rape or incest. Every court watcher considered it inevitable that Donald Trump's appointees would erode, if not eliminate, *Roe v. Wade.* The decision in the case would likely redirect the long arc of American legal history that had seemed to bend irreversibly toward sexual freedom, until it didn't.

Joe Biden had long struggled with the issue of abortion. Catholicism wasn't an incidental part of his identity. It was his connection to the past, a place he yearned for, despite all the pain that lay buried there. On his wrist, he sometimes wore rosary beads that Beau Biden once purchased in Mexico. Religion, the possibility of a benevolent God, brought him comfort, as did the trappings of religion that evoked the Scranton childhood he imagined as Eden. "Wherever there were nuns," he once wrote, "there was home."

The fate of the liberal Catholic politician is torment. He had bonded with Nancy Pelosi over their shared angst. Their religious leaders told them that to be a good Catholic, they needed to stand firmly against abortion. To be a good liberal—and an effective Democratic politician—they needed to champion the cornerstone of female autonomy. Biden felt torn between competing authorities and competing imperatives. It was genuinely an uncomfortable place to reside.

To fulfill his ambitions, he needed to make concessions to the sentiments of his party. During the 2020 primary campaign, he surrendered his longtime support for the Hyde Amendment, which prevented government monies from ever funding abortions. But he did so only grudgingly, after dragging his feet, as if he were still worried about disappointing the nuns back in Scranton.

THEN, ON MAY 2, the future was shockingly clear. *Politico* published a leaked draft of Samuel Alito's majority opinion in *Dobbs v. Jackson*. Of all the institutions in Washington, the Supreme Court had the least trappings of modernity. Preserving its remoteness, an unapproachable mystique, helped guard its legitimacy. It didn't permit cameras to record its proceedings. Justices and their clerks hewed to a code of omertà, which denied the public any behind-the-curtain sense of the court's internal politics. The *Politico* leak transgressed that ethos.

That Alito served as the mouthpiece for the majority was probably all one needed to know. Where Chief Justice John Roberts cuts a genteel figure, Alito wages Kulturkampf with the ferocity of a man who views himself as civilization's last best hope. He has the zeal of the late Antonin Scalia without the humor or the need to be liked.

The decision, in draft form, wasn't Solomonic reasoning. It read like a strident essay in *National Review*, not even bothering with the pretense of persuading the other side. He wrote, "*Roe* was egregiously wrong from the start. Its reasoning was exceptionally weak, and the decision has had damaging consequences."

For months, the White House knew there was a possibility a decision like this might land. A small working group, led by Jennifer Klein (director of the White House Gender Policy Council) and Dana Remus (White House counsel), prepared options for the president—a slate of policies and executive orders that he could roll out in the event of a decision like *Dobbs*. With the *Politico* leak, the White House was no longer dealing with hypotheticals. It knew roughly what it would confront. The time had arrived to get Biden's take.

BIDEN KNEW what he didn't like. He said that he hated how the Obama administration debated policy in the Roosevelt Room, where experts and aides, many of whom the president barely knew, crowded around the table and strutted their wonkish stuff. Biden didn't like the self-important performances.

Biden preferred to figure out policy in a safe space, where he trusted the faces and could test arguments and work through frustrations without having to worry about aides rushing to leak his stray, unformed comments to *The New York Times*. There were issues where he needed that protective insulation of his innermost circle of advisers, and abortion was foremost among them.

As Klein and Remus walked Biden through his options, he kept stopping to explain himself. Biden seemed to feel the need to remind the room of his personal views. "I'm for *Roe* modified by *Casey*," he kept repeating. It was an allusion to the Supreme Court's 1992 ruling in *Planned Parenthood v. Casey*, which gave states the power to regulate abortion. In other words, Biden explained, he favored an unregulated right to abortion in the first trimester, believed that states could impose restrictions in the second, and didn't believe that late-term abortion should exist at all, except in narrow circumstances.

For a man of his generation, Joe Biden was open-minded on most questions of sexual freedom. Back in the Obama administration, he was part of a vanguard arguing for the legalization of gay marriage, so much so that

Politico proclaimed him "Joe Biden, Gay Icon." He felt strongly about protecting transgender rights, and had no hesitation about racing ahead of public opinion on that issue. But whenever abortion came up, even tangentially,
he hesitated. His mind went straight to worrying about how a policy might
impinge on the conscience of health care providers who didn't want to perform the procedure on religious grounds.

Listening to the litany of proposals, he quickly accepted a few. It was an
outrage that women could be arrested for traveling to another state to get
an abortion, and he felt strongly about protecting that right. But he hesitated
to endorse other proposals that Klein and Remus presented to him.

"We can't replace fifty years of constitutional protections with an executive order," he said.

And in the broadest sense, he was right. *Dobbs* was a political problem,
only solvable by passing federal legislation restoring *Roe.*

Biden saw the need to protect access to the drug mifepristone. It is the
drug that induces miscarriage, as well as abortion, but would disappear in
the bans that states would pass in the aftermath of *Dobbs.* One of Klein and
Remus's proposals would protect the availability of the drug for the sake of
facilitating miscarriages. But Biden kept asking if the drug would be abused
to perform abortions in states that banned them. "I know it's exploited," he
said.

The implication of his objection was that he was more worried about how
his administration might expand access to abortion than the fact that the
Supreme Court was about to take away the right. Some of his aides left the
meeting dazed, and unclear about how the administration would ultimately
respond when *Dobbs* finally arrived. On the way out the door, he told the
group, "Just to be clear, I didn't agree to any of this."

ON JUNE 24, the Department of Homeland Security issued a bulletin that
placed its regional offices on alert, advising them to bulk up security at
courthouses. That felt ominous. But when colleagues mentioned it to Dana

Remus, she told them that the Supreme Court wasn't likely to rule on *Dobbs* that day, because the justices would wait until the very end of the term to unleash such an explosive opinion.

Still, that was just an educated guess, and this was the week when decisions emerged from the court at a furious rate. Jen Klein sat in her office in the Old Executive Office Building; another aide, Rachel Vogelstein, stationed herself at a table in the corner. Vogelstein kept SCOTUSblog open on her laptop. The site contained a live stream of news from within the court's chambers.

At 10:01 a.m., Vogelstein shouted across the room that the court had ruled on a case about Medicare. "It's not it." Then at 10:10 a.m., it was there, staring at her on the screen, the moment they had spent months preparing for but still couldn't truly fathom.

They printed out the decision, along with the accompanying concurrence and dissent, and began to scour the text. One of Klein's special assistants who was reading along with her had just boarded a plane for South Dakota. Klein knew that by the time she landed at her destination, that state would have already banned abortion because of a trigger law it had passed in anticipation of the arrival of a ruling like *Dobbs*.

An hour after the decision, Klein entered the Oval Office to brief Biden. Despite the opinion's leak to *Politico*, Biden still felt gobsmacked by the moment. With his optimism and his faith in institutions, he had hoped John Roberts would curb the instincts of his conservative colleagues, to moderate the outcome. "They just overturned a precedent of fifty years," he exclaimed. "I don't believe that they have ever overturned a fundamental constitutional right." He asked Remus if she could have her office fact-check that assertion so that he could add it to his public remarks.

Working his way through the decision, he seized on Clarence Thomas's concurrence. He stopped to dwell on a line that seemed to confirm his worst fears. Thomas wrote, "[I]n future cases, we should reconsider all of this Court's substantive due process precedents, including *Griswold*, *Lawrence*, and *Obergefell*. Because any substantive due process decision is 'demonstrably erroneous' . . . we have a duty to 'correct the error' established in those precedents."

The passage struck Biden with force. Back in the eighties, privacy was Biden's issue. It was one of the bludgeons that he wielded to destroy the Supreme Court nomination of Robert Bork. Biden had argued that erosion of privacy was the end goal of the right-wing agenda—and that Bork's ascent to the Supreme Court would make it possible. And here in Thomas's concurrence, the conservatives were finally saying the quiet part aloud, intimating that the majority would eventually erode every other precedent grounded in a right to privacy. After *Dobbs*, the court would advance to the next phase in its agenda: ending gay marriage and eliminating the right to contraception.

Biden was going to deliver his remarks about *Dobbs* shortly—and unveil a truncated set of proposals to blunt the decision. Deputy chief of staff Jen O'Malley Dillon had coordinated everything in advance of the moment. Because Biden was about to attend a NATO summit in Madrid, she had planned for likely scenarios, including the dreaded possibility that the decision would arrive while he was midflight. His remarks were written and approved long in advance of the moment.

But now, he wanted to rewrite them at the last minute, emphasizing his revelation about the threat to privacy.

Aides sensed the psychological dynamic at play. Biden wanted to avoid talking about the issue that tortured him. He seized on privacy, because it allowed him to avoid directly wading into the abortion wars and kept him on comfortable terrain.

Mike Donilon, the closest thing the president has to an alter ego, tried to nudge him back to the sentiment of the remarks as originally scripted. "Here's what people are experiencing," Donilon told him. "They are feeling anger and worry. You need to address those fears head on."

Donilon was also a political consultant who understood the potential potency of the abortion issue for Biden. The Supreme Court had handed Biden an issue that could transform the contours of the coming election. All those Democrats who were dispirited were primed to rally to his side because of their fury over the decision.

Biden seemed to agree. But when he gave his speech, he couldn't quite rise to the occasion. Squinting into the teleprompter, he said, "I know so many of us are frustrated and disillusioned that the Court has taken something away that's so fundamental. I know so many women are now going to face incredibly difficult situations. I hear you. I support you. I stand with you." The tone was more sorrowful than angry, a little distant, and stood in contrast to images of protesters at the Supreme Court.

And the world seemed to intuit all of the doubts he expressed in private. He was supposed to have a raft of policies and executive orders ready to unveil in this speech. But he hadn't agreed to them yet. It made him look flat-footed and indifferent.

Rebecca Traister, the feminist essayist, wrote a piece titled "Joe Biden's *Dobbs* Response Has Been Breathtakingly Awful." *The Washington Post* reported the speech "lacked the urgent tone that many Democrats felt was required, and [that] even some White House officials later said they wished the president had been more fiery."

THE DISPLEASURE of the Left was perfectly foreseeable—and it sent Biden's inner circle scrambling. But dislodging the president from stubbornly held positions could be excruciating.

It didn't help that the Left set out to highlight the administration's flaccid response by trumpeting policies that sounded righteous but were either implausible or politically self-defeating. Elizabeth Warren advocated setting up abortion clinics on the outskirts of national parks and suggested that government should cover the costs for women who now needed to travel to obtain legal abortions.

White House aides felt besieged by friends and allies, sometimes annoyingly so. An article on CNN's website argued that the administration's failure to act quickly "gets to questions of basic management." Biden's advisers resented being accused of incompetence when they felt the core problem was their boss's indecision.

Biden's failure to channel his base's anger with the Supreme Court began to cost him in the polls. According to a You Gov survey, one in four Democrats disapproved of his handling of the abortion issue. Among his most loyal supporters, his approval rating began to noticeably plummet, a worrying omen for the midterm elections.

But Biden seemed entrenched, and kept privately citing statements that the United States Conference of Catholic Bishops published, excoriating him from the right. It was as if the group understood that it could prey on his guilty conscience. Faced with the messy psychological dynamic at play, aides debated enlisting Biden's sister, Valerie, to make the case for signing executive orders.

Their best ally, in the end, turned out to be the radicalism of the anti-abortion zealots in the states, who were quickly availing themselves of *Dobbs* to institute draconian restrictions. In Ohio, a trigger law imposed a sweeping ban on abortions after the sixth week of pregnancy. Reports began circulating about a ten-year-old girl from Columbus, raped and pregnant. Because of Ohio's ban, she needed to travel to Indiana to find a doctor to perform the abortion. This was the sort of morality tale that roiled Biden's imagination, the bullying of the defenseless that set him off, allowing him to shift into the role of fatherly protector.

Two weeks after *Dobbs*, he signed an executive order protecting access to medication abortion. As he did, he found himself growing unexpectedly emotional, invoking the case that rattled him so badly. "Ten years old—ten years old!—raped, six weeks pregnant, already traumatized." He chopped at the air with his hands and seemed to almost vibrate with anger. "Imagine being that little girl."

Compared with his performance on June 24, he sounded far more convincing; that was because he was far more convinced. This was Biden's method for working through issues that conflicted him. He needed to vent, brood, and process his own doubts.

On August 2, Kansans went to the polls to vote on a referendum to amend the state's constitution to remove the right to abortion from the document. Most prognosticators predicted that Kansas, hardly a bastion of social liberalism, would remain true to its social conservative self. But women, roused by *Dobbs*, turned out en masse and overwhelmingly rejected the amendment. It lost by a margin of 18 percent. Districts that Trump had won decisively, like the swath of suburbs and farmland north of Wichita, voted pro-choice.

The referendum affirmed Biden's strategic instinct. It would have been counterproductive to embrace the more aggressive response to *Dobbs* proposed by the likes of Elizabeth Warren. But as he watched the results, he couldn't quite believe what he saw. Whatever his qualms, he now possessed the issue that provided his party with a fighting chance of surviving November's midterms. The issue that tormented him was the issue that could save him.

44

The Bath

THERE WERE, at most, ten people in Washington who understood how close Chuck Schumer was to reviving Biden's domestic agenda with an unlikely last-minute triumph—or how close it was to slipping away.

The possibility of collapse was what had begun to bother Schumer. For a year, the primary obstacle to his legislative dreams was the obstreperous Joe Manchin. But Schumer's policy director, Gerry Petrella, had spent the past two months negotiating with Manchin's chief of staff, Lance West. In a conference room in the basement of the Capitol, the pair kept pushing toward an agreement for the ages, which they felt sure would shock the world when they could finally reveal it.

They worked through the details of prescription drug reform and an extension of Affordable Care Act benefits. They hashed out tax increases on corporations and hedge fund managers that would help pay for billions of dollars of investments in clean energy.

It was all there, agreed to by their bosses, nearly ready to be printed as legislative text, except for the last, hardest details. They needed to agree on a program that would reduce carbon emissions. But even with the most contentious sections of the bill, they were on a trajectory to finish.

Schumer's new enemy was the calendar. Senators were about to leave town for the Fourth of July, and Labor Day was looming in the near distance.

This was an election year, and he couldn't plausibly pass the bill once Congress headed to the hustings. Working backward, Schumer's staff figured that they really needed to vote a bill into law before Congress fled Washington for the August recess. That left roughly a month to rush things to completion.

If they were passing a normal piece of legislation, he wouldn't have worried. But this was a massive bill, which needed to comply with the exacting constraints of the reconciliation process, enforced by a persnickety parliamentarian.

The parliamentarian represented a bottleneck in the process. She would need to scrutinize each provision, judging whether it fell within the acceptable bounds of the rule governing reconciliation, an audit known as a Byrd Bath—in honor of the West Virginia senator Robert Byrd, who created the arcane rules back in the seventies. Every provision in a reconciliation bill needed to have a "fiscal implication." Otherwise, the parliamentarian would rule it out of bounds and excise it from the bill. If she rejected a provision, Schumer would be sent scrambling for a last-minute fix. The fragile structure that Schumer and Manchin had concocted might collapse.

Before the Senate dispersed, Schumer summoned Manchin to his office. He felt as if he needed to light a fire under Manchin, to convince him that it was time to rush.

THERE WAS a plan that Schumer had cooked up. Instead of waiting to hand the parliamentarian a final bill, he would submit it to her in chunks, starting with the prescription drug piece. By disaggregating the legislation, he would avoid slamming the parliamentarian at the end with a massive ream of paper. And this piecemeal approach meant that even if he failed to negotiate a climate deal, he would still have a piece of legislation at the ready.

"Maybe we get a big bill, maybe we get something piecemeal," Schumer told Manchin. "But it's time to go."

Schumer told him that once they submitted a section to the parliamentarian, the rules demanded that they also give Republicans access to the legislative text. Rather than let the Republicans leak the details, Schumer preferred to have his press office plant stories about their progress.

Manchin told him, "Chuck, you've got to be the one who drives the train. I'll support you, but you need to be the one who drives this." But he was all in favor of steaming forward.

After more than a year of false dawns, Schumer told his staff that he felt as if they just might pull it off.

THAT FEELING of optimism lasted approximately forty-eight hours. Schumer bumped into Manchin on the floor of the Senate. He pulled him aside and wanted to know, "Are we still good?"

Since their last meeting, Schumer had submitted the prescription drug section of their deal to the parliamentarian. It was now public. And once their progress was available for the world to see, the inevitable counteroffensive began.

The nature of the reconciliation process is that it doesn't leave the minority party with many obstructionist options. But Mitch McConnell was determined to test them all. He announced that if the Democrats moved forward with reconciliation, he would sink the bipartisan CHIPS bill, which needed at least ten Republican votes to pass. The bill would invest nearly $300 billion in developing the American semiconductor industry, reducing the economy's dependence on the foreign import of the single most important component of modern life. After a year of wallowing in limbo, CHIPS was weeks away from finally passing. McConnell felt that his threat might deter Schumer, who considered CHIPS a pet project.

More worryingly, McConnell knew how to exploit Manchin's vulnerabilities. He gave a speech on the floor explaining how the Schumer-Manchin program would destroy small businesses in West Virginia.

But those were the tactics that Schumer could see with his own eyes.

He knew that over the Fourth of July break, Manchin would go back home. Manchin would be inundated with friends imploring him that he couldn't abandon them, who told him that he needed to hold firm and save the nation from socialism.

But Manchin assured him that he had nothing to fear. "We're good, buddy. Keep the staff working."

After Manchin returned from recess, Schumer planned on sticking close to him so he could cajole him and ward off legislative saboteurs. But these were still pandemic times. Just as he was about to fly back from New York, Schumer tested positive for COVID. Instead of giving Manchin the LBJ treatment, Schumer was stuck in his Brooklyn apartment.

He was going to be at a distance on the most precarious day of the month, July 13. That's when the monthly inflation report descended from the Bureau of Labor Statistics. All along, Manchin invoked inflation as his primary objection to spending hundreds of billions of dollars on a reconciliation bill.

But when the fresh report arrived, it felt as if it were crafted by Mitch McConnell to doom the bill. Inflation had risen to a level unseen since the early eighties. For months the Biden administration had described inflation as "transitory," but these numbers debunked that claim.

That afternoon, Lance West met with Gerry Petrella and told him that Manchin wanted to wait another month before moving forward with the tax and climate parts of the bill. He just didn't feel as if he could spend money in good conscience, with the number so high.

"If you've run out of time, we understand," West told him.

Manchin would support a reconciliation bill that would reform prescription drug pricing and renew Affordable Care Act subsidies, which congress temporarily expanded during the pandemic. But, if Schumer were willing, Manchin would be happy to wait around to see how the August inflation numbers turned out. He still believed that there was a deal to be had.

But Petrella knew that Manchin's stance was a mortal blow to their efforts. "Dude," he told West, "you know the next month's numbers won't look any different. It will still be too high."

This felt like betrayal, and Petrella couldn't hide his despair. "All the fucking work we've done . . . All the work our bosses have done . . ." he vented, "You're really going to blow it up, now?"

Then he found himself begging. "Come on, man, you've got to go back to Manchin."

"I will, but I'm telling you where this is," West told him.

Two hours later, Schumer called Manchin from his sickbed.

"What are you doing? We're so close. This is going to be a history-making bill."

Manchin felt attacked and clung even more fiercely to his objections.

"I'm not going to do something, and overreach, that causes more problems."

Schumer told him that he saw no choice but to move forward with the fragments of the bill where they had agreement. It would give them an achievement to tout in November. For decades, Democrats had promised prescription drug reform. It always tested off the charts in focus groups. They were missing their chance to save the planet, but at least they would have something to trumpet.

THAT AFTERNOON, Gerry Petrella scheduled a Zoom with dozens of staffers who had worked on Senate committees. Over the months, he had asked them for help cobbling together the details of policies, even though Petrella was coy about the purpose of his requests. But now, he was informing them that all their hard work had been in vain. He watched as the news washed over the faces on his screen. In boxes across his computer, staffers began tearing up.

When the press reported the death of the climate negotiations, Manchin's Senate colleagues allowed their pent-up frustrations to come rushing out.

They wanted to hold him personally responsible for the government's failure to avert climate catastrophe. Martin Heinrich of New Mexico tweeted that Democrats should consider stripping Manchin of his committee chairmanship. That seemed restrained compared with what activists said about Manchin on Twitter. It felt especially painful to learn that they had been so close to a climate bill—as if a generational opportunity had drifted away.

MANCHIN NEVER ENJOYED playing the villain. And whenever he felt discomfort, he liked to talk through his feelings with his friends, desperate for approval. He called Steve Ricchetti at the White House, even though he was obviously an interested party in the saga.

It struck Ricchetti that Manchin didn't understand the situation clearly. Manchin kept saying, "It's over."

"It doesn't have to be," Ricchetti told him. "It's only over because you told Schumer that you weren't ready."

Ricchetti felt that he needed to dislodge Manchin from his sense of fatalism. All along, Ricchetti considered himself the last optimist in the White House, the only one who truly believed that a climate bill would eventually land on the president's desk. His role was to keep everyone talking at moments like this, when collapse seemed inevitable.

He told Manchin that if he wanted to come back to the table—and to make something happen—he could.

"We want this deal," he pleaded with Manchin. "Tell us what you need."

"I'll think about it," Manchin replied.

It felt like a polite rejection.

45

Truth and Reconciliation

On Monday morning, five days after Manchin sank the biggest, best version of their bill, Schumer joined his staff's daily conference call. In the storm of Democratic fury, Schumer hadn't actually voiced a public opinion about the collapse, since he remained quarantined.

That morning, however, he tested negative. He planned on returning to Washington later in the day. As party leader, he needed to explain the piecemeal bill that he intended to pass—and why it still qualified as a worthy achievement.

As Schumer talked through the remarks he sketched in his head, his chief negotiator, Gerry Petrella, received a text from Lance West. There wasn't much to the message, just a terse invitation to meet in Manchin's hideaway office in the Capitol in an hour's time. A few minutes later, a subsequent text arrived, asking Petrella if he minded Brian Deese's joining them. "Of course not," he replied.

When Petrella and Deese arrived, West handed them a document.

The Manchin course was never linear. After talking with Ricchetti on Friday night, the senator decided that he didn't want to be the bad guy in the story. He spent Saturday huddling with West, sketching out a fresh offer for a climate bill, assembling a compromise he deemed worthy.

When West passed along the document to Petrella and Deese, he told them that some fine-tuning might be required, but he thought it was a fair deal that Schumer and the White House could accept.

As Petrella scanned the offer, he braced himself for the worst. But as he read, he absorbed the reality that Manchin had confounded his expectations. The plan was actually ambitious, not that far from the substance of their negotiations.

Manchin had his demands, to be sure. They had covered most of this ground before. He wanted approval of the Mountain Valley Pipeline, which would transport natural gas from wells in north-central West Virginia, turning his state into a major player in that energy market. He asked for the Democratic leadership's support for a separate bill reforming the process for permitting new energy infrastructure so that it could be built without having to surmount so many bureaucratic impediments. And he needed hundreds of millions of dollars set aside for deficit reduction, to assuage his centrist conscience. But that was just horse trading. The only thing that truly mattered was his proposing more than $300 billion in tax credits that would incentivize the nation to rapidly embrace clean energy. If Congress passed his proposal, carbon emissions would fall by 40 percent of the 2005 levels by 2030.

Petrella, who felt at once elated and frustrated by Manchin's wild swings, told West, "Lance, I've been sticking my neck out, defending you guys, saying that you were going to fucking do something here, for a year. I'm willing to do it one more time, but it's got to be before the August recess, and this has got to be it. This is the deal. We're locking arms."

West told Petrella that the document in his hands was the "flight plan." They were going to finally land the plane.

THAT AFTERNOON, Schumer made it back to DC. His aides scoped out a basement room in the maze of corridors, with exposed pipes and brick walls, beneath the Capitol's formal chambers and gilded offices.

"I didn't know about this place," Schumer said. His staff explained that it officially belonged to him. Schumer posted aides to watch the corridors so that no reporters could witness him and Manchin furtively converging on the same locale. He staggered their arrivals, to further guard against unwanted attention.

When Manchin finally entered the room, he joked, "You did it. You guys finally beat the shit out of me."

Over the course of a fifteen-minute conversation, they shook hands and agreed to finalize the legislation that Manchin had sketched. They vowed to treat the last stage of negotiation as the closest-held secret in Washington. They weren't going to keep the White House in the loop, since that is a building where secrets go to die. To finish by the August recess, they would need to sprint.

They also needed a name: Manchin toyed with calling it the Energy Security Act. Together they dubbed it the Inflation Reduction Act. The moniker didn't really capture the contents of the bill, or its grandeur. But the tax credits and health care provisions would make life cheaper. That might be a touch disingenuous, and it certainly wasn't a title that would echo through the ages, but it had the feel of good politics.

THE SUMMER OF 2022 proved to be unexpectedly prolific. In the dazed aftermath of a massacre at an elementary school in Uvalde, Texas, bipartisan gun legislation passed in June. It strengthened background checks, especially for prospective buyers under the age of twenty-one. It incentivized states to enact red flag laws, which would allow judges to temporarily confiscate the guns of those they deemed an imminent threat. By allocating nearly $15 billion for mental health treatment, it also doubled as a meaningful piece of health care legislation.

Throughout the Biden administration, centrists in the Senate yearned to assert their own relevance, to prove themselves the indispensable power brokers of the era. After the gun legislation, they were ready to push hard to finish CHIPS.

In search of sixty votes, CHIPS grew more expansive. To the White

House's delight, undecided Republican senators bartered for investment in research and development in their home states. The bill began to hark back to the Cold War, when the menace of a foreign enemy provided a pretext for expanding universities and erecting research laboratories. CHIPS now poured billions into the National Science Foundation, to fund research and development in artificial intelligence and nanotechnology. It set money aside to develop a deeper pool of American scientists, mathematicians, and engineers.

But Mitch McConnell's threats hovered over the calendar. He publicly threatened to kill CHIPS if Schumer moved forward with his reconciliation bill. Thus the need for secrecy—and choreography. To protect CHIPS, Schumer needed McConnell to believe that reconciliation was a distant fantasy. He needed to expeditiously pass the semiconductor bill before word of his deal with Manchin leaked. But he also wanted to avoid embarrassing the Republicans who intended to vote for CHIPS. His plan was to wait a day after passing the semiconductor bill before announcing his deal.

But this was summer in Washington. A thunderstorm grounded flights into the city. Schumer delayed the CHIPS vote for a day as he waited for senators to return. That meant two of the momentous accomplishments in his career were crammed into a single afternoon.

At lunchtime on July 27, the Senate passed CHIPS, with seventeen Republican votes. It passed because Schumer and Manchin, two of the biggest kibitzers on Capitol Hill, restrained themselves.

Schumer was too anxious to revel in his first victory. He needed to see Nancy Pelosi, to let her know about his deal with Manchin. A year earlier, Pelosi felt blindsided by Schumer when he failed to tell her about how he signed a surreptitious agreement with the West Virginia senator. Now, he was ready to spring a much happier surprise on her, although he wasn't sure how she would respond to Manchin's demands, which he worried might irk Alexandria Ocasio-Cortez and her comrades on the Left. But Schumer couldn't relay his revelation to Pelosi, because he couldn't reach her. She was in a secure room in the basement of the Capitol, receiving a briefing on

Ukraine, without access to a cell phone. When she finally emerged, Schumer trekked to her office.

It came as an enormous relief that she didn't think twice about agreeing to Schumer's side deals with Manchin. Schumer asked her to call the West Virginia senator to relay her assent.

That left one last task before they could tell the world about their deal. Manchin, who now had his own case of COVID, needed Biden's formal endorsement of their agreement.

All along, Manchin was convinced that the White House was going to hate provisions in the deal expanding oil and gas leases. But many in the White House, like Brian Deese, were perfectly comfortable with what Manchin wanted. Given the conflict in Ukraine and the spike in energy prices, they were happy to expand domestic production of energy. It was politically expedient, at the very least—and might help lower prices in the middle of a crisis.

When Biden came on the line and greeted Manchin, he purred, "Joe-Joe!"

After nine months of emotionally exhausting back-and-forth, they were done.

THAT AFTERNOON, Manchin and Schumer published a joint statement revealing their secret agreement to the world. And the world couldn't quite believe it. *Politico* deemed it a "shocker." And when that outlet relayed the news to Tiernan Sittenfeld, the League of Conservation Voters' top lobbyist, she could only manage to blurt, "Holy shit." In Washington, these sorts of surprises were usually spoiled by the city's high concentration of reporters and its cultural proclivity for leaking.

After so many months of false dawns, it felt only prudent to view this as another moment of bloated expectations. But this was unlike every other plot point. This wasn't hearsay evidence of Manchin's endorsement of a theoretical deal, but a definitive statement issued in his name.

Secrecy, however, came at a cost. Every Democratic senator greeted the announcement with euphoria, except for one. Kyrsten Sinema learned about the agreement on the floor of the Senate, when Republican senator John Thune mentioned it to her. And she instantly unleashed her fury on Schumer.

In fairness, Joe Manchin knew that the legislation would needle her. Over the past year, the pair struggled to suppress their rivalry. They both enjoyed being the fiftieth senator, the vote on which their party's agenda depended. It was the point of maximum leverage—and it came with the plaudits of tycoons, who cheered them for spoiling the Democratic agenda.

Despite their shared centrism, there was an ideological difference that separated them. They championed different constituencies. Where Sinema built an alliance with Wall Street, Manchin enjoyed occasionally sticking it to the bankers, like a good old-fashioned populist from the hollers. And where Manchin felt a home-state duty to the fossil fuels industry, and personally benefited from its success, Sinema wanted to break its stranglehold over climate policy.

In the course of negotiations with Schumer, Manchin had insisted on a provision ending the carried-interest loophole—a gaping unfairness in the tax code that allows hedge fund and private equity managers to count their revenue as capital gains and avoid the income tax. But Sinema had a history of defending that loophole. Manchin had every reason to believe that Sinema would despise his proposal—and that she would likely consider it a red line— but he insisted on pushing forward with it, regardless.

Schumer didn't fight Manchin. He wasn't going to worry about his Sinema problem when it was theoretical. But now her objection was more than a theoretical source of worry. Sinema constituted the primary obstacle to the realization of Schumer's greatest achievement, and he was stuck.

The simple solution was for Manchin to concede. He could just give Sinema her win—and find another way to pay for the bill. But Manchin wasn't in a yielding mood. "I'm not going to let *her* define this bill," he told Steve Ricchetti.

To dislodge the pair of obstinate senators, Schumer enlisted Mark Warner, one of their fellow centrists. Warner considered both of them friends and had a history of skillfully steering them in leadership's favored direction.

Warner's first task was getting Manchin to relent, which meant a late-night visit to his houseboat. A summer storm soaked Warner's suit, and he lounged around in a borrowed T-shirt and a pair of Manchin's flip-flops. "Show generosity of spirit," he urged. He had an ally in Manchin's wife, Gayle, who had access to emotional weaponry that Warner didn't. "You can't be greedy on this," she told her husband.

Having worked through his anger, Manchin could see that he had little choice but to grant Sinema her win.

But that didn't solve Schumer's problem. Sinema had promised her Republican friend John Thune that she would vote for an amendment protecting the carried-interest loophole. But Thune had slipped a poison pill into his legislative text. His amendment would extend a Trump-era provision capping the state and local tax deduction. That sounded esoteric enough. But moderate Democrats from wealthy districts in the Northeast loathed this provision, which riled their constituents. If the Thune amendment prevailed, then the whole Inflation Reduction Act could plausibly collapse.

Warner and Schumer stayed up until three in the morning, trying to talk Sinema out of her commitment to Thune. But her stubbornness exceeded Manchin's. There was no way, she said, that she would break her word.

But after many tortured hours, they found a way forward. Sinema would vote for the Thune amendment, then vote for an amendment that Warner offered, undoing her vote. It was an exhausting finale to a never-ending process. And it required the senators to huddle, in the cloak room, splaying binders of legislative text across couches, scribbling on a copy of the bill, to make sure that the new provisions were properly inserted.

On August 7, Gerry Petrella watched the roll call on the floor of the Senate. With no margin for failure, he worried about the potential for a last-minute development that might ruin everything. During the Trump administration, he watched John McCain emerge from his cancer treatment and flash the Senate clerk a thumbs-down, scuttling the Republican attempt to overturn Obamacare. The conjuring of that memory filled him with anxiety.

But after twenty hours of debate, an all-night session, the vice president cast a tie-breaking vote, passing the Inflation Reduction Act.

For a time, this legislative saga looked like one of the great embarrassments in the recent history of the presidency. A year earlier, Biden had thrown his prestige and time into the bill—and failed spectacularly. Yet here were the fruits of patient persistence. It was his resurrection.

THERE'S A HISTORIC standard by which Democratic presidents are judged: Have they meaningfully extended the reach of the social welfare state? By that metric, the Inflation Reduction Act is a dud. Every provision in the original version of Build Back Better that created new programs to care for the vulnerable fell to the side. Joe Manchin spiked plans for childcare subsidies and universal pre-K and paid family leave. After his yearlong pursuit of a legacy-worthy piece of legislation, Joe Biden failed to create an arm of the government that will be forever attached to his name, nothing like Obamacare or remotely resembling social security.

But the thrust of the Inflation Reduction Act can still be described as transformational—and it will change American life.

The theory of the legislation is that the world is poised for a momentous shift. For a generation, the economy has taken tentative steps away from its reliance on fossil fuels. New technologies emerged that lowered the costs of solar panels and wind turbines and batteries; the mass market showed genuine interest in electric vehicles and heat pumps. But the pace of adaptation was slow, painfully slow given the looming changes to the climate. On its own, the economy was never going to evolve in time to avert the worst consequences of climate change. What was needed was a massive nudge in the right direction.

In the past, the stick of regulation and the rod of taxation were the methods that environmentalists believed could break the fossil fuel economy. But the Inflation Reduction Act doesn't rely on such punitive tactics, because Manchin culled them from the bill. Instead, it imagined that the United States could become the global leader of a booming climate economy, if the government provided tax credits and subsidies, a lucrative set of incentives.

There was a cost associated with the bill. By the Congressional Budget Office's score, it offered $386 billion in tax credits to encourage the production of wind turbines, solar panels, geothermal plants, and battery storage. Tax credits would reduce the cost of electric vehicles so that they would become the car of choice for Middle America.

But $386 billion was an estimate, not a price tag, since the legislation didn't cap the amount of money available in tax credits. If utilities wanted to build more wind turbines or if demand for electric vehicles surged, the government would keep spending. When Credit Suisse studied the program, it estimated that so many businesses and consumers will avail themselves of the tax credits that the government could spend nearly $800 billion.

If Credit Suisse is correct, then the tax credits will unleash $1.7 trillion in private sector spending on green technologies. Within six years, solar and wind energy produced by the US will be the cheapest in the world. Alternative energies will cross a threshold: it will become financially irresponsible not to use them.

Even though Joe Biden played a negligible role in the final negotiations, the Inflation Reduction Act exudes his preferences. He romanticizes the idea of factories building stuff. It is a vision of the Goliath of American manufacturing, seemingly moribund, sprung back to life. At the same time that the legislation helps to stall climate change, it allows the United States to dominate the industries of the future.

This was a bill that, in the end, climate activists and a broad swath of industry could love. Indeed, strikingly few business lobbies, other than finance and pharma, tried to stymie the bill in its final stages. It was a far cry from the death struggles over energy legislation in the Clinton and Obama administrations, when industry scuppered transformational legislation.

The Inflation Reduction Act will allow the United States to prevent its own decline. And not just economic decline. Without such a meaningful program, the United States would have had no standing to prod other countries to respond more aggressively to climate change. It would have been a marginal player in shaping the response to the planet's greatest challenge. The bill was an investment in moral authority.

46

War Games

JOE BIDEN had a metaphorical conceit that he kept wielding to explain his sense of worry. There were three clocks, all of them simultaneously ticking down. If any reached zero, then the Ukrainians would be in existential peril.

One clock counted down to the moment when the European allies would lose patience with the war. The depth of European solidarity with Ukraine had stunned the whole of his national security team. But that support was going to be tested in the coming months, as temperatures dropped across the Continent. It was easy to sanction the Russian energy sector when Europeans didn't need Russian gas to warm their homes. But the average German or French citizen would soon face outrageous heating bills and inevitably moan to their politicians about them. At some point—and it didn't require much of an imagination to flash forward to that day—Emmanuel Macron and Olaf Scholz would want to press Ukraine to end the war.

The second clock was Biden's own. An influential set of his Republican adversaries had furtively supported his approach to the war. Many in the White House regarded Mitch McConnell as an unsung hero of the conflict, since he kept quietly helping move funding for arms through the Senate. But inflation was an issue—and it was only a matter of time before enterprising Republican politician began laying blame for the predicament on the White House's aggressive support of the war. And with the growing possibility that the Republicans would control the House after the midterms, with the balance of power resting with MAGA isolationists, it felt unavoidable that the White House would eventually struggle to send arms in such abundance.

Finally, there were the Ukrainians themselves. Biden believed that the toll of a war of attrition could be sustained for only so long. While life in Kyiv had reverted to something resembling normal, the economy was anemic. Over the first burst of war, it had contracted by a third. And while the Ukrainians didn't provide a census of the dead, the body count was in the tens of thousands, at least. Eventually, the Ukrainians would begin to run out of weapons, too. The United States didn't have an infinite arsenal to give them.

With the pressure of the clocks, Biden believed that the Ukrainians needed to change the contours of the war, to shift the narrative. After the triumph of the Battle of Kyiv, the Ukrainians were locked in a stalemate. The war had become a slog fought in the Donbas, in the east of Ukraine, with each side hammering the other, killing in large numbers, without ever shifting the balance of the conflict. Would the Europeans, would the American Congress, subsidize a war with slim hope of future victories?

Over the summer, the administration worked with the Zelensky government to formulate a new strategy. With the help of US war planners, the Ukrainians would launch a counteroffensive that would shift momentum on the battlefield—and that, in turn, would strengthen the Ukrainian hand for a diplomatic offensive that would follow military success. Mark Milley boiled the plan down to a football metaphor. "The military needs to open up a gap in the defensive line so that the diplomacy can be the fullback rushing through it."

The State Department circled a date on the calendar. In September, the UN General Assembly would convene in New York. Zelensky might attend it, his first trip out of Kyiv. At the very least, he would give an important virtual address there. It was too early to say, but that might be the moment the Ukrainians would begin pushing for a political end to the war.

ZELENSKY HAD A VISION for the counteroffensive. It was bold and maximal-ist. One prong of the Ukrainian attack would rescue the port city of Kher-son, which the Russians had occupied since March. The city was the locale of an extravagant attempt to strip residents of their culture and identity—an object lesson in the Russian campaign of cultural genocide—and therefore a potent symbol of reclamation. In the second prong of the Zelensky plan, the army would push across the Zaporizhzhya region, toward the Sea of Azov. Taken together, the twin axes of assault would collapse the Russian occupation of the south.

Lloyd Austin thought the Ukrainians had a more-than-decent chance of pulling off the plan, despite its grandiosity. His instinct was that American intelligence was still overstating the strength of the Russian military. Aus-tin kept telling aides that Russian generals had put their army "through a woodchipper." He would quip that Putin's military consisted only of a navy and an air force, because its army was so threadbare. In meetings with the Pentagon's crisis management team, he would look at the maps they pre-sented him, with little squares representing Russian divisions, and kept ask-ing leading questions. "Have they been eating regular meals? . . . What's the morale level?" He was in search of evidence that would confirm his suspicions.

But Mark Milley and many of Austin's colleagues in the Pentagon didn't fully share his faith in the Ukrainian plan. They worried that the Ukraini-ans were seduced by an inflated sense of their own abilities, ballooned by the stories that the Western media told about their battlefield bravura. And the Ukrainians didn't have the doctrinal sophistication or the armored equip-ment or the trained soldiers to attack such heavily entrenched positions on two separate fronts. The Zelensky plan would exhaust artillery caches with-out gaining back much territory.

To work through the plans, the Pentagon hosted a war game at an army base in Wiesbaden, Germany, presided over by Major General Chris Donahue, the head of the 82nd Airborne. Donahue—tactically creative and a savvy adapter of new technologies—had become Washington's favorite soldier. After he oversaw the evacuation of Hamid Karzai International Airport in Kabul, the last American to board the last C-17 out of Afghanistan, he was stationed in Europe, in anticipation of the Russian invasion. He led what came to be known as the Assure and Deter Force.

Several dozen Ukrainian officers and war planners descended on Wiesbaden, along with some of the Pentagon's sharpest tacticians and their UK counterparts. Each nation took the same battle plan and disappeared into a separate room, to simulate Zelensky's two-pronged counteroffensive, mapping out logistics and calculating munitions rates. An exercise scheduled to take two days was extended over a week.

None of the teams could make Zelensky's expansive plans work. The Ukrainians lacked the mechanized forces to pull it off. But in the course of the back-and-forth, Donahue and the Pentagon planners helped propel the Ukrainians to consider an alternative, which exploited a weakness in the enemy.

It was clear that the Russians expected an imminent Ukrainian offensive in the south. They had begun to redeploy troops from the north, to bolster their presence around Kherson. According to intelligence reports, the forces that remained in the north, in the Kharkiv region, consisted of riot police and other poorly led units. In the town of Izyum, which had served as an arsenal and hub for the occupying military, only half of the Russian force remained in place. This presented a juicy target for a surprise attack. At the very least, an offensive near Kharkiv might force the Russians to shuffle troops back to the north.

It was an inventive tactic—and the product of a relationship that was rapidly deepening. In advance of Wiesbaden, the Ukrainians had sent the Pentagon a mere fragment of a battle plan, with few of the details in the actual document. They apparently didn't trust the Pentagon to sit silently with such precious material. It was simply the latest in a long line of strange omissions in the course of the conversations between the two countries. Despite Ukraine's reliance on the United States, it resisted the idea of a transparent relationship with it. But by the end of the conference, the Ukrainians began to treat Donahue as one of their own—they adopted him as a coach. He became not just Washington's favorite soldier, but Kyiv's, too.

ON SEPTEMBER 8, Tony Blinken arrived in Kyiv by train, his second visit of the war. His first stop in town was the reopened US embassy, a squat, charmless fortress on the city's western outskirts, where he received a briefing from the military attaché and intelligence officers. He hadn't timed his trip to coincide with the onset of the counteroffensive, but the aides passed along fresh reports from the first hours of the battle. There were modest Ukrainian gains in the north, and an initial report of troops punching through the Russian lines.

Blinken had steeled himself for his next stop: a meeting with Zelensky and the entirety of his wartime cabinet. His purpose was to focus their minds on a subject, one that they probably preferred to avoid—diplomacy. The theory of the counteroffensive was that it would strengthen Ukraine's hand when the time came for negotiating an end to the conflict, but diplomacy took planning, too. And Blinken wanted to encourage Zelensky to plan for negotiations, whenever they might happen, with the same level of forethought that his government had applied to its military preparations. He needed Zelensky to begin thinking ahead to the end—what he was prepared to negotiate away, what security guarantees he needed.

But by the time Blinken arrived at the office of the presidential administration, that whole line of conversation suddenly felt beside the point. When Zelensky greeted him, he was bursting. The preliminary reports that Blinken received in the embassy a few hours earlier hadn't fully captured the extent of Ukrainian gains, which kept increasing. Ukrainian forces had barely met resistance. In fact, the Russians were simply abandoning their positions, not even bothering to cart away crates of ammunition. The Ukrainians had barreled forward at an astonishing clip in the direction of the Russian border.

Blinken tried to run Zelensky's assessment through a mental filter, accounting for the high probability of exuberant hyperbole. But if Zelensky was right, he was describing a victory that exceeded the highest hopes of the war planners and the collapse of the enemy.

STILL, THE success in the north wasn't supposed to be the main event, just an opportunistic land grab and a bit of misdirection, distracting Russian attention from the counteroffensive in the south. But in the weeks that followed Blinken's visit to Kyiv, the southern counteroffensive was largely notional. The Ukrainians were heaving munitions in the Russian direction, but not moving troops or gaining ground. The stagnation disturbed Lloyd Austin.

The secretary of defense began to doubt that the counteroffensive would ever happen. Move quicker, he told Ukraine's defense minister, Oleksii Reznikov. But Reznikov said it wasn't possible. The Ukrainians needed more time to prepare.

It was understandable why the Ukrainians might hesitate before sending troops into Kherson. The Russians had dug trenches in the farmland around the city, which was flat and provided little cover for an attacking army. And if there was a chance that the Russians might vacate Kherson of their own accord, even if that was not exceedingly likely, it was preferable to conquering it through block-by-block combat. The Ukrainians didn't want another of their great cities in ruins.

Because the Ukrainians never seemed to share their true intentions, Austin felt uncertain that he had the full view of their plans. Perhaps all the bombardment of Russian positions was just a feint. That would be incredibly annoying. The Pentagon's own arsenals of certain munitions were drawing low. It was a risk to American security to deplete stocks like this. And Austin grumbled to his aides about the possibility that all those rockets and missiles might be frittered away, with no territorial gains to show. The Ukrainians were poised for a decisive moment in the war, but perhaps they wouldn't seize it.

47

Waves Crashing

As JOE BIDEN worked over a draft of a speech he described as his closing argument for the midterm campaign, he received a devastating piece of news. On October 28, a carpenter named David DePape broke a glass window and entered Nancy Pelosi's home in the Pacific Heights neighborhood of San Francisco. He found his way to the bedroom and awakened her eighty-two-year-old husband, Paul. "Where's Nancy?" DePape wanted to know. She was, in fact, in Washington. DePape, a QAnon enthusiast who wrote blog posts with titles like "It's OK to Be White," told Paul Pelosi that he intended to break his wife's kneecaps and then kidnap her. "We've got to take them all out," he said.

When the police arrived at the scene, DePape took a hammer and smashed Pelosi's skull, leaving him unconscious in a pool of blood.

Biden struggled to shake the image of a stricken Paul Pelosi. Political violence, out there in the nation, kept moving ever closer to home. He asked Mike Donilon to revise his capstone speech of the campaign season to begin with this terrible incident.

Ever since 2017, after the hateful rally in Charlottesville, Virginia, where neo-Nazis marched with tiki torches through the university town shouting "Jews will not replace us," Biden had warned about this danger. Trump was transporting noxious extremism into the mainstream. Despite his long lingering sense of foreboding, Biden's alarm kept growing. As the election approached, he read fresh warnings about militias using the term *civil war*.

Beginning in May, he kept trying to trumpet his worries in a series of speeches. Because Joe Biden was Joe Biden, he didn't quite manage to nail any of these addresses. As he spoke in front of Philadelphia's Independence Hall in prime time, the lighting of the historic edifice was distractingly ominous, almost a little kitsch. Within camera shot, marines stood perched over his shoulder, which television pundits judged an inappropriate exploitation of the armed forces, a Trump-like sin. *The Washington Post* editorial board chided him for touting his domestic achievements in the course of defending the foundations of the republic, "too often sounding more like a Democrat than a democrat."

But he would go again, six days before the election. Standing in a room in Union Station, a few blocks from the Capitol, the site of the insurrection, Biden made his final appeal to the electorate. He wanted it to feel personal, which required him to address his audience in the second person. With a bank of flags behind him, he tried to describe the crisis of American democracy in the most urgent terms he could muster:

> This is no ordinary year. So I ask you to think long and hard
> about the moment we're in. In a typical year, we're often not
> faced with questions of whether the vote we cast will preserve
> democracy or put us at risk. But this year, we are. This year, I
> hope you will make the future of our democracy an important
> part of your decision to vote and how you vote.

None of the oratory qualified as eloquent. And it bombed with pundits. CNN's Chris Cillizza called the speech "head scratching." A headline in *Politico* described it as "puzzling." According to Biden's critics, his speech was an epic blunder, since it did next to nothing to address the economic worries that voters told pollsters was their motive force.

The Biden inner circle read these criticisms with annoyance. Did the pollsters and pundits really want Biden to spend his time talking about crime and the economy? Nothing he could say would persuade voters on those fronts. Biden desperately wanted to avoid a referendum on his performance. It needed to be a Manichaean choice: Biden or Trump, democracy or authoritarianism, take your pick.

Having drubbed Biden's speech, political analysts began to pre-write the Democratic obituary. They forecast a red wave, or even a red tsunami. A columnist in *The New York Times* declared, "When [elections] break, they usually break in one direction. And right now, all the indicators on my political dashboard are blinking red—as in, toward Republicans."

HISTORY ALSO SUGGESTED the inevitability of Joe Biden's defeat. In American politics, the president's party almost always hemorrhages House seats in midterm elections. After holding power for two years, incumbents are ritualistically reprimanded by the public for having rushed to fulfill their agenda, flogged for overreaching, and penalized for all the ugliness that legislating entails. They are subjected to what Barack Obama once described, after his own dismal performance in a midterm election, as a "shellacking."

In the fall of 2022, the Democrats weren't just vulnerable to the predictable vicissitudes of fickle voters. They stood in front of the electorate in economic conditions that could be objectively described as painful. In September, inflation stabilized at 8.2 percent, which meant that basic necessities were measurably more expensive. Gas prices, which fell during the summer, began to creep upward in October. Quotidian existence felt like it would quickly drain a life savings, and voters wailed to pollsters about that.

Some in the Biden inner circle believed his enemies were conspiring to make things worse. Back in October, the kingdom of Saudi Arabia had pressured OPEC to curtail production of petroleum, despite the energy crisis induced by the war in Ukraine. It sure seemed like Crown Prince Mohammed bin Salman was rooting for the return of the coddling presence of

Donald Trump. The fact that he went ahead with production cuts after the Biden administration asked him to delay, and after the president had traveled to the kingdom in July and offered the monarch a reputation-redeeming fist bump, made it feel like an especially malicious ploy.

The domestic fossil fuel industry was acting just as vindictively, dumping money into Republican coffers and (aides insinuated) artificially keeping prices high at the pump. After Biden signed legislation that would help wean the country from oil and gas, the victims of his policies were returning the favor.

Despite all these omens of impending catastrophe, Joe Biden stubbornly believed that he would defy the cycles of political history. Every time he left the White House to campaign—which wasn't all that frequently, given his low approval ratings—he returned with stories about how the polls failed to capture what he saw on the trail. None of the vulnerable Democratic incumbents told him that they feared a red wave. And in Joe Biden's epistemology, he trusted the instincts of his fellow politicians more than the scientific pretensions of pollsters.

Like so many other moments in the first two years of his presidency, it was hard to tell if he was painfully out of touch or better able to channel the national mood than anyone credited him.

ON THE MORNING of Election Day, the president summoned his deputy chief of staff Jen O'Malley Dillon so that he could pump her for intelligence.

He wanted to know if she was seeing any evidence of voter suppression.

Law enforcement hadn't issued any specific warnings about Election Day violence. But that threat was on Biden's brain. The media had reported that armed militia members planned on inserting their menacing presence at polling places to ward off Democratic voters.

Fears of antidemocratic meddling sufficiently spooked the White House that the president pushed back his plans to fly to a G20 summit in Bali. He wanted to be on call in Washington for the day after the election, to respond to whatever emerged. The most likely scenario was that Republicans would replicate Trump's tactics from 2020. They would call on states to stop counting mail-in ballots, if those ballots risked eroding a Republican lead in the initial vote count. He thought it was important that he remain on American soil to rebut any lies, to issue any reassurances about the integrity of the process.

It was early in the day, but O'Malley Dillon told him that she wasn't hearing anything troubling from the field. In fact, there were hopeful early signs.

A year earlier, in the Virginia governor's race, the White House had an early premonition of the Democrats' defeat almost as soon as voting began. This time, O'Malley Dillon told him that she didn't see a similar swell in rural polling stations or any inkling of overwhelming Republican turnout.

That evening, Biden asked his staff to order pizza so that his political aides could gather with him in the Roosevelt Room and watch television. As he chewed on a slice, the first wave of results arrived from Florida. They weren't even close. The state's Republican governor Ron DeSantis and senator Marco Rubio triumphed in romps, which television analysts hinted might portend the beginning of a terrible night for Biden.

Biden moved to the dining room off the Oval. With nothing to do but wait, he wanted to start making calls to candidates, to console Democrats whose early returns suggested they had lost their careers, or to congratulate those who had cruised to victory.

Every few hours, O'Malley Dillon arrived from the ad hoc data center she had erected in the Diplomatic Room of the Old Executive Office Building, a far more formal setting than any election night boiler room she had ever set up. She kept briefing Biden on returns from House races on the outer fringes of suburban Virginia, which she considered the most telling gauge of the night. What she saw in those races suggested that the evening might take a pretty wild swerve from the early depressing news out of Florida. Something history defying might be in the works.

VICTORY COMES in many shades. By 9:00 p.m., it became clear that a red wave wouldn't materialize; not even close. The Democrats had a solid chance of holding their majority in the Senate—and if everything fell their way, in the House, too. This sounded like bare survival. But relative to the patterns of American politics, it was a miracle.

There were just three previous instances in the last hundred years of American history when the president's party held its seats in the Senate—and lost fewer than ten in the House. Each of those antecedents can be explained away as an outlier. In 1934, Franklin Roosevelt benefited from the fact that the nation still blamed the opposition party for the Great Depression. In 1962, John Kennedy basked in the immediate aftermath of the Cuban missile crisis, and voters rewarded him for averting nuclear Armageddon. In 2002, a nation traumatized by terrorism stood by George W. Bush's hawkish party.

Perhaps it says something about this moment in time—when each partisan tribe views the other as an existential threat—that Biden achieved his pattern-defying results without a national security threat to buoy him. Certainly, he benefited from good fortune, with the *Dobbs* decision motivating his party's demoralized base. But the victory was also the product of strategic savvy.

Biden prided himself on his rapport with the blue-collar voters. That constituency was said to be forever migrating to the Republican party—and that change would make it difficult to win in the states once described as the industrial Midwest. But the Democrats managed to hang on to governorships in Michigan, Wisconsin, and Pennsylvania. John Fetterman picked up a Senate seat in Pennsylvania, where Biden campaigned more heavily than in any other battleground.

The success in the Rust Belt—where he managed to advance a multicultural agenda without gratuitously inflaming the anxieties of white voters—confirmed his theory of politics. He notched progressive victories without rubbing it in the faces of the culturally vanquished. The election showed the wisdom of his approach to abortion, however painful it was to watch him initially navigate the issue. By refusing to make himself the issue, by rejecting Elizabeth Warren's and Alexandria Ocasio-Cortez's aggressive proposals, he let Republicans damage themselves as he stood to the side, a mere defender of the status quo.

Biden calls himself a "fingertip politician"—and it's the second part of that label that helped him exceed electoral expectations. He made strategic choices to protect his coalition, even when those decisions earned him the derision of editorial pages. To counteract inflation, or at least how it's most directly experienced, he emptied the Strategic Petroleum Reserve to tamp down gas prices at the pump. To win young voters and fulfill a campaign promise to Elizabeth Warren, he agreed to student-debt relief, even if it wasn't a policy he especially liked.

Where the pundits lampooned Biden for trying to define the election as a battle for democracy, his argument carried the day. Despite inflation, voters felt compelled to punish politicians with authoritarian tendencies. Trump-backed election deniers went down in defeat in races for governor and secretary of state in each of the battleground states.

His strategy protected the machinery of democracy from a hostile takeover. For the second consecutive election, he staved off the threat of authoritarianism. This was the standard he set for judging his own success. It wasn't a permanent achievement, of course. But he had averted disaster, and it was unrealistic to expect that he could do any more than that in the circumstances.

THE NEXT DAY, the president couldn't resist gloating. He held a press conference in the State Dining Room, where he reveled in his success. "A good day for democracy and a good day for America," he averred.

As he soaked up praise, he received news of another triumph. Victory in the domestic struggle for democracy was followed by a decisive victory in the struggle abroad.

It was the culmination of the most intense fighting in the nine months of the war. The Ukrainian counteroffensive in the south, which stalled for much of September, finally pushed forward in October, after the Ukrainians changed commanders in the field. American-supplied Guided Multiple Launch Rocket Systems, GMLRS (pronounced "gimmlers"), knocked out bridges and pummeled entrenched Russian outposts around the city of Kherson. The rockets were fired from systems mounted on the backs of trucks, called HIMARS (pronounced "hi-mars"), so agile that they could quickly appear and then just as quickly disappear.

GMLRS were the height of precision, and they surgically eliminated every possible route of escape from the occupied city of Kherson, stranding nearly thirty thousand Russian troops on the west side of the Dnipro River, cut off from their supply lines.

The Russian position in Kherson was untenable. Avoiding the slaughter of well-trained troops, exhausted and demoralized, necessitated retreat.

On November 9, the day after the US midterms, in a meeting broadcast live on Russian television, defense minister Sergei Shoigu told his commanders, "Go ahead with the pullout of troops and take all measures to ensure safe transfer of troops, weapons and equipment to the other bank of the Dnipro River." It was a humiliating concession of defeat. Tellingly, it was announced without Putin present.

Retreat was the one maneuver that the Russian army could effectively execute in Ukraine. When it had time to plan, it was adept at ferrying troops out of danger and extricating equipment. But in so doing, it ceded the only regional capital of Ukraine that it had captured in the course of the war. It handed Ukraine a morale-boosting victory that would carry the nation through the coming winter's freeze.

UKRAINE'S GOVERNMENT had survived more than eight months of war. It had prevailed in three battles—in Kyiv, Kharkiv, and Kherson—that will be enshrined in military history. The victories could be ascribed, in significant measure, to the United States, and to Joe Biden, too.

It was his skills as a politician that mattered most. He brought along his compatriots—and his allies—so that they went beyond their comfort zone, to provide the Ukrainians the sort of robust support that the United States might bestow upon an ally in a world war. By November, the Biden administration had supplied Ukraine with $50 billion in aid, both humanitarian and military, including some of the most advanced weapon systems in the American arsenal. When he saw the defining battle for global democracy, he poured himself into winning it.

None of this was inevitable. Donald Trump certainly wouldn't have executed this strategy; neither, in all likelihood, would any of Biden's competitors for the 2020 Democratic nomination. Bolstering the Ukrainians in unprecedented fashion risked an unrestrained escalation of tensions with Russia. Biden's wartime leadership drew on his weathered instincts and his robust self-confidence. He never ignored his own stubborn doubts when the emotions of the moment tempted him to take steps that he considered imprudently provocative—or a waste of resources. Like a woodworker who can make cuts without measuring, he practiced statecraft without much external advice about when to push hard and when to resist political pressures. He just knew.

For most of his presidency, Democratic voters griped to pollsters about his advanced years. They seemingly preferred a president who projected vigor or who possessed oratorical chops. And his advanced years were a hindrance, depriving him of the energy to cast a robust public presence or the ability to easily conjure a name. It was striking that he took so few morning meetings or presided over so few public events before 10 a.m. His public persona reflected physical decline and time's dulling of mental faculties that no pill or exercise regimen can resist. In private, he would occasionally admit to friends that he felt tired.

But with Ukraine, the advantages of having an older president were on display. He wasn't just a leader of the coalition, he was the West's father figure, whom foreign leaders could call for advice and look to for assurance. It was his calming presence and his strategic clarity that helped lead the alliance to such an aggressive stance, which stymied authoritarianism on its front lines. He was a man for his age.

Acknowledgments

It has been my professional good fortune to work with some of the best editors in the English language. At *The Atlantic*, I'm grateful to Jeffrey Goldberg, Adrienne LaFrance, John Swansburg, Yoni Appelbaum, Gal Beckerman, and Juliet Lapidos. In addition to their intellectual and literary gifts, they are some of my favorite people in the world. And I couldn't have written this book without their support.

Ann Godoff had the idea for this book, even before it was clear that Joe Biden would win the presidency. Her oracular wisdom, dispensed with casual ease, kept propelling me in the right direction. Each time we touched base and toured the horizon, I walked away shrewder about politics and authorial craft. She also knows how to hire. Thanks to everyone at Penguin Press: William Heyward, Casey Denis, Patricia Clark, Sarah Hutson, and Victoria Lopez, and copyeditor Angelina Krahn. Rafe Sagalyn has been my agent for twenty-five years, and I've always felt lucky to be represented by someone with so much integrity.

At the White House, I benefited from the fact that my primary intermediary was Remi Yamamoto. She's both wickedly smart and wickedly funny, admirably tough and wonderfully warm.

Thanks to Amanda Tust, Sheera Avi-Yonah, and Kirk Steyer for their research help. Hilary McClellen was my indispensable backstop, a ruthless enemy of error and unfailingly delightful. There are friends who listened to me yammer on about this project, and then offered wise counsel in response: Jonathan Alter, Kevin Arnovitz, Kenneth Baer, David Bradley, Jonathan Chait, Andrei Cherney, Nicole Elkon and Neal Wolin, Beth and Curtis Groves, Ted Kaufman, Mike Kinsley, Mark Leibovich, Molly Levinson and Josh Wachs, Ryan Lizza, Barry Lynn, David Marchick, Jonathan Martin, George Packer, Simon Rosenberg, Noam Scheiber, Max Stier, Derek Thompson, and Geoffrey Wheatcroft. Along the way, a few friends agreed to read the book. They are my heroes: Isaac Chotiner, Jonathan Cohn, Tom Freedman, John Judis, Jodi Kantor, David Plotz, and Scott Stossel.

Thanks also to Walter and the good folks he manages at the Compass Coffee on Massachusetts Avenue. My colleague David Leonhardt simultaneously wrote his book there. Having the chance to talk shop with him every morning was one of the great pleasures of this project.

My parents, as always, were my most important focus group—and I love getting the chance to tell them stories and to test their reactions to ideas. I need to apologize to my extremely understanding mother-in-law for working over a trip we took to celebrate her birthday. Sadie and Theo are my bottomless reservoirs of joy. Abby is the most loving, supportive partner, and my first reader.

Sources and Notes

T HIS BOOK RELIES on nearly three hundred interviews conducted between November 2020 and February 2023. Some of these interviews
were "on record," most of which were conducted on "deep background"—
where I agreed not to directly attribute information to a source.

Every book written about Joe Biden owes a debt to Richard Ben Cramer's masterpiece, *What It Takes: The Way to the White House.* Mine is no different. My psychological understanding of the president is ultimately derived
from Cramer's big, beautiful book. It says something about both the author
and his subject that Biden spoke at Cramer's memorial service in 2013. In a
statement that Biden issued after Cramer's death, he said, "It is a powerful
thing to read a book someone has written about you, and to find both the
observations and criticisms so sharp and insightful that you learn something
new and meaningful about yourself."

Cramer had access to Biden that I never managed. But the great thing
about Biden as a subject is his verbosity. He does a terrible job at suppress-
ing his internal monologue. His staff and friends have a clear understanding
of his mind, because they are exposed to so much of it. This is the reason
that I felt comfortable writing about him with intimacy.

Of course I'm indebted to my colleagues in the press. I relied on excel-
lent retrospective studies of the Afghanistan withdrawal by Matthieu Aikins

and George Packer. I also leaned heavily on the *Washington Post* series on Ukraine "The Road to War" and the *New York Times* investigation "Putin's War." Bob Woodward and Robert Costa published their book, *Peril*, just as I was ramping up my reporting. It has essential reporting on the American Rescue Plan and Biden's decision to withdraw from Afghanistan.

The reconstruction of dialogue is an inherently imperfect activity. Unless a conversation is recorded—and understandably, most governmental officials don't record their sensitive conversations—every attempt at recapturing a verbal exchange will fail to precisely capture it. When sources recounted conversations to me, sometimes they referred to notes; other times, they relied on memory. With full awareness of the limitations of memory, I still used it as the basis for my narrative, relying on instinct to gauge its precision.

Prologue
1   **The consistent underestimation:** Richard Ben Cramer, *What It Takes: The Way to the White House* (New York: Random House, 1992).
2   **But when that day:** Eli Stokols and Chris Megerian, "'Grim and Beautiful,' Biden's Inauguration a Day of Jarring Juxtapositions," *Los Angeles Times*, January 20, 2021.
2   **The inaugural dais:** Luke Broadwater, "'Trump Was at the Center': Jan. 6 Hearing Lays Out Case in Vivid Detail," *New York Times*, June 9, 2022.
2   **Instead of a democratic extravaganza:** Howard Altman, "26,000 National Guard Troops Came to DC and Protected the Inauguration without Incident," *Military Times*, January 21, 2021.
2   **On January 19, the eve:** Christina Maxouris and Jason Hanna, "US Surpasses 400,000 Deaths from Covid-19," CNN, January 20, 2021.
2   **To fill the expanse:** Elissa Nadworny, "Nearly 200,000 Flags on National Mall Represent Those Who Cannot Attend Inauguration," NPR, January 20, 2021.
2   **Postmortems of his victory:** Michael Grunwald, "America Votes to Make Politics Boring Again," *Politico*, November 7, 2020.
3   **It required him to tangibly:** Nicole Gaouette, "Biden Says US Faces Battle to 'Prove Democracy Works,'" CNN, March 26, 2021.
3   **Politics is the means:** Bernard Crick, *In Defence of Politics* (Chicago: University of Chicago Press, 1962).
7   **"the strong and slow":** Max Weber, *Charisma and Disenchantment: The Vocation Lectures* (New York: New York Review Books, 2020), 115.

1: Day One
11   **Inauguration Day began:** Rob Crilly, "Trump Travel Pool Reports of January 20, 2021," American Presidency Project, UC Santa Barbara.
11   **This was the lone inauguration:** Joey Garrison, "A President Hasn't Refused to Attend the Inauguration of His Successor in 152 Years. Donald Trump Will Change That," *USA Today*, January 8, 2021.
11   **"Hopefully, it's not":** Peter Nicholas, "What I Saw at the White House on Trump's Last Day," *The Atlantic*, January 20, 2021.
11   **Minutes after Trump:** Michael S. Rosenwald, "Biden Attends Mass at St. Matthew the Apostle Ahead of Inauguration," *Washington Post*, January 20, 2021.
12   **When Klain was:** Dan Slater, "Biden Picks Former O'Melveny Partner Klain for Chief of Staff," *Wall Street Journal*, November 14, 2008.

12   **While Biden proudly:** Emily Czachor, "Fact Check: Would Joe Biden Be the First President in 80 or 90 Years Who Is Not an Ivy League Graduate?," *Newsweek*, October 12, 2020.

13   **When Biden officials:** Gavin Bade, "Trump-Appointed Staff at USTR Delay Biden Transition," *Politico*, December 22, 2020.

13   **Trump appointees at the Office:** Niels Lesniewski, "Budget Process, COVID Spending Being Undermined by OMB, Biden Transition Says," *Roll Call*, December 30, 2020.

14   **When Biden walked:** Ben Leonard, "Everything You Need to Know to Follow the Biden-Harris Inauguration," *Politico*, January 19, 2021.

15   **This desire to:** David Smith, "Neil Kinnock on Biden's Plagiarism 'Scandal' and Why He Deserves to Win: 'Joe's an Honest Guy,'" *Guardian*, September 7, 2020.

15   **"He understood me":** Joe Biden, *Promise Me, Dad: A Year of Hope, Hardship, and Purpose* (New York: Flatiron Books, 2017), 87.

16   **inauguration ceremony itself:** White House, "Inaugural Address by President Joseph R. Biden, Jr.," January 20, 2021.

17   **Biden transition received:** Annie Karni and Katie Rogers, "Can Someone Please Open the Door?," *New York Times*, January 21, 2021.

17   **When Joe and Jill:** Karni and Rogers, "Can Someone Please Open the Door?"

18   **Presidential historians speculated:** Peter Baker, "Copying Roosevelt, Biden Wanted a Fast Start. Now Comes the Hard Part," *New York Times*, January 30, 2021.

19   **Ever since the Ford Administration:** Michael M. Grynbaum, "White House Press Secretary Gets a New 'Flak Jacket': A Women's Blazer," *New York Times*, May 20, 2022.

2: Taking the Call

22   **His old boss referred:** Scott Wilson, "Obama Dismisses Russia as 'Regional Power' Acting Out of Weakness," *Washington Post*, March 25, 2014.

22   **Four days later:** White House, "Readout of President Joseph R. Biden, Jr. Call with President Vladimir Putin of Russia," January 26, 2021.

23   **intelligence community would review:** Ellen Nakashima, "Biden Administration Preparing to Sanction Russia for SolarWinds Hacks and the Poisoning of an Opposition Leader," *Washington Post*, February 23, 2021.

3: Visions of Rescue

24   **Back when he was vice:** Carl Hulse, Jeremy W. Peters, and Michael D. Shear, "Obama Is Seen as Frustrating His Own Party," *New York Times*, August 18, 2014.

24   **He asked his friend:** Larry Buchanan and Matt Stevens, "The Art in the Oval Office Tells a Story. Here's How to See It," *New York Times*, May 5, 2021.

25   **Just over a week:** Nelson D. Schwartz, Ben Casselman, and Ella Koeze, "How Bad Is Unemployment? 'Literally Off the Charts,'" *New York Times*, May 8, 2020.

26   **But as the pandemic entered:** Brian Bennett, "COVID-19 Is Spiking—and Donald Trump Has Pulled a 'Disappearance Act,'" *Time*, November 17, 2020.

26   **The magnitude of human suffering:** Abha Bhattarai and Hannah Denham, "Stealing to Survive: More Americans Are Shoplifting Food as Aid Runs Out during the Pandemic," *Washington Post*, December 10, 2020.

26   **described as "secret code":** Jonathan Alter, "Barack and Joe's Secret Code," *Politico*, January 19, 2017.

27   **Over time, Biden had come:** Carl Hulse, "Ghosts of 2009 Drive Democrats' Push for Robust Crisis Response," *New York Times*, January 31, 2021; and Adam Entous, "The Untold History of the Biden Family," *New Yorker*, August 15, 2022.

27   **This was very near a:** Michael Sean Winters, "Biden and the Dignity of Work," *America*, August 28, 2008.

28   **campaign's abrupt reversal:** Edward-Isaac Dovere, "The Mastermind Behind Biden's No-Drama Approach to Trump," *The Atlantic*, November 30, 2020.

30   **And though they might have:** Catie Edmondson, "'Do You Believe This?' Chilling Footage Shows Congressional Leaders on Jan. 6," *New York Times*, October 13, 2022.

31   **He spoke to them on:** Rachael Bade, Tara Palmeri, Ryan Lizza, and Eugene Daniels, "Schumer and His Flip Phone Get Their Moment," *Politico*, March 4, 2021.

32   **But in recent years, Republicans:** Rebecca Rainey, "Romney Proposes Child Care Benefit for Families, Fueling Democrats' Push," *Politico*, February 4, 2021.

32   **Thanks to DeLauro's tenacity:** Annie Linskey, "How Biden Quietly Created a Huge Social Program," *Washington Post*, March 22, 2021.

32   **And the bill began:** Laura Reiley, "Relief Bill Is Most Significant Legislation for Black Farmers Since Civil Rights Act, Experts Say," *Washington Post*, March 8, 2021.

33   **According to the Columbia tabulation:** "The American Rescue Plan Could Cut Child Poverty by More Than Half," Center on Poverty & Social Policy at Columbia University, March 11, 2021.

4: Waiting for the Jab

34   **In Florida, retirees:** Madeline Holcombe, "Florida Seniors Face Long Lines and a Haphazard Registration System to Get Covid-19 Vaccines," CNN, January 7, 2021.

35   **He grew up in DC:** Juliet Eilperin and Zachary A. Goldfarb, "Jeff Zients Helped Salvage HealthCare .gov. Now He'll Be Obama's Go-To Guy on Economy," *Washington Post*, December 22, 2013.

35   **As a kid, he traded:** Monica Langley, "The Businessman behind the Obama Budget," *Wall Street Journal*, July 13, 2012.

35   **But his responsibilities morphed:** Josh Hicks, "Who Is Jeffrey Zients, and How Is He Qualified to Fix HealthCare.gov?," *Washington Post*, October 24, 2013.

36   **rallied a team:** Steven Brill, *America's Bitter Pill: Money, Politics, Backroom Deals, and the Fight to Fix Our Broken Healthcare System* (New York: Random House, 2015).

36   **"It's all about the execution":** Jeffrey Zients, commencement address, American University Kogod School of Business, May 12, 2018.

38   **She hadn't been able to:** Dan Diamond, "The Crash Landing of 'Operation Warp Speed,'" *Politico*, January 17, 2021.

38   **Zients and Quillian sketched:** Ariana Eunjung Cha, "Biden Makes Tackling Racial, Ethnic Inequities during Coronavirus Pandemic a Priority," *Washington Post*, December 15, 2020.

39   **Like Zients, Slavitt had trained:** Jonathan Cohn, *The Ten Year War: Obamacare and the Unfinished Crusade for Universal Coverage* (New York: St. Martin's Press, 2021).

39   **Slavitt didn't especially:** Andy Slavitt, *Preventable: The Inside Story of How Leadership Failures, Politics, and Selfishness Doomed the U.S. Coronavirus Response* (New York: St. Martin's Press, 2021).

41   **Kessler hadn't officially worked:** Nicholas Florko, "A Former FDA Chief, Brimming with Experience but Lacking in Niceties, Surprises Washington by Winning Biden's Trust," *STAT*, December 21, 2020.

41   **To challenge an industry:** David Kessler, *A Question of Intent: A Great American Battle with a Deadly Industry* (New York: PublicAffairs, 2001).

42   **One of the Biden administration's:** Dan Merica and Veronica Stracqualursi, "Biden Administration to Retire 'Operation Warp Speed' Moniker," CNN, January 15, 2021.

43   **While Moderna, Sanofi:** Sydney Lupkin, "Pfizer's Coronavirus Vaccine Supply Contract Excludes Many Taxpayer Protections," NPR, November 24, 2020; and Philip Bump, "No, Pfizer's Apparent Vaccine Success Is Not a Function of Trump's 'Operation Warp Speed,'" *Washington Post*, November 9, 2020.

43   **In July 2020:** Sharon LaFraniere, Katie Thomas, and Noah Weiland, "Trump Administration Passed on Chance to Secure More of Pfizer Vaccine," *New York Times*, December 7, 2020.

44   **Trump felt cheated:** Tom Whipple, "Billions at Stake, Endless Waiting, an Angry Trump: the Pfizer CEO's Great Vax Hunt," *Sydney Morning Herald*, April 9, 2022.

44   **Even though Pfizer:** Sharon LaFraniere and Katie Thomas, "Pfizer Nears Deal with Trump Administration to Provide More Vaccine Doses," *New York Times*, December 22, 2020.

44   **Zients assigned that job:** Isaac Stanley-Becker, "Biden Harnesses Defense Production Act to Speed Vaccinations and Production of Protective Equipment," *Washington Post*, February 5, 2021.

45   **He knew how to invoke:** Betsy Klein, "Biden Administration to Use Defense Production Act for Pfizer Supplies, At-Home Tests and Masks," CNN, February 5, 2021.

45   **The administration pushed:** Sharon LaFraniere, "Biden Got the Vaccine Rollout Humming, with Trump's Help," *New York Times*, March 10, 2021.

46   **On January 26:** White House, "Remarks by President Biden on the Fight to Contain the COVID-19 Pandemic," January 26, 2021.

46   **At nine o'clock that night:** Robert Kuznia, Katie Polglase, and Gianluca Mezzofiore, "In Quest for Vaccine, US Makes 'Big Bet' on Company with Unproven Technology," CNN, May 1, 2020.

47   **he moved that date:** White House, "Fact Sheet: President Biden to Announce All Americans to Be Eligible for Vaccinations by May 1, Puts the Nation on a Path to Get Closer to Normal by July 4th," press release, March 11, 2021.

5: The Nod of the Head

48   **Nine days into:** Cleve R. Wootson Jr., "Harris TV Interview in West Virginia Provokes Flare-Up With Manchin," *Washington Post*, February 1, 2021.

49   **Biden had just delivered:** White House, "Inaugural Address by President Joseph R. Biden, Jr.," January 20, 2021.

49   **An outgrowth of an obscure:** Richard Kogan and David Reich, "Introduction to Budget 'Reconciliation,'" Center on Budget and Policy Priorities, May 6, 2022.

50   **Donilon and Klain went to:** Theodoric Meyer, Alex Thompson, and Daniel Lippman, "Klain, Get Me Rewrite!," *Politico*, March 18, 2021.

50   **During the Trump years, Klain:** Adam Cancryn, "Progressives, Once Skeptical of Biden, Rally around His Chief of Staff," *Politico*, November 21, 2022.

51   **With appointments to administration jobs:** Michael D. Shear, Katie Glueck, Maggie Haberman, and Thomas Kaplan, "Biden Names Ron Klain as White House Chief of Staff," *New York Times*, November 11, 2020.

51   **Reed had been:** Alex Thompson and Nick Niedzwiadek, "Bruce Reed, Summoner of the Techlash," *Politico*, September 14, 2021.

51   **Good old Fritz:** Joe Biden, *Promises to Keep: On Life and Politics* (New York: Random House, 2007).

51   **"I will always be":** Carol E. Lee, "Biden Says Goodbye to the Senate," *Politico*, January 15, 2009.

52   **"I'm crazy about her":** Emily Cochrane, "Empowered by an Odds-Defying Win, Susan Collins Is Ready to Deal," *New York Times*, November 27, 2020.

52   **Where the president proposed:** Fadel Allassan, "GOP Senators Release Details of $618 Billion COVID Relief Package," *Axios*, February 1, 2021.

6: Take Me Home

56   **lived on a houseboat:** Ben Terris, "Washington's Hottest Club Is Joe Manchin's Houseboat," *Washington Post*, August 6, 2021.

57   **In February, Manchin announced he:** Marianne Levine and Caitlin Emma, "Manchin to Oppose Tanden for OMB, Imperiling Major Biden Nomination," *Politico*, February 19, 2021.

57   **Progressives found it a bit:** Nick Wing, "Joe Manchin Shoots Cap-and-Trade Bill with Rifle in New Ad," *HuffPost*, October 11, 2010.

57   **"I worked with them for":** Robert Costa and Bob Woodward, *Peril* (New York: Simon & Schuster, 2021), 319.

58   **"macroeconomic stimulus on":** Lawrence H. Summers, "The Biden Stimulus is Admirably Ambitious, But It Brings Some Big Risks, Too," *Washington Post*, February 4, 2021.

59   **unemployment benefits reduced:** Emily Cochrane, "Senate Is on Track for Stimulus Vote after Democrats Agree to Trim Jobless Aid," *New York Times*, March 5, 2021.

59   **He told Schumer:** Burgess Everett and Marianne Levine, "'I Have No Idea What He's Doing': Manchin Perplexes with Covid Aid Power Play," *Politico*, March 5, 2021.

60   **"Geneva Convention applies":** Jim Newell, "How Joe Manchin Brought the Senate to a Screeching Halt," *Slate*, March 5, 2021.

60   **"wasn't always pretty":** Emily Cochrane, "Divided Senate Passes Biden's Pandemic Aid Plan," *New York Times*, March 6, 2021.

60   **Two weeks after the Rescue:** Kate Sullivan, "Gayle Manchin Nominated to Be Federal Co-chair of Appalachian Regional Commission," CNN, March 26, 2021.

60   **More than a month later:** "Jill Biden, Manchin, Actress Jennifer Garner to Visit WVa," Associated Press, May 12, 2021.

61   **"first step toward":** Jordan Weissmann, "Biden's COVID Bill Is His First Step toward an FDR-Style Presidency," *Slate*, March 9, 2021.

7: Normal People

62   **In December, the Kaiser Family:** Liz Hamel, Ashley Kirzinger, Lunna Lopes, Audrey Kearney, Grace Sparks, and Mollyann Brodie, "Vaccine Hesitancy," in *KFF COVID-19 Vaccine Monitor: January 2021*, Kaiser Family Foundation, January 27, 2021.

62   **The scale of the problem:** Ashley Parker and Matt Viser, "'The Former Guy': Biden and His Aides Work to Ignore Trump—but It Won't Be Easy," *Washington Post*, February 22, 2021.

63   **Andy Slavitt knew:** Andy Slavitt, "The Unvaccinated and Taking On Marjorie Taylor Greene (with Frank Luntz)," July 12, 2021, in *In the Bubble with Andy Slavitt*.

63 **In January 2020:** Joe DePaolo, "Frank Luntz Reveals He Suffered a Stroke, Recalls Heartwarming Meeting with Biden Afterwards: He 'Gave Me the Biggest Hug. And He Didn't Let Go,'" *Mediaite*, October 1, 2020.

64 **And in his self-conception:** Jordan Weissmann, "Joe Biden's Promise to Be a President for All Americans Isn't Just Cheesy Rhetoric," *Slate*, October 16, 2020.

65 **"shoot straight from the shoulder":** White House, "Remarks by President Biden in a CNN Town Hall with Anderson Cooper," February 17, 2021.

65 **Through the pandemic:** Manisha Aggarwal-Schifellite, "3 Ways to Strengthen a Child's Mental Resilience," *Harvard Gazette*, August 11, 2021.

66 **Over the decades, Jill Biden's:** Jada Yuan, "Jill Biden Returns to the Classroom, Live and In Person," *Washington Post*, September 3, 2021.

68 **On January 21, Jill Biden:** Jill Biden, "Education Forum with First Lady Jill Biden," C-SPAN, January 21, 2021, video, 21:36.

68 **In Chicago, Mayor Lori Lightfoot:** Amelia Nierenberg, "Chicago Fights over In-Person Learning," *New York Times*, January 5, 2022.

69 **That year, the school board:** Steven Greenhouse and Sam Dillon, "School's Shake-Up Is Embraced by the President," *New York Times*, March 6, 2010.

70 **Data showed a precipitous:** Neal Rothschild and Sara Fischer, "Boring News Cycle Deals Blow to Partisan Media," Axios, June 29, 2021.

70 **"Sorry not sorry":** Ron Klain (@WHCOS), "Sorry, not sorry," Twitter, June 29, 2021.

70 **Jen Psaki explained:** Collin Binkley, "Is One Day a Week Enough? Biden's School Goal Draws Blowback," Associated Press, February 10, 2021.

8: The Captain Cook Incident

71 **The two most powerful:** White House, "Readout of President Joseph R. Biden, Jr. Call with President Xi Jinping of China," February 10, 2021.

71 **In 2011, Barack Obama had dispatched:** Edward Wong, "Cooperation Emphasized as Biden Visits China," *New York Times*, August 18, 2011.

72 **A good Biden story:** Glenn Kessler, "Biden's Repeated Claim He's 'Traveled 17,000 Miles with' Xi Jinping," *Washington Post*, February 19, 2021.

72 **"He doesn't have a democratic":** Reuters Staff, "Biden Says China's Xi Doesn't Have a 'Democratic Bone' in His Body," Reuters, March 25, 2021.

74 **Campbell sat at a table:** "U.S.-China Summit in Anchorage, Alaska," C-SPAN, March 18, 2021.

75 **"I settled on":** Barack Obama, *A Promised Land* (New York: Random House, 2020), 476.

75 **"Mao made the Chinese nation":** Josh Rogin, *Chaos under Heaven: Trump, Xi, and the Battle for the Twenty-First Century* (Boston: Houghton Mifflin Harcourt, 2021), 11.

76 **"eating our lunch":** Donald J. Trump (@realDonaldTrump), "Wake Up America—China is eating our lunch," Twitter, August 3, 2011.

76 **He participated in:** Salman Ahmed, Wendy Cutler, Rozlyn Engel, David Gordon, Jennifer Harris, Douglas Lute, Daniel M. Price et al., *Making U.S. Foreign Policy Work Better for the Middle Class* (Washington, DC: Carnegie Endowment for International Peace, 2020).

76 **Carnegie report argued:** Ahmed et al., *Making U.S. Foreign Policy Work Better for the Middle Class*.

77 **He promised a pivot to Asia:** Kurt M. Campbell, *The Pivot: The Future of American Statecraft in Asia* (New York: Twelve, 2016).

77 **"The era of engagement":** Kurt M. Campbell and Jake Sullivan, "Competition without Catastrophe: How America Can Both Challenge and Coexist with China," *Foreign Affairs*, September/October 2019.

77 **"Our intent is":** US Department of State, "Secretary Antony J. Blinken, National Security Advisor Jake Sullivan, Director Yang and State Councilor Wang at the Top of Their Meeting," press release, March 18, 2021.

78 **nickname "Tiger Yang":** Kinling Lo, "Beijing's 'Tiger' Diplomat Takes Decades of China-US Negotiation into Crucial Meeting with Mike Pompeo," *South China Morning Post*, June 18, 2020.

79 **"So you know Vladimir Putin":** "Joe Biden, interview by George Stephanopoulos," ABC News, March 16, 2021.

79 **"The name you":** Anna Chernova, Zahra Ullah, and Rob Picheta, "Russia Reacts Angrily after Biden Calls Putin a 'Killer,'" CNN, March 18, 2021.

79 **In all the strategic documents:** Joseph R. Biden Jr., "Interim National Security Strategic Guidance," White House, March 2021.

9: Border Crush

82   **As a kid, he would:** Joe Biden, *Promises to Keep: On Life and Politics* (New York: Random House, 2007), 20.

82   **Now he stood:** White House, "Remarks by President Biden in Press Conference," March 25, 2021.

84   **He was getting terrible marks:** Zolan Kanno-Youngs, Jonathan Martin, and Alexander Burns, "Biden Received Early Warnings That Immigration and Inflation Could Erode His Support," *New York Times*, May 1, 2022.

84   **But Biden had always styled:** Asma Khalid, "An Old Friend of Law Enforcement, Biden Walks a Thin Line on Police Reform," NPR, July 8, 2021.

84   **But winning the Democratic nomination:** Zolan Kanno-Youngs, Michael D. Shear, and Eileen Sullivan, "Disagreement and Delay: How Infighting over the Border Divided the White House," *New York Times*, April 9, 2022.

84   **During the campaign, he said:** Myah Ward, "Biden Finds Himself Once More in a Title 42 Bind," *Politico*, December 31, 2022.

84   **Whatever the justifications:** Zolan Kanno-Youngs and Michael D. Shear, "Biden Faces Challenge from Surge of Migrants at the Border," *New York Times*, March 8, 2021.

84   **The plight of these children:** Miriam Jordan, "Thousands of Migrant Children Detained in Resumption of Trump-Era Policies," *New York Times*, February 26, 2021.

85   **In theory, kids:** Jonathan Easley, "Biden: No Child Should Be in Border Facility for More Than 72 Hours," *The Hill*, March 25, 2021.

85   **Children remained stuck:** Miriam Jordan, Simon Romero, and Zolan Kanno-Youngs, "Children Are Sleeping on Mats in Overcrowded Border Facilities," *New York Times*, March 15, 2021.

86   **On February 12, the administration:** Zeke Miller, Aamer Madhani, and Julie Watson, "After Outcry, Biden Plans to Lift Refugee Cap in May," Associated Press, April 17, 2021.

87   **On April 16, the White House:** Steve Holland and Mica Rosenberg, "Biden Keeps U.S. Refugee Cap at Trump-Era 15,000—for Now," Reuters, April 16, 2021.

87   **"Say it ain't so":** Dick Durbin (@SenatorDurbin), "Say it ain't so, President Joe. This is unacceptable," Twitter, April 16, 2021, 4:25 p.m.

87   **"This cruel policy":** Richard Blumenthal (@SenBlumenthal), "Turning our back on the worst refugee crisis in modern history is a tragic mistake. This cruel policy is no more acceptable now than it was during the Trump Admin. Biden's decision reverses his previous commitment & denies safe haven to refugee seekers who have been fully vetted," Twitter, April 16, 2021, 4:36 p.m.

88   **Without any further:** Sean Sullivan, "Biden Says He Will Raise Refugee Cap from 15,000 to 62,500, after Widespread Criticism for Extending Trump-Era Levels," *Washington Post*, May 3, 2021.

10: Biden's War

92   **The meeting went so badly:** Zalmay Khalilzad, *The Envoy: From Kabul to the White House, My Journey through a Turbulent World* (New York: St. Martin's Press, 2016).

92   **On two separate visits:** Michael Hirsh, "From Moral Responsibility to Magical Thinking: How Biden Changed His Mind on Afghanistan," *Foreign Policy*, April 16, 2021.

93   **"Listen to me":** Barack Obama, *A Promised Land* (New York: Random House, 2020), 318–19.

98   **As Robert Kagan:** Robert Kagan, "Power and Weakness," *Policy Review*, no. 113 (June and July 2002): 3–28.

101   **As Biden prepared his final:** Bob Woodward and Robert Costa, *Peril* (New York: Simon & Schuster, 2021).

103   **On April 14:** White House, "Remarks by President Biden on the Way Forward in Afghanistan," April 14, 2021.

104   **Eventually, the Biden administration:** Zeke Miller and Aamer Madhani, "'Overdue': Biden Sets Aug. 31 for US Exit from Afghanistan," Associated Press, July 8, 2021.

11: Hug Bibi Tight

105   **On May 10:** Patrick Kingsley and Isabel Kershner, "More Than 30 Dead in Gaza and Israel as Fighting Quickly Escalates," *New York Times*, May 11, 2021.

106   **Biden came from:** Shmuel Rosner, "Israel Will Be Perfectly Happy with President Biden," *New York Times*, August 9, 2020.

107   **"Bibi, I don't":** Lucy McCalmont, "Biden: Tell Bibi We're Still Buddies," *Politico*, November 10, 2014.

107   **A headline in *Haaretz*:** "No Phone Call from Biden Is a Wake-Up Call," *Haaretz*, February, 15, 2021.

108   **Israel had just finished:** Adam Rasgon, "Israel Has Its 4th National Election in 2 Years. Here's Why," *New York Times*, March 17, 2021.

109   **Bernie Sanders, who had:** Bernie Sanders, "The U.S. Must Stop Being an Apologist for the Netanyahu Government," *New York Times*, May 14, 2021.

109   **Even Gregory Meeks:** Jacob Magid, "Top Democrat Looking to Delay $735 Million Sale of Precision Missiles to Israel," *Times of Israel*, May 18, 2021.

109   **Four days into:** "Israel Destroys Gaza Tower Housing AP and Al Jazeera Offices," Reuters, May 15, 2021.

12: Rabbit Ears

112   **When Joe Biden watched:** Kamala Harris, "Harris Speaks Out on Why She Hasn't Traveled to Southern Border," interview by Lester Holt, NBC News, video, 6:09, June 8, 2021.

114   **Constantly in search of:** Jonathan Martin and Alexander Burns, *This Will Not Pass: Trump, Biden, and the Battle for America's Future* (New York: Simon & Schuster, 2023).

116   **When she read:** Edward-Isaac Dovere and Jasmine Wright, "Exasperation and Dysfunction: Inside Kamala Harris' Frustrating Start as Vice President," CNN, November 18, 2021.

116   **Instead of diligently:** Noah Bierman, "Kamala Harris' Biggest Assignment is in Latin America. But She Hasn't Gone There Much," *Los Angeles Times*, June 6, 2022.

13: Go Left, Young Man

117   **In 1955, when the world:** Frank Swoboda, "To Renovate Headquarters, AFL-CIO Renegotiates Its Space," *Washington Post*, June 17, 1997.

118   **Before his foray:** Ian Kullgren, "Marty Walsh's Story Gives Him an Edge in Biden Labor Messaging," *Bloomberg Law*, February 17, 2021.

118   **Then in early February:** Noam Scheiber and Karen Weise, "Amazon Warehouse in Alabama Is Set to Begin Second Union Election," *New York Times*, February 4, 2022.

119   **Although Ricchetti hardly:** Michael Scherer and Sean Sullivan, "Lobbyist Brother of Top Biden Adviser Poses Challenge to President's Ethics Promises," *Washington Post*, June 14, 2021.

119   **"I made it clear":** "President Biden on Workers' Right to Organize and Unionize," YouTube, February 28, 2021, video, 2:21.

119   **As part of the American:** Emily Cochrane, "Top Senate Official Disqualifies Minimum Wage from Stimulus Plan," *New York Times*, February 25, 2021.

120   **He stood in front:** White House, "Remarks by President Biden in Address to a Joint Session of Congress," April 29, 2021.

120   **"In any other country":** Quint Forgey, "AOC: 'In Any Other Country, Joe Biden and I Would Not Be in the Same Party,'" *Politico*, January 6, 2020.

120   **During the primaries:** Zephyr Teachout, "'Middle Class' Joe Biden Has a Corruption Problem—It Makes Him a Weak Candidate," *Guardian*, January 20, 2020.

122   **When he would describe:** David Axelrod, "Episode 205: Jake Sullivan," January 4, 2018, in *The Axe Files with David Axelrod*, produced by CNN, podcast, 1:08:44.

122   **After starring on the high:** Mark Leibovich, "Jake Sullivan, Biden's Adviser, a Figure of Fascination and Schadenfreude," *New York Times*, November 30, 2021.

123   **Richard Holbrooke once:** Michael Crowley, "Hillary Clinton's Secret Iran Man," *Politico*, April 3, 2015.

124   **"I have the humility":** Greg Jaffe, "Lessons in Disaster: A Top Clinton Adviser Searches for Meaning in a Shocking Loss," *Washington Post*, July 14, 2017.

125   **One of Sullivan's close:** Rebecca Traister, "Biden's Big Left Gamble," *Intelligencer*, New York, July 5, 2021.

125   **When Sullivan put together:** Jake Sullivan, "The New Old Democrats," *Democracy*, June 20, 2018.

125   **He loved to deliver:** Max Greenwood, "Biden Pitches Himself as 'Union Man' in First Major Campaign Speech," *The Hill*, April 29, 2019.

126   **His fidelity to Delaware's:** Byron York, "The Senator from MBNA," *National Review*, August 23, 2008.

126   **A Rhodes Scholar from Idaho:** Orion Donovan-Smith, "Biden Taps Longtime Adviser and Coeur d'Alene Native Bruce Reed as Deputy Chief of Staff," *Spokesman-Review*, December 29, 2020.

126   **When he left government:** Robin Toner, "Jackson Urges Support for 'Special Interests,'" *New York Times*, June 23, 1987.

127   **Reed was depicted:** Robert Kuttner, "Will Biden Name a Deficit Hawk to Head OMB?," *American Prospect*, November 19, 2020.

127 **Reed once wrote:** Bruce Reed, "Bruce Reed on Washington's Warring Subcultures," *Washington Monthly*, November 1, 2009.

127 **Leaving the Obama White House:** Alex Thompson and Nick Niedzwiadek, "Bruce Reed, Summoner of the Techlash," *Politico*, September 14, 2021.

127 **The more he saw:** Joseph Menn, "Top Biden Adviser Seen as Making Tech Regulation More Likely," Reuters, November 22, 2020.

128 **To Biden this was an:** Andrea Hsu, "Biden Moves to Restrict Noncompete Agreements, Saying They're Bad for Workers," NPR, July 9, 2021.

128 **In her twenties, she published:** Robinson Meyer, "How to Fight Amazon (Before You Turn 29)," *The Atlantic*, July/August 2018.

129 **It tied together:** Zach Montague, "Biden's Order Includes 72 Initiatives That Take Aim at Very Specific Practices the White House Wants Changed," *New York Times*, July 9, 2021.

129 **"Capitalism without competition":** White House, "Remarks by President Biden at Signing of an Executive Order Promoting Competition in the American Economy," July 9, 2021.

130 **"Forty years ago, we":** White House, "Remarks by President Biden at Signing of an Executive Order."

130 **Back when he was chair:** Mark Gitenstein, *Matters of Principle: An Insider's Account of America's Rejection of Robert Bork's Nomination to the Supreme Court* (New York: Simon & Schuster, 1992).

14: Face to Face

133 **Biden had just described:** Joe Biden interviewed by George Stephenapolous, "Biden Talks Cuomo, Putin, Migrants, Vaccine," ABC News, March 16, 2021.

134 **The Europeans signed on to:** Nectar Gan and Ben Westcott, "China May Not Be a Member of the G7, but It's Dominating the Agenda," CNN, June 11, 2021.

134 **Even Emmanuel Macron suspended:** Michel Rose and Steve Holland, "America Is Back with Biden, France's Macron Says," Reuters, June 12, 2021.

134 **The site for the meeting:** Isabella Kwai, "An 18th-Century Villa Was Again a Stage for History," *New York Times*, June 16, 2021.

15: Independence Day

137 **An article in The Atlantic:** James Hamblin, "A Quite Possibly Wonderful Summer," *The Atlantic*, February 19, 2021.

137 **Susan Collins exclaimed:** Libby Cathey, Cheyenne Haslett, and Stephanie Ebbs, "CDC Director Grilled over Mask Guidance in Heated Capitol Hill Hearing," ABC News, May 11, 2021.

137 **Walensky, a celebrated:** Mike Stobbe, "New CDC Director Takes Over Beleaguered Agency amid Crisis," Associated Press, January 20, 2021.

140 **Delta infected 414,188:** Holly Ellyatt, "After Being Ravaged by the Delta Covid Variant, How Is India Doing Now?," CNBC, July 23, 2021.

141 **"We are emerging":** Sean Sullivan and Matt Viser, "Biden Heralds U.S. Emergence from the Pandemic, but He Risks Celebrating Too Soon," *Washington Post*, July 4, 2021.

141 **Only 67 percent:** Alexander Tin, "U.S. Falls Short of Biden's July 4 COVID-19 Vaccine Goal," CBS News, July 4, 2021.

16: The Highway to Bipartisanship

142 **In the Oval Office, in:** White House, "Readout of Oval Office Meeting with Senators Capito, Barrasso, Blunt, Crapo, Toomey, and Wicker," May 13, 2021.

144 **But, notably, they largely directed:** Alexander Bolton and Amie Parnes, "GOP Says Ron Klain Pulling Biden Strings," *The Hill*, March 1, 2021.

144 **There was an obvious dividing:** Sarah Ewall-Wice, "Biden's American Jobs Plan and American Families Plan: What's in Them and Where the Funding Will Come From," CBS News, May 1, 2021.

145 **As a self-styled car guy:** Alan Rappeport, "How Biden Uses His 'Car Guy' Persona to Burnish His Everyman Image," *New York Times*, October 26, 2022.

145 **Just as the New Deal:** Nicholas Kristof, "Joe Biden Is Electrifying America like F.D.R.," *New York Times*, May 1, 2021.

145 **The officially sanctioned Republican:** Emily Cochrane, "In Infrastructure Talks with Biden, Capito Faces Fraught Path to Deal," *New York Times*, May 12, 2021.

146 **They had agreed to boost:** Trevor Hunnicutt, David Morgan, and Susan Cornwell, "Biden Shifts Infrastructure Talks to New Bipartisan Senate Group," Reuters, June 9, 2021.

146 **In the press, the collapse:** Seung Min Kim and Tyler Pager, "White House Infrastructure Talks with Capito Collapse, Leading to Fingerpointing as Biden Shifts Strategy," *Washington Post*, June 8, 2021.

147 **Cutting a bipartisan deal:** Burgess Everett and Marianne Levine, "Portman Under Pressure to Deliver on Big Bipartisan Deal," *Politico*, July 28, 2021.

147 **For his primary negotiating:** Emily Cochrane, "An Unlikely Pair, Portman and Sinema Steer Infrastructure Deal," *New York Times*, July 30, 2021.

147 **When she first ran:** Jonathan Martin, "A Senate Candidate's Image Shifted. Did Her Life Story?," *New York Times*, September 24, 2018.

147 **In a short time, she:** Brian Slodysko, "Sinema's Shift: 'Prada Socialist' to Corporate Donor Magnet," Associated Press, November 13, 2021.

148 **After Biden dispatched:** Emily Cochrane, Jim Tankersley, and Michael D. Shear, "'Not My Intent': How Biden's Impromptu Comments Upended a Political Win," *New York Times*, June 26, 2021.

149 **"Neither side got":** Jonathan Lemire, Josh Boak, and Lisa Mascaro, "Biden Extols Bipartisan Infrastructure Deal as a Good Start," Associated Press, June 24, 2021.

149 **Jittery Democrats were:** Ella Nilsen, "Progressive Groups Are 'Fed Up' with Biden's Infrastructure Playbook," *Vox*, June 5, 2021.

150 **One hour after appearing:** White House, "Remarks by President Biden on the Bipartisan Infrastructure Deal," June 24, 2021.

150 **Lindsey Graham said:** Rachael Bade, Ryan Lizza, Tara Palmeri, and Eugene Daniels, "Graham: Biden Made GOP Look Like 'F—ing Idiots,'" *Politico*, June 25, 2021.

150 **"My comments also created":** Cochrane, Tankersley, and Shear, "'Not My Intent.'"

151 **"these RINO Republicans":** Steve Benen, "To Derail Infrastructure Talks, Trump Ups the Pressure on GOP," MSNBC, July 27, 2021.

151 **In the end, Mitch McConnell:** Emily Cochrane, "Senate Passes $1 Trillion Infrastructure Bill, Handing Biden a Bipartisan Win," *New York Times*, August 10, 2021.

152 **The nation was still capable:** Jim Tankersley, "How Biden Got the Infrastructure Deal Trump Couldn't," *New York Times*, July 29, 2021.

152 **But the bill did more:** Emily Cochrane, Christopher Flavelle, and Alan Rappeport, "Here's What's in the Infrastructure Bill That Biden Signed Today," *New York Times*, November 15, 2021.

152 **It subsidized a network:** Madeleine Ngo, "Amtrak in the Infrastructure Bill: $66 Billion in New Funding, and an Adjusted Mandate," *New York Times*, August 2, 2021.

17: Gut Check

155 **Plans to withdraw:** Michael R. Gordon, Gordon Lubold, Vivian Salama, and Jessica Donati, "Inside Biden's Afghanistan Withdrawal Plan: Warnings, Doubts but Little Change," *Wall Street Journal*, September 5, 2021.

156 **rehearsal of concept drill:** Gordon, Lubold, Salama, and Donati, "Inside Biden's Afghanistan Withdrawal Plan."

156 **speed meant safety:** George Packer, "The Betrayal," *The Atlantic*, January 31, 2022.

158 **When Biden met with Ghani:** White House, "Readout of President Joseph R. Biden, Jr. Meeting with President Ghani and Chairman Abdullah of Afghanistan," June 25, 2021.

159 **Its armed forces were massive:** Daniel Dale, "Fact-Checking Biden's Assertion that the Afghan Military Was '300,000 Strong,'" CNN, August 17, 2021.

159 **Yet the Taliban:** Patrick Wintour, "A Tale of Two Armies: Why Afghan Forces Proved No Match for the Taliban," *Guardian*, August 15, 2021.

159 **Pompeo's deal had freed:** Mujib Mashal and Fatima Faizi, "Afghanistan to Release Last Taliban Prisoners, Removing Final Hurdle to Talks," *New York Times*, August 9, 2020.

159 **Meanwhile, corrupt government commanders:** Kathy Gannon, "Afghan Forces Struggle, Demoralized, Rife with Corruption," Associated Press, May 27, 2021.

160 **"I am not a military":** "Excerpts of Call Between Joe Biden and Ashraf Ghani July 23," Reuters, August 31, 2021.

18: The Kill List

162 **Just after the group:** Michael Rubin, "Taking Tea with the Taliban," American Enterprise Institute, February 1, 2010.

163 **As secretary of state, she:** Preeti Aroon, "Clinton to Afghan Women: 'We Will Not Abandon You,'" *Foreign Policy*, May 10, 2014.

19: Withdrawal

166   **Tony Blinken headed off:** Nahal Toosi, "Afghan Crisis Puts Blinken in a Rare Position: The Hot Seat," *Politico*, September 13, 2021.

166   **The president escaped:** Ashley Parker, Tyler Pager, and Annie Linskey, "72 Hours at Camp David: Inside Biden's Lagging Response to the Fall of Afghanistan," *Washington Post*, August 17, 2021.

167   **Within the State Department, there:** Michael R. Gordon, Gordon Lubold, Vivian Salama, and Jessica Donati, "Inside Biden's Afghanistan Withdrawal Plan: Warnings, Doubts but Little Change," *Wall Street Journal*, September 5, 2021.

167   **Of course, there were plans:** Dan Lamothe, "Declassified Afghanistan Reports Back U.S. Commanders Who Said Biden Team Was Indecisive during Crisis," *Washington Post*, February 12, 2022.

167   **Every intelligence assessment:** Mark Mazzetti, Julian E. Barnes, and Adam Goldman, "Intelligence Warned of Afghan Military Collapse, Despite Biden's Assurances," *New York Times*, August 17, 2021.

168   **By Sunday, the Taliban:** Bryan Bender, Alexander Ward, Lara Seligman, Andrew Desiderio, and Alex Thompson, "'This Is Actually Happening'. Inside the Biden Team's Five-Day Scramble as Afghanistan Collapsed," *Politico*, August 20, 2021.

168   **That was a rattling:** Mazzetti, Barnes, and Goldman, "Intelligence Warned of Afghan Military Collapse."

171   **He wanted updates:** Dan Lamothe and Alex Horton, "Documents Reveal U.S. Military's Frustration with White House, Diplomats over Afghanistan Evacuation," *Washington Post*, February 8, 2022.

172   **The noise of gunshots:** George Packer, "The Betrayal," *The Atlantic*, January 31, 2022.

173   **Instead of testing:** Matthieu Aikins, "Inside the Fall of Kabul: An On-the-Ground Account," *New York Times Magazine*, December 10, 2021.

173   **At approximately 1:45:** Aikins, "Inside the Fall of Kabul."

174   **Well before Ghani's departure:** Aikins, "Inside the Fall of Kabul."

174   **Baradar wasn't just:** Jessica Donati and Margherita Stancati, "A Taliban Leader Emerges: Hunted, Jailed and Now Free," *Wall Street Journal*, August 16, 2021.

174   **In 2010, Pakistani intelligence:** Mark Mazzetti and Dexter Filkins, "Secret Joint Raid Captures Taliban's Top Commander," *New York Times*, February 15, 2010.

174   **When the American envoy:** Mujib Mashal and Lara Jakes, "At Center of Taliban Deal, a U.S. Envoy Who Made It Personal," *New York Times*, March 1, 2020.

176   **Soon after McKenzie and Baradar:** Hamza Mohamed and Ramy Allahoum, "Taliban Enters Afghan Presidential Palace after Ghani Flees," Al Jazeera, August 15, 2021.

177   **The runway at Hamid:** Alex Horton and Dan Lamothe, "Inside the Afghanistan Airlift: Split-Second Decisions, Relentless Chaos Drove Historic Military Mission," *Washington Post*, September 27, 2021.

178   **The crew of the plane:** Helene Cooper and Eric Schmitt, "Body Parts Found in Landing Gear of Flight From Kabul, Officials Say," *New York Times*, August 17, 2021.

178   **Videos taken from:** Luke Harding and Ben Doherty, "Kabul Airport: Footage Appears to Show Afghans Falling from Plane after Takeoff," *Guardian*, August 16, 2021.

178   **They showed, in the distance:** Gerry Shih, Niha Masih, and Dan Lamothe, "The Story of an Afghan Man Who Fell from the Sky," *Washington Post*, August 26, 2021.

21: John Bass Stands at the Gates of Despair

183   **It was hard for John Bass:** Jennifer Hansler, "US Ambassador to Afghanistan Leaves Post in Expected Departure," CNN, January 6, 2020.

183   **He planted a garden:** U.S. Embassy Kabul, Facebook, April 15, 2019.

183   **the country's coterie:** U.S. Embassy in Afghanistan, "Remarks by Ambassador John R. Bass on International Day to End Impunity for Crimes against Journalists," October 29, 2018.

185   **Bass rushed to:** "State Dept. Sending Official to Manage Evacuation," Associated Press, August 17, 2021.

187   **The most chaotic:** Joshua Kaplan, Joaquin Sapien, Brian J. Conley, Mohammad J. Alizada, Samira Nuhzat, Mirzahussain Sadid, and Abdul Ahad Poya, "Hell at Abbey Gate: Chaos, Confusion and Death in the Final Days of the War in Afghanistan," ProPublica, April 2, 2022.

22: Sullivan's Choice

192   **To his colleagues:** Mark Leibovich, "Jake Sullivan, Biden's Adviser, a Figure of Fascination and Schadenfreude," *New York Times*, November 30, 2021.

193 **All day long, she:** Benoit Faucon, "Afghan Female Musicians Evacuated to Qatar after Prior U.S.-Led Effort Fell Short," *Wall Street Journal*, October 4, 2021.

194 **Along with a small:** Gary Fineout, "Waltz Rips Biden Administration over Afghanistan—Murphy 'Disappointed' by Troop Drawdown—Fed Offer Supports to Schools with Mask Mandates—Toll Grows From Haiti Earthquake," *Florida Playbook*, *Politico*, August 16, 2021.

194 **As Murphy watched:** Samantha-Jo Roth, "Rep. Stephanie Murphy, a Former Vietnamese Refugee, Pushes to Help Afghans in Peril," Spectrum News 13, August 25, 2021.

23: Lily Pads

197 **In anticipation of an evacuation:** Conor Finnegan and Josh Margolin, "In Private, Qatar Warn US Officials of 'Growing Crises' at Bases Housing Afghans: Internal Report," ABC News, August 25, 2021.

197 **As the numbers swelled:** Christina Goldbaum and Najim Rahim, "'What Will Happen to Me?' An Uncertain Future Awaits Afghans Who Fled," *New York Times*, August 29, 2021.

197 **The Qataris didn't:** International Labour Organization, "ILO Publishes Report on Work-Related Deaths and Injuries in Qatar," November 18, 2021.

197 **But they were also determined:** Josh Lederman and Raf Sanchez, "From Pariah to Partner: How Qatar's Role in Afghanistan Helped to Restore U.S. Relations," NBC News, September 13, 2021.

197 **Every other day in late:** Jim Garamone, "Austin, Blinken Thank Qatari People for Support in Afghan Evacuation," US Department of Defense, September 7, 2021.

198 **Refugees would fly:** Michael D. Shear, Lara Jakes, and Eileen Sullivan, "Inside the Afghan Evacuation: Rogue Flights, Crowded Tents, Hope and Chaos," *New York Times*, September 3, 2021.

198 **Just as the Biden:** Jenna Portnoy, "Six Afghan Children Who Arrived in Virginia Have Measles," *Washington Post*, September 14, 2021.

198 **every forty-five minutes:** Jim Garamone, "Austin Gives Senate Hard Truths of Lessons from Afghanistan," US Department of Defense, September 28, 2021.

199 **"After seven months":** David E. Sanger, "For Biden, Images of Defeat He Wanted to Avoid," *New York Times*, August 15, 2021.

24: The Red Dot

200 **Unlike any other foreign:** Matthieu Aikins, "Inside the Fall of Kabul: An On-the-Ground Account," *New York Times Magazine*, December 10, 2021.

201 **Her husband had achieved:** Guy Delauney, "Kosovo's Love Affair with the Clintons," BBC, October 27, 2016.

25: The Bitter End

203 **As the Taliban stormed:** David Guttenfelder, "At an Abandoned American Base, a Notorious Prison Lies Empty," *New York Times*, December 21, 2021.

204 **The British had been screening:** Helene Cooper, Eric Schmitt, and Thomas Gibbons-Neff, "As U.S. Troops Searched Afghans, a Bomber in the Crowd Moved In," *New York Times*, August 27, 2021.

205 **The Irish journalist:** Fintan O'Toole, "The Designated Mourner," *New York Review of Books*, January 16, 2020.

205 **Even before Biden began:** Matt Viser, "'Don't You Ever Forget That Name': Biden's Tough Meeting with Grieving Relatives," *Washington Post*, August 30, 2021.

208 **In total, the United States:** Karen DeYoung, Dan Lamothe, John Hudson, and Karoun Demirjian, "America's 20-Year War in Afghanistan Ends as Last U.S. Military Cargo Plane Lumbers into the Sky over Kabul," *Washington Post*, August 30, 2021.

26: Mr. Zelensky Comes to Washington

213 **For two years, Volodymyr Zelensky:** Joshua Yaffa and Adam Entous, "A Ukrainian Push for a White House Visit Gave Trump Leverage over Zelensky," *New Yorker*, September 28, 2019.

213 **Or rather, he offered Zelensky:** Michael Balsamo and Zeke Miller, "Memo: Trump Prodded Ukraine Leader to Investigate Bidens," Associated Press, September 25, 2019.

214 **Zelensky felt as if:** Jonathan Swan and Dave Lawler, "Zelensky 'Surprised' and 'Disappointed' by Biden Pipeline Move," Axios, June 6, 2021.

214 **To obstruct the Biden administration's:** Betsy Woodruff Swan, Alexander Ward, and Andrew Desiderio, "U.S. Urges Ukraine to Stay Quiet on Russian Pipeline," *Politico*, July 20, 2021.

27: Manchinema

216 **On September 2, Joe Manchin:** Joe Manchin, "Why I Won't Support Spending Another $3.5 Trillion," *Wall Street Journal*, September 2, 2021.

217 **On September 22, Biden:** Ryan Lizza, Rachael Bade, Tara Palmeri, and Eugene Daniels, "Inside the Room of Biden's Talks with Dems," *Politico*, September 23, 2021.

218 **When Biden aides tried:** Manu Raju, "Inside the Manchin-Sanders Feud That Has Democrats Nervous about Biden's Agenda," CNN, October 8, 2021.

219 **They wanted her to guarantee:** Sarah Ferris and Heather Caygle, "Anatomy of a Power Play: How 9 House Dems Cut Their Deal with Pelosi," *Politico*, August 24, 2021.

219 **But that deadline slipped:** Tony Romm and Marianna Sotomayor, "House Democrats Huddle amid Simmering Tensions over Biden's Big Economic Agenda," *Washington Post*, September 27, 2021.

220 **behind home plate:** Carl Hulse, "With Their Agenda in the Balance, Biden and Pelosi Work the Congressional Baseball Game," *New York Times*, September 30, 2021.

220 **In a memo dated July 28:** Burgess Everett, "Manchin Proposed $1.5T Top-Line Number to Schumer This Summer," *Politico*, September 30, 2021.

28: Mark Milley's Map

222 **Back in April:** Isabelle Khurshudyan, "Russian Troops Massed near Ukrainian Border Begin Pullback," *Washington Post*, April 23, 2021.

223 **On a Sunday in mid-October:** Shane Harris, Karen DeYoung, Isabelle Khurshudyan, Ashley Parker, and Liz Sly, "Road to War: U.S. Struggled to Convince Allies, and Zelensky, of Risk of Invasion," *Washington Post*, August 16, 2022.

225 **"I trust her":** John Hall, "Vladimir Putin Says He Didn't Intend to Scare Dog Phobic Angela Merkel When He Brought His Labrador to a Meeting," *The Independent*, July 11, 2016.

226 **Meeting with Blinken, Austin:** Harris et al., "Road to War."

226 **This was a climate:** Nahal Toosi, "The Putinologist: CIA Chief's Long History with Putin Gives Him Special Insight," *Politico*, May 30, 2022.

226 **He understood the Russian:** William J. Burns, *The Back Channel: A Memoir of American Democracy and the Case for Its Renewal* (New York: Random House, 2019), 206.

29: The Big Ask

230 **On October 24:** Sean Sullivan and Seung Min Kim, "From Charm Offensive to Scorched Earth: How Biden's Fragile Alliance with Manchin Unraveled," *Washington Post*, December 19, 2021.

230 **Scranton Joe loved:** Richard Ben Cramer, *What It Takes: The Way to the White House* (Random House: New York, 1992).

232 **On his way to Europe:** Geoff Bennett, Dartunorro Clark, and Kristen Welker, "Biden Expected to Meet with House Democrats, Push Progressives to Pass Infrastructure Bill," NBC News, October 27, 2021.

232 **Don't do it:** Heather Caygle, Sarah Ferris, and Laura Barrón-López, "Jayapal Warned Klain Not to Push an Infrastructure Vote. Then Chaos Ensued," *Politico*, October 29, 2021.

233 **He came bearing flowers:** Lisa Mascaro, Aamer Madhani, and Farnoush Amiri, "Biden Announces 'Historic' Deal—but Still Must Win Votes," Associated Press, October 28, 2021.

233 **Upon hearing the word:** Lauren Gambino, "Biden Urges Democrats to Unite around 'Historic' $1.75tn Investment Package," *Guardian*, October 28, 2021.

234 **With Pelosi unexpectedly:** Marianna Sotomayor, "Once More unto the Breach: Pelosi Strives to Deliver an Agenda That Has Divided Her Caucus, Testing Her Power," *Washington Post*, November 15, 2021.

235 **"He did not ask":** Caygle, Ferris, and Barrón-López, "Jayapal Warned Klain."

235 **The trio of old pros:** Clare Foran, Manu Raju, Daniella Diaz, and Annie Grayer, "House Democrats Again Delay Infrastructure Vote amid Party Divisions," CNN, October 28, 2021.

30: Pressure Drop

236 **"I'm open to":** Emily Cochrane, Jonathan Weisman, and Margot Sanger-Katz, "Manchin Raises Doubts on Safety Net Bill, Complicating Path to Quick Vote," *New York Times*, November 1, 2021.

237 **By Friday, November 5:** Sarah Ferris, Heather Caygle, and Nicholas Wu, "Pelosi Amps Up Domestic-Agenda Pressure Campaign, Pressing Friday Votes," *Politico*, November 4, 2021.

237 **The angriest of:** Sarah Ferris, "Stephanie Murphy's Defiant Long Game to Keep Dems in Power," *Politico*, November 3, 2021.

238 **But the more Pelosi listened:** Jonathan Weisman and Carl Hulse, "How a $1 Trillion Dollar Infrastructure Bill Survived an Intraparty Brawl," *New York Times*, November 6, 2021.

240 **But Jayapal wouldn't let:** Mike Lillis, "Progressives Leave Black Caucus Leader Waiting Outside Meeting," *The Hill*, November 5, 2021.

241 **After four years in Congress:** Justin Wingerter, "Colorado's Joe Neguse Continues Rapid Rise within U.S. House Leadership," *Denver Post*, November 30, 2020.

241 **The child of Eritrean:** Abdi Latif Dahir, "This Eritrean-American Is Now Colorado's First Black Congressman," *Quartz*, November 8, 2018.

242 **Pocan once denounced:** Zack Budryk, "Progressive Democrat after Border Defeat: Since When Did Problem Solvers Become 'the Child Abuse Caucus,'" *The Hill*, June 27, 2019.

242 **Jayapal asked to:** Sarah Ferris, "The Real Power in the New Congress Isn't Where Matt Gaetz Thinks It Is," *Politico*, January 13, 2023.

243 **Biden had assiduously:** Robert P. Baird, "Inside the Democrats' Battle to Build Back Better," *New Yorker*, November 8, 2021.

244 **And on November 19:** Emily Cochrane and Jonathan Weisman, "House Narrowly Passes Biden's Social Safety Net and Climate Bill," *New York Times*, November 19, 2021.

31: Variant of Concern

245 **But just after breakfast:** Ewen Callaway, "Heavily Mutated Omicron Variant Puts Scientists on Alert," *Nature*, November 25, 2021.

245 **spike of cases:** Peter Beaumont, "Omicron Driving Record Rate of Covid Infection in South African Province," *Guardian*, December 3, 2021.

246 **Given how little they knew:** Zolan Kanno-Youngs and Sheryl Gay Stolberg, "United States Will Bar Travelers from 8 Countries in Southern Africa," *New York Times*, November 26. 2021.

247 **In anticipation of visiting:** Giulia Heyward and Sophie Kasakove, "Americans Hunt for Virus Tests and the Assurance of Safe Holiday Gatherings," *New York Times*, December 23, 2021.

247 **On December 6, NPR's:** White House, "Press Briefing by Press Secretary Jen Psaki, December 6, 2021."

248 **But the Biden administration simply:** Annie Linskey, "Inside the Administration's Failure to Avert a Covid Testing Shortfall," *Washington Post*, December 23, 2021.

248 **In fact, Parliament eventually:** UK House of Commons Committee of Public Accounts, *Tests and Trace 2*, October 27, 2021.

248 **During the summer, the pharmaceutical:** Sheri Fink, "Maker of Popular Covid Test Told Factory to Destroy Inventory," *New York Times*, August 20, 2021.

248 **The president would eventually admit:** Donald Judd and Maegan Vazquez, "Biden Says 'Nothing's Been Good Enough' as Covid Hotspots See Testing Shortages," CNN, December 22, 2021.

32: The Eruption

250 **At first, he spoke:** Joe Manchin, "Why I Won't Support Spending Another $3.5 Trillion," *Wall Street Journal*, September 2, 2021.

250 **Then he told friends:** Steve Clemons, "White House Incivility Is What 'Lost' Joe Manchin," *The Hill*, December 20, 2021.

251 **That evening, he had:** Sean Sullivan and Seung Min Kim, "From Charm Offensive to Scorched Earth: How Biden's Fragile Alliance with Manchin Unraveled," *Washington Post*, December 19, 2021.

252 **Because Manchin stripped:** Jeff Stein and Tyler Pager, "How the White House Lost Joe Manchin, and Its Plan to Transform America," *Washington Post*, June 5, 2022.

252 **He considered himself a man:** Clemons, "White House Incivility."

253 **When lefty protesters paddled:** Nick Visser, "'Kayaktivists' Protest Outside Joe Manchin's Houseboat over Budget Bill," *HuffPost*, September 28, 2021.

253 **Kyrsten Sinema couldn't even:** Bryan Pietsch, "Immigration Activists Follow Sinema into Bathroom, Demanding Action on Reconciliation Bill," *Washington Post*, October 4, 2021.

253 **There were other, darker incidents:** Clemons, "White House Incivility."

254 **"My team and I":** White House, "Statement from President Biden on the Build Back Better Act," December 16, 2021.

254 **He texted Ricchetti:** Stein and Pager, "How the White House Lost Joe Manchin."

256 **When Manchin appeared:** Ronn Blitzer, "Manchin Says He 'Cannot Vote' for Build Back Better: 'I've Done Everything Humanly Possible,'" Fox News, December 19, 2021.

257   **The president absorbed:** Stein and Pager, "How the White House Lost Joe Manchin."

257   **"will have to explain":** White House, "Statement from Press Secretary Jen Psaki," press release, December 19, 2021.

33: Where Have the Better Angels Gone?

261   **Part of why Biden:** Joe Biden, "We Are Living through a Battle for the Soul of This Nation," *The Atlantic*, August 27, 2017.

266   **"Abraham Lincoln or Jefferson Davis?":** White House, "Remarks by President Biden on Protecting the Right to Vote," January 11, 2022.

267   **But an hour before:** Matt Viser and Seung Min Kim, "'One of Those Weeks': From Voting Rights to Vaccines, Biden Experiences the Limits of His Office—and the Fragility of His Presidency," *Washington Post*, January 15, 2022.

267   **While he was in:** Viser and Kim, "'One of Those Weeks.'"

267   **"I've known, liked":** Alex Rogers, "Mitch McConnell Calls Biden's Speech 'Incoherent' and 'Beneath His Office,'" CNN, January 12, 2022.

267   **Rather than accepting:** Viser and Kim, "'One of Those Weeks.'"

34: Get Caught Trying

269   **Russia understood this:** Steven Pifer, "Russia's Draft Agreements with NATO and the United States: Intended for Rejection?," Brookings Institution, December 21, 2021.

269   **On December 17:** Patrick Reevell, "Russia Makes Sweeping Demands for Security Guarantees from US amid Ukraine Tensions," ABC News, December 17, 2021.

270   **"It depends on what":** Myah Ward, "White House Looks to Clarify Biden's 'Minor Incursion' Comment on Russia and Ukraine," *Politico*, January 19, 2022.

271   **"We want to remind":** Volodymyr Zelensky (@ZelenskyyUa), "We want to remind the great powers that there are no minor incursions and small nations. Just as there are no minor casualties and little grief from the loss of loved ones. I say this as the President of a great power," Twitter, January 20, 2022, 2:29 p.m.

271   **On January 21, Tony:** Shane Harris, Karen DeYoung, Isabelle Khurshudyan, Ashley Parker, and Liz Sly, "Road to War: U.S. Struggled to Convince Allies, and Zelensky, of Risk of Invasion," *Washington Post*, August 16, 2022.

271   **Rather, there were usually:** "Chain-Smoking Lavrov Takes Turn as Mr. Nyet," *Moscow Times*, August 7, 2012.

271   **The other Lavrov:** David M. Herszenhorn and Michael R. Gordon, "Veteran Diplomat Fond of Cigars, Whiskey and Outfoxing U.S.," *New York Times*, September 16, 2013.

274   **Mark Milley told:** Jacqui Heinrich and Adam Sabes, "Gen. Milley Says Kyiv Could Fall Within 72 Hours If Russia Decides to Invade Ukraine: Sources," Fox News, February 5, 2022.

35: Vacancy

275   **On January 27, Stephen Breyer:** Adam Liptak, "Stephen Breyer to Retire from Supreme Court," *New York Times*, January 26, 2022.

275   **Back in the primaries:** Meg Kinnard, "Clyburn, Architect of Biden's Court Pledge, Pushes His Pick," Associated Press, January 30, 2022.

276   **And then illness:** Chris Cameron and Emily Cochrane, "Senator Ben Ray Luján Recovering after Suffering Stroke," *New York Times*, February 1, 2022.

276   **Through his involvement:** Isabella B. Cho, "Harvard Alum Ketanji Brown Jackson '92 Confirmed to Supreme Court," *Harvard Crimson*, April 8, 2022.

276   **Jackson had clerked:** Linda Greenhouse, "The Court Ketanji Brown Jackson Knew," *The Atlantic*, March 20, 2022.

277   **"Stated simply," she wrote:** Josh Gerstein, "That Time Jackson Shredded Trump in a Federal Court Ruling," *Politico*, February 25, 2022.

277   **She had spent:** Charlie Savage, "As a Public Defender, Supreme Court Nominee Helped Clients Others Avoided," *New York Times*, February 26, 2022.

277   **Months earlier, nobody:** Michael S. Schmidt, "A Top Biden Ally Has a Favored Candidate to Replace Justice Breyer: Judge J. Michelle Childs," *New York Times*, January 26, 2022.

277   **His expertise was rounding:** Jeff Zeleny, Kevin Liptak, and Phil Mattingly, "South Carolina Judge Is at the Center of a Political Whirlwind around Biden's Supreme Court Decision," CNN, February 4, 2022.

278   **Where Collins and:** Aaron Blake, "Mitt Romney's Historic Flip on Ketanji Brown Jackson," *Washington Post*, April 5, 2022.

278   **But he told Ricchetti:** Blake, "Mitt Romney's Historic Flip."

278   **But then he heard:** Cleve R. Wootson Jr. and Marianna Sotomayor, "Jim Clyburn Saved Biden's Candidacy—and Now Has the President's Ear on Supreme Court Picks," *Washington Post*, February 16, 2022.

36: The Way to Joe Manchin's Heart

281   **Manchin, an old quarterback:** Ivan Maisel, "The Coach and the Senator: Nick Saban and Joe Manchin Have Friendship That Dates to 1950s," On3, August 19, 2021.

37: "I Know What You're Doing"

289   **Once Russia postponed:** Shane Harris, Ashley Parker, and Ellen Nakashima, "New Intelligence Suggests Russia Plans a 'False Flag' Operation to Trigger an Invasion of Ukraine," *Washington Post*, February 11, 2022.

290   **Russia, it seemed:** Kayleen Devlin, Jake Horton, and Olga Robinson, "Ukraine Crisis: Is Russia Staging 'False Flag' Incidents?," BBC, February 23, 2022.

290   **In early February, the American:** Julian E. Barnes, "U.S. Exposes What It Says Is Russian Effort to Fabricate Pretext for Invasion," *New York Times*, February 3, 2022.

290   **Sullivan set up:** Ashley Parker, Shane Harris, Michael Birnbaum, and John Hudson, "13 Days: Inside Biden's Last-Ditch Attempts to Stop Putin in Ukraine," *Washington Post*, February 25, 2022.

290   **On February 10, the intelligence:** Harris, Parker, and Nakashima, "New Intelligence Suggests."

295   **At eleven in:** President of Russia, "Address by the President of the Russian Federation," February 24, 2022.

297   **"Do whatever you can":** Shane Harris, Karen DeYoung, Isabelle Khurshudyan, Ashley Parker, and Liz Sly, "Road to War: U.S. Struggled to Convince Allies, and Zelensky, of Risk of Invasion," *Washington Post*, August 16, 2022.

38: The End of the Dream

298   **Antonov Airport was:** "'Dream' Destroyed: World's Largest Plane Lies 'Ruined' after Russian Retreat from Hostomel," Yahoo! News, April 2, 2022.

298   **In Putin's war plan:** James Marson, "Putin Thought Ukraine Would Fall Quickly. An Airport Battle Proved Him Wrong," *Wall Street Journal*, March 3, 2022.

298   **Since Kyiv would:** Paul Sonne, Isabelle Khurshudyan, Serhiy Morgunov, and Kostiantyn Khudov, "Battle for Kyiv: Ukrainian Valor, Russian Blunders Combined to Save the Capital," *Washington Post*, August 24, 2022.

298   **More than a month before:** Sonne et al., "Battle for Kyiv."

299   **But the Americans:** Joshua Yaffa, "Inside the U.S. Effort to Arm Ukraine," *New Yorker*, October 17, 2022.

299   **Then, in February, Zaluzhnyi:** Yaffa, "Inside the U.S. Effort."

299   **Early in the morning:** Sonne et al., "Battle for Kyiv."

299   **At the air base:** Sonne et al., "Battle for Kyiv."

299   **The remaining three hundred:** Sonne et al., "Battle for Kyiv."

300   **"Who's in control":** "Russia Unleashes on Ukraine with More Attacks, Airstrikes," *Erin Burnett Outfront*, CNN, February 24, 2022.

300   **Kyiv was filled:** Mari Saito and Maria Tsvetkova, "How Russia Spread a Secret Web of Agents across Ukraine," Reuters, July 28, 2022.

300   **To fend off the threat:** "Ukrainian TV Broadcasts Instructions for How to Make Molotov Cocktails," CNN, February 25, 2022.

300   **Around the world, rumors:** Valerie Hopkins, "In Video, a Defiant Zelensky Says, 'We Are Here,'" *New York Times*, February 25, 2022.

301   **"I'll try to move":** Volodymyr Zelensky (@ZelenskyyUa), "Today at 10:30 am at the entrances to Chernihiv, Hostomel and Melitopol there were heavy fighting. People died. Next time I'll try to move the war schedule to talk to #MarioDraghi at a specific time. Meanwhile, Ukraine continues to fight for its people," Twitter, February 25, 2022, 6:36 a.m.

301   **"The fight is here":** "Zelenskyy Declines US Offer to Evacuate Kyiv," Associated Press, February 25, 2022.

301 **The New York Times ran:** Amanda Holpuch, "U.S. Flag Makers are Rushing to Fill Orders for Ukrainian Flags," *New York Times*, March 3, 2022.

301 **Blue and yellow flags:** Audra D. S. Burch, Jennifer Medina, Jazmine Ulloa, and Maya King, "Russia's Attack Rallies a Divided Nation: The United States," *New York Times*, March 16, 2022.

302 **The Germans announced:** Sarah Marsh and Madeline Chambers, "Germany Freezes Nord Stream 2 Gas Project as Ukraine Crisis Deepens," Reuters, February 22, 2022.

302 **Europeans agreed that:** Philip Blenkinsop, "EU Bars 7 Russian Banks from SWIFT, but Spares Those in Energy," Reuters, March 2, 2022.

303 **On Sunday evening, two days:** David E. Sanger and William J. Broad, "Putin Declares a Nuclear Alert, and Biden Seeks De-escalation," *New York Times*, February 27, 2022.

303 **He seemed to be amplifying·** Vladimir Isachenkov, Dasha Litvinova, Yuras Karmanau, and Jim Heintz, "Russia Attacks Ukraine as Defiant Putin Warns US, NATO," Associated Press, February 23, 2022.

303 **Bill Burns considered:** Jonathan Landay and Michael Martina, "U.S. Cannot 'Take Lightly' Threat Russia Could Use Nuclear Weapons— CIA Chief," Reuters, April 14, 2022.

303 **Before the war started, Sullivan:** David E. Sanger, Eric Schmitt, Helene Cooper, and Julian E. Barnes, "U.S. Makes Contingency Plans in Case Russia Uses Its Most Powerful Weapons," *New York Times*, March 23, 2022.

39: The Battle of Kyiv

306 **On the first evening:** Paul Sonne, Isabelle Khurshudyan, Serhiy Morgunov, and Kostiantyn Khudov, "Battle for Kyiv: Ukrainian Valor, Russian Blunders Combined to Save the Capital," *Washington Post*, August 24, 2022.

307 **By adjusting their strategy:** Sonne et al., "Battle for Kyiv."

311 **After it recovered:** Daniel Michaels, "The Secret of Ukraine's Military Success: Years of NATO Training," *Wall Street Journal*, April 13, 2022.

311 **And to the White House's:** Edward Wong and Julian E. Barnes, "Russia Asked China for Military and Economic Aid for Ukraine War, U.S. Officials Say," *New York Times*, March 13, 2022.

312 **Serendipitously, the evidence:** Richard Pérez-Peña and David E. Sanger, "The U.S. Warns China Not to Give Russia Military or Economic Aid," *New York Times*, March 14, 2022.

314 **On the afternoon:** Shannon Pettypiece, "Biden Rallies Support for Ukraine in Speech from Warsaw: 'We Stand with You,'" NBC News, March 26, 2022.

314 **It was overwhelming:** "Biden Takes Selfie with Ukrainian Girl," Reuters, March 26, 2022.

315 **Speaking at an excited:** "Biden on Putin: 'For God's Sake, This Man Cannot Remain in Power,'" Bloomberg, March 26, 2022.

315 **"A dictator bent":** White House, "Remarks by President Biden on the United Efforts of the Free World to Support the People of Ukraine," March 26, 2022.

315 **"For God's sake":** White House, "Remarks by President Biden."

316 **The Washington Post reminded:** Tyler Pager and Matt Viser, "How Biden Sparked a Global Uproar with Nine Ad-Libbed Words about Putin," *Washington Post*, March 26, 2022.

40: Bankova

317 **On March 25, an apparatchik:** Carole Landry, "Russia Says Focus Is Shifting Away From Kyiv, Toward Eastern Ukraine," *New York Times*, March 25, 2022.

317 **hard to know if this:** Carole Landry, "Russia Signals a Shift," Russia-Ukraine War Briefing, *New York Times*, March 25, 2022.

317 **In the town of Bucha:** Liz Sly and Kostiantyn Khudov, "Accounting of Bodies in Bucha Nears Completion," *Washington Post*, August 8, 2022.

317 **One of the weapons:** Lorenzo Tondo, "Dozens of Bucha Civilians Were Killed by Metal Darts from Russian Artillery," *Guardian*, April 24, 2022.

318 **To make room:** Sly and Khudov, "Accounting of Bodies."

318 **When the Biden administration described:** Amy B. Wang, "Biden Signs Ukraine Lend-Lease Act into Law, Expediting Military Aid," *Washington Post*, May 9, 2022.

318 **It pulled weapons:** Niki Kitsantonis and Anatoly Kurmanaev, "Sleepy Greek Port Becomes U.S. Arms Hub, as Ukraine War Reshapes Region," *New York Times*, August 18, 2022.

319 **That meant that the military:** Eric Schmitt, "Special Military Cell Flows Weapons and Equipment into Ukraine," *New York Times*, July 27, 2022.

322   **"Grateful to @POTUS":** Volodymyr Zelensky (@ZelenskyyUa), Twitter, April 29, 2022, 1:40 p.m.

41: The Gorge

330   **phenomenon as "transitory":** Christopher Condon, "Yellen Sticks with 'Transitory' View of U.S. Inflation," Bloomberg, October 12, 2021.

330   **Federal Reserve chair thought:** Christopher Rugaber, "Fed's Powell Says High Inflation Temporary, Will 'Wane,'" Associated Press, June 22, 2021.

331   **Then Biden tried to brand:** White House, "Remarks by President Biden on Gas Prices and Putin's Price Hike," June 22, 2022.

331   **He kept ordering:** Clifford Krauss, "Even as Oil Prices Ease, U.S. Keeps Tapping Strategic Reserve," *New York Times*, September 29, 2022.

331   **Over the months, after he:** Arathy Somasekhar, "U.S. Emergency Oil Reserves Tumble to Lowest Since 1984," Reuters, September 12, 2022.

332   **"unprepared and unresponsive":** Edward-Isaac Dovere, "Biden Leaves Democrats Hanging as Midterms Burst into Full Swing," CNN, January 20, 2022.

333   **Several elections back:** Alexander Nazaryan, "Why Biden Is Deploying Trump's MAGA Brand against the GOP," Yahoo! News, May 15, 2022.

333   **"a potential dog-whistle":** Center for American Progress, "GOP Branding Project," April 2022, 24.

334   **When Biden debuted:** Parker and Scherer, "Biden Sees a New Threat."

334   **Ultra-MAGA sounded:** Alex Thompson, Adam Cancryn, and Max Tani, "Is 'Ultra-MAGA' Lame?," *Politico*, June 27, 2022.

334   **"I'm ultra-MAGA":** Parker and Scherer, "Biden Sees a New Threat."

43: Dobbs v. Biden

335   **On his wrist:** Matt Hadro, "Biden Mentions Our Lady of Guadalupe, Shows Rosary Beads, in Meeting With Mexican President," *Catholic News Agency*, March 2, 2021.

335   **"Wherever there were nuns":** Joe Biden, *Promises to Keep: On Life and Politics* (New York: Random House, 2007), 7.

336   **To fulfill his ambitions:** Katie Glueck, "Joe Biden Denounces Hyde Amendment, Reversing His Position," *New York Times*, June 6, 2019.

336   **Then, on May 2:** Josh Gerstein and Alexander Ward, "Supreme Court Has Voted to Overturn Abortion Rights, Draft Opinion Shows," *Politico*, May 2, 2022.

336   **"*Roe* was egregiously wrong":** Gerstein and Ward, "Supreme Court Has Voted."

341   **Squinting into the teleprompter:** "President Biden Reacts to Supreme Court Decision Overturning Roe v. Wade," C-SPAN, June 24, 2022, video, 12:03.

341   **"I know so many of us":** White House, "Remarks by President Biden on the Supreme Court Decision to Overturn Roe v. Wade," June 24, 2022.

341   **Rebecca Traister, the feminist:** Rebecca Traister, "Joe Biden's *Dobbs* Response Has Been Breathtakingly Awful: Why Can't the President Show Some Fight?," *The Cut*, July 12, 2022.

341   **"lacked the urgent tone":** Ashley Parker, Yasmeen Abutaleb, and Tyler Pager, "Two Long Weeks: Inside Biden's Struggle to Respond to Abortion Ruling," *Washington Post*, July 9, 2022.

341   **should cover the costs:** "Warren, Murray Lead Over 20 Senators Urging President Biden to Issue Executive Order to Defend Americans' Right to an Abortion," warren.senate.gov, June 8, 2022.

341   **"gets to questions":** Edward-Isaac Dovere, "After String of Supreme Court Setbacks, Democrats Wonder Whether Biden White House Is Capable of Urgency Moment Demands," CNN, July 6, 2022.

342   **According to a You Gov:** Parker, Abutaleb, and Pager, "Two Long Weeks."

342   **Two weeks after *Dobbs*:** Mariana Alfaro, "Biden Decries Case of 10-Year-Old Rape Victim Forced to Travel for Abortion," *Washington Post*, July 8, 2022.

343   **On August 2, Kansans:** Mitch Smith and Katie Glueck, "Kansas Votes to Preserve Abortion Rights Protections in Its Constitution," *New York Times*, August 2, 2022.

343   **Districts that Trump:** Keith Collins and Allison McCann, "Where Trump Counties in Kansas Chose to Preserve Abortion Rights," *New York Times*, August 3, 2022.

44: The Bath

349   **Martin Heinrich of New Mexico:** Anthony Adragna, "Martin Heinrich Says He's Questioning Why Joe Manchin Continues to Lead the Energy Committee amid His Waffling on Climate Spending," *Politico*, July 15, 2022.

45: Truth and Reconciliation

354 **Politico deemed it:** Burgess Everett and Marianne Levine, "Manchin's Latest Shocker: A $700B Deal," *Politico*, July 27, 2022.

354 **And when that outlet:** Zack Colman, Josh Siegel, and Kelsey Tamborrino, "'Holy S—t': Surprise Senate Deal Sets Stage for Record Climate Change Package," *Politico*, July 27, 2022.

355 **Despite their shared:** Manu Raju and Lauren Fox, "Patience Wanes as Democrats Demand Sinema and Manchin Reveal Views on Biden Agenda," CNN, September 29, 2021.

355 **personally benefited from its success:** Christopher Flavelle and Julie Tate, "How Manchin Aided Coal, and Earned Millions," *New York Times*, March 17, 2022.

356 **She would vote for an amendment:** Marianne Levine, Burgess Everett, and Jordain Carney, "Senate Dems Pass Long-Awaited Climate, Tax and Health Care Bill," *Politico*, August 7, 2002.

357 **What was needed:** Robinson Meyer, "The Climate Economy Is about to Explode," *The Atlantic*, October 5, 2022.

358 **When Credit Suisse:** "US Inflation Reduction Act: A Catalyst for Climate Action," Credit Suisse, November 11, 2022.

359 **The Inflation Reduction Act will:** "US Inflation Reduction Act," Credit Suisse.

359 **The bill was an investment:** Robinson Meyer, "'The Biggest Thing to Happen in International Climate Diplomacy in Decades,'" *The Atlantic*, August 31, 2022.

46: War Games

362 **Zelensky had a vision:** Isabelle Khurshudyan, Paul Sonne, Serhiy Morgunov, and Kamila Hrabchuk, "Inside the Ukrainian Counteroffensive That Shocked Putin and Reshaped the War," *Washington Post*, December 29, 2022.

363 **Several dozen Ukrainian:** Joshua Yaffa, "Inside the U.S. Effort to Arm Ukraine," *New Yorker*, October 17, 2022.

47: Waves Crashing

367 **"Where's Nancy?" DePape:** Paul LeBlanc, "Suspect in Paul Pelosi Attack Awoke Him by Standing over His Bedside, Documents Show," CNN, November 2, 2022.

368 **Within camera shot:** Brianna Keilar, "Biden's Use of Marines during Philadelphia Speech Adds to Debate over Politicization of the Military," CNN, September 4, 2022.

368 **"too often sounding":** "Democracy Is in Danger. Biden Should Invoke Patriotism, Not Partisanship, to Make That Point," editorial, *Washington Post*, September 2, 2022.

368 **But he would go:** Peter Baker, "Biden Warns That 'Big Lie' Republicans Imperil American Democracy," *New York Times*, November 2, 2022.

368 **"This is no ordinary":** White House, "Remarks by President Biden on Standing Up for Democracy," November 3, 2022.

368 **None of the oratory:** Chris Cillizza, "Joe Biden's Head-Scratching Democracy Speech," CNN, November 3, 2022.

368 **A headline in *Politico* described:** Eugene Daniels and Ryan Lizza, "Biden's Important, Puzzling Democracy Speech," *Politico*, November 3, 2022.

369 **"When [elections] break":** Blake Hounshell, "Democrats' Feared Red October Has Arrived," *New York Times*, October 19, 2022.

369 **circle believed his enemies:** Mark Mazzetti, Edward Wong, and Adam Entous, "U.S. Officials Had a Secret Oil Deal with the Saudis. Or So They Thought," *New York Times*, October 25, 2022.

372 **There were just three:** Harry Enten, "How Joe Biden and the Democratic Party Defied Midterm History," CNN, November 13, 2022.

374 **The Ukrainian counteroffensive:** Isabel van Brugen, "How U.S. HIMARS Helped Ukraine Retake Kherson," *Newsweek*, November 14, 2022.

374 **GMLRS were the height:** Samantha Schmidt and Serhii Korolchuk, "After Kherson, Ukraine's Military Ponders New Push South and East," *Washington Post*, December 3, 2022.

374 **On November 9, the day:** Marc Santora, Andrew E. Kramer, Dan Bilefsky, Ivan Nechepurenko, and Anton Troianovski, "Russia Orders Retreat from Kherson, a Serious Reversal in the Ukraine War," *New York Times*, November 9, 2022.

375 **By November, the Biden administration:** Jonathan Masters and Will Merrow, "How Much Aid Has the U.S. Sent Ukraine? Here Are Six Charts," Council on Foreign Relations, December 16, 2022.

Index